Leaders at War

A VOLUME IN THE SERIES

Cornell Studies in Security Affairs

edited by Robert J. Art, Robert Jervis, and Stephen M. Walt

A list of titles in this series is available at www.cornellpress.cornell.edu.

Leaders at War

How Presidents Shape Military Interventions

Elizabeth N. Saunders

CORNELL UNIVERSITY PRESS
ITHACA AND LONDON

Cornell University Press gratefully acknowledges receipt of a subvention from
The George Washington University, which aided in the publication of this book.

First published 2011 by Cornell University Press
Printed in the United States of America

Library of Congress Cataloging-in-Publication Data

Saunders, Elizabeth N. (Elizabeth Nathan), 1978–
   Leaders at war : how presidents shape military interventions / Elizabeth N.
Saunders.
       p. cm. — (Cornell studies in security affairs)
   Includes bibliographical references and index.
   ISBN 978-0-8014-4922-2 (cloth : alk. paper)
   1. War and emergency powers—United States—History—20th century.
2. Politics and war—United States—History—20th century.   3. Presidents—
United States—History—20th century.   4. Political leadership—United
States—History—20th century.   5.. Intervention (International law)—
History—20th century.   6. United States—Military policy—History—20th
century.   7. United States—Foreign relations—1945–1989.   I. Title.
II. Series: Cornell studies in security affairs.
   JK558.S38 2011
   973.92092'2—dc22

                                                                    2010040738

Cloth printing   10   9   8   7   6   5   4   3   2   1

Contents

Acknowledgments

During the years I have worked on this book I have been lucky to receive advice and support from many people whom it is now a pleasure to thank. First, I thank my advisers at Yale University, who helped guide this project from its inception: Bruce Russett, Keith Darden, and John Lewis Gaddis. Each contributed valuable advice and continually pushed me to refine my arguments and my research. Their different areas of expertise and collective intellectual energy improved the project immensely. I am indebted to the many other members of the Yale faculty and my fellow students who gave assistance, comments, and support along the way. I also thank my undergraduate adviser, Patrick Thaddeus, for his advice and encouragement as I shifted from studying physics and astronomy to political science.

I am grateful for the generous financial support I received for the project. A Harvard-Cambridge Scholarship helped me transition to studying international relations, and a National Science Foundation Graduate Research Fellowship supported several years of graduate school. The research itself was made possible by grants and support from the Smith Richardson Foundation (through Yale's International Security Studies Program); the Yale Center for International and Area Studies (now MacMillan Center); and George Washington University. A Brookings Research Fellowship in Foreign Policy Studies allowed me to spend a year at the Brookings Institution, and I thank the many Brookings scholars who took time to discuss the project with me. A Bryce Fund Grant from the American Political Science Association supported my stay at APSA's Centennial Center, which was a congenial place to finish writing an early draft. A fellowship at the John M. Olin Institute for Strategic Studies at Harvard allowed me to spend a year revising the manuscript. I thank Olin's director, Steve Rosen, and my Olin colleagues for providing extremely useful feedback at the Olin seminar and during countless conversations throughout the year.

I am also grateful to the many archivists who facilitated my research, and especially to Valoise Armstrong, Catherine Cain, and Chalsea Millner at the Eisenhower Library; Michael Desmond, Sharon Kelly, and Stephen Plotkin at the Kennedy Library; Allen Fisher and John Wilson at the Johnson Library; and Edward Barnes, Michael Hussey, and Martin McGann at the National Archives facility in College Park, Maryland.

The political science department at George Washington University (GW) has been a wonderful environment to finish the final version of the manuscript. My colleagues were very supportive and helpful, particularly in our young faculty summer colloquium. I owe special thanks to Marty Finnemore, who was a great source of encouragement and advice; Jim Goldgeier, who literally took the manuscript out of my hand and demanded to read the whole thing; Jim Lebovic, who shared his insights about Vietnam and Iraq in weekly Friday afternoon chats; and Charlie Glaser, who organized a book workshop (with the able assistance of Sarah Bulley) and provided excellent feedback. I am also grateful to Robert Adcock, Mike Brown, Llewelyn Hughes, Gina Lambright, Harris Mylonas, Chad Rector, and the late Lee Sigelman for their very helpful comments and suggestions on various drafts. In the history department at GW, I also thank Hope Harrison and Ron Spector for useful comments. For excellent research assistance, I thank Morgan Cotti, Kate Irvin, Shannon Powers, Amir Stepak, and Rachel Whitlark.

This project has benefited from feedback from many people throughout its development (though of course I alone bear responsibility for its flaws). I particularly thank seminar participants at the Yale International Relations Workshop; the Yale International Security Studies Colloquium in International History and Security; the Olin Institute at Harvard; the Institute for Global and International Studies at GW; the GW Cold War Group; Princeton University; the University of Chicago's Program on International Security Policy; the University of Notre Dame's International Security Program; and the University of Virginia's Miller Center of Public Affairs colloquium. I am grateful to GW's Institute for Security and Conflict Studies for sponsoring the book workshop, and I thank the outside readers, Andy Bennett, Larry Berman, and Jack Snyder, for taking the time to provide detailed feedback and lively discussion. In addition to those already mentioned, for their valuable advice and comments I am grateful to Deborah Avant, Davy Banks, Sara Berndt, Ted Bromund, Jonathan Caverley, Carolyne Davidson, Alexander Downes, Andrew Erdmann, Tom Flores, Benjamin Fordham, Dan Galvin, Lilach Gilady, Michael Glosny, Brendan Green, Alexandra

Guisinger, Dan Hopkins, Susan Hyde, Richard Immerman, Andrew Kennedy, Andrew Krepinevich, Sarah Kreps, Austin Long, Jason Lyall, Tanvi Madan, Siddharth Mohandas, David Nickerson, Irfan Nooruddin, Tom Schwartz, Todd Sechser, Vivek Sharma, Mark Sheetz, Caitlin Talmadge, Jennifer Tobin, Stephen Watts, Vesla Weaver, Salim Yaqub, and Philip Zelikow. Rafaela Dancygier, Jim Goldgeier, Mark Lawrence, and Jim Lebovic, as well as the book workshop participants, deserve special thanks for reading and commenting in detail on the whole manuscript. I apologize to anyone I may have forgotten.

At Cornell University Press, I thank Roger Haydon for his support of the project throughout the publication process; the series editor Robert Jervis for his extremely helpful comments and suggestions; an anonymous reviewer for very useful feedback; and Susan Specter, Kimberley Vivier, and the able staff at Cornell for guiding it through the editorial and production processes. Dave Prout prepared the index. Portions of chapters 1, 2, 4, and 5 were published as "Transformative Choices: Leaders and the Origins of Intervention Strategy," *International Security* 34, no. 2 (2009): 119–161. I thank the journal and MIT Press for permission to use this material in the book.

The process of writing this book would have been far more difficult without the support and good humor of friends too numerous to name. I owe special thanks to Rafaela Dancygier, Lilach Gilady, Alexandra Guisinger, Dan Hopkins, Susan Hyde, and Helen LaCroix for countless rounds of advice, comments, and pep talks, even as they navigated their own academic projects.

Finally, I could not have completed this project without the support of my family. John and Catherine Nathan, in addition to being wonderful parents, instilled in me a love of international relations, science, and writing, influences that have come together in this project. My sister, Caroline Nathan Horn, has been a tremendous source of support and an invaluable friend. And my wonderful husband, Tom Saunders, was always ready to be my sounding board, proofreader, and cheerleader, and also provided vital comments on more drafts than I can count. He lived with this project—and put up with its author—with an unfailing patience and good humor that sustained me throughout this process. I dedicate this book to my family, with deepest thanks.

1

When and How States Intervene

For over a century, military interventions have bedeviled U.S. presidents. At least since the United States acquired the ability to project power overseas in the late nineteenth century and especially since 1945, American leaders have grappled with difficult questions about the scope and purpose of U.S. interventions. From Vietnam to Somalia, Iraq, and Afghanistan, the debate has often centered on whether to use force merely to restrain other states' international actions or instead to reshape the domestic institutions of countries that threaten U.S. interests. At an even more basic level, there has also been significant debate over whether to undertake these interventions at all.

The decision to intervene and the choice of intervention strategy have important implications for both the intervening and the target state. The Obama administration's 2009 deliberations over strategy in Afghanistan, for example, highlighted the trade-off between a more intrusive nation-building strategy designed to prevent Afghanistan from once again becoming a terrorist haven, but at a higher cost to the United States, and a more limited and sheltered counterterrorism posture that might contain the external threat from al Qaeda but leave the Afghan people at the mercy of the Taliban.[1] Interventions may also affect the balance of power and a state's ability to pursue other security goals. American policymakers, for instance, now debate whether the U.S. military should prepare for future unconventional wars like those in Iraq and Afghanistan, or whether such operations threaten America's ability to confront other, more conventional threats.[2] More generally, Richard N. Haass, director of policy planning in the first administration of George W. Bush, has recently argued that the "difference between a foreign policy designed to manage relations between states and one that seeks to alter the nature of states is critical, and constitutes the principal fault line in the contemporary foreign policy debate."[3]

American presidents have taken sharply different sides in this debate. Across many different international settings, presidents have varied significantly in how deeply they have used U.S. forces to reshape the domestic institutions of target states. The nation-building operations in Haiti and the Balkans in the 1990s were highly intrusive; other interventions, such as the 1958 intervention in Lebanon and the 1965 intervention in the Dominican Republic, far less so. Successive leaders have even approached the same conflict differently: the first President Bush limited intervention in Somalia to humanitarian aid, for example, whereas Bill Clinton at least initially allowed the mission to expand to address underlying domestic problems. For international relations scholars, the crucial issue is whether variation in intervention choices stems from the international environment, from domestic politics, or from differences among the presidents themselves.

This book seeks to explain when and why great powers such as the United States choose to transform foreign institutions and societies through military interventions.[4] Why do some military interventions explicitly try to transform the domestic institutions of the states they target whereas others do not, instead attempting only to reverse foreign policies or resolve disputes without trying to reshape the internal landscape of the target state? In other words, what explains how deeply an intervention intrudes on the internal affairs of target states? Many definitions of military intervention assume that it involves interference in other states' domestic affairs, rather than allowing the extent of internal interference to vary—thus leaving an important and timely aspect of intervention unexplored.[5] Even regime change can vary in intrusiveness, from operations that change only the leader of the target state while leaving institutions intact, to interventions that thoroughly alter the domestic order. The choice of strategy is intertwined with a more basic question about military intervention: Why do great powers like the United States undertake overt intervention in some conflicts or crises but not in others? It is important not only to explain interventions that happened but also to address interventions that plausibly might have occurred but did not. I seek to explain both when *and* how states intervene.

It is impossible to answer these questions, I contend, without exploring a crucial but often-overlooked factor in international relations: the role of individual leaders. Many analysts see individual leaders as too idiosyncratic to study analytically, on the one hand, or assume that leaders respond to international or domestic conditions in similar ways, on the other. I argue, by contrast, that leaders vary systematically in how they perceive threats, and that these different threat perceptions help explain when and how states intervene. The critical variable distinguishing leaders is the degree to which they believe that the internal political, economic, or social characteristics of other states are the ultimate source of threats. Leaders who diagnose threats as emerging from the domestic institutions of other states are more likely to use intervention to attempt to transform those institutions. Leaders who instead see threats as arising from another state's foreign and security policies are more likely to intervene without interfering deeply in the target state's domestic affairs.

To home in on the role of leaders and show that their beliefs shape intervention choices, even within a single state in a single international system, the book concentrates on U.S. military interventions during the Cold War, focusing on the presidencies of Dwight D. Eisenhower, John F. Kennedy, and Lyndon B. Johnson. Using archival and historical evidence, I show that leaders' causal beliefs about the origin of threats—beliefs formed long before leaders face actual crises and even before they take office—shape, in two ways, the cost-benefit calculation leaders make when they confront intervention decisions. First, these beliefs influence how leaders value the benefits of transforming target states, and second, they affect how leaders allocate scarce national security resources as they prepare to undertake certain forms of intervention. Leaders' causal beliefs about the origin of threats have profound consequences for the decision to intervene and for the choice of intervention strategy, as well as implications for the probability of intervention success.

Individual leaders are particularly critical to intervention decisions. Important variation in how states approach interventions over time cannot be explained by theories that rely on stable or slow-changing factors such as the structure of the international system or regime type. In addition, most great-power military interventions in smaller powers are "wars of choice," that is, they do not result from a direct or existential threat to the state.[6] There remain many more potential threats than states can confront directly, however, and within the same state, reasonable people can disagree about the nature and importance of these threats. As Fred Greenstein and Richard Immerman observe, though leaders often argue that they have no choice but to act, decisions to intervene are close calls: different leaders might make different choices.[7] Leaving leaders out of the equation risks missing important dynamics and changes in intervention choices.

Yet scholars have tended to do just that. In the last few decades, international relations theorists—with the notable exception of those who take a psychological approach—have rarely incorporated a central role for leaders, especially since Kenneth Waltz's dismissal of individual-level explanations in *Man, the State, and War*.[8] Some analysts simply do not expect leaders to have a significant effect on state behavior independent of the domestic or international setting. Others acknowledge that leaders are important but despair of making simple, generalizable predictions about *how* leaders matter.[9] Recently, scholars of international relations have taken a renewed interest in making leaders the unit of analysis, but there remains much room for exploring how leaders themselves vary.[10]

This book charts a middle course between the two extremes of studying leaders as a series of "great men," on the one hand, and excluding leaders by assuming that they respond to domestic or international conditions in similar ways, on the other. Although analysts often refer to decisions made by "leaders," they typically mean leaders operating within the constraints of domestic institutions or the international environment, which do the real explanatory work. I suggest that within states, the identity of the individual leader is profoundly significant. But since leaders can vary in many different ways—including their goals, means, psychological biases, and political effectiveness—scholars want to know *how* leaders shape crucial foreign policy choices. In this book, I focus on how leaders differ in the substantive beliefs they hold about the origin of threats. This claim is more specific than arguing that ideas matter: it is individual leaders who determine which threat perception dominates at a particular moment. The book contributes to the recent revival of interest in the role of leaders in international relations by developing a simple but powerful typology of leaders, as well as a rigorous way to conceptualize and measure leaders' beliefs and test their influence on intervention decisions.

How Leaders Shape Interventions: Overview of the Argument

A decision to intervene involves not only a commitment to deploy a state's military forces in a particular conflict or crisis but also a choice about how much domestic interference the intervention will involve. I therefore analyze both the decision to intervene and the choice of intervention strategy. In this book, I define military intervention as an overt, short-term deployment of at least one thousand combat-ready ground troops across international boundaries to influence an outcome in another state or an interstate dispute; it may or may not involve explicit interference in the target state's internal affairs. This definition is intended to provide an apples-to-apples comparison of intervention choices across different presidencies; covert operations are excluded because their secret and less costly nature means they may be selected through a different process than overt interventions. I elaborate on the rationale for this definition and the restrictions it employs in chapter 2.

"Intervention strategy" refers to the initial strategy a leader intended to use rather than the actual outcome on the ground. The actual intervention strategy may be the product of other factors that interact with intentions, such as the preferences and performance of the military or the target environment. Understanding the leader's intended policy choice is still crucial, however, because it may consume significant resources and affect the course of the intervention even if it is not implemented successfully.[11]

If leaders choose to intervene, we can think in terms of two ideal-typical intervention strategies on either end of a spectrum. On one end of the spectrum are *transformative* strategies, which specifically seek to interfere in the domestic affairs of targets at either the national or local level (or both, since local-level change is usually intended to further change at the national level). On the other end of the spectrum are *nontransformative* strategies, which do not explicitly aim to interfere directly in the domestic organization of the target state, even if such interventions have inadvertent effects on local domestic institutions or the civilian population.

The distinction between transformative and nontransformative strategies holds even at the dramatic level of regime change operations, because such operations can vary significantly in their goals and scope. Leadership change that accompanies institutional change qualifies as transformative. But an intervention that changes only the leadership of the target state without fundamentally altering its domestic institutions—a "decapitation"—is considered nontransformative.

The most important source of willingness to intervene is the perception of a threat to national security, but even within the same state, leaders may differ in how they identify such threats. As different individual leaders survey the landscape of international hazards, they use causal beliefs, or "beliefs about cause-effect relationships," to sort and prioritize the many possible threats they face.[12] In terms of threat perception, leaders can be categorized according to one of two ideal types. *Internally focused* leaders see a causal connection between threatening or aggressive foreign and security policies and the internal organization of states. These leaders may perceive the very nature of another state's domestic order, or conflicts that may challenge that order, as threatening. For example, they may believe that another state's domestic order may cause it to be aggressive. Alternatively, they may see another state's domestic institutions as likely to lead to unfavorable foreign or security policies or outcomes that endanger the balance of power. These leaders will therefore concentrate on the domestic aspects of the conflict or crisis—including the domestic institutions of crisis actors—as potential sources of threat, and may also see crises that are primarily domestic as potentially meriting intervention. In contrast, *externally focused* leaders diagnose threats directly from the foreign and security policies of other states regardless of domestic institutions, and thus are likely to focus primarily on the international dimensions of interstate or intrastate crises.

Causal beliefs about the origin of threats shape the cost-benefit calculation leaders make when they confront intervention decisions, through two mechanisms.

First, these beliefs influence the value leaders place on transforming the domestic institutions of target states. Internally focused leaders will see more value in ensuring a particular domestic order within the target state as a way to secure favorable foreign and security policies from the target state in the future. In contrast, externally focused leaders prioritize intervention outcomes that ensure desired foreign and security policies from the target state in the short term, without paying much attention to the target's domestic form. These differences shape how leaders see the benefits of successfully transforming target states, even though both leader types aim for favorable foreign and security policies from the target state in the long term and may share a long-term commitment to a favored form of domestic institutions, such as democracy.

A second mechanism through which beliefs shape intervention choices is by influencing how leaders allocate scarce national security resources to confront threats. Much planning and strategizing for intervention happens long before crises arise. Based on their threat perceptions, leaders make initial "policy investments" at the outset of their tenure—choices that affect the material, bureaucratic, and intellectual capabilities available for different intervention strategies and thus shape preparedness for intervention. Internally focused leaders are more likely to develop significant capabilities for transformative strategies whereas externally focused leaders are more likely to invest in capabilities for nontransformative strategies. These policy investments occur through several channels, such as staffing decisions, overall strategy and the defense posture, budgetary allocations, and institutional creation and change. Preparedness, in turn, affects estimates of costs and the probability of success associated with different strategies, and thus a leader's willingness to initiate intervention with a particular strategy. Although the book does not deal directly with the determinants of intervention success, the preparedness mechanism suggests that choices made early in a presidency are an important factor in the outcome of interventions on the ground.

These two mechanisms affect whether leaders believe a particular crisis constitutes a threat—and thus merits intervention at all—as well as how deeply they are likely to get involved in the target state's institutions if they choose to intervene. The two decisions are intertwined: if a preferred strategy is not feasible or is estimated to be particularly costly, the leader may be dissuaded from intervening at all. One manifestation of the impact of causal beliefs is that leaders may have different views on what counts as an opportunity to intervene. If leaders face multiple opportunities to intervene at the same time, they are more likely to choose the target that best suits their favored strategy (i.e., the strategy most likely to secure the intervention outcome they prioritize and for which they are best prepared). If they face only a single opportunity, the feasibility of their preferred strategy may affect their willingness to intervene at all. Even if the two leader types agree that a conflict or crisis warrants intervention, their different diagnoses of threat may lead them to choose different strategies. When they intervene, internally focused leaders are more likely to undertake transformative strategies whereas externally focused leaders are more likely to pursue nontransformative strategies. Thus within political or environmental constraints, given multiple opportunities for intervention or the choice of strategy within a single intervention, leaders try to channel their response toward the strategy most likely to produce their favored outcome.

Leaders do not necessarily have the luxury of choosing their intervention opportunities, however. Domestic or international audiences may provide political imperatives to intervene *somewhere*. Under such pressures, a leader might intervene in a conflict he would otherwise forgo. He may feel forced to pursue a nonpreferred strategy for which he has not made policy investments and is thus less prepared, or he may employ his preferred strategy even though it is ill-suited to the conflict at hand. In such cases, a decision to intervene may result in a gap between ends and means that can have important consequences on the ground. Finally, although I focus on the initial decision to intervene and the choice of strategy, my argument has implications for the probability of intervention success. In addition to the initial odds of success (which are affected by the preparedness mechanism), even if leaders try to change strategies they must still live with their policy investments and may find it difficult to shift policy effectively on short notice.

Much of the intervention literature does not address how states choose an intervention strategy, but there are two arguments that could, in principle, account for variation in intervention choices, and they are the main alternative explanations I explore. The "structural/material conditions" hypothesis, drawn partly from realist arguments, suggests that intervention decisions, including strategy, are driven by structural or material factors such as available capabilities or the situation in the target state. A second alternative, the "domestic competition" hypothesis, posits that while leaders may vary in their beliefs, it is political interaction among domestic actors—including not only leaders but also bureaucrats, advisers, advocacy groups, parties, and the public—that produces decisions. In chapter 2, I outline the observable implications of these alternative explanations and my argument, allowing me to adjudicate among competing accounts.

The two leader types I identify are, of course, ideal types. In reality, leaders may have a more complex understanding of the nature of threats. Differences in leader type may also be tempered by the dominant paradigm of a given time period, such as the Cold War, when all presidents were dedicated to stopping the spread of communist institutions. Furthermore, at lower levels of cost, internal meddling may be more attractive. Each president in this book, for example, succumbed to the temptation to use covert operations to interfere in other states' domestic affairs, including the externally focused Dwight D. Eisenhower and the internally focused John F. Kennedy. Yet even within the Cold War, there was considerable variation in the degree, scope, and strategy of interference—differences that despite a shared commitment to fighting communism, reflected the degree to which presidents connected the domestic affairs of these states to U.S. national security.

There are important connections between the two leader types and the realist and liberal traditions, but the categories here do not overlap completely with the realist and liberal labels. Some realists, notably Henry Kissinger and Stephen Walt, have considered internal processes such as revolutions to be sources of threat.[13] Furthermore, while liberalism in its most general form can simply refer to the importance of domestic factors in international politics, in international relations theory liberalism usually refers to a specific set of propositions about the effects of democracy and economic openness.[14] The theory developed in this book could also be applied in nondemocratic settings: for example, Soviet leaders could be more or less internally focused, perhaps accepting less thoroughly communist regimes if they were strong allies. Furthermore, the argument is not equivalent to claiming that "ideology matters." One can believe in an ideology, and even champion the superiority of an ideology (as all Cold War presidents did), without necessarily connecting changes in another state's internal order to security threats.[15]

An important concern is that causal beliefs may simply be an expression of some other underlying factor. For example, perhaps certain leaders, such as those who have served in the military, are more likely to hold certain beliefs.[16] The empirical chapters, however, identify diverse pathways through which leaders acquire causal beliefs, such as experience and self-education, illustrating that causal beliefs do not spring from a single source. Political parties are another potentially confounding factor: as discussed below, there is an apparent correlation between threat perception and party, with Republicans tending to be externally focused, and Democrats internally focused.[17] But there are also important exceptions, notably the externally focused Lyndon Johnson and the internally focused Ronald Reagan, suggesting that it is important to pin down threat perceptions for each individual. Leaders with certain beliefs may be drawn to one party over another or may join parties irrespective of these particular foreign policy beliefs. The empirical chapters suggest that parties do not formally socialize leaders to hold causal beliefs about the origin of threats.

The connection to parties implies, however, that in the United States the two ideal-typical causal beliefs are not arbitrary, but rather stem from long-standing currents of political thought. Leaders tap into these currents of thought, one focusing on other states' domestic institutions as a source of threat (which in the United States usually takes the form of a concern about the degree of popular legitimacy) and the other focusing on external behavior. These currents of thought stem from powerful shared ideas that persist over time in American political culture and may even be older than the U.S. capability to intervene overseas (often dated from the late nineteenth century and the Spanish-American War). From the founding era, American leaders have debated whether to evaluate other states based on their domestic institutions, as illustrated by the vehement debate in the 1790s over which side to favor in the European war. Thomas Jefferson saw revolutionary France, with its emphasis on liberty and equality, as a natural ally of the American republic and thus wished to preserve the Franco-American connection. Alexander Hamilton, in contrast, argued that republics were just as "addicted to war" as monarchies and that "momentary passions . . . and immediate interests" governed human affairs, leading him to favor at least a temporary alignment with Britain to secure access to British commerce and avoid another war with Britain until the United States grew stronger.[18]

Some political scientists and historians have gone so far as to posit a single dominant national pattern of intervention. In this vein, some argue that the United States has a national tendency to promote institutional change abroad. Tony Smith, for example, documents a long-standing "democratizing mission" in U.S. foreign policy, including interventions.[19] In the Cold War context, Odd Arne Westad argues that the American ideological tradition led the United States to promote its vision of liberty and reform in its Cold War interventions.[20] In a review of what he terms "America's long 'regime change' century," Stephen Kinzer emphasizes that regime change has long been a feature of U.S. foreign policy.[21] Robert Kagan goes even further, tracing the U.S. tendency to promote its ideals back to the founding era.[22] Additionally, shared ideas at the international level undoubtedly shape and constrain the way states intervene in certain eras, as Martha Finnemore's study of the evolving purpose of intervention shows.[23]

Yet even within strong national traditions of intervention or prevailing international conditions, there remains shorter-term variation in how leaders perceive threats and in the way states use intervention, differences that can provoke fierce debate. In the early twentieth century, for example, Theodore Roosevelt and Woodrow Wilson took quite different approaches to intervention in the Caribbean. Roosevelt focused on internationally oriented behavior such as the collection of debt whereas Wilson saw the form of local governments as an inherent source of threat to U.S. security and declared that he would "teach the South American republics to elect good men."[24] During the Cold War, the international environment and its norms conditioned the superpowers to use intervention to ensure stability within their respective spheres of influence, perhaps constraining the number of truly transformative interventions until the fall of the Berlin Wall ushered in an era of more intrusive interventions, often for humanitarian purposes.[25] Yet even within the Cold War, as John Lewis Gaddis chronicles, there were dramatic shifts—very much driven by presidents themselves—in how the United States pursued containment, including intervention in the Third World.[26]

My findings suggest that it is individual leaders whose causal beliefs decisively assert which of the two traditions of American intervention dominates during their tenure. The research design and empirical evidence help to illustrate that leaders' intervention choices vary even within the dominant paradigm of a particular era, and that policy shifts do not stem from some other domestic source. In the book's empirical chapters, I show, for example, that leaders actively shape their advisory circles and are not merely prisoners of others' ideas, and that leaders' threat perceptions do not merely reflect the electorate's preferences.

In the remainder of this chapter, I outline my strategy for identifying the role of leaders in the face of several theoretical and empirical problems and discuss the research design and case selection. Readers primarily interested in the general argument and the case studies should find the main points and the rationale for the design of the book outlined in this chapter; those interested in the details of the theory, method, and measurement strategy will find a complete discussion in chapter 2.

Identifying the Role of Leaders

We have an intuitive understanding that leaders play an important role in shaping military interventions, but actually demonstrating that leaders' threat perceptions have an independent effect on intervention choices is a major challenge. One significant difficulty is separating the role of individuals from the influence of domestic politics or the structure of the international system. To isolate the effect of leaders, the empirical heart of this book concentrates on U.S. military interventions during the Cold War. By examining only the United States (by that time firmly entrenched as a great power) within one international system (a bipolar world), I hold domestic institutions, great-power status, and the structure of the international system relatively constant. I focus on U.S. actions in the Third World, since the extent to which the international behavior and domestic institutions of Third World states constituted threats to U.S. interests was a major source of debate during the Cold War, and the Third World was the locus of Cold War military interventions.

I investigate the presidencies of Eisenhower, Kennedy, and Johnson, leaders who provide strong leverage for examining both the impact of causal beliefs and alternative hypotheses. To avoid conflating beliefs and behavior, and to address the possibility that beliefs are merely justifications for action, I use archival and historical evidence from the pre-presidential period to show that each president held his beliefs before confronting crises and even before taking office. For each president, I examine both actual interventions and those that might have occurred but did not, since leaders' causal beliefs may lead them to choose nonintervention. I focus my archival efforts on the pre-presidential period, relying on published primary sources and secondary accounts for tracing intervention decisions in order to cover more ground in the case studies.

The Cold War should be a relatively easy case for realist and rationalist approaches and a harder test for a theory based on leaders' causal beliefs about the origin of threats. We might expect a particularly strong "threat consensus" during the Cold War, when each side had a clear adversary. Indeed, it might seem somewhat odd to argue that American leaders varied in their threat perceptions during this period since all Cold War presidents were anticommunist; by definition, each perceived threats at least in part based on the internal arrangements of other states. Despite the Cold War consensus, however, the nature of the communist threat remained subject to interpretation. Was communism a threat because it represented a particular internal organization for other states, or was it a threat because of the Soviet Union's challenge to the balance of power and attempt to bring as many allies as possible into its sphere of influence?[27] In terms of the Third World, where most Cold War interventions occurred, some presidents (such as Kennedy, Carter, and Reagan) focused on preventing Third World states from "going communist" as a result of domestic weakness, particularly feeble or illiberal institutions that left them susceptible to a communist takeover from within or vulnerable to an attack from outside. Others (such as Eisenhower, Johnson, and Nixon) concentrated on outside aggression against Third World states, or subversion of institutions that was directed from the outside and could threaten any state regardless of its domestic order. The threat of "communism" could thus mean merely the threat of further Soviet bloc advances on the world map, or it could take on the additional meaning of a threat from the domestic institutions of Third World states that might go communist from within.

U.S. presidents confronting decolonization and revolution in the Third World thus arrived at very different diagnoses and prescriptions for American security. While U.S. interventions during the Cold War shared an anticommunist aim, presidents chose a wide variety of responses to Cold War crises, including choosing *not* to intervene. As Yuen Foong Khong notes, "the correlation between containment and military intervention raises as many questions as it answers."[28] Another significant Cold War concern was maintaining credibility, but leaders showed considerable flexibility in where they believed credibility was at stake and how they demonstrated toughness.

Given the apparent Cold War consensus, demonstrating variation in and the importance of leaders' threat perceptions during the Cold War provides stronger evidence for the theory than if I tested it in another period such as the immediate post–Cold War era, when many observers have argued there was little consensus about the nature of threats.[29] One might still be concerned that the Cold War is a special case because it gave the United States reason to be particularly worried that leftist regimes would threaten American interests. Chapter 6, however, extends the argument both before and after the Cold War, showing that the pattern holds in other international settings. The variation in leaders' causal beliefs is not unique to a particular time period, though it can be shaped and constrained by the conditions of each era and by different substantive concerns about the nature of other states' regimes.

As a liberal democracy, the United States also provides a tough test for the role of leaders, since we might expect leaders to have a greater independent impact in autocracies.[30] Furthermore, although the president has strong informational and agenda-setting powers on foreign policy issues,[31] the public and other domestic elites have more opportunities to influence policymaking than in other systems. One might argue that concentrating on the United States runs the risk of focusing on American "exceptionalism" in promoting institutions abroad. But in the twentieth century and in other periods, as John Owen has shown, both democracies and autocracies have sought to impose domestic institutions on other states.[32] The argument could be extended to other countries, including autocracies. Even in the Soviet Union, in which political ideology was based on transforming societies, leaders varied in how actively they imposed their vision on Third World states.[33] Focusing on the United States serves a methodological purpose, but understanding U.S. intervention choices is important in its own right since the United States will likely remain the only state with the capability to undertake large-scale and distant interventions for the immediate future.

Capturing Causal Beliefs

There remain two common pitfalls for any attempt to trace the effect of beliefs on behavior. First, leaders may say and do things under the pressure of crisis decision making that may not reflect what they actually believe. It is therefore dangerous to use these responses as evidence of their "revealed" preferences. We cannot simply observe, for example, an intervention that changes the target state's institutions and infer that the leader of the intervening state was internally focused. Second, how do we know that the stated beliefs are not merely "hooks" that leaders employ to justify decisions already made?[34]

To avoid these pitfalls, I use three strategies, all designed to conceptualize and measure causal beliefs independent of the phenomenon being explained.[35] First, I shift my measurement of causal beliefs to the pre-presidential period, to show that leaders arrived in office with a set of ideas already in place and held those beliefs before they faced actual crises. This temporal separation avoids conflating beliefs and behavior, as well as the "ideas-as-hooks" problem.[36] The measurement strategy also makes theoretical sense: scholarship has shown that leaders draw on their experience when confronting decisions, and that these beliefs are highly "sticky."[37] As Henry Kissinger put it, "the convictions that leaders have formed before reaching high office are the intellectual capital they will consume as long as they continue in office."[38] This argument raises the question of whether leaders learn over time. I find only limited evidence of learning, consistent with arguments that people use their existing beliefs as a prism through which they view new information.

As a second strategy to avoid conflating beliefs and behavior, I develop a set of indicators to capture causal beliefs independent of intervention behavior. For each president and administration that I examine in depth, I use a common set of questions and indicators. The indicators for threat perception (discussed in detail in chapter 2) investigate the future president's views on the nature of threats; on alliances and the American sphere of influence, especially whether he focused on a Third World state's internal institutions or its external alignment; and on the nature and purpose of foreign aid, a useful measure of how the future president saw threats that is not necessarily correlated with intervention strategy. These indicators probe threat perception, and not simply a belief in the efficacy of a particular strategy, since relying on the latter would risk a tautological explanation. I also examine any views the future president expressed on strategy and policy investments in the years before he took office, especially in terms of intervention in the Third World. Understanding how a leader's beliefs translated into positions on strategy and even the interventions of his predecessors is useful evidence because it is separated in time from the future leader's intervention decisions and helps establish both how his beliefs translated into policy preferences in his pre-presidential career and whether his views changed from this period to his time in office. Finally, I examine policy investments made early in each administration, before leaders faced crises, as an observable implication of causal beliefs that is also temporally separated from intervention decisions.

I evaluate the effect of causal beliefs on intervention decisions using case studies and process tracing. In light of the difficulties involved in isolating the role of leaders, this method is a useful way to identify the causal mechanisms at work within a set of cases chosen to hold other factors relatively constant and to gain maximum analytical leverage. Process tracing can illuminate the mechanisms behind both the decision to intervene (including noninterventions) and the choice of intervention strategy.

Case Selection

In choosing presidents to study, I seek to maximize leverage in terms of leaders' threat perceptions (the primary explanatory variable) while controlling for potentially confounding factors. Table 1.1 details the threat perceptions of U.S. presidents from Truman to George W. Bush, along with their major interventions and a list of significant noninterventions (the list of noninterventions is not exhaustive, but rather highlights major decisions).[39] The codings are binary, but there are differences in degree. Kennedy, for example, was much more firmly focused on the internal characteristics of other states than was Truman, although both are classified as internally focused.

For in-depth study, I examine the administrations of Eisenhower, Kennedy, and Johnson, who governed when the superpower conflict was well under way and the international system was relatively stable. Both Kennedy and Johnson served in Congress during Eisenhower's presidency, so all three considered many of the same issues and crises.

Most importantly, these three presidents provide variation in causal beliefs. Eisenhower, whom I code as externally focused, and Kennedy, whom I find to be internally focused, are relatively clear examples of each ideal type. Eisenhower was certainly anticommunist, and in this sense, like all Cold War presidents, he was concerned about other states' regimes. But as long as states were noncommunist and reliably pro-American, the nature of their internal order mattered little. His concern was thus a negative concern—focused on what regimes were *not*—rather than a positive concern about how other states were organized internally. This argument might seem surprising because Eisenhower is so often identified with covert operations designed to prevent the rise of supposedly communist regimes in the Third World. But Eisenhower embraced such operations in part because he saw them as quick fixes that would ensure noncommunist regimes and prevent the loss of client states to the Soviet Union without requiring extensive institution building within target states. In contrast, Kennedy believed strongly that U.S. national security was threatened by domestic conditions in Third World countries. Domestic conditions might lead to aggression or leave states vulnerable to a communist takeover, and therefore the United States had to help guide the development of these states' domestic institutions, especially in the direction of increased popular legitimacy.

TABLE 1.1.
U.S. presidents, interventions, and major noninterventions, 1945–2008

President	Threat perception	Interventions (strategy in parentheses)[a]	Major noninterventions
Truman	Internal	Korea, 1950 (NT, briefly T)	Chinese Civil War, 1948; carrying Korean War into China
Eisenhower	External	Lebanon, 1958 (NT)	Indochina, 1954; Suez, 1956; Iraq, 1958
Kennedy	Internal	Vietnam counter-insurgency, 1962 (T)	Cuba, 1961 (overt); Laos, 1961; Cuba, 1962
Johnson	External	Vietnam, 1965 (NT); Dominican Republic, 1965 (NT)	Panama, 1964
Nixon	External	Cambodia, 1970 (NT)	Yom Kippur War, 1973
Ford	External		Angola (overt), 1975
Carter	Internal		Nicaragua, 1978–1979; Afghanistan, 1979; Iran, 1979–1980
Reagan	Internal	Lebanon, 1982 (NT); Grenada, 1983 (T)	El Salvador/Nicaragua (overt), 1980s
George H. W. Bush	External	Panama, 1989 (T); Gulf War, 1991 (NT); Somalia, 1992 (NT)	Carrying Gulf War to Baghdad; Bosnia, 1992
Clinton	Internal	Somalia, 1993 (T); Haiti, 1994 (T); Bosnia, 1995 (T); Kosovo, 1999 (T)	Rwanda, 1994
George W. Bush	External (initially); change after 9/11?	Afghanistan, 2001 (initially NT?); Iraq, 2003 (initially NT?)	Darfur, 2003–2008

[a] NT = nontransformative; T = transformative.

Johnson provides a somewhat unlikely case for an externally focused leader, particularly in light of his arguably transformative efforts at home through the Great Society. Comparing Kennedy and Johnson provides especially useful analytical leverage. Given that Johnson shared Kennedy's party affiliation, served as Kennedy's vice president, inherited much of Kennedy's national security apparatus, and emphasized continuity to the public in the wake of Kennedy's assassination, the policy differences Johnson had with Kennedy are all the more striking.[40] Furthermore, the assassination meant that the transition did not arise from factors correlated with intervention, and thus changes in intervention policy across the two presidencies did not stem from voters electing a president with particular intervention preferences. Despite the many factors that might lead us to expect otherwise, Johnson did not share Kennedy's focus on threats from the domestic order of Third World states. Rather, Johnson's evaluation of threats was relatively similar to Eisenhower's even though the two men differed strongly in many other respects.

For each president, my approach is first to examine his causal beliefs and policy investments. Then I turn to the universe of potential and actual interventions. One might argue that leaders are more likely to intervene when there are more opportunities to do so.[41] Yet opportunities do not seem to significantly affect the general intervention picture: Eisenhower and Kennedy each had many opportunities, but each intervened overtly only once, for example.

The type of intervention opportunity might also be critical. The potential costs and benefits of an intervention vary with the nature of the conflict, such as whether it is a civil or an interstate war, as well as conditions within the target state, such as terrain and the intensity of fighting.[42] I do not argue that leaders ignore a sobering confrontation with the realities of the target environment, but I attempt to show that causal beliefs influence decisions even once we account for such realities. Leaders obviously consider costs and the likelihood of success, but Americans are painfully aware that the United States has intervened in difficult contexts such as Korea and Vietnam.

In choosing cases within each presidency to examine in depth, I aim to explore how leaders' causal beliefs influence intervention decisions within each leader's tenure, as well as how beliefs explain variation in decisions across presidencies. For each president, I select one intervention and one nonintervention, closely spaced in time and within the same region. This case selection strategy helps control for as many factors as possible, such as available capabilities, regional effects, international conditions, and domestic politics within the United States. These paired comparisons of interventions and noninterventions illustrate how the causal mechanisms shape intervention decisions within each presidency.

To show how causal beliefs affect decisions within an ongoing conflict across multiple presidencies, I also discuss the approaches of all three presidents to the Vietnam War. A conflict such as Vietnam undoubtedly attracted American interest in part because the nature of the government was at stake within the larger context of the Cold War. Furthermore, each president sought to protect U.S. credibility and avoid the "loss" of Vietnam.

Despite this consensus, however, the three presidents differed in the extent to which they identified the domestic institutions of South Vietnam as the source of the problem. As a result, their responses varied in terms of how much they tried to reshape those institutions as part of their strategy for keeping South Vietnam noncommunist and demonstrating U.S. resolve, rather than simply being satisfied with any government or leader so long as South Vietnam did not "go communist." The circumstances of the conflict in Vietnam changed, of course, across the three presidencies. But we can still get useful leverage by examining what the three leaders said and wrote about Vietnam at points when they confronted similar circumstances. Both Kennedy and Johnson expressed views while Eisenhower was deciding whether to intervene in Indochina in 1954, for example. Furthermore, we have the record of the views Johnson expressed when he served as Kennedy's vice president, a period in which he sat in on many meetings on Vietnam. Johnson's escalation in Vietnam can be considered an especially difficult case for the theory because in addition to the Cold War consensus, Johnson felt pressure to demonstrate continuity with Kennedy's policies.

For Eisenhower, I first briefly explore his approach to Latin America, setting up a comparison with Kennedy and especially Johnson, who intervened overtly in the region. I also discuss Eisenhower's decision not to intervene in Indochina in 1954. I then turn to a paired comparison of the crises in the Middle East in July 1958, when Eisenhower intervened in Lebanon but not in Iraq. For Kennedy, I also briefly discuss his policies in Latin America for comparative purposes. For a paired comparison within his presidency, I investigate Kennedy's decision not to intervene in Laos but to initiate a counterinsurgency war in Vietnam. For Johnson, the paired comparison is less obvious. However, Johnson's handling of the 1964 crisis in Panama provides a useful comparison with his intervention in the Dominican Republic in 1965. I also examine his escalation of the war in Vietnam. Table 1.2 summarizes the cases I explore in depth.

Collectively, these cases provide evidence, within a relatively controlled domestic and international environment, that leaders' causal beliefs about the origin of threats strongly influence decisions about where and how to intervene. Eisenhower demonstrated an externally focused threat perception throughout his pre-presidential career, concentrating on other states' foreign policies and alignment with the United States rather than their internal affairs. As president,

TABLE 1.2.
Cases examined in chapters 3–5

President	Threat perception	Interventions (strategy in parentheses)[a]	Noninterventions
Eisenhower	External	Lebanon, 1958 (NT)	Indochina, 1954; Iraq, 1958
Kennedy	Internal	Vietnam counterinsurgency, 1962 (T)	Laos, 1961
Johnson	External	Vietnam, 1965 (NT); Dominican Republic, 1965 (NT)	Panama, 1964

[a] NT = nontransformative; T = transformative.

Eisenhower confronted revolution in the more strategically important Iraq and comparatively minor instability in Lebanon, and faced pressure to demonstrate American resolve. But he declined to intervene in Iraq and chose a limited, nontransformative intervention in Lebanon, where he would not have to get deeply involved in building or rebuilding domestic institutions. In contrast, Kennedy held clear beliefs that located the source of threats in the internal institutions of other states. He formed these beliefs long before taking office, as early as 1951, when he toured the Middle East and Asia in search of a better understanding of Third World politics. Almost immediately after taking office, he devoted considerable attention to policy investments in transformative strategies. Despite calls from many of his advisers for a nontransformative intervention in Laos to signal credibility, Kennedy instead accepted a negotiated settlement. He also shaped the intended U.S. strategy in Vietnam, repeatedly overruling advice to use a conventional strategy and arguing instead for a transformative counterinsurgency policy (which the military resisted). Kennedy's Vietnam strategy culminated in his consideration of a coup against South Vietnamese president Ngo Dinh Diem, a U.S. ally whom Kennedy deemed an obstacle to reform.

Johnson did not share Kennedy's diagnosis of threats. Despite his commitment to domestic reform within the United States, Johnson's pre-presidential years demonstrate a clear external focus. As president, Johnson intervened in the Dominican Republic to preserve stability. In Vietnam, where Johnson faced more difficult circumstances than Kennedy, his initial approach rejected Kennedy's counterinsurgency emphasis in favor of conventional warfare. Changing circumstances within Vietnam are insufficient to explain Johnson's choice of strategy for the initial escalation. Johnson's vice presidential record is particularly helpful in identifying the role of his beliefs.

In general, I find that leaders' threat perceptions are relatively consistent from the pre-presidential period through the presidency, and that presidents are slow to change their beliefs about the origin of threats. It is especially difficult to assess learning during an ongoing intervention because changes in strategy may be driven by battlefield or political circumstances rather than true changes in beliefs. The theory therefore has more to say about the initial choice of strategy than about changes in strategy as the intervention unfolds. But as the cases of Vietnam and Iraq illustrate, the initial choice of strategy may be critical to the overall course of the intervention.

After establishing my claims in the Cold War, chapter 6 demonstrates that the theory applies outside this period. I briefly compare how Theodore Roosevelt and Woodrow Wilson approached intervention in the Dominican Republic and then turn to the post–Cold War period, contrasting how George H. W. Bush and Bill Clinton approached intervention in Somalia. I also discuss how the argument applies to the Iraq War.

Including leaders in the analysis of state behavior need not doom scholars to studying a series of contingencies or "great men."[43] It is possible to distinguish among leaders in a systematic, rigorous way that identifies their role in shaping how states use force.

Defining and Explaining Intervention

How do leaders' causal beliefs about the origin of threats shape both the initial decision to intervene and the choice of intervention strategy? Given the discretionary nature of intervention, the ambiguity of national interests, and the large number of potential threats in the international environment, leaders need some way to assess and prioritize the many possible hazards they confront.[1] Unlike analysts who posit a single logic for how states confront threats, I suggest that different leaders, even within the same state, hold one of two ideal-typical causal beliefs, depending on whether they diagnose threats as emerging from a state's domestic order or whether they instead view threats as arising primarily from external behavior. By directly and indirectly influencing how leaders view the benefits, costs, and probability of success of interventions, leaders' causal beliefs about the origin of threats exert a strong independent effect on both when and how states intervene. Although the theory is framed generally, throughout the chapter I frequently refer to U.S. foreign policy for ease of exposition.

What Is Military Intervention? Defining the Universe of Cases

Many definitions of intervention focus on interference in the domestic affairs of target states.[2] But as Finnemore persuasively argues, these definitions exclude many forms of intervention.[3] Furthermore, such a definition obscures variation in the depth of internal interference. Many interventions that technically involve some interference in the domestic affairs of the target state do not attempt to change the target state's institutions directly, even if the intervention itself has long-term internal consequences. The 1958 U.S. intervention in Lebanon, for example, ostensibly shored up Lebanon's domestic order but stopped short of direct interference in Lebanese domestic institutions. The intervention was largely a demonstration of the credibility of U.S. security guarantees in the wider context of the Cold War in the Middle East. Additionally, many scholars analyze the problem in terms of specific types of intervention, such as interventions in civil wars, humanitarian crises, alliance defense, or democratization, resulting in largely separate literatures. There remains little general theorizing about when states undertake certain types of intervention or choose among different options for intervention in a single crisis.

Rather than define intervention too narrowly, I follow Finnemore in treating variation in the purpose and nature of intervention as part of the phenomenon to be explained, and I argue for a definition that allows the depth of domestic interference to vary. I therefore define military intervention as an overt, short-term deployment of at least one thousand combat-ready ground troops across international boundaries to influence an outcome in another state or an interstate dispute; it may or may not interfere in another state's domestic institutions.

The components of this definition help bound the universe of cases. For example, "short-term" may encompass a wide range of time frames but is intended to capture the idea that intervention is not aimed at conquest or colonialism. The universe of potential interventions encompasses both interstate and intrastate crises, including state failure and humanitarian crises. Both interstate and intrastate crises have attracted intervention, and both can be undertaken with varying degrees of internal interference. Depending on the leader's threat perception, there may also be a subjective element in what "counts" as a potential intervention. An internally focused leader, for example, may see domestic changes in other states as grounds for intervention, increasing the number of potential interventions for that leader. Furthermore, the same crisis may attract the attention of potential interveners for different reasons because many crises contain both international aspects and dimensions associated with the domestic politics of the potential target state. In other crises, the nature of the conflict may be ambiguous. In defining the universe of potential interventions, I exclude cases in which leaders were restrained by a clear risk of nuclear escalation, as in the Berlin crisis of 1961 and other cases in which the United States might have intervened in Eastern Europe.

Several other restrictions help ensure comparability across cases. First, I limit the universe of cases to overt military interventions and exclude covert operations because overt deployments involve an explicit, visible decision to commit forces for potentially costly actions. Other forms of intervention, such as covert operations, do not risk extensive military losses or put national prestige on the line to the same degree. A covert operation is usually much less costly, and if it remains secret, involves no audience costs. Even externally focused leaders may be tempted to use covert operations to meddle in other states' internal affairs because they offer the promise of a quick, relatively low-cost way to effect change. Thus the causal process that governs decisions to intervene covertly is theoretically very different from that governing the decision to intervene overtly.[4] In overt military interventions, as Bruce Jentleson and Ariel Levite note, leaders cross a "critical threshold . . . from other forms of intervention to the direct and massive commitment of combat troops."[5]

Second, to further facilitate comparability, and because ground troops are likely required for transformative strategies, I exclude operations involving only air or naval power. Other analysts have emphasized that "boots on the ground" are required for transformative strategies such as democratization and thus exclude air and naval incursions.[6] Covert, air, or naval operations may be relevant, however, when they are part of ongoing overt interventions. Similarly, I discuss how other elements of foreign policy such as foreign aid relate to a leader's threat perception and intervention choices.

Third, I include only deployments of at least one thousand combat-ready ground troops, a restriction intended to capture significant deployments in which troops were prepared to use force (thus excluding rescue missions or disaster relief).[7] Additionally, wars such as the 1991 Gulf War are included if they involved an outside power choosing to intervene in a dispute.[8] Finally, intervention may be used either in support of or in opposition to a government.[9] Even a transformative strategy can be used in support of an incumbent government (for example, by helping the government improve its relationship with its people through institutional reform or creation).

Three Intervention Options

The theory developed in this chapter addresses both the decision to intervene and the choice of intervention strategy. For leaders who choose to intervene, I distinguish between two ideal-typical strategies, according to whether the strategy involves significant interference in the target state's domestic institutions.

A *nontransformative* strategy aims to resolve an international or civil conflict or crisis, or restrain or roll back a foreign policy action, without the explicit intention to alter domestic institutions within the target state. Examples include interventions designed to aid local allies against outside aggression (as in the 1991 Gulf War). Leaders can also choose a nontransformative strategy in humanitarian interventions, as in George H. W. Bush's limited approach in Somalia. For a civil conflict, a nontransformative strategy would focus on stopping the fighting or preventing international consequences such as conflict spillover, but without nation building. Of course, a nontransformative strategy may have a dramatic effect on civilians and institutions, and it is possible that internal change may occur as a by-product. Furthermore, nontransformative interventions usually involve some treading on the state's domestic affairs. But the coding is intended to distinguish limited or collateral involvement from deliberate institutional interference. Even highly destructive or brutal strategies are treated as nontransformative if they do not aim to ensure a particular set of institutions. Some interventions that shore up existing governments may also be considered nontransformative. Some interventions on behalf of another regime try to reform or build domestic institutions in an attempt to stop internal change that would otherwise occur, but others are considered nontransformative if they try to protect the status quo with limited or no institutional interference, or if they merely try to block unfavorable leaders or regimes without a real preference for alternative institutions. In the 1965 Dominican Republic intervention, for example, Johnson merely tried to forestall the appearance of a communist government but otherwise paid little attention to the nature of governmental institutions.

In contrast, a *transformative* strategy explicitly aims to interfere in or actively determine the target state's domestic order. For example, Woodrow Wilson's approach to intervention in the Dominican Republic contrasts sharply with that of Theodore Roosevelt. Whereas Roosevelt limited his intervention to protecting the Dominican customhouses amid domestic instability that threatened the collection of debt, Wilson sent U.S. troops to occupy the country from 1916 until 1924 and sought to remake Dominican domestic institutions.[10] To be considered transformative, the intervention strategy must attempt to change, construct, or rebuild the target state's domestic institutions (usually political institutions but potentially also economic, social, or military institutions). An intervention on the side of an incumbent government may be considered transformative if it keeps the leadership in place but changes or reforms underlying institutions. National-level institutions, such as legislatures and ministries, are an obvious source of transformational change, but transformation may also occur through local-level institutions, either in tandem with national-level change or as a way to spur national-level reform or bolster an existing regime.

At the national level, one might imagine that leadership change would constitute transformation. As John Owen and others have pointed out, however, institutional change is distinct from changing only the leader or a small group of elites.[11] Thus we cannot assume that regime change is necessarily transformative. Leadership change that occurs alongside or in the service of institutional change is considered transformative. But a "decapitation" that targets only the leadership of the target state without actively engaging in underlying institutional change is insufficient to categorize an intervention as transformative. Leadership change itself must be a deliberate strategy: change that occurs as a by-product of intervention, without the explicit targeting of military power against the regime, would not qualify. Thus one indicator for national-level institutional change is how deeply the intervening state intended any leadership change to extend. But at least one other indicator of national-level change must be present for the intervention to be coded as transformative. Since interventions may occur on behalf of an incumbent government, however, leadership change is not a necessary condition for transformation. Other indicators for national-level change, developed in more detail at the end of this chapter, include whether the intervention aimed at national-level institutional reform or construction and whether nonmilitary issues were well integrated with, and considered part of, the overall military strategy.

A transformative strategy may also aim to change local-level institutions, usually as a means of achieving national-level change, but with most of the actual institution building occurring at the local level. Indicators for intended local-level change are similar to those at the national level: whether the overall strategy aimed to employ the military in building or reforming local-level institutions; the integration of local-level nonmilitary issues with the overall military strategy; and whether troops aimed to interact with the local population. Examples of local-level transformative strategies include nation building and post-conflict reconstruction. Furthermore, some (though certainly not all) forms of counterinsurgency incorporate institution building into the war-fighting strategy and thus have an explicitly transformative character. Population-centered counterinsurgency, especially as understood in the 1950s and 1960s, calls for deep involvement in local institutions.[12] In such a strategy, counterinsurgency forces must not only drive away guerrillas but also build local security institutions to protect the population, as well as, ideally, political and civic institutions that can foster loyalty to the government and separate the insurgents from their base of support in that population. The *U.S. Army and Marine Corps Counterinsurgency Field Manual*, updated during the Iraq War, explicitly embraces this view of counterinsurgency.[13] Institution building and interaction with the population are critical to this kind of counterinsurgency, but conventional, mechanized force using regular units is counterproductive. Population-centered counterinsurgency can take the form of local-level transformation in support of an existing government and thus does not necessarily require leadership change.[14]

There are important differences within each class of intervention, but it makes theoretical sense to treat the distinction between transformative and nontransformative strategies as a binary choice.[15] There is a fundamental difference between actively involving a state's military in the internal affairs of the target state and fighting a more conventional battle that seeks no such interference.[16] There may be gradations of transformation, however: installing new leadership and enforcing or holding elections (as in the 1989 U.S. intervention in Panama) would be less transformative than full-scale transformation of national-level institutions. Changing both national- and local-level institutions would be even more transformative.

Leaders have a third option, of course: they can choose not to intervene at all. Far from being a residual category, noninterventions are a critical element of intervention decisions and emerge from the mechanisms proposed by the theory. The category is inherently somewhat ambiguous because leaders may opt against intervention for different reasons: because they did not deem a conflict or crisis threatening or because they wished to intervene but judged the estimated cost of their chosen strategy to be too high or their preparedness insufficient. Leaders must also weigh the expected utility of nonintervention in its own right: if the expected costs of not intervening are sufficiently high, perhaps from anticipated domestic or political audience costs, leaders may feel forced into intervening.

Explaining Intervention Choices

Alternative Explanations

Scholarship on intervention has tended to focus on why states initiate intervention,[17] or on particular forms of intervention, such as peacekeeping, peacemaking, democratization, or occupation.[18] There remains little theorizing, however, about the specific issue of how deeply intervention interferes in the domestic institutions of target states or how states choose from among different intervention strategies.[19]

Several theories could be extended to include the choice of intervention strategy. Many formulations, however, are not well suited to explaining variation in intervention choices within states over time because in attempting to explain broad trends in intervention outcomes, they rely on international or domestic factors that are either stable or slow to change. Furthermore, although they differ widely on the specifics, many of these explanations suggest that states with given international or domestic characteristics respond to intervention opportunities in similar ways, leaving no independent role for leaders. For example, most realist theories share the assumption that the anarchic international system—the structure of which changes rarely—produces external threats, such as shifts in relative capabilities, the balance of power, or international alignments. Thus states with a given level of power should respond in similar ways across space and time, regardless of who is in charge. In terms of intervention, Stephen Krasner, for example, argues that during the Cold War, the superpowers generally did not intervene in the Third World to alter "basic institutional arrangements" because these states were not particularly important in security terms.[20] Yet in assuming that all leaders see security threats in the same way, this argument misses interesting variation in strategy.

At the domestic level, many theories, including some that do address intervention strategy, also focus on either cross-national trends or the continuity of national intervention tendencies, rather than on changes in strategy within a given domestic setting. Theories that center on domestic political institutions predict, for example, that democracies are unlikely to intervene against each other.[21] Other domestic-level explanations address the choice of strategy but stress continuity rather than change. For example, Owen argues that both democracies and autocracies try to promote their own institutions; others have specifically noted the tendency for the United States to promote liberal democratic institutions.[22] Some theories that operate within the state also focus on continuity. Bureaucratic or institutional perspectives posit that organizations favor particular doctrines: for example, the U.S. Army has traditionally disliked transformative operations.[23] Although these analyses highlight consistent patterns in intervention strategy, changes in how states intervene within relatively short time periods can have important consequences.

Constructivists focus on a potentially rich source of within-country variation: the ideas that inform state behavior. But in practice, constructivists emphasize the social or shared nature of ideas and thus also tend to focus on long-term trends. Finnemore, for example, details how shared understandings of the purpose of intervention have evolved. During periods such as the Cold War, however, most states share one understanding of the legitimate purpose of intervention.[24] This approach is not necessarily incompatible with my argument, but it focuses on a more general, long-term understanding of the purpose of intervention rather than microlevel changes in how states wield intervention as a tool. Domestically, scholars have explored how shared ideas among elites affect policy choice, including strategy.[25] But a leader may hold distinct beliefs and may try to change the dominant framework by hiring advisers or government officials who share those beliefs.

Certain variants of existing approaches are better suited to addressing changes in intervention strategy over time, and they are the principal alternative explanations I address in the empirical chapters. One simple explanation is that states make intervention decisions (including the choice of strategy) through a cost-benefit analysis that is independent of individual leaders.[26] In this view, leaders may (or may not) hold different initial beliefs, but when they actually confront decisions, they do not vary systematically in how they view the benefits of intervening, which derive primarily from the international security situation. Leaders initiate interventions and determine strategy based on structural or material factors, including available capabilities in the intervening state and the characteristics of a given intervention opportunity (such as terrain or the intensity of a conflict), and try to choose the most appropriate strategy for the situation at hand. Under this approach, any variation in intervention outcomes is driven by the logic of the situation rather than by leaders. This argument suggests the following hypothesis:

Structural / Material Conditions Hypothesis

Leaders evaluate intervention opportunities based on structural and material conditions in the international environment, within their own state, and within the potential intervention target. Given a set of conditions, leaders will make similar cost-benefit calculations about whether and how to intervene, regardless of their own personal beliefs.

Another set of alternative explanations involves competition among domestic actors and thus could account for changes in intervention strategy within a state over time. Here domestic political actors, including leaders, may vary in the way they view the benefits of intervening, but it is the political struggle among these actors that accounts for variation in intervention decisions, not variation in leaders' beliefs alone. For example, a bureaucratic politics model that focuses on how leaders vary in their interactions with bureaucracies, or how much they defer to or override organizations such as the military, could account for variation over time.[27] Intervention decisions might also be a product of interactions or logrolling among advisers, other elites, domestic groups, or parties, all of whom may also respond to public opinion.[28] In this view, we would expect to see leaders get their way on some occasions but at other times defer to other domestic actors. An even stronger version of this argument might suggest that if advisers or advocacy groups within or outside the government drive intervention policy, then leaders should routinely defer to advisers who are exposed to similar information or be persuaded by such groups in policy debates. The following hypothesis encapsulates this family of arguments:

Domestic Competition Hypothesis

Competition among domestic actors, including not only leaders but also the bureaucracy, the public, advisers, parties, and advocacy groups, drives intervention policy. Intervention decisions, including the choice of strategy, are a product of political interaction among these actors rather than leaders' preferences.

It is important to note that these hypotheses are alternative explanations in the sense that they might be sufficient to account for intervention decisions and do not predict a systematic, independent role for leaders. But my argument does not imply that structural and material conditions or domestic competition do not matter; rather, the argument is that these factors are insufficient to explain intervention choices, and that leaders' causal beliefs have an effect on decisions independent of structural and material conditions or domestic competition.

THREAT PERCEPTION AND THE INDIVIDUAL LEVEL

In addition to these two explanations, a logical hypothesis for when and how states intervene is that states respond to perceived threats. Yet even explanations that connect intervention to the perception of threat make oversimplified or ambiguous predictions. Realists, for example, often argue that leaders intervene to protect vital national interests, but they provide little guidance for studying how states prioritize among the kinds of threats that often attract intervention.[29] At the domestic level, normative explanations for the democratic peace suggest that democracies tend to see autocracies as threatening, but these explanations usually do not specify how threat perceptions among or within democracies might vary.[30] Indeed, Margaret Hermann and Charles Kegley warn that scholars should not assume that all democratic leaders subscribe to the perceptions suggested by democratic peace theory.[31] More generally, as Robert Jervis emphasizes, the perception of danger is an inherently subjective process.[32] Yet despite frequent nods to its importance in international relations, there has been relatively little direct work on threat perception.[33]

To account for the subjectivity of threat perception, as well as variation in intervention choices over time, we can look to the individual level. Recently, international relations scholars have shown renewed interest in leaders.[34] One strand of research explores how a leader's desire to stay in office affects his policy choices.[35] In these theories, however, domestic political institutions or electoral incentives, rather than the attributes of individual leaders, drive policy choice. Substituting one leader for another does not change the predicted outcome. Another strand examines how leaders' reputations vary in terms of competence, honesty, or credibility.[36] But these arguments leave much variation among individual leaders unexplored. If leaders have an incentive to demonstrate resolve through costly actions, for example, where and how will they choose to make a stand?

There is also a rich individual-level tradition that draws on psychological theories. These theories highlight factors that may produce error or bias in the way individuals gather information or make decisions, such as misperception or the analogies and schemas that help decision makers make sense of a complex world.[37] Scholars have also explored traits such as differences in risk tolerance or aggressive tendencies, age, personality, and leadership style.[38] I do not focus on error or bias in threat perception or information processing,[39] or differences in the way leaders carry out policies, but rather concentrate on how their substantive beliefs shape conceptions of threats. As discussed below, however, psychological mechanisms may be one of several pathways through which leaders acquire beliefs. Furthermore, the argument could be extended to include psychological factors. For example, Khong shows that the use of different analogies influenced how Kennedy and Johnson intervened in Vietnam. The typology of leaders developed in this book suggests that certain leaders may be disposed to invoke certain analogies.[40]

A Theory of Intervention Decision Making

SCOPE AND LIMITS OF THE THEORY

Building on research showing that people vary in the prior beliefs and assumptions they employ when confronting decisions, I focus on individuals' substantive beliefs.[41] I argue that causal beliefs, or "beliefs about cause-effect relationships," guide leaders' understandings of the nature and origin of threats.[42] While the theory argues that leaders act to protect national security and make intervention decisions based on a cost-benefit calculation, it does not assume that all leaders facing the same constraints will view threats similarly. And while it argues that ideas inform the expected utility calculation and help define national interests, it makes no assumptions about how widely these ideas are shared among governing elites.

Before I elaborate the argument, however, it is important to note what this theory does *not* do. First, it does not address the likelihood of long-term intervention success or the durability of postconflict settlements. Second, it does not fully address the issue of strategic interaction. Some scholars have argued that both military doctrine and decisions to fight are contingent on the choices of adversaries.[43] But I concentrate on policymaking in the intervening state to explain variation within countries; moreover, leaders often do not know *ex ante* where they will be intervening when they make policy investments early in their tenure.[44] Third, while the argument acknowledges the role of domestic politics, in focusing on the decision maker I do not address the influence of public opinion or mass beliefs on elite preference formation itself. Scholars have shown that leaders have an agenda-setting role and that elite discourse has a significant shaping effect on public opinion (which can, in turn, act as a constraint).[45] Fourth, the theory does not address several other aspects of intervention choices, such as the overall size of the intervention. It describes only how the causal beliefs of leaders shape the cost-benefit calculation they make in a given situation. Fifth, as discussed at the end of this chapter, the theory does not make predictions about overall "interventionism," that is, the propensity for each leader to intervene. Finally, as discussed above, I do not address psychological biases that affect information processing, but I discuss connections with psychological approaches that suggest areas for future research.

Causal Beliefs: Two Paths to Threat Perception

This book is primarily concerned with great-power interventions in smaller powers. Smaller powers cannot threaten the great power's survival directly, but their alliance decisions or fate in conflicts can affect the global or regional balance of power. Smaller powers can also make direct moves, such as regional aggression or the expropriation of property or natural resources, that threaten the great power's interests. There are many more potential threats from smaller powers than leaders can confront directly, however. Even if there is a broad national consensus about an overarching threat—such as a superpower rival—different leaders within the same state may see different ways of prioritizing the many possible intervention opportunities they confront.

Leaders confront this problem by invoking causal beliefs about the origin of threats. In this framework, two different ideal-typical causal beliefs lead to perceptions of threat. One belief, held by *externally focused leaders*, is that threats are associated with other states' foreign and security policies or international orientation. Such leaders do not see a causal connection between these outcomes and the domestic institutions of smaller powers. When externally focused leaders consider threats against a smaller power's security or alignment, they do not connect such threats to the smaller power's internal institutions. In terms of more direct threats to the great power's interests, such as the seizure of a strategic asset, the expropriation of natural resources, or the initiation of regional or civil aggression, externally focused leaders treat smaller powers relatively similarly since, in this view, any state might engage in such behavior regardless of its internal organization. Any concern an externally focused leader has about domestic crises within other states centers primarily on the international dimensions of those crises, such as whether civil strife results in conflict spillover, produces a change in the state's alliances, or threatens a state's ability to meet its international obligations, as in Roosevelt's concern about the Dominican custom-houses. While this path to threat perception is consistent with many formulations of realism, some realists (such as Kissinger and Walt) address threats from within other states, as discussed in chapter 1.

To be sure, externally focused leaders may still have a general preference for other states' institutions, but they care less about the specific form of those institutions. During the Cold War, for example, some externally focused leaders, including Eisenhower and Johnson, were sensitive to changes in the domestic politics of other countries and reacted to the rise of regimes they believed to be communist or susceptible to communism, but they held primarily negative preferences—that these regimes be noncommunist. Furthermore, when considering Cold War issues such as credibility, externally focused leaders are less likely to worry about the domestic institutions of states they seek to protect in order to demonstrate resolve.

In contrast, *internally focused leaders* believe that a smaller power's foreign and security policies are intimately connected to its domestic institutions. Internally focused leaders bear some relation to those who use what Waltz calls "second image" thinking, concentrating on factors related to the internal structure of states.[46] Leaders who hold this causal belief care about threatening foreign and security policies or outcomes but also view the smaller power's domestic order as a genuine source of threat. Internally focused leaders might make several different connections between domestic institutions and threat. Most generally, leaders may believe that a particular regime is likely to produce a particular kind of foreign policy. One manifestation of such a belief, for example, is the view that democracies are likely to be peaceful whereas nondemocracies are aggressive. Some democratic leaders may thus subscribe to the liberal proposition that nondemocracies are inherently threatening or link aggressive behavior to internal institutions (as Wilson did in characterizing German aggression in his war message to Congress in 1917).[47] Alternatively, leaders may affirmatively prefer the certainty of a stable autocracy,[48] although it is important to distinguish such a preference from viewing autocrats as a short-term expedient to solve a foreign policy problem. Leaders may also believe that a state's domestic institutions are likely to determine its alliance choices, in turn raising concerns about the balance of power.

A second way to link internal institutions to threat is through the belief that revolutionary states may disrupt the international status quo. Walt argues that revolutionary states may be seen as threatening for a variety of reasons, including the increased uncertainty they engender and the potential threats they pose to other states' existing interests.[49] Leaders who hold this belief may not wait for actual revolutions before inferring threat, instead viewing conditions conducive to revolution or instability within a smaller power as potential sources of threat.

A third pathway through which internally focused leaders may perceive threats arises from the fear of "demonstration effects." Alternative authority structures in other states may cause leaders to perceive a threat to their own security (as when the Soviets saw West Berlin as a dangerous alternative that had to be sealed off).[50] Leaders may also worry about more direct "contagion" effects if a particular regime provided aid to rebels elsewhere. Thus for internally focused leaders, internal institutions can be threatening both as the ultimate source of foreign and security policy and in their own right.

Internally focused leaders can see the domestic institutions of smaller powers as a source of threat through two other pathways with particular relevance to the Cold War. Most leaders are likely to be concerned about the risk that a regional ally or friendly state will be attacked, or in the Cold War context, that a client state will fall under the other superpower's sphere of influence. But an internally focused leader might blame the smaller power's internal institutions for leaving it vulnerable to either external attack or takeover from within. Leaders also worry about maintaining credibility—indeed, credibility was a Cold War preoccupation. But an internally focused leader might see the demonstration of credibility as connected to domestic institutions. For internally focused leaders, an intervention that nominally results in victory but that does not leave the target state's regime resting on a firm institutional footing is not a complete victory. To an internally focused U.S. president, demonstrating credibility entails not merely showing that the United States has the will to fight but also ensuring that victory will last. Thus standing firm just anywhere, without taking the internal institutions of the target state into account and ensuring a favorable domestic outcome, is not enough to demonstrate resolve. An internally focused U.S. president who prefers democracy might also be concerned that attempting to demonstrate credibility by propping up weak or repressive institutions would only embolden other dictators.

Given that the Cold War provides so many reasons for leaders to focus on the internal institutions of other states, one might reasonably ask if it is possible to distinguish between internally and externally focused leaders during this period. Indeed, one might argue that U.S. presidents during the Cold War were unusually focused on the nature of other states' regimes, with a corresponding tendency to infer behavior from internal institutions. Yet the broad tendency—which all U.S. presidents during the Cold War indeed shared—to see the nature of other states' regimes as a matter of concern for U.S. policy still left significant variation in the extent to which leaders diagnosed threats from internal institutions. Given the strong Cold War tendency to react (or even overreact) to the slightest hint of communist advancement in the Third World, any variation we see in how presidents assessed threats is even stronger evidence that the pattern I identify holds.

It is important to note that both leader types are ultimately concerned with other states' foreign and security policies and position in the international system; the difference arises from how the two types diagnose the source of those policies and outcomes. Internally focused leaders, while concerned with international behavior and outcomes, pay additional attention to domestic organization because they see domestic institutions as causally connected to these outcomes. Internally focused leaders may expect that over time a government with a favorable domestic order will moderate any unacceptable foreign policies. The short-term risk that the state will have unfavorable foreign policies may be worth the long-run reward. Externally focused leaders may prefer to see certain institutions over the long run but are less willing to risk current foreign and security policies that are unfavorable.

Leaders form these causal beliefs before they arrive in office. The theory is agnostic about how leaders acquire beliefs. Indeed, the many pathways through which leaders develop beliefs strengthen the theory because they show that causal beliefs are not reducible to a single alternative explanation. These pathways may include psychological mechanisms, such as the influence of past experience (as in the case of Eisenhower), although direct experience is not necessary. Causal beliefs about the origin of threats may relate to other beliefs, such as domestic political orientation, although it is important to establish whether such a relationship is causal or coincidental.[51] Leaders may also acquire beliefs from work on policy issues, self-education, or contact with groups that hold shared beliefs. Kennedy provides an interesting twist on the latter two pathways: he expressed an early interest in threats from domestic conditions in the Third World, and as a congressman in 1951 he traveled on his own initiative to the Middle East and Asia. Later, as a senator and then as president, he surrounded himself with development economists and modernization theorists, although his decision making in Southeast Asia stayed even closer to a transformative agenda than did many of the recommendations from these advisers. Elite consensus and shared beliefs are thus possible and even likely, given that leaders can choose like-minded advisers.[52] In the case of intervention decisions, however, it may be sufficient for the leader alone to hold a belief. A leader may also bring to office beliefs that are shared with a certain group but not necessarily with other governmental elites (especially outside his chosen advisory circle). The important point is that these causal beliefs are installed in power in the person of the leader, and do not necessarily reflect the underlying preferences of the public or an existing elite consensus.

This argument raises the question whether beliefs change over time, perhaps through learning. Andrew Bennett's study of Soviet interventionism finds, for example, that Soviet and Russian leaders' experience with intervention led to changes in their beliefs that explain patterns in Soviet and Russian intervention behavior over time. Theoretically, learning is possible in this framework, but it is important to assess whether leaders who shift policies (such as intervention strategy) over time have undergone a true "change in cognitive structures as the result of experience or study," as Bennett defines learning, or whether changes in strategy reflect reluctant adjustments in the face of situational or political realities.[53] Situational pressures make assessments of learning particularly challenging during ongoing interventions, and thus the theory has less explanatory power as the intervention evolves. But the initial choice of strategy may have a lasting impact on the intervention even if leaders later try to shift strategies. Empirically, I look for evidence that leaders' beliefs changed through learning, but in practice I find little evidence of fundamental changes in causal beliefs, consistent with research showing that people assimilate new information through the framework of existing beliefs.[54]

How Causal Beliefs Influence Intervention Decisions

The Direct Mechanism: Causal Beliefs Shape Leaders' Valuation of Benefits

We can identify two mechanisms through which causal beliefs shape the way leaders confront intervention decisions. The leader's type *directly* shapes the cost-benefit calculus of intervention decisions by influencing how the leader values the benefits of successfully transforming target states. To see how this mechanism works, we must consider not only whether a crisis is resolved or instead continues but also *how* the crisis ends, in terms of both the target state's domestic institutions and its foreign and security policy. Leaving aside whether there is an actual intervention, we can disaggregate the outcome of a conflict or crisis into its international and domestic terms. The international terms concern the smaller power's alignment and security, as well as whether the smaller power continues to engage in foreign policy behavior that is unacceptable or hostile to the great power (or one of its clients) once the conflict is over. The domestic terms of a conflict outcome relate to whether the domestic order of the smaller power is favorable or acceptable to the great power after the conflict. This domestic order need not match the regime of the great power exactly. A "favorable" domestic outcome simply means that the smaller power has whatever domestic institutions the great power prefers.

Externally focused leaders prioritize favorable international outcomes. If forced to choose, they rank foreign policy success over achieving the "right" domestic institutions in the target state. U.S. presidents, for example, frequently have tolerated "friendly dictators"—the external benefit of friendliness outweighing the internal shortcoming of dictatorship. As Franklin Roosevelt was said to have remarked after Anastasio Somoza overthrew the elected government of Nicaragua in 1936, "He may be a son-of-a-bitch, but he is our son-of-a-bitch."[55] Most Cold War presidents accepted dictators that were reliably anticommunist. Even if the dictator is unfriendly, as long as his unfavorable foreign policy actions can be stopped, an externally focused leader may not see significant additional gains from removing him. Thus George H. W. Bush successfully ejected Saddam Hussein from Kuwait but left him in power after the 1991 Gulf War.

In contrast, internally focused leaders prioritize favorable internal outcomes. Internally focused leaders see greater benefits from achieving domestically successful crisis outcomes since they believe such outcomes are the ultimate key to securing favorable foreign and security policies. These benefits may outweigh the costs even if the target state's foreign and security policies are less favorable in the short term. One example stems from the dilemma of democratization. A smaller power might have democratic institutions after a conflict, but democratic elections could produce a government that is hostile to the great power or does not pursue the great power's preferred policies.[56] Of course, internally focused leaders would also welcome friendly foreign policies from the smaller state. But if forced to choose, internally focused leaders may be willing to sacrifice favorable foreign policies—at least in the short term—in exchange for long-term institutional success.

THE INDIRECT MECHANISM: POLICY INVESTMENTS

Leaders' causal beliefs also influence the cost-benefit calculus of interventions through a second, *indirect* mechanism: by influencing how leaders allocate scarce resources to confront threats. Before specific crises arise, leaders transmit their causal beliefs through the policy process by making policy investments that place more or less weight on capabilities for different intervention strategies. Of course, the availability of resources for a particular strategy will also be affected by the overall size of the military and related civilian agencies. Eisenhower, for example, constrained the size of conventional, non-nuclear forces so that these forces had more limited options. But given the level of conventional forces available, he still placed far more emphasis on nontransformative strategies.

The most important moment for policy investments is at the outset of the leader's tenure, when leaders have the most leverage to make significant changes, and policy investments have the most time to take hold.[57] Policy investments are also an observable implication of causal beliefs themselves, since by allocating scarce resources in advance of specific crises, leaders in effect declare what threats they believe are most important and how they intend to counter those threats. Military forces, military and civilian bureaucratic institutions, and non-military factors such as foreign aid programs can all place more or less weight on transformative or nontransformative strategies. While there will be institutional and bureaucratic constraints, leaders have a central agenda-setting role in selecting priorities.

Leaders' policy investments may not be implemented successfully. Bureaucratic resistance may hamper investments, as many have argued about Kennedy's attempts to institutionalize a counterinsurgency capability. Furthermore, investments may not take effect quickly enough to influence intervention outcomes significantly. But particularly if policy investments revert capabilities to a state's "normal" distribution of resources, the effect may be more immediate. Johnson's relaxation of Kennedy's pressure on the army to invest in counterinsurgency and George W. Bush's reversal of Clinton-era efforts to increase nation-building capacity, for example, returned the military to its preferred emphasis on regular war fighting. And the mere attempt to make policy investments is an important indicator of a leader's preferences, even if changes in capabilities lag.

Policy investments occur through several mechanisms. I concentrate on four indicators (developed in more detail at the end of this chapter): staffing decisions, strategy and the defense posture, budgetary allocations, and institutional creation and change (particularly within the bureaucracy). Some factors, such as bureaucratic institutions, are more difficult to change than others. The relationship between investments and preparedness is thus not necessarily linear.

Collectively, these policy investments affect the distribution of material, bureaucratic, and intellectual capabilities available for transformative or nontransformative strategies, and in turn, preparedness for different intervention strategies. There will be some inherent risk to any overt military intervention. Transformative strategies may also be inherently riskier, since they may lead to contact with domestic forces, engender domestic opposition, or provoke unforeseen political dynamics within the target state. All leaders presumably factor inherent risk into their estimates of costs and the probability of success.

But another form of risk stems from preparedness for different intervention strategies, which may raise the estimated probability of success or reduce the estimated cost of a particular strategy. This additional risk depends, in part, on policy investments and thus causal beliefs. Leaders make the initial policy investments, so they have information about the degree to which they have attempted to adjust capabilities in favor of a given intervention strategy.[58] Even if leaders

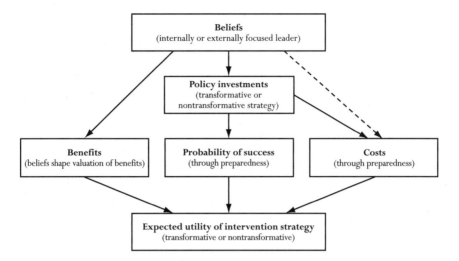

Figure 2.1. How leaders' causal beliefs influence the expected utility of an intervention strategy.

are not completely successful, however, merely attempting to change the distribution of capabilities to reflect their priorities may affect their perceptions of what capabilities are available when crises arise.

Intervention Decisions: Benefits, Costs, and the Probability of Success

When a leader confronts an opportunity to intervene, these two mechanisms—the valuation of benefits, and policy investments—combine to shape his overall cost-benefit calculation. We can conceptualize a leader's decision as the simultaneous evaluation of the expected utility of the two types of intervention (transformative or nontransformative), as well as the expected utility of not intervening.[59]

The Expected Utility of Intervention

Benefits. As shown on the left side of figure 2.1, the most direct way that causal beliefs influence the expected utility of a given intervention strategy is through the valuation of benefits. Internally focused leaders place more value on domestically successful outcomes, and thus the expected benefits of those outcomes contribute more to these leaders' expected utility for a transformative intervention.

Costs. As shown in the center and on the right side of figure 2.1, the effect of causal beliefs on the expected costs of intervention is channeled indirectly through policy investments. We would expect leaders to factor the inherent risk and cost of a given intervention opportunity into their decisions. But leaders must also consider the potentially higher or lower costs of intervening with a certain strategy, depending on preparedness for that strategy. For example, a leader might estimate that for a given target, a transformative strategy is likely to be inherently more costly than a nontransformative strategy. But good preparation might mitigate the inherent risk and cost whereas lack of preparation or improvised changes in strategy are likely to increase the risk of setbacks.

One might ask why there is no direct pathway through which beliefs influence costs. The effect of causal beliefs about the origin of threats on the estimated cost of a given strategy is ambiguous, as indicated by the dashed line in figure 2.1. Since each leader can, in theory, consider using either strategy, the question is whether different leaders considering the *same* strategy for a given intervention opportunity perceive different cost estimates. It is possible that the leader's type is correlated with systematically lower estimated costs for a particular strategy. Perhaps internally focused leaders are more likely to believe that transformation is easy to accomplish from the outside, just as in American domestic politics Democrats tend to see government intervention as feasible and desirable. But there are other possibilities that point in the opposite direction. For example, internally focused leaders may be more aware than their externally focused counterparts of just how difficult or costly successful transformation would be, leading them to be especially sensitive to the difficulty of transformative interventions. Such leaders might believe that since the internal structure of the target state would be at stake in a transformative intervention, the opposition will fight even harder. It is a theoretical and empirical matter beyond the scope of this book to assess whether causal beliefs about the origin of threats systematically correlate with these other types of beliefs. It is also possible that psychological biases combine with causal beliefs to influence estimates of costs. A leader who holds strongly entrenched causal beliefs, or who has undertaken an especially vigorous program of policy investments, may feel pressure to believe that his preferred strategy can be undertaken at low cost. But such effects would result from psychological bias and are thus also beyond the scope of the theory. Since the leader's type may have ambiguous effects on perceptions of costs, I indicate this possible pathway with a dashed line, and I bracket theorizing it directly here.

Probability of Success. As shown in the middle of figure 2.1, the final pathway for causal beliefs to influence the expected utility of intervention is through the estimate of the probability of success. Just as it influences estimates of costs, preparedness will affect estimates of the probability of both an internally and externally successful outcome. As with estimates of costs, factors related to the target environment will also affect the probability of success independent of leaders' causal beliefs and policy investments. But investing heavily in transformative tools, for example, will improve the chances of domestic success within the target state.

The Expected Utility of Nonintervention

The cost-benefit analysis for choosing nonintervention is in some respects simpler than for intervention because, by definition, nonintervention requires no military action. Nevertheless, it is complicated by political dynamics. Leaders cannot control which crises break out and may be under pressure to act even when the opportunity does not seem quite right.

Benefits and the Probability of Success. If there is no intervention, the international and domestic outcomes of a crisis simply result from whatever happens as the crisis plays itself out. Leaders still value the benefits of these outcomes according to their causal beliefs. An externally focused leader who expects that even without intervention the crisis will end with favorable foreign policy consequences but an unfavorable domestic order in the smaller power would see little additional benefit in intervening to ensure a favorable internal outcome, and thus might be more likely to choose nonintervention. An internally focused leader might view that same set of outcomes from nonintervention as less desirable. The probability of success for nonintervention is largely a function of factors related to the conflict or crisis itself.

Costs. Political dynamics play a particularly important role in the costs of nonintervention. In this case, there are no material costs to the intervener. The costs of nonintervention stem primarily from audience costs (both domestic and international). If the expected costs of doing nothing are high, leaders may feel pressure to act even when they do not perceive a direct threat. These pressures may lead them to gamble on an intervention they would otherwise forgo. Domestic audiences that may put pressure on presidents to intervene include other branches of government, the bureaucracy, and the public.[60] Leaders may also look prospectively at anticipated shifts in public opinion. A leader who hopes to stay in office may fear that even if the public does not appear to favor intervention now, it will blame him in the future if nonintervention results in a poor foreign policy outcome.[61] Leaders may also feel pressure to demonstrate toughness or competence.[62] Internationally, leaders may want to signal to allies that they will make good on security guarantees or show their resolve to deter future aggression.

When the expected costs of nonintervention overwhelm leaders' threat perceptions, their causal beliefs may still affect *how* they intervene given that they feel compelled to do so. Leaders may gamble on a riskier intervention even when the probability of success along their preferred dimension—international or domestic—is low. Such a gamble could involve an internally focused leader who perceives the probability of domestic success within the target state to be low but chooses a transformative intervention anyway. Leaders may also intervene in situations in which we would not expect their "type" to initiate a deployment. For example, toward the end of his term George H. W. Bush faced mounting pressure to do something about the crises in Somalia and Bosnia, which he did not perceive as threats.[63] Depending on the parameters of the given opportunity, an externally focused leader might decide to gamble on switching to a transformative strategy, or more likely, he might follow Bush's action in Somalia and stick with a nontransformative strategy, for which he is better prepared.

When a leader feels pushed into intervening, there may be implications for the probability of intervention success. Leaders may choose a strategy that reflects their policy investments but is ill-suited to the conflict, resulting in a "mismatched" intervention. Although this theory does not make predictions about the *misperception* of threats—partly because the nature of threats can be ambiguous—there may be cases in which the nature of a conflict lends itself more readily to a particular strategy. For example, recent research has shown statistically what counterinsurgency theorists have long argued: that highly mechanized forces are ineffective in combating an insurgency.[64] Interventions triggered by conventional aggression by the smaller power are likely to require regular combat operations against the smaller power's military forces. Thus in some cases, we can identify interventions in which the strategy is mismatched to the conflict. Johnson's escalation of the Vietnam War is arguably an example: his initial choice of a nontransformative strategy was ineffective against the insurgency within South Vietnam. Thus even if leaders initiate intervention for reasons beyond the scope of the theory, their causal beliefs may still affect the choice of strategy and influence the probability of success.

Hypotheses and Observable Implications

Given these cost-benefit calculations, we can derive hypotheses for how causal beliefs shape intervention decisions, both within a single leader's set of choices and across the decisions of different leaders. The theory does not predict that leaders blindly follow their beliefs. The threat of nuclear war was enough to close off consideration of direct U.S. intervention in Soviet satellites, for example. On the nonintervention side, we would similarly expect that when the probability of a conflict resolving itself favorably without intervention is high, intervention is less likely. And at very low levels of estimated costs, we would expect intervention to be more likely regardless of the leader's beliefs.

Within the large class of conflicts for which the probabilities and costs are in some intermediate or ambiguous range, however, causal beliefs become more influential. Consider a leader deciding whether to intervene in a single crisis. He may choose nonintervention because he does not perceive a threat or because the crisis does not present a threat along the dimension he cares most about. If he does perceive a threat, his diagnosis of the source of the threat will still affect both his decision to intervene and his choice of strategy. A leader would be more likely to intervene if he estimates the strategy needed to achieve his preferred result (for example, domestic success within the target state) to be feasible. Conversely, a leader would be more likely to choose nonintervention if he estimates that he cannot employ his favored strategy successfully, even if the situation on the ground and available capabilities suggest that intervention using a different strategy is possible. For example, an internally focused leader who perceives successful transformation as infeasible would be less likely to launch a nontransformative intervention that would achieve only an internationally successful outcome. Kennedy's unwillingness to use a nontransformative strategy in Laos to demonstrate American resolve, despite repeated pressure to do so from his advisers, illustrates this case. Kennedy was reluctant to intervene in Laos without a firm basis for domestic success, and he accepted a negotiated settlement rather than apply what he saw as an inappropriate conventional strategy. Eisenhower was more willing to consider intervening in Laos since he contemplated a nontransformative show of resolve that would simply keep the communists out of power. Thus there are two ways—threat perception and the choice of strategy—that causal beliefs affect an individual leader's initial decision to intervene.

When a leader decides to intervene, his causal beliefs affect the choice of strategy. Strictly speaking, leaders do not have preferences over strategies but rather have preferences over outcomes, and thus they must gauge whether a transformative or nontransformative strategy is more likely to produce their preferred outcome. In some cases, it is likely that leaders who place more value on domestically successful outcomes, for example, will narrow their consideration of options to a transformative strategy or no intervention at all. In other cases (such as Laos), the option less likely to produce the favored outcome may still be considered, perhaps because it is favored by advisers or is the only feasible alternative. Overall, given that a leader decides to intervene, an internally focused leader is more likely to choose a transformative strategy and an externally focused leader is more likely to choose a nontransformative strategy.

A leader's causal beliefs may also influence the selection of intervention targets in the face of multiple concurrent crises. A leader facing two different crises would be more likely to intervene where he perceives the bigger threat or in the target that best suits his favored strategy. Cases in which leaders could choose targets in this way include Kennedy's consideration of the conflicts in Laos and Vietnam, Eisenhower's decisions in Lebanon and Iraq in 1958, and George H. W. Bush's choices in Somalia and Bosnia in 1991 and 1992.

Comparing across leaders, it is possible that two leaders may disagree that a given crisis or conflict represents a threat. An internally focused leader might perceive civil war or internal strife as inherently threatening whereas an externally focused leader might not (or would be concerned only about international consequences). Leaders may also agree that a given crisis or conflict represents a threat but may disagree about the source of the threat. For example, both leader types might perceive threats from aggressive behavior by another state or from the potential loss of territory within their sphere of influence. But internally focused leaders would connect such behavior or the potential loss of territory to the domestic institutions of the state in question whereas externally focused leaders would not. Crises with multiple or ambiguous dimensions may also lead to disagreement about the source of the threat. Finally, both leader types might conclude that a crisis or conflict merits intervention, but not because they agree it represents a threat. For example, an externally focused leader may feel domestic or international pressure to intervene in an internal crisis, leading to high estimated costs of nonintervention, whereas an internally focused leader might see the internal crisis as more directly threatening. Under the scenarios in which leaders either agree that a crisis constitutes a threat or agree only that it merits intervention, given that a leader decides to intervene, he will choose the strategy most likely to achieve his preferred outcome.

To summarize, the theory yields the following hypotheses:

General Causal Beliefs Hypothesis

1. Leaders' causal beliefs about the origin of threats systematically affect how they make cost-benefit calculations when faced with an intervention decision.

Leader-Specific Hypotheses

2. A leader's causal beliefs about the origin of threats influence the way he values the benefits of intervention outcomes. Leaders will vary in how they value

the benefits of domestically versus internationally successful outcomes. Leaders take these valuations into account when deciding to intervene and choosing strategies.

3. A leader's causal beliefs affect how he allocates scarce resources early in his tenure to prepare for interventions. Leaders take these policy investments, and their effects on preparedness, into account when deciding to intervene and choosing strategies.

4. A leader will be more likely to intervene in a given conflict if he estimates that the strategy most likely to produce his favored outcome is feasible. Conversely, a leader will be less likely to intervene (and more likely to choose nonintervention) if he estimates this strategy to be infeasible, even if the alternative strategy is an option. Rather than simply consider the choice between intervening or not intervening, leaders will evaluate options for strategy alongside the possibility of nonintervention.

5. Within material and political constraints, given that a leader decides to intervene, internally focused leaders are more likely to choose a transformative strategy whereas externally focused leaders are more likely to choose a nontransformative strategy.

6. A leader facing multiple crises will choose a target based on threat perception and on where he estimates his favored strategy to be more suitable and more likely to be successful.

Across-Leader Hypothesis:

7. Two leaders considering the same ongoing crisis may or may not agree that a crisis constitutes a threat. Even if both leaders agree that a crisis constitutes a threat (or merits intervention for other reasons), they may disagree on the source of the threat and thus make different initial decisions to intervene or choose different strategies.

These hypotheses come with an important caveat. They make predictions about a leader's intervention decisions, but they do not say anything about a leader's *overall* propensity to intervene, that is, the relative frequency with which the two leader types intervene. It is possible that internally focused leaders are more cautious because transformative interventions may be riskier. This higher risk for transformative strategies might be one reason that transformative interventions are relatively rare. But nontransformative strategies may also be very costly and can damage relations between the great power and the target state. Furthermore, a leader's overall propensity to use force may be related to psychological or political factors beyond the scope of this theory.

Testing the Theory and Its Alternatives

Table 2.1 summarizes the predictions generated by the theory, as well as by the two primary alternative explanations. Each of the three explanations—causal beliefs, structural/material conditions, and domestic competition—generates different predictions for how leaders will confront decisions to intervene, making the theory elaborated here falsifiable. If causal beliefs strongly influence intervention decisions, we would expect leaders to vary systematically in how they make cost-benefit calculations, valuing the benefits of successful transformation differently and making policy investments that reflect their causal beliefs. We would also expect that leaders evaluate not only whether to intervene but how, and that their preferred outcome (with its associated strategy) influences their initial decision to intervene; that their type correlates with the choice of strategy; that they choose from multiple intervention targets based on threat perception and the feasibility of their preferred strategy; and that they may differ from other leaders in how they view the same ongoing crisis.

In contrast, the structural/material conditions hypothesis predicts that leaders do not vary systematically in how they make cost-benefit calculations. Leaders should not vary in how they perceive threats or how they value the benefits

TABLE 2.1.
Summary of predictions

	Structural/material conditions hypothesis	Domestic competition hypothesis	Causal beliefs hypothesis
Do leaders vary in how they make cost-benefit calculations?	No: Given a set of conditions, leaders make similar cost-benefit calculations.	Maybe, but not decisive: Cost-benefit calculations result from interaction among domestic actors.	Yes: Leaders' causal beliefs systematically influence their cost-benefit calculations.
Do leaders vary in threat perception and how they value benefits?	No: Threat perception and the valuation of benefits are driven by international security factors.	Maybe, but not decisive: Threat perception and the valuation of benefits result from interaction among domestic actors.	Yes: Leaders vary systematically in threat perception and how they value benefits.

(TABLE 2.1—cont.)

	Structural/material conditions hypothesis	Domestic competition hypothesis	Causal beliefs hypothesis
Do attempted policy investments reflect causal beliefs?	No: Policy investments are driven by anticipated security needs.	Maybe, but not decisive: Policy investments are the product of competition among domestic actors.	Yes: Leaders attempt to invest in the capabilities that reflect their threat perception.
Does a leader's preferred strategy influence the decision to intervene?	No: Strategy may influence the decision to intervene but is driven by structural and material factors.	Maybe, but not decisive: Leaders' preferences are only one input into domestic competition.	Yes: A leader will be more likely to intervene if he estimates his favored strategy to be feasible.
Do leaders' causal beliefs affect the choice of strategy?	No: Strategy is driven by the situation on the ground and available capabilities.	Maybe, but not decisive: Strategy is a product of interaction among domestic actors.	Yes: Internally focused leaders are more likely to intervene transformatively; externally focused leaders are more likely to intervene nontransformatively.
If there are multiple crises, do leaders' causal beliefs affect intervention targets?	No: Target selection results from available capabilities, the target environment, and the security importance of targets.	Maybe, but not decisive: Target selection is a product of interaction among domestic actors.	Yes: Leaders choose targets based on threat perception and where they estimate their favored strategy to be more likely to succeed.
Do leaders considering the same ongoing crisis differ in their evaluations?	No: Any variation results from changes in capabilities or the situation on the ground.	Maybe, but not decisive: Any variation results from changes in interactions among domestic actors.	Yes: Leaders may not agree that there is a threat or may disagree about the source of the threat and choose different strategies.

of intervention outcomes because these are driven by the structure of the international environment. Similarly, there is no leader-driven variation in resource allocation or how strategy influences initial decisions. If multiple intervention opportunities arise, leaders should choose targets based on available capabilities, feasibility, and the relative security importance of targets. If different leaders confront the same ongoing crisis, we would expect any variation in intervention choices to be driven by changes in available capabilities or the situation on the ground.

Finally, the domestic competition hypothesis allows that leaders may vary along many of these dimensions, but it predicts that leaders' threat perceptions are not necessarily decisive for intervention outcomes because other domestic actors also play important roles. Overall cost-benefit calculations, valuations of benefits, and policy investments result from political interaction among domestic actors. When leaders choose strategy or select intervention targets, variation results not from leaders' preferences but rather from variation in the outcome of domestic competition. Leaders may get their way occasionally, but other actors' preferences may be decisive at other times. Similarly, different leaders considering the same ongoing crisis may choose different paths, but the outcomes are driven by political interaction rather than variation among leaders themselves.

Empirically, the main alternative explanations have observable implications that help distinguish them from the effects of causal beliefs. For example, if available capabilities drive intervention decisions, we can ask whether certain kinds of interventions are more likely when the relevant capabilities increase, and we can examine whether leaders with similar views about total capabilities made different policy investments and decisions. If structural and material conditions drive decisions, we would also expect to see leaders evaluating intervention opportunities in terms of the conditions on the ground. Alternatively, we might expect leaders to respond similarly to pressure to signal credibility, for example by undertaking only difficult interventions to demonstrate resolve.

To explore the domestic competition hypothesis, we can examine whether other powerful domestic actors influenced intervention decisions. If leaders routinely disagree with and overrule advisers who are exposed to similar information, we have evidence that executive leadership is crucial.[65] We can examine whether leaders react differently to similar sets of advisers or bureaucracies with similar preferences, such as a military strongly committed to conventional strategies. The hypothesis that partisan or ideological considerations drive intervention behavior would predict that Democratic presidents would be similar in their intervention decisions and would be more likely to invest in transformative capabilities. We can also examine empirically the extent to which actual or anticipated public pressure drove intervention choices.

Measurement and Methodology

Following Alexander George and Andrew Bennett's assertion that setting out general, standardized questions for each case is a crucial research design task, I use a standard set of indicators to code leaders' beliefs, policy investments, and intervention choices in all three presidencies.[66]

Measuring Intervention Choices

To construct a list of noninterventions—cases in which the United States might plausibly have intervened but did not—I examine interstate and intrastate crises in the Third World.[67] Theoretically, crises are not required to trigger interventions. Internally focused leaders may see threats brewing merely by observing the domestic politics of target states. In practice, however, an internal or external crisis is often the proximate trigger of an intervention decision, and thus these crises provide a useful baseline universe of potential interventions.[68] Looking only at the Third World excludes cases in which there was an obvious risk of nuclear escalation that might have inhibited intervention, as in Eastern European crises. While measuring the fact of a nonintervention is straightforward, I also examine why leaders decided against intervention. I focus on whether a leader considered intervening at all; whether he considered intervening using a particular strategy, and how that potential strategy affected his decision calculus; and whether he pursued any alternative policies instead of intervention, including foreign aid and alliances.

For interventions that did occur, I code an intervention as transformative if it explicitly attempts to interfere in the target state's national or local institutions, or both.[69] For an intervention to qualify as attempting national-level institutional change, leadership change alone is insufficient; at least one other indicator of national-level institutional change must be present. All these indicators are measured in terms of the goals of the intervention and the intended strategy. At the national level, a crucial indicator is *institutional reform or construction*: if the intervention strategy aimed to reform or construct national-level institutions, it is considered transformative. Reform of political institutions is the most important factor here, but reform of other institutions (especially economic or military institutions) is also possible in a transformative intervention. Another indicator examines the *integration of nonmilitary issues* at the national level into the overall military strategy. There is some overlap here with the indicator for institutional reform. But it is also useful to gauge the degree to which nonmilitary issues at the national level are explicitly incorporated into the military strategy, as we would expect in a transformative strategy, rather than considered separately.

Indicators for intended local-level change are similar to those for the national level. First, to measure intended *institutional reform or construction* at the local level, I examine whether the strategy aimed to employ the military and related civilian agencies in building or reforming local-level institutions, including local political institutions, security institutions such as the police, and economic or social institutions. *Integration of nonmilitary issues* is also an important indicator at the local level: a transformative strategy should incorporate nonmilitary changes such as local economic development into the military strategy rather than treat such issues separately. Finally, an indicator specific to the local context concerns *interaction with the local population*: in a strategy that is transformative at the local level, troops are likely to be interacting closely with the population (rather than fighting in static positions or remaining on bases). Such interaction excludes collateral or deliberate damage from regular warfare.

To measure these indicators, I draw on published primary document collections (such as the *Foreign Relations of the United States* series) and secondary sources. Concentrating my archival research on measuring causal beliefs in the pre-presidential period and relying on published sources (much of which is primary material) for presidential decisions allows me to cover numerous cases while still conducting detailed process tracing.

Measuring Causal Beliefs

To measure my main explanatory variable—causal beliefs about the origin of threats—I ask a common set of questions for each future leader, measured in the pre-presidential period. These indicators avoid tautology by investigating threat perception rather than a belief in the efficacy of transformative or nontransformative strategies.

The first set of questions directly investigates the future president's views on the *nature of threats*. Did he see the domestic conditions of Third World states as the ultimate source of threats? Did he tend to focus on the domestic or international dimensions of potential threats, and did he see connections between them? For example, when considering the security of client states, was he more concerned about internal threats or outside aggression? Did he see a client state's domestic institutions as connected to its ability to withstand such aggression? More generally, did underlying conditions within a society affect future threat potential, or did he focus simply on proximate conditions?

A second set of questions probes views on *alliances and America's sphere of influence*. Although all Cold War presidents were anticommunist, they varied in how they viewed potential allies, particularly in the Third World. Did they want as many allies and clients as possible, regardless of domestic structure, and thus did they focus mainly on Third World states' international alignment and pro-American stance? Or did they want allies with particular domestic institutions? A related question concerns the future president's views on "neutralism," a significant Cold War issue that emerged when states such as India declared their intention to remain nonaligned in the superpower struggle.[70] Was neutralism acceptable, particularly if the neutral state's domestic structure might develop along favorable lines? Or did nonalignment with the United States represent a potential threat? Additionally, how tolerant was the future president of domestic developments such as nationalism? Such developments could be seen as threatening to short-term foreign policy success but healthy for institutional stability, particularly in states emerging from colonial rule.

The third set of questions gauges the future president's views on *foreign aid*, a frequently debated political issue, particularly during the Cold War. Which form of aid did the future president see as more useful, military or nonmilitary? What kind of military aid did he emphasize: internal security aid or military aid designed to help countries protect borders and defend against aggression? For nonmilitary aid, what connection, if any, did he see between economic or political aid and domestic reform within recipient states?

In addition to these three indicators, I examine any pre-presidential views each future leader expressed on *strategy and policy investments*, especially with respect to intervention in the Third World and the policies of his predecessors. These statements help establish how the future leader's causal beliefs translated into policy preferences in the pre-presidential period, facilitating comparison with his leadership years. This evidence is particularly informative for my examination of Kennedy and Johnson, whose years in Congress required them to comment on Eisenhower's policies. Johnson's vice-presidential years also yield a picture of his views on Kennedy's policies. To be sure, future leaders may make instrumental comments about interventions and especially their predecessors' actions. But if their statements are temporally separated from their later intervention decisions, it is less likely that their instrumental motives result from the same kinds of pressures and constraints they would face as leaders. I include in this section any views that future leaders expressed about the cases I examine for their presidential years (for example, the views that all three future presidents expressed on the conflict in Indochina before they arrived in the Oval Office). This strategy ensures that I use pre-presidential views of these cases to establish a baseline of how leaders' beliefs informed preferences concerning these cases in the years before they took office, not as a direct measure of the way leaders viewed threats.

To answer the common set of questions for each future leader, I use primary sources from the pre-leadership period, drawn from archival and published document collections, including presidential libraries (which contain extensive pre-presidential collections). The use of archival sources in this case has its limits. One way to analyze the documents would be to perform content analysis on the archival data, using measures such as the frequency with which a future president employed a particular phrase in his pre-presidential years. But several problems preclude such an analysis. First, reducing the categories "internally focused" and "externally focused" to even a small number of phrases risks missing much of the interesting variation in language across individuals. Second, the nature of the pre-presidential documentary record varies across the three future leaders, not only because of their different career paths but also because of variation in the nature and scope of the records they created. Furthermore, the way records from the pre-presidential period were preserved undoubtedly varied among the three, since at that point in their careers there was not necessarily a preservation system in place comparable to the way presidential records are preserved and catalogued. Some of the material comes from public or semipublic documents, such as speeches or letters to constituents, which must be seen in the appropriate context. But some of these statements—for example, Kennedy's public push for more attention to domestic conditions in the Third World—were not particularly popular, giving them more weight as statements of personal beliefs. All the statements came before each man assumed the presidency. While there is significant variation in the universe of pre-presidential documents, the existing records still provide a useful basis on which to examine the three future presidents' beliefs.

MEASURING POLICY INVESTMENTS

I also use policy investments as an observable implication of causal beliefs. Here again, I employ a common set of indicators for each president. I measure policy investments in the early period of each presidential administration, when there is the most scope for change. As with intervention decisions, I make use of published primary sources as well as secondary literature.

The first indicator for policy investments concerns *staffing decisions*. The initial selection of White House, cabinet, and other staff positions within the government, as well as the distribution of power among these actors, can be an important indicator of a leader's preferences, as well as a source of and constraint on intellectual capacity when crises arise. If presidents fill a particularly important post with someone who is not inclined to think in terms of a transformative or nontransformative strategy, for example, that strategy may be less likely to be chosen. Of course, leaders may still vary in how much they defer to or are persuaded by the advisers they choose, as the domestic competition hypothesis predicts.

A second indicator concerns official policy on *strategy, the defense posture, and the use of force*. This mechanism refers generally to the way military forces and nonmilitary programs are configured to deal with threats, in terms of the relative weight placed on transformative versus nontransformative strategies. How do transformative strategies figure into overall national strategy, if at all? A nonmilitary aspect of strategy would be the size and orientation of the state's foreign aid program, which can also place more or less emphasis on transformation. What was the balance between military and nonmilitary aid? If military aid is an important component of overall strategy, what form did it take? For example, military aid to a government might aim to strengthen the target state's resistance to outside aggression by building up conventional forces, and thus would be considered nontransformative. Although building up the target state's conventional army alters a security institution, it focuses on defending the state from external forces rather than internal threats. Such aid may aim to deter external attacks, or in the case of a military government, to ensure the military promotes policies that favor the donor state. Military aid that aims to build up the existing regime's ability to defend against internal threats, however, alters the distribution of power between the state and internal actors, and in certain forms (such as counterinsurgency aid) may also play an explicitly transformative role. Similarly, nonmilitary aid such as economic development assistance might vary in the extent of its domestic interference. Some economic aid might aim to benefit the existing regime whereas other kinds of aid might seek to further political, economic, or social reform.

Budgetary allocations are another crucial mechanism for distributing resources to implement strategy. Within the U.S. defense budget, for example, what weight is given to specialized programs for counterinsurgency, nation building, policing, and civil affairs programs aimed at institution building in target states? How is the foreign aid budget distributed? A fourth indicator addresses *institutional creation and change*, including budgetary and political support for institutions related to intervention. Presidents might create, retask, or even eliminate institutions within the bureaucracy.[71] Which institutions get priority? What new institutions are created or eliminated? Kennedy created the Alliance for Progress and the Peace Corps, for example, as well as an interagency group based in the White House to oversee efforts to build counterinsurgency capabilities.

As indicators of leaders' beliefs, policy investments also have their limitations. They are very difficult to compare consistently over time. How do we compare, for example, the founding of an institute for counterinsurgency with the decision to stockpile more nuclear weapons? Even within the U.S. defense budget, spending categories are not disaggregated in enough detail to provide fine-grained distinctions between transformative and nontransformative capabilities, and of course many categories overlap or change over time. A second limitation is that policy investments depend to some degree on the actions and legacies of previous leaders. Some policy investments may take effect only over a period of several years; others may be so entrenched that significant action is required simply to return to a previous baseline level. A leader starting from a strong set of capabilities along his preferred dimension needs to invest less than a leader whose views differ substantially from those of his predecessor. A related issue is that the overall size of the military might affect preparedness and the share of capabilities allotted to different strategies, as well as perceptions of threat.[72] Process tracing is a useful way to account for these issues.

Military intervention decisions are complex. The theory makes probabilistic statements: it does not imply, for example, that an externally focused leader will *never* respond to domestic crises within other states or choose a transformative strategy. Structural, material, and domestic factors matter, but leaders, who may have fundamentally different views about the nature of threats, help give national strategy its content and orientation.[73] By influencing expectations of costs, benefits, and the probability of success, causal beliefs shape intervention decisions and may also leave an imprint on outcomes. Leaving out leaders' beliefs, or studying only a particular type of intervention, may mask important variation in intervention choices. I now turn to the empirical evidence, tracing the causal beliefs, policy investments, and intervention decisions of Eisenhower, Kennedy, and Johnson.

3

Dwight D. Eisenhower

Dwight D. Eisenhower took office with his World War II command experience less than a decade in the past. His presidency was marked by many crises, particularly in the Third World. Yet Eisenhower's only overt military intervention as president was a limited operation in Lebanon in July 1958, near the end of his two-term presidency. Meanwhile, in neighboring Iraq, on July 14, 1958, a bloody coup overthrew the Hashemite monarchy. Despite pressure to widen the operation beyond Lebanon, Eisenhower declined to intervene in Iraq, just as he declined to intervene in other crises, such as Indochina in 1954. The Lebanon operation lasted only a few months; as CIA agent Wilbur Eveland wrote of the intervention, "I found it hard to believe that we'd accomplished anything at all."[1]

This chapter argues that Eisenhower's externally focused beliefs about the origin of threats shaped his intervention decisions. Eisenhower was, of course, concerned about the nature of other states' regimes in a broad sense. His World War II experience was dedicated to defeating—and implicitly, transforming—Germany, and he was a committed anticommunist. But in terms of immediate American foreign policy, Eisenhower focused on the external foreign and security policies of other states, and if these policies were satisfactory, he was willing to largely ignore domestic issues in those states. Thus my claim is not that Eisenhower did not care at all about internal issues, but rather that he saw them as relatively insignificant, in terms of how the United States should prioritize threats. Eisenhower's beliefs, traceable throughout his well-documented military career, were particularly well formed by the time he ran for the presidency.[2] Once in office, Eisenhower worked to limit U.S. defense spending and

capabilities for conventional ground warfare, and he made few policy investments in transformative capabilities. His overall strategy did not pay significant
attention to the Third World except to defend U.S. credibility or ensure that
particular states did not fall under communist control.

As with other presidents, however, Eisenhower's beliefs were only one factor
in his intervention decisions. Like Kennedy and Johnson, Eisenhower tended to
overreact to any hint of communist advances in the Third World. The claim that
he was externally focused may seem odd, for example, in light of his adventur-
ous use of covert operations. Although Eisenhower refrained from using force in
the Indochina and Suez crises, he had no such scruples about using the CIA to reinstall the Shah in Iran in 1953, overthrow the Arbenz regime in Guatemala in 1954,
apparently attempt a coup in Syria in August 1957, foment a rebellion in Indonesia,
and set in motion the Bay of Pigs operation.[3]

Yet as discussed in chapter 1, it is important to distinguish between covert
operations and overt military interventions because the decision to intervene
covertly may be governed by a different causal process than decisions to intervene overtly. It is possible that Eisenhower connected domestic institutions to
threats, but he may also have reacted to the mere possibility that a left-leaning
regime would go communist—as he feared in the cases of leaders such as
Mohammad Mossadegh in Iran and Jacobo Arbenz in Guatemala—without actually holding a substantive belief that the particular institutional form of states
like Iran and Guatemala left them at risk for such a communist takeover.

Even given this distinction, however, Eisenhower's fondness for this particular kind of covert operation is consistent with a nontransformative pattern.
Eisenhower favored these covert operations because they appeared to offer relatively quick, cheap fixes. Furthermore, they aimed to harness local forces and
institutions that were either already in place or easily reinstalled, so that no significant building or rebuilding of institutions would be necessary. In Guatemala,
the CIA relied on psychological warfare, aimed especially at the urban and military elite, to convince Arbenz and his supporters that a major rebellion was
under way, in the hope that Arbenz would simply resign—which he did. The
intention in these operations was a sort of palace coup rather than a wholesale
change in domestic institutions.[4]

More generally, while operations like those in Iran and Guatemala demonstrate a form of concern with other states' regimes, it was a negative concern—
that the regimes not be communist or anti-American—rather than a positive
concern. The long-term internal consequences of the operations in Iran and
Guatemala were deeply significant, but Eisenhower's goal in both cases was to
ensure a noncommunist government using the smallest possible U.S. footprint.[5]
The details of the resulting government were of little interest to him. In the long

run, Eisenhower might well have welcomed institutional change, possibly in the direction of democracy, just as his ultimate preference in the Cold War would have been to see the Soviet Union turn away from communism and its satellites liberated. But in terms of short-term U.S. foreign policy, a pro-American, non-communist government would suffice. Though he tended to view most nationalist and left-leaning governments as likely to go communist, Eisenhower sometimes showed tolerance for internal change or accommodated U.S. policy to such change—as long as it came with a pro-American, or at least not anti-American, line. For example, as Kenneth Lehman notes, the lack of hostility of Bolivia's revolutionary leaders toward the United States was one reason the Eisenhower administration was surprisingly tolerant of Bolivia in the 1950s, giving it significant economic aid even as its government was arguably more radical than that of the ill-fated Arbenz regime in Guatemala.[6] In Indonesia, the United States supported a rebellion against the government of President Sukarno, which took a firmly neutralist posture in the Cold War. But when the covert intervention failed, the Eisenhower administration made the "opportunistic switch" back to Sukarno as the likeliest leader to support American policies.[7] And as discussed below, Eisenhower accepted the assurances of the revolutionary government in Iraq that it wished to remain pro-Western. Eisenhower also worried extensively about externally backed "indirect aggression" against Third World states of any stripe, regardless of their internal institutions.[8] In contrast, for the internally focused Kennedy, other states' domestic institutions (particularly those of repressive autocracies) left them vulnerable to communist takeovers from within and thus in need of reform.

I begin by establishing Eisenhower's beliefs, using evidence from some critical episodes in his pre-presidential years, according to the indicators laid out in chapter 2. I then turn to his policy investments in office, and finally, to his intervention decisions. After a brief discussion of his Latin America policy—useful for comparison with Kennedy and Johnson—I look at Eisenhower's decision not to intervene in Indochina in 1954 and then examine in depth his decision making in the dual crises in the Middle East in July 1958. Methodologically, the Eisenhower period is critical because it lays the groundwork for later comparisons with Kennedy and Johnson, both of whom served in Congress throughout the Eisenhower presidency and vied to succeed him. Eisenhower's actions also allow me to assess alternative explanations, including the influence of structural and material conditions and the role of other domestic actors. Many historians agree that despite the public perception at the time that Secretary of State John Foster Dulles was dominant, Eisenhower played the leading role in foreign policy decision making through what Fred Greenstein has termed the "hidden-hand presidency."[9]

Eisenhower's Beliefs

"The striking feature of [Eisenhower's] beliefs . . . ," Richard Immerman notes, "is that Eisenhower formulated them long before he decided to run for political office."[10] Eisenhower's early years of service, particularly a formative experience in the Panama Canal Zone,[11] and later in the Philippines, gave him significant exposure to national security problems, including in the developing world. Yet as his career took off during World War II, he often expressed frustration at having to deal with local domestic problems that he saw as a distraction from his military campaign and the international politics it served. While such an approach was arguably predictable given Eisenhower's responsibilities, many—including the statesmen he served—took issue with how he handled local political problems, especially during the North African campaign.

THE NATURE OF THREATS

In his pre-presidential military career, Eisenhower displayed an early tendency to concentrate on the international dimensions of security problems, despite significant exposure to what would become known as the Third World. In late 1929, he was sent to serve in the War Department in Washington and began working on preparedness for a future world war. During this period, in line with the international political situation, he focused on readying the military to fight a large-scale conventional war. In 1930, however, as part of his work on the mobilization of industry, he went to Mexico to investigate an alternative source of rubber. His diary entries from this trip reflect little interest in local affairs, except to note that the "people in this section seem impoverished—and dejected. Under the best of conditions it would appear no easy task to wrest a living from this desert region."[12] His report cited the "stability of government and fair treatment for investors" as a factor affecting expansion of the rubber industry, but otherwise paid local affairs little attention.[13]

Eisenhower's service on the staff of Douglas MacArthur in the Philippines from the fall of 1935 to the winter of 1939 gave him firsthand experience with a nation on the brink of independence and struggling to form new institutions. The U.S. military mission was charged with building an army for the defense of the Philippines, which was scheduled to gain full independence in 1946. Eisenhower's nation building centered almost exclusively on building up the Philippine Army, and he concentrated on the external threat to Philippine security. Before the mission left Washington, planners worked out the basics of a Defense Plan for the Philippines, which, as Eisenhower acknowledged in his diary, had been prepared "before gaining an intimate knowledge of local conditions."[14]

The official U.S. goal, as summarized by Eisenhower, was to create by 1945 a "defensive force capable of assuring a high degree of security for each inhabited island in the Archipelago, against either foreign aggression or internal disturbance."[15] But in practice, Eisenhower spent most of his time organizing a conventional army into combat units rather than an internal security force. There was a constabulary already in existence for the purpose of keeping domestic order, but the goal was to convert much of it into the new conventional force.[16] As Peter Lyon points out, there is "no evidence that [Eisenhower] troubled . . . to determine why the countryside, especially in central Luzon, sporadically seethed with agrarian revolt."[17] To Eisenhower, defending against internal threats in the Philippines was a mission quite distinct from the task he had been sent to accomplish.

In Manila, Eisenhower occasionally expressed some interest in local affairs, as in a 1937 letter to his father-in-law in which he described the scene in the Philippines as "a very interesting experiment in self-government." He detailed the social and political divisions and expressed interest in proposed economic reforms, saying that "it is most interesting to be here watching the early stages of a development that is certain to have far reaching effects in the coming years."[18] But he did not connect these issues to his main task. Eisenhower might best be described as a reluctant nation builder, and one whose experience was confined to conventional army building.

During his career in World War II, Eisenhower consistently tried to treat military and international affairs as separate considerations from local domestic politics, and he did not see the nuances of domestic issues within his theater of operations as particularly relevant to the Allied effort. His first test came in North Africa, where he again concentrated on the international dimensions of the crises he faced at the expense of local issues. At the time of the Allied invasion (Operation TORCH) in the fall of 1942, North Africa was controlled by Vichy France, officially neutral but fascist in orientation. It was unclear whether local French forces would resist the invasion. Before TORCH got under way, U.S. and British officials had approved in principle backing a Vichy official to govern in North Africa, in the hope of obviating the need for combat and a military occupation. Rather than find a non-Vichy or relatively palatable Vichy figure to take over, Eisenhower struck a deal with the commander of Vichy forces, Admiral François Darlan. The deal ensured local law and order in North Africa and allowed Anglo-American forces to land unopposed. As Stephen Ambrose summarizes, "Eisenhower's sole criterion for picking a French leader was simple: 'Who can control?'"[19] Eisenhower saw dealings such as the alliance with Darlan as essential to achieving his international goal: the defeat of Germany (which, in a larger sense, would result in the transformation of Germany and by extension, Vichy

France). But to an even greater extent than some of his civilian and military superiors wished, he subordinated concerns about local politics to the ultimate goal of defeating Germany.

Eisenhower, as Ambrose writes, "knew practically nothing of the political complexities and was only interested in finding a Frenchman who could deliver up Algeria and allow his armies to move on into Tunis."[20] The choice came down to Darlan or General Henri Giraud, who also bore some Vichy taint but was deemed more palatable and trustworthy. The British concurred in the selection of Giraud as the top French official, but as Arthur Funk notes, Darlan "was not ruled out."[21] Despite the basic Allied agreement, Eisenhower stood out in the ensuing events for the degree to which he concentrated on military and international affairs and at least hoped to ignore local political matters. In a note to Army Chief of Staff George C. Marshall two days after the TORCH landings, Eisenhower wrote that he was "so impatient to get eastward . . . that I find myself getting absolutely furious with these stupid Frogs."[22] With the political machinations still ongoing, Eisenhower wrote his deputy, Mark Clark, "It is important also that we do not create any dissension among the tribes or encourage them to break away from existing methods of control. To organize this country in support of the war effort, we must use French officials and we do not want any internal unrest or trouble. I don't see why these Frenchmen, that are jockeying for personal power, do not see these things and move with speed. Give them some money if it will help."[23]

When Giraud proved unable to deliver on his promises—precisely because he had no place in the French hierarchy whereas Darlan did—Eisenhower flew to Algiers on November 13 and approved what became known as the Darlan deal.[24] The deal with such a high-ranking Vichy official was greeted in the United States and Britain with extreme distaste, prompting Churchill, among others, to worry about a threat to the Allied cause. Ambrose concludes that the "basic factor in the Darlan deal was political naïveté."[25] Eisenhower was not naive in the sense that he lacked political purpose in making the deal, which had a distinct international political purpose: to speed the defeat of Germany. But it was precisely Darlan's record that prompted an unanticipated American and British public reaction, which was fiercely critical of Eisenhower. Though he later wrote his brother that he *had* recognized the political difficulties in advance, his note to his chief of staff, Walter Bedell Smith, on the day he approved the Darlan deal was matter-of-fact and did not give any hint of anticipated problems with Darlan.[26] The British, though they had tacitly approved of approaching Darlan, reacted violently. Churchill wrote Roosevelt on November 17 that dealing with "local Quislings" could do "serious political injury" to the Allied advance.[27] In the United States, the public outcry was so strong that for several days Eisenhower's friends had to push Roosevelt to make a public statement of support for the general. Finally, on November 16, Roosevelt issued a statement accepting the arrangement but calling the Darlan deal a "temporary expedient" to save lives and obviate the need for a " 'mopping-up' period" in North Africa.[28] But Roosevelt also warned Eisenhower that "it is impossible to keep a collaborator of Hitler and one whom we believe to be a Fascist in civil power any longer than is absolutely necessary."[29]

Regardless of the military and international political value of the deal with Darlan, it is interesting to note how Eisenhower justified it. On November 18, he wrote Bedell Smith that his "whole interest now is Tunisia. When I can make the Allies a present of that place [Churchill] can kick me in the pants and put in a politician here who is as big a crook as the chief local skunk."[30] Eisenhower summed up his frustrations to Marshall on November 30, telling his boss that the "sooner I can get rid of all these questions that are outside the military in scope, the happier I will be! Sometimes I think I live ten years each week, of which at least nine are absorbed in political and economic matters."[31] As Rick Atkinson writes, Eisenhower "averted his gaze" as Darlan took repressive action, imprisoning thousands and leaving anti-Jewish laws in effect.[32] Months later, Assistant Secretary of War John McCloy, visiting North Africa, wrote in a memorandum to Eisenhower that "things are moving too slowly toward the liberalization of restrictions on personal freedom. I can find no good reason why the Nazi laws still obtain here."[33] On December 11, the Joint Chiefs of Staff (JCS) cabled Eisenhower to say they were "disturbed" by reports of "our inability to exercise control over the local French authorities in internal administrative matters." The JCS warned that military operations might ultimately be "endangered" by the lack of control.[34] But Eisenhower wanted a Frenchman, any Frenchman, to keep order in North Africa, and he hoped to ignore most other local issues.

In the closing phases of the war and the postwar period, Eisenhower emphasized the international rather than the domestic dimensions of the potential threat from communism. Indeed, during the war and even into the postwar period, he had relatively optimistic views on whether the United States could coexist and even cooperate with the Soviet Union. Eisenhower was not alone in such a view: Roosevelt himself also hoped for postwar U.S.-Soviet cooperation.[35] As the war drew to a close, Eisenhower was open and generous with the Russians to the point of drawing criticism from Churchill. In a May 1945 conversation with his aide Harry Butcher, Eisenhower argued, "It should be possible to work with Russia if we will follow the same pattern of friendly cooperation that has resulted in the great record of Allied unity."[36] In August 1945, with Truman's approval, Eisenhower visited Moscow. He told the press that he saw "nothing in the future that would prevent Russia and the United States from being the closest possible friends."[37]

Eisenhower's optimism persisted even as U.S. attitudes toward Russia began to shift. In 1946 and even into 1947, after a period marking what Gaddis calls "a decisive turning point in American policy toward the Soviet Union," Eisenhower continued to suggest that peaceful coexistence with the Soviets might be possible.[38] In a speech in March 1946, he noted that Lincoln's famous statement about a house divided had *not* said that "two houses constructed differently, of different materials, of different appearance could not stand in peace within the same block." Eisenhower argued, "We must learn in this world to accommodate ourselves so that we may live at peace with others whose basic philosophy may be different—and in practice we will often find very great differences."[39] The following month, he again invoked Lincoln's house metaphor, adding, "Good neighbors do not pry into the domestic life of each other's families even while they observe common standards of conduct in their daily association."[40] And in October 1946, he told an audience in New York City, "If there is room in our own country for every shade of political and social and religious thinking and expression, there is room in the world for different philosophies of government, so long as none is dedicated to the forceful imposition of its political creed on others."[41]

Eisenhower's stance finally shifted as the evidence of a nascent Cold War proved increasingly difficult to ignore. In a D-Day address in Kansas City in June 1947, he said, "We do not dictate to any nation what it does internally but we intend to continue the firm champion of those who seek to lead their own lives in peace with world neighbors."[42] By August 1947, his rhetoric had shifted, though he still emphasized the possibility of cooperation and explicitly focused on Soviet international behavior rather than the nature of Soviet institutions. He told the American Legion Convention,

> We must face the hard fact that, during the two years since hostilities ended, the cooperative spirit has lost ground. The world comprises two great camps, grouped on the one side around dictatorships which subject the individual to absolute control and, on the other, democracy which provides him a free and unlimited horizon. In my view, conflicting political theories can exist peacefully in the same world provided there is no deliberate effort on the part of either to engage in unjust coercion or unwarranted interference against the other. But as long as deliberate aggression against the rights of free men and the existence of free government may be a part of the international picture, we must be prepared for whatever this may finally mean to us.[43]

In an overarching sense, Eisenhower did, of course, see the communist camp as threatening. But his views of how to deal with the Soviet Union may have been similar to those of George Kennan. The Soviet system would change, perhaps even collapse, of its own accord over the long term, so the best course for the United States was "patience and firmness," refraining in the meantime from interference in the internal affairs of other states, particularly in peripheral regions.[44]

Once his Cold War attitude hardened, what little attention Eisenhower paid to the emerging Third World largely concerned either drawing a line against communist aggression or maintaining access to raw materials, natural resources, and trading partners, all while mostly ignoring domestic political and economic issues within the states themselves. For example, as discussed below, Eisenhower saw the conflict in Indochina in terms of the domino theory as early as 1951. Third World states also drew Eisenhower's attention in terms of another external dimension: keeping supply and trading lines open. In 1951, when Iran nationalized the British-owned Anglo-Iranian Oil Company, Eisenhower wrote his childhood friend Swede Hazlett that the situation was "tragic." "Frankly," he wrote, "I have gotten to the point that I am concerned primarily, and almost solely, in some scheme or plan that will permit that oil to keep flowing to the westward."[45] He wrote Martin Clement, former president of the Pennsylvania Railroad Company, that "the simple rule that should dictate our relationships with other nations is to determine with what countries and peoples we *must* preserve a friendly and mutually profitable trade in order that our particular type of economy can continue to flourish, and how to do it!" He continued,

We begin to think of Malaya in terms of available tin, rubber, and tungsten; of India in manganese and other valuable products; of Central Africa in cobalt and uranium; of the Mid-East in oil; of Chile in copper; of Bolivia in tin; and so on around the world. To trade with these countries, we need, of course, to maintain sure access to them and, after that, we must know that they *want* to trade with us. This last is assured through the existence of governments that are not antagonistic to us or to trading with us on a mutually profitable basis.[46]

Beyond this friendly attitude toward trade with the United States, Eisenhower listed no other requirements for governments in the Third World.

Eisenhower's inattention to Third World domestic politics also tied in with one aspect of his threat perception that would form a bedrock principle of his strategy as president: his perception that meeting external threats could actually pose a risk to the institutions of the United States, by expanding the national security apparatus so much that the economy and other institutions would suffer.[47] The United States would have to decide which interests were really vital and thus worth protecting. As the Cold War took shape, Eisenhower increasingly saw the necessity for making such choices. Initially, in May 1946, he wrote, "Our most effective security step is to develop in every country, where there is any chance or opportunity, a democratic form of government to the extent that individualism rather than statism is the underlying concept of government."[48] But by May 1947, he was more discriminating, writing in his diary that there were "so many nations needing our help that the whole job seems appalling, even though it is clear that help to some of them is definitely in our own interest."[49] As he wrote to Hazlett in 1950, America had for too long avoided facing "the problem arising out of the conflicting considerations of national security on the one hand and economic and financial solvency on the other."[50] America would have to make choices about which threats it decided to meet—or what counted as a threat in the first place. An external focus fit naturally with this kind of thinking, since as we have seen, Eisenhower viewed threats as arising primarily from international considerations and rarely connected threats to the domestic institutions or internal problems of other states.

ALLIANCES AND AMERICA'S SPHERE OF INFLUENCE

Once Eisenhower accepted the Cold War frame of reference, he took an externally focused approach to alliances and America's sphere of influence. For example, he was dismissive of the idea of neutrality in the emerging Cold War. Eisenhower wanted states lined up on one side or the other. In a press conference on a trip to West Germany in January 1951, he told a reporter who asked about possible German neutrality, "in this day and time to conceive of actual neutrality . . . is an impossibility," adding that "the more people on my side the happier I will be."[51] To Martin Clement, Eisenhower wrote that the "whole struggle has developed such a level of intensity that the word 'neutrality' has become almost meaningless. Magnetically, our globe is one whole; if a magnetic needle anywhere in the world does not point specifically to North or South, then it is untrustworthy and useless. Almost in the same way, if any country in the world today is not oriented toward Communism . . . then it must be specifically a part of the organization of free nations, determined to preserve its integrity against a Communistic threat. To attempt to do otherwise is silly and suicidal."[52] This view of allies and neutrality would contrast with that of Kennedy, who was more interested in the long-term strength of potential allies' domestic institutions. Kennedy was willing to sacrifice short-term alliance considerations and allow states to stay neutral if it meant they would be stronger in the long run.

In his search for allies, Eisenhower was willing to overlook the past or domestic differences if he could win more states to his side. As NATO's Supreme Commander, he made an overture to Tito, telling Army Chief of Staff J. Lawton Collins, who was traveling to Yugoslavia, "The contribution that Yugoslavia can make towards the security of my southern flank is brought into focus here every time we consider plans and forces required for the defense of Southern Europe, particularly Italy. I am <u>heartily in favor</u> of your visit."[53] Ambrose likens the overture to a "sort of Darlan Deal in reverse" that drew Republican ire. But Eisenhower, "as in November 1942, would take allies wherever he could find them."[54] His tolerance also extended to Franco's Spain: as he told Truman at the end of January 1951, "I feel about the question of keeping Spain out [of NATO] the same as I feel about keeping a sinner out of church. . . . You can't convert the sinner unless you let him inside the front door."[55]

Though Eisenhower strongly opposed colonialism, his pre-presidential views on nationalism, particularly as a force that might or might not destabilize the U.S. sphere of influence, are difficult to assess. By the time of his transition to the presidency, in early January 1953, he wrote in his diary that the "free world's hope of defeating the Communist aims does not include objecting to national aspirations."[56] His hostile view of colonialism would only grow stronger. But Eisenhower also saw danger from nationalism—not so much from its internal consequences but rather because the Soviets might "take advantage of the confusion resulting from [the] destruction of existing relationships" as a way to expand their global position.[57] Though he continued to profess a relatively tolerant view of nationalism even after assuming the presidency, such a view was ultimately inconsistent, as Gaddis points out, with his tendency to see communist conspiracies everywhere, resulting in "hyperactivity" in the Third World.[58]

FOREIGN AID

Eisenhower's pre-presidential views on foreign aid and particularly its role in the Third World are difficult to discern, partly because aid to the Third World had not yet developed into the major political issue it would become in the Cold War. The few comments he made were generally consistent with his external focus and his emphasis on military considerations. Like Kennedy and Johnson, he was a supporter of the Marshall Plan. But as H. W. Brands notes, Marshall Plan aid "represented, first, a response to the devastation of the war in Europe, and second, a policy directed principally at countries that would become American allies."[59] Eisenhower wrote in his diary in May 1947 (several weeks before Marshall announced his plan) that "the best thing we could now do would be to post 5 billion to the credit of the secretary of state and tell him to use it to support democratic movements wherever our vital interests indicate."[60] For countries that counted as "vital interests," then, Eisenhower was enthusiastic about shoring up democracy.

Unsurprisingly, given his position, most of Eisenhower's comments on aid before assuming the presidency concerned military aid. As chief of staff of the army, Eisenhower signed a paper on behalf of the JCS that dealt with military assistance to Turkey; the aid would "stiffen the Turkish will and ability to resist" Soviet pressure and "improve the Turkish military potential."[61] A few months later, Eisenhower wrote a memo to the JCS titled "United States Assistance to Other Countries from the Standpoint of National Security." He noted that the Western Hemisphere would be "the main base of our war potential" and thus aid might be required "to safeguard the security and the warmaking capacity of this hemisphere," including Canada and Latin America.[62] Though he rarely dealt with aid before becoming president, his focus on military aid, coupled with his fiscal conservatism, laid the groundwork for his presidential tendency to focus on military rather than nonmilitary aid to the Third World.

STRATEGY AND POLICY INVESTMENTS: PRE-PRESIDENTIAL EVIDENCE

Eisenhower's pre-presidential comments on strategy and policy investments are obviously too vast to explore fully, but it is interesting to note how his beliefs about the nature of threats translated into policy preferences and choices about strategy before his election. One nontransformative trend in Eisenhower's military thinking that manifested itself during World War II was his aversion to occupation and his view that the military should not be involved in the process of domestic transformation. Initially, for example, he did not want to liberate Paris directly.[63] And as the end of the war approached, Eisenhower declined to drive for Berlin. Many factors, including the fact that the Russians were far closer to Berlin, contributed to his decision to push through the center of Germany and leave Berlin to the Russians. But by the time the Allies were within striking distance of Berlin, Eisenhower saw the city as far less valuable militarily. In March 1945, he wrote British general Bernard Montgomery, who was angling to lead the charge into Berlin, that Berlin had "become, so far as I am concerned, nothing but a geographical location, and I have never been interested in these. My purpose is to destroy the enemy's forces and his powers to resist."[64] The fear that the Nazis would organize a guerrilla force to resist occupation played an important role in Eisenhower's wish to defeat the German forces as quickly and thoroughly as possible. He also believed, based on estimates, that taking Berlin would involve major casualties and would involve risky urban warfare.[65] But whereas Roosevelt (and later Truman) wanted to avoid postwar political issues, Churchill objected strongly, arguing not only that Berlin was crucial to defeating Germany but also that if the Russians were allowed to take the city, there might be "grave and formidable difficulties in the future."[66]

After the war ended, Eisenhower gave a somewhat limited definition of postwar occupation in a speech in April 1946, saying, "It is the job of the men of the Armed Forces to see that the enemies of humanity cannot again make war. 'Occupation' may be defined as simply as that."[67] Nearly a year later, he told an audience at the National Press Club that occupation was "a problem apart from the Army's normal mission. We didn't want it but it was assigned to the Army as the only agency in a position to conduct the overall program."[68] A few weeks later, he argued in Atlanta that the United States should "see if we cannot make [enemy countries] peaceable democracies rather than aggressive autocracies." But he was careful to say that the "policy was made by the government and the Army is merely doing its job, nothing more."[69] The view that occupation was outside the army's "normal" mission may have dovetailed with the prevailing outlook of the time but nonetheless reflected Eisenhower's external focus.

Unsurprisingly, Eisenhower's conventional, nontransformative approach to the use of force remained evident after the war. During the Korean War, in a letter to Hazlett, Eisenhower wrote that even in peacetime the army had to keep some sort of "task force" or "striking force" that "would give us a splendid 'fire department' basis on which to meet actual aggression."[70] Dealing with trouble spots on a "fire department" basis—an attitude that Kennedy would later specifically attack—does not suggest that those trouble spots would receive transformative treatment.

Before he assumed the presidency, Eisenhower also expressed views on the conflict in Indochina, where he would later face his own intervention decision. He concentrated on the international dimension of the crisis and, indeed, falling dominoes, with little concern for domestic issues inside Indochina. In March 1951, when he met with French general Jean de Lattre de Tassigny, commander of the French forces in Indochina, Eisenhower (by then commanding NATO) said that he "viewed the whole thing from a global point of view and that he realized that this was holding the danger away not only from Siam and Burma, but also perhaps even as far as India."[71] On the same day, he wrote in his diary that if the French "quit [and] Indo China falls to Commies, it is easily possible that the entire [Southeast] Asia [and] Indonesia will go, soon to be followed by India. That prospect makes the whole problem one of interest to us all."[72] In his meeting with de Lattre, Eisenhower also expressed his anticolonial sentiments, urging that the French promise of independence be highlighted.[73] But apart from this concern about independence, Eisenhower did not dig deeper into the domestic aspects of the conflict. His focus on the international consequences of a French defeat was perhaps appropriate to his role as NATO commander. But as discussed in chapter 4, just a few months later Kennedy would visit Saigon and home in on domestic aspects of the war.

Finally, it is interesting to note Eisenhower's views of how Truman conducted the Cold War. While Eisenhower agreed with much of his predecessor's foreign and defense policy, he took issue with Truman's expansive defense spending, which he felt might threaten America's own domestic institutions.[74] Evidence of his pre-presidential commitment to keeping military budgets in line abounds, suggesting that his fiscal caution was a constraint on many different types of military capabilities, not simply those for transformative strategies. In 1949, he wrote in his diary, "We must hold our position of strength without bankrupting ourselves."[75] A 1952 diary entry noted that the United States was "risking . . . the danger of internal deterioration through the annual expenditure of unconscionable sums on a program of indefinite duration, extending far into the future."[76] But Eisenhower's views on defense spending were not merely economic preferences; they helped define his vision of national interests. A nation that expanded its military capabilities without limits might destroy its institutions in the process of defeating its enemy.

In summary, Eisenhower concentrated on external threats and the international dimensions of multifaceted crises. He did not see much of a connection between local domestic institutions and U.S. national security, as long as someone was available to maintain local stability and a pro-American stance. Initially, he was relatively optimistic about cooperation with the Soviet Union. Once Cold War attitudes hardened, he viewed America's alliances and sphere of influence through an external lens, hoping to attract as many allies as possible. He took a dim view of neutralism, preferring states to choose sides regardless of their domestic order. He viewed foreign aid in primarily military terms, and his strategic outlook was decidedly oriented toward conventional, nontransformative warfare. His fiscal conservatism informed his view of threats to the United States and how to meet them. He would translate these beliefs into policy soon after moving into the White House.

Eisenhower as President: Strategy and Policy Investments

Eisenhower favored a formal system of planning that yields a rich record of his strategy and policy investments.[77] Minimizing cost was an overarching concern. This concern affected capabilities—and thus preparedness—for both transformative strategies and nontransformative strategies, however, and thus need not inevitably have led to a deemphasizing of transformative capabilities. Nevertheless, the Third World, and particularly its domestic institutions, would have a very limited role in Eisenhower's strategy.

STAFFING DECISIONS

The staffing decisions Eisenhower made helped put him on a path to implementing his strategy. He was surrounded by fiscal conservatives (such as Treasury Secretary George Humphrey), but as Gaddis notes, "it would be a mistake to see Eisenhower as merely reflecting the influences of those around him on this issue."[78] The highest-profile figure in the administration was Secretary of State Dulles, who also tended to focus on Soviet intentions to expand rather than the domestic institutional weaknesses of states that might go communist.[79] At lower levels, Eisenhower and Dulles pushed out those in the State Department with reformist views of the Third World.[80] Eisenhower's staffing decisions did not, therefore, suggest that his administration would be particularly interested in Third World domestic issues.

STRATEGY, DEFENSE POSTURE, AND THE USE OF FORCE

Once Eisenhower was in office, his vision of both external threats to the United States and the threat to American institutions from the high costs of an expansive defense policy became codified as national security policy.[81] The administration's statement of Basic National Security Policy, NSC 162/2, did not contain an option for rolling back communism using military force.[82] In Eisenhower's formulation, limited wars could themselves constitute a threat.

In practice, Eisenhower's "New Look" strategy aimed to reduce military spending by relying on the threat of nuclear force through "massive retaliation," at the expense of conventional force. Eisenhower cut funds for conventional forces, telling JCS chairman Arthur Radford in 1956 that a "few Marine battalions or Army units" would be available for small wars but that "participation in small wars . . . is primarily a matter for Navy and Air."[83] While Eisenhower's fiscal conservatism encompassed preparedness for conventional war generally (rather than transformative strategies alone), transformative operations would be difficult to mount under these constraints and did not figure significantly in overall strategy.

With combat forces limited under the "New Look," the Third World got relatively short shrift in Eisenhower's strategy. Eisenhower sought to keep as much of the Third World from going communist as possible with minimal U.S. expenditure and overall footprint. NSC 162/2 devoted very little space to this effort: only two paragraphs followed the heading "The Uncommitted Areas of the World."[84]

This relative inattention was also reflected in Eisenhower's foreign aid policy, at least until near the end of his presidency. When Eisenhower took office, he advocated a policy of "trade not aid," opposing large-scale public expenditures for foreign aid and instead relying on trade—an externally oriented solution—and private investment to fuel growth abroad.[85] NSC 162/2 argued for giving only "limited" aid.[86] What assistance the United States gave was heavily weighted toward military rather than economic assistance, a balance that Kennedy would challenge during the 1950s.[87]

In his study of Eisenhower's foreign economic program and the "trade not aid" policy, Burton Kaufman finds that the Eisenhower administration adjusted its policies over time, gradually shifting to more support for development aid that aimed less at short-term crisis management and more at long-term development of local institutions. But Kaufman also suggests that these adjustments came in response to events in the Third World, which "compelled the White House to pay more attention to the development needs of Third World Nations."[88] After months of debate following the French defeat in Indochina, Eisenhower began to support the idea of a development fund for Asia. Some of the proposals circulating within the administration included a study by MIT professors Walt Rostow and Max Millikan, whose ideas about development and domestic transformation would be highly influential in the Kennedy administration.[89] But in announcing the policy in a special message to Congress in April 1955, Eisenhower sounded cautious, saying that the "major responsibility must necessarily lie with the countries themselves."[90] This language was quite different from the explicit goal of building up institutions in the Third World, a goal that Kennedy would embrace from the start of his presidency. Eisenhower continued to shift his policy to what Kaufman terms "trade and aid," backing the Development Loan Fund in 1957. But although Kaufman concludes that the new moves were a "significant departure for U.S. foreign economic policy," he notes that the aid amounts were "considerably less than many proponents of foreign aid, including Millikan and Rostow, believed was necessary for Third World economic development," and the "White House still intended to rely heavily on foreign trade and private investment as part of its overall foreign economic program."[91]

Eisenhower's anticolonialism and somewhat sympathetic view of nationalism seem at odds with another important aspect of his strategy: his fondness for covert operations and psychological warfare. But here again costs played a role. With limited war so sharply circumscribed, some other tool had to substitute for conventional war in situations where politics had to be continued by other means. These tools were also "relatively inexpensive" and thus fit into Eisenhower's overall goal of keeping costs down.[92] As Robert Bowie and Richard Immerman describe, the 1953 operation to restore the Shah in Iran "reinforced the administration's confidence that a Third World cancer as overtly malignant as it perceived Mossadegh to be could be isolated and surgically removed, a confidence buttressed by the ouster of Guatemala's Jacobo Arbenz in 1954."[93] Such "surgical" operations could change regimes without involving the United States in a transformative action requiring deep involvement in local domestic institutions.

Budgets

Keeping the defense budget under control was an overriding goal for Eisenhower. Though he started from the increases authorized by Truman in the wake of NSC 68 and the early Cold War, Eisenhower nonetheless imposed his own stamp on the budget. As Gaddis points out, across the entire Eisenhower presidency the defense budget was relatively stable, but both the percentage of the total budget and the overall share of GDP devoted to defense declined significantly.[94] In his first two budgets Eisenhower cut the defense portion by 32 percent in 1954 and 11 percent in 1955.[95] Additionally, the army took a significant hit in both dollars and corresponding manpower, decreasing in size from 1.5 million to 1 million men by 1955.[96] Reflecting the administration's emphasis on military assistance and "trade not aid," as well as limiting aid overall, international development and humanitarian assistance declined by nearly 46 percent in 1954 while international security assistance dropped by 24 percent.[97]

Institutional Creation and Change

Eisenhower also made changes domestically and internationally to institutionalize his priorities. In the foreign aid field, for example, he sided with the fiscally conservative Humphrey over Dulles in the 1953 fight over which agency would control the Export-Import Bank. Humphrey wanted to return control to Treasury and to limit the bank's lending.[98] In later years, as discussed, Eisenhower supported aid-oriented development programs such as the Development Loan Fund. But his initial policy investments in aid-related institutions aimed to constrict U.S. aid, leaving him much work to do when pressures in the Third World threatened to overwhelm existing U.S. policy.

Eisenhower—still a committed internationalist—invested heavily in alliances, a policy critics labeled "pactomania." The administration sought to build up a network of alliances in key areas, particularly along the periphery of the Soviet Union and its sphere of influence. The Southeast Asia Treaty Organization

(SEATO) was one such pact that emerged from the Indochina crisis. The administration failed to create a Middle East Development Organization, but Dulles pushed for a grouping of so-called Northern tier states such as Turkey and Iran. This grouping became the Baghdad Pact, which, as discussed below, had serious implications for the Iraqi regime that chose to ally openly with the West. These internal implications do not seem to have concerned the administration much, however. Rather, Eisenhower saw regional alliances as helpful in terms of both deterring Soviet-directed external aggression and keeping costs down, because local allies would provide the bulk of the ground forces to deal with "brush fire" wars.[99] The practice of building walls without regard to the domestic politics of the countries that formed the bricks and mortar would come back to haunt the administration in the Middle East in 1958.

Intervention Choices: Latin America

Those who sought to persuade Eisenhower to undertake military intervention, from his own advisers to the French in 1954 and Lebanese leaders in 1958, faced high hurdles. In Latin America, Southeast Asia, and the Middle East, Eisenhower would pursue largely nontransformative policies. Although he did not intervene overtly in Latin America, in this section I briefly review his approach to the region, setting up later comparisons with Kennedy and Johnson.

For most of his presidency, Eisenhower's Latin America policy was decidedly nontransformative. As Stephen Rabe argues, Eisenhower was the dominant figure in U.S. policy toward Latin America during his administration, which had a "coherent, consistent strategy" focused on getting "Latin Americans to support the United States in the Cold War, adopt free trade and investment principles, and oppose communism."[100]

According to Walter Bedell Smith (by then serving as undersecretary of state), the administration's first statement of policy toward Latin America, NSC 144/1, was prepared "in some haste and represented a shotgun approach."[101] The document, as Rabe notes, paid little attention to the domestic affairs of Latin American states (beyond anticommunism); it was also consistent with the "trade not aid" approach in emphasizing private investment, trade, and only a "limited economic grant program."[102] Eisenhower "heartily" backed military assistance to Latin America, however, as a way of bolstering and ensuring the pro-American sentiment of the military class in Latin American countries, where the military often dominated.[103] This aid was also oriented toward helping Latin American states defeat outside aggression, consistent with what one Defense Department official called an "obsessive concentration" on "external aggression resistant armies."[104] Using the protective gloss of the nonintervention principle, Eisenhower embraced dictators in the region as a source of anticommunist stability. The administration "fawned over some of Latin America's most unsavory tyrants," even awarding some the Legion of Merit.[105] As mentioned, the covert operation in Guatemala can be considered nontransformative.

Like Kaufman, Rabe finds that Eisenhower shifted his policies over time. But in tracing the evolution of Eisenhower's policies in Latin America, Rabe notes that a true change in the administration's policy in the region did not come until 1960, at the very end of Eisenhower's presidency. Following Vice President Richard Nixon's trip to Latin America in 1958, when he was harassed at several stops and in some danger in Venezuela amid protests over U.S. policy, the administration adjusted its policies but stuck to the fundamental premise of its stance toward the region. The United States moved away from its embrace of dictators but maintained an emphasis on military aid. Rabe attributes this "failure" to "fundamentally change" the policy to Eisenhower and Dulles themselves.[106] In Cuba, the administration curtailed its warm relations with the Cuban dictator Fulgencio Batista. But Eisenhower chastised the U.S. ambassador to Cuba for going too far in criticizing a Batista police action, saying it was "not a good idea for any Ambassador to make statements about local conditions."[107]

It was not until Fidel Castro turned toward the Soviet Union in 1960 that Eisenhower's policy finally moved toward a more transformative position. Once U.S. policy shifted to one of antagonism toward Castro, Eisenhower's anticommunism took a new form: the administration "decided that it had to lead and direct a reform of Latin America's basic institutions . . . both to overthrow radicals and to eliminate conditions that might spawn future Fidel Castros in the Western Hemisphere."[108] In 1960, Eisenhower took a goodwill trip to the region that heightened his interest in its problems. He now saw both leftists *and* right-wing dictators that might create conditions for revolution as potential threats, and accordingly looked more favorably on programs aimed at bolstering domestic institutions. As discussed in chapters 4 and 5, Kennedy came to office with this dual threat perception already in place, but Lyndon Johnson was closer to Eisenhower's original position. The Act of Bogotá of September 1960 laid the foundation for Kennedy's Alliance for Progress, launching transformative social and economic programs.[109]

But we should be cautious about interpreting this policy shift. It is important to note that it came at the very end of Eisenhower's presidency. "Until 1960," Rabe writes, "the Eisenhower administration continued to hold that a secure and stable hemisphere could be achieved basically with free trade and investment policies, military aid, and admonitions to Latin Americans not to form ties with Moscow or with local Communist parties."[110] Only the attack on Nixon and the shift to overt hostility from Cuba finally swayed U.S. policy, making it difficult to assess whether the policy shift was a pragmatic reaction to events or instead represented true learning, in the sense of a change in Eisenhower's beliefs about the origin of threats.

Intervention Choices in Southeast Asia: Indochina

Eisenhower's external focus also informed his decision not to intervene to save the collapsing French position in Indochina in 1954, as well as his handling of the fledgling nation of South Vietnam. In the 1954 crisis, he opposed a unilateral ground intervention with U.S. combat forces and, to the extent he considered intervening, focused primarily on an air and naval strike. Once he decided firmly against intervention, he backed off his previous statements that the loss of Indochina itself was crucial to keeping all of Southeast Asia from going communist and instead initiated several nontransformative programs (including the SEATO alliance) to keep the remainder of the region in the Western camp. He also made a commitment to the regime of Ngo Dinh Diem in South Vietnam. But despite initial demands that Diem carry out reforms to build a strong, popularly supported base for his regime, the Eisenhower administration largely left him alone. Though well aware of the problems with Diem, Eisenhower cared mainly about Diem's anticommunist, pro-Western stance. As Melanie Billings-Yun makes clear in her study of Eisenhower's decision not to intervene, Eisenhower remained in control throughout the crisis.[111]

As we have seen, by the time he took office Eisenhower had already expressed the view—consistent with the Truman administration's policy—that Indochina was part of the global anticommunist struggle.[112] In 1954, when the French poured their remaining hopes for winning the war in Indochina into defending their garrison at Dien Bien Phu, Eisenhower tried to keep his options open and delay a final decision, but ultimately he made clear his aversion to using ground forces in Indochina and concentrated on whether to approve an intervention involving air and naval power (possibly including nuclear weapons). For example, in a conversation with Dulles on March 24, 1954, Eisenhower expressed opposition to getting involved but said "he did not, however, wholly exclude the possibility of a single strike, if it were almost certain this would produce decisive results."[113] During this period, U.S. military planners made some preparations for intervention, centering on air and naval strikes. In March 1954, Eisenhower put the Seventh Fleet on alert.[114] In the NSC meeting on March 25, he expressed faith in the domino theory, saying he "believed that the collapse of Indochina would produce a chain reaction which would result in the fall of all of Southeast Asia to the Communists" and asking for guidance on "the extent to which we should go in employing ground forces to save Indochina from the Communists." He also suggested that Vietnam invite a grouping of states to defend it through a treaty, thus laying the groundwork for SEATO.[115]

As the French position deteriorated, Eisenhower tried to postpone any firm decision but made increasingly clear his strong stance against using ground troops. On April 4—the day after Dulles met with congressional leaders, who urged that no U.S. action take place except under certain conditions, including allied support—Eisenhower laid down three conditions for U.S. intervention in Indochina. These conditions, which were unlikely to be met, were the active participation of countries such as Britain, Australia, New Zealand, Thailand, and the Philippines; a "full political understanding" with France, likely meaning independence for the Associated States of Indochina and French participation in the rest of the war; and advance congressional approval.[116]

At the NSC meeting on April 6, Eisenhower finally made his position explicit. "As far as he was concerned," Eisenhower said with "great emphasis," there was "no possibility whatever of U.S. unilateral intervention in Indochina, and we had best face that fact." Later in the meeting, Eisenhower "expressed his hostility to the notion that because we might lose Indochina we would necessarily have to lose all the rest of Southeast Asia," and he referred to "saving the rest of Southeast Asia in the event that Indochina were lost." Eisenhower here moved the goalposts on U.S. policy. Having decided against intervention, he was willing to move the line back and make a stand elsewhere. He now "expressed warm approval" for the regional alliance idea, declaring it "better than emergency military action." When Vice President Nixon pointed out that the real problem in Indochina was internal subversion—a problem the proposed regional organization would do little to address—Eisenhower simply reiterated his belief in the regional grouping. He later interrupted again "to state with great conviction that we certainly could not intervene in Indochina and become the colonial power which succeeded France."[117] He was exasperated with the French, whom he later condemned for using "weasel words in promising independence."[118] As Billings-Yun concludes, by April 26, with Dien Bien Phu not yet fallen, Indochina "had lost its place at the head of the agenda."[119]

Eisenhower declined to intervene in Dien Bien Phu for a variety of reasons. As Billings-Yun summarizes, his stand had been fairly consistent in the month leading up to the fall of the French garrison: he thought the French "exaggerated the military importance of Dien Bien Phu"; that the French would never win without granting independence; that the West must realize the importance of Southeast Asia to its security; and that local armies alone, perhaps with regional assistance, could provide security.[120] But we can also trace the decision to his external focus. Eisenhower believed that the American stake in Indochina had little to do with the domestic institutions of Indochina itself, and he saw few benefits to the domestic transformation of Indochina. Furthermore, his preferred form of intervention—a nontransformative effort to help France and secure an internationally successful outcome—was not necessarily feasible because it risked evolving into a far more intrusive operation than he was prepared to undertake. Indeed, he feared that any U.S. intervention might take on a transformative cast and that the United States risked inheriting France's status as a colonial power. Eisenhower therefore changed his definition of drawing a line in Southeast Asia and seized on the SEATO alliance. Keeping costs down and relying on local proxies also made the SEATO alternative much more attractive. As he told Republican legislative leaders at a meeting on April 26, "there are plenty of people in Asia, and we can train them to fight well. I don't see any reason for American ground troops to be committed in Indo China."[121] His policy would give the United States what it "wanted at the least cost."[122] He thus chose not to intervene in Indochina because he diagnosed the threat in external terms and perceived the costs of intervening to secure a favorable international outcome—with the additional risk of getting drawn into a transformative operation—to far exceed the benefits. He did not really consider using a transformative strategy. As George Herring notes, Dulles even declined to add a Marshall Plan–like component to SEATO, hoping that the "mere existence of the alliance" would be a deterrent to communist aggression.[123]

Even after the Dien Bien Phu decision and the Geneva conference of 1954, however, there remained the problem of U.S. policy toward the newly independent and partitioned Vietnam. For the remainder of his presidency, Eisenhower committed his administration and U.S. prestige to the Diem regime, despite significant awareness of Diem's shortcomings as a leader. As William Duiker notes, the administration "went into the Diem experiment with its eyes wide open."[124] In the following months and years, the United States gave substantial support to South Vietnam, putting the country near the top of the list of U.S. aid recipients. U.S. support to the fledgling nation, however, was heavily weighted toward military aid, which formed over 70 percent of American assistance; some economic aid even went toward projects with a military purpose, such as roads.[125] David Anderson observes that this imbalance in aid was consistent with a view that "placed a higher priority on stability than reform."[126] From Washington's perspective, the program began with some of the spirit of building up a stable South Vietnamese government. But Eisenhower's personal views shaped its concentration on such international factors as South Vietnam's ability to resist outside aggression. As Herring notes, the administration hoped the effort would be "limited" in the spirit of the Iran and Guatemala operations.[127] At an August 1954 NSC meeting to discuss a new policy statement for Southeast Asia, Eisenhower confessed to being "frankly puzzled by the problem of helping defeat local subversion."[128] At the October 22 NSC meeting, U.S. officials debated increased military aid, including training the Vietnamese Army, and discussed whether political stability was a prerequisite to any military program. Eisenhower broke in "with conviction" and invoked his own experience in the Philippines: "What we wanted . . . was a Vietnamese force which would support Diem. Therefore let's get busy and get one, but certainly not at a cost of $400 million a year. The President said that he knew something from personal experience about doing this kind of job in this kind of area. He therefore was sure that something could be done and done quickly." Later Eisenhower "said that the obvious thing to do was simply to authorize General O'Daniel [head of the U.S. military mission] to use up to X millions of dollars—say, five, six, or seven—to produce the maximum number of Vietnamese military units on which Prime Minister Diem could depend to sustain himself in power."[129] On October 23, Eisenhower had a letter delivered to Diem offering an aid package whose purpose was "to assist the Government of Viet-Nam in developing and maintaining a strong, viable state, capable of resisting attempted subversion or aggression through military means. The Government of the United States expects that this aid will be met by performance on the part of the Government of Viet-Nam in undertaking needed reforms."[130] As Anderson points out, however, this kind of "crash program" could only be a "stopgap."[131]

Indeed, Eisenhower never enforced his condition that Diem undertake reforms. At one point in 1955, the administration considered replacing Diem.[132] Apart from this episode, however, Eisenhower was uncritical, despite plenty of information that Diem himself was the source of many problems. As Anderson notes, over time Eisenhower and Dulles "devoted less of their personal attention to the inscrutable politics of Vietnam." After 1955, Eisenhower's "contribution was basically an unreflective reiteration of the domino theory and of the earlier decisions to support Diem and to continue the pursuit of containment in South Vietnam."[133]

Thus while many lower-level U.S. officials would toil away diligently at political, economic, and social problems in South Vietnam,[134] Eisenhower concentrated on the country's international position. From Eisenhower's perspective, "nation building" primarily meant "army building," as it had in the Philippines. And even here, the focus of the U.S. effort remained overt aggression rather than Diem's lack of popular support and the growing insurgency inside South Vietnam. As Ronald Spector details, the men in charge of training the new army made preparation to meet a conventional attack from the North the center of the new army's mission. Internal security or counterinsurgency operations were seen either as a secondary mission that could be dealt with by regular forces or as an outright distraction from conventional preparedness.[135] These views partly reflected the U.S. Army's lack of attention to the problem of guerrilla warfare during the 1950s and its conventionally oriented doctrine (discussed in more detail in chapter 4).[136] And as Herring notes, in a way the emphasis on conventional warfare, which the U.S. Army knew best, can be seen as logical from the perspective of the time, given that the U.S. was trying to build "from scratch" an army that would face "two quite diverse missions" and the countryside was relatively calm until 1958.[137]

The U.S. Army's preferences no doubt influenced the development of the South Vietnamese Army. But another important factor was the lack of unified guidance from Washington in this period. What attention Eisenhower paid to Vietnam remained nontransformative in orientation.[138] By May 1957, Eisenhower was busy playing host to Diem in Washington and touting the South Vietnamese leader as a "miracle man."[139] When the North Vietnamese significantly stepped up their insurgent campaign in 1959, therefore, Washington was largely taken by surprise.[140] Only in March 1960 did the U.S. advisory command begin to develop a counterinsurgency plan.[141] But as Spector notes, the plan "was really not a new departure" and was largely an expansion of existing conventional measures.[142] As Duiker summarizes, the Eisenhower administration was "not blind" to South Vietnam's internal problems, but "in general, Washington appeared to view the problem as primarily military in nature."[143] In emphasizing military issues and stability, nation building in Vietnam under the Eisenhower administration did not go deep.

Eisenhower's successor, John F. Kennedy, would make many of the same mistakes in dealing with South Vietnam. But even before he became president, Kennedy paid far more attention to the domestic structure of South Vietnam and to the problem of guerrilla warfare. Indeed, in 1958 he joined other senators in pressing the Eisenhower administration to shift the emphasis in foreign aid from military to economic aid in Vietnam.[144] The key point is that for Eisenhower—and later, for Johnson—U.S. credibility was based primarily on not losing Vietnam, with little concern for the final shape of the South Vietnamese state.

Intervention Choices in the Middle East: The Lebanon and Iraq Crises of 1958

Eisenhower's inclination to collect allies and build walls without regard to the domestic institutions of Third World states also manifested itself in his handling of the 1958 crises in Lebanon and Iraq. Many historians argue that Eisenhower intervened in Lebanon to protect U.S. credibility.[145] Most analyses of the U.S. response to the Iraq coup conclude that the United States did not seriously entertain a rollback plan because the coup plotters rapidly gained control and there was no plausible alternative leader for the West to support.[146] But Eisenhower was careful to ensure that U.S. credibility would be on the line only where he would be able to back it up with a limited, nontransformative response. Since the July 1958 crises in Lebanon and Iraq unfolded almost simultaneously, I first discuss the background in the region and in each country, and then turn to the two crises themselves.

THE POST-SUEZ ENVIRONMENT

The general trend in the Middle East in the mid-1950s was one of rising Arab nationalism. In July 1956, after a period of tension in U.S.-Egyptian relations, Egyptian leader Gamal Abdel Nasser nationalized the Suez Canal Company. Eisenhower was furious when, in October 1956, the British, French, and Israelis conspired to attack Egypt, overthrow Nasser, and retake the canal.[147] Believing strongly that force must not be used for seemingly imperial aims and that allies must consult each other, Eisenhower came down firmly against the British, French, and Israelis. The Suez debacle—culminating in November 1956 with Eisenhower putting strong economic pressure on Britain, France, and Israel to withdraw their forces from Egypt—decimated the British position in the Middle East, leaving a power vacuum in the region.

Both Lebanon and Iraq occupied somewhat curious positions in this regional turmoil. Initially, the Eisenhower administration was optimistic about Lebanon's prospects as a U.S. ally, especially when Camille Chamoun, a pro-Western Maronite Christian, became president in 1952. The Suez crisis, however, forced Chamoun out on something of a limb. Domestic strife in Lebanon emerged as Chamoun came under fire from Muslims for not breaking off diplomatic relations with Britain and France and for trying to act as a mediator during the crisis.[148] Meanwhile, the government in Iraq was also out on a limb with respect to its Arab neighbors because of its orientation toward the West. The British, the colonial power in Iraq until 1932, were still very much involved in Iraqi affairs in the 1950s, especially the Iraq Petroleum Company. The Hashemite king Faisal II ruled Iraq, but its government was run by Prime Minister Nuri al-Said.[149]

"Pactomania" was to some extent responsible for Iraq's precarious position in the Middle East. In 1955, Iraq had concluded a mutual security treaty with Turkey, a treaty that became known as the Baghdad Pact (and later included Iran, Pakistan, and Britain). Dulles concluded that various schemes for a Middle East defense organization centered on Egypt were unworkable and instead proposed the "Northern tier" concept: a pact based on such states as Turkey and Iran, which bordered the Soviet Union. But reaction to the Baghdad Pact in the rest of the Arab world, led by Nasser, was hostile, leaving Iraq isolated as the only Arab participant. The Eisenhower administration, including Dulles, distanced itself from the pact, despite strong pressure to join from both Britain and the pact countries (especially Iraq) and even some administration officials.[150]

Another dimension of U.S. policy would shape the U.S. response to the July 1958 coup: a consistent policy of avoiding responsibility for bolstering Iraqi institutions and instead actively encouraging the British to take the lead in Iraqi politics and military affairs. In February 1954, the United States and Britain signed a secret Memorandum of Understanding (MOU) stating that "the Iraqi Government should continue to look primarily to the United Kingdom Government" for its arms and training needs.[151] Even after Suez, despite warnings that both Britain and Nuri were in "precarious" positions,[152] the State Department only reluctantly beefed up aid, emphasizing that the MOU still applied and that U.S. help would be "temporary."[153] Washington seemed unwilling to bolster Nuri, even as he presented an opportunity to balance against Egypt and tried to keep Iraq in the Western camp while shifting his emphasis from Britain to the United States. Why this reluctance? Scholars have suggested that the Arab-Israeli conflict, a preoccupation with the communist threat, and a generally full plate led the United States to keep its distance from Iraq.[154] These arguments make sense but must also be seen in the context of Eisenhower's beliefs. As long as Iraq retained its pro-Western orientation and participated in security arrangements that suited the United States, Eisenhower worried little about Iraqi domestic institutions and even ignored the domestic political damage Nuri's regime suffered as a result of its pro-Western stance. Furthermore, from Eisenhower's perspective, taking on a new ally like Iraq when the British already had a strong position there would be redundant and costly. Replacing the British might also leave the United States looking like a colonial power and burdened with responsibility for building up Iraqi military institutions. Aid to Lebanon came with less colonial taint and was less risky in terms of Arab-Israeli politics.

THE EISENHOWER DOCTRINE

Almost immediately after the Suez cease-fire, Eisenhower ordered a major review of U.S. policy in the region, with a particular emphasis on the Soviet threat. The review culminated in the 1957 Eisenhower Doctrine. As presented to Congress, the doctrine called for an aid program, backed up with the threat to use force to defend states in the Middle East "against overt armed aggression from any nation controlled by International Communism."[155] For Arab governments, however, embracing the doctrine meant openly associating with the

West, a stance not likely to go over well with their domestic audiences.[156] As Gaddis notes, by this time Eisenhower had privately expressed some skepticism about the wisdom of a black-and-white alliance policy that had no room for gray areas such as neutralism, writing to his brother Edgar in 1956 that "it is a very grave error to ask some of these nations to announce themselves as being on our side." But his reasoning concerned the international and military consequences of forcing states to declare their allegiance rather than the potential domestic repercussions for these states: Eisenhower worried that the United States would have the "impossible task" of arming new allies that were militarily weak and that new military allies would potentially invite a Soviet or communist attack.[157] At the time of the Eisenhower Doctrine, he did not consider the local domestic consequences of asking Arab regimes to publicly trumpet their relationship with the United States, consistent with his externally focused view of alliances.

The form of the Eisenhower Doctrine itself also emphasized international matters. Administration officials decided that the doctrine should be directed only at the threat from communism rather than also at intra-Arab rivalries or other regional threats. The doctrine also explicitly stated that the United States would only use force to protect nations "requesting such aid"; Eisenhower himself suggested the provision requiring a request, though Dulles objected.[158] In July 1958, in light of this provision, Eisenhower would emphasize the Lebanese government's invitation to intervene.

The Lebanese Civil War and the U.S. Commitment to Lebanon

Following congressional approval of the Eisenhower Doctrine in March 1957, both Lebanon and Iraq publicly embraced it. But the administration was more forthcoming with support for Lebanon than for Iraq. The June 1957 Lebanese parliamentary elections became what Salim Yaqub calls "a referendum on the Eisenhower Doctrine," not for any particular Lebanese domestic reasons but in the context of the international stakes.[159] To this end, CIA agent Wilbur Eveland began showing up at the presidential palace late at night with briefcases full of cash for Chamoun, who rigged the elections in his own favor.[160] The widely perceived electoral fraud prompted the Lebanese opposition, composed to this point mainly of Muslims angry with Chamoun and his embrace of the doctrine, to expand to include many moderate Christians. The disparate opposition factions could agree on one point: that they must halt Chamoun's rumored effort to amend the constitution to allow himself to seek a second term as president. This effort, a distinctly Lebanese issue, would precipitate Lebanon's domestic crisis in 1958. But in the meantime, Lebanon's symbolic importance and its increasing reliance on the West were not lost on Eisenhower, who in October 1957 discussed with British prime minister Harold Macmillan the possibility of a joint

British-American intervention in Lebanon or Jordan (another weak regime); a few weeks later, Dulles requested contingency plans for intervention.[161]

Tensions in the Middle East ratcheted up another notch when, in February 1958, Egypt and Syria united to form the United Arab Republic (UAR). In response, Jordan and Iraq formed the Arab Union that same month. Meanwhile, Chamoun continued to press for U.S. support, citing communist infiltration. Chamoun decided officially to seek reelection on May 7; tensions erupted into civil war on May 8. Even the leader of the Lebanese Army, the Maronite Christian general Fuad Shihab, actively opposed Chamoun's reelection bid, arguing that the "sole cause of [the] present revolutionary crisis in Lebanon is Chamoun's selfish determination to succeed himself in office."[162]

But the United States would soon become even more committed to Lebanon and to Chamoun himself. Eisenhower worried primarily about U.S. credibility, focusing on the international dimension of the problem rather than connecting the crisis to Lebanon's domestic issues. On May 13, Chamoun forced Eisenhower's hand by demanding to know whether the United States would answer a request for intervention if the need arose. Chamoun's question prompted a high-level meeting the same day at the White House, where credibility dominated the thinking of both Eisenhower and Dulles, though both were well aware of the dangers of intervening. Eisenhower "observed that it was well to consider such problems, but that we also had to take into account the apparently much larger problems which would arise if the Lebanese needed our intervention and we did not respond." Dulles immediately agreed but noted that the Eisenhower Doctrine did not apply because the UAR, thought to be helping the Lebanese rebels, was not under communist control, though a provision known as the Mansfield Amendment (which noted that "the United States regards as vital to the national interest and world peace the preservation of the independence and integrity of the nations of the Middle East") might provide a basis for intervention.[163] Later that day, Dulles cabled the U.S. ambassador, Robert McClintock, with the official U.S. response: the United States would honor a request for military intervention under restrictive conditions.[164] The United States and Britain worked in concert to update their contingency plans for joint U.S.-U.K. intervention. Thus by mid-May 1958, the Eisenhower administration had further committed itself to Chamoun, despite his own contribution to the very instability that might require intervention. As Yaqub puts it, "Chamoun now symbolized the U.S. commitment to freedom and independence, and it was imperative for the United States that he avoid public failure."[165]

In the next two months, Lebanon oscillated between the verge of chaos and moves toward stabilization. Chamoun and Lebanese foreign minister Charles Malik continued to press the charge of outside subversion from the UAR. There was some limited UAR infiltration through Syria, and Nasser channeled aid to the rebels through the UAR embassy in Beirut and broadcast radio attacks on Chamoun. But Chamoun and Malik exaggerated the extent of the infiltration.[166] Eisenhower and Dulles privately recognized that outside aggression was not the cause of the conflict, but they concentrated on its international dimensions. Thus when Nasser himself proposed a solution that would allow Chamoun to serve out his term but not seek reelection, Eisenhower and Dulles refused to endorse it lest Nasser get credit, even though they recognized the plan as "not wholly unreasonable."[167]

As the situation in Lebanon deteriorated again in mid-June, Eisenhower contemplated acting, but out of concern for the international repercussions rather than for Lebanon's domestic situation. On June 15, the president called an emergency meeting at the White House. Frustrated, he asked, "How can you save a country from its own leaders?" and "said he had little, if any, enthusiasm for our intervening at this time." He further "commented that what was really needed in Lebanon was a strong leader whom we could back strongly." But Eisenhower concurred with the credibility arguments, noting that if intervention were necessary, the United States should "attempt to bolster the Lebanese army as soon as possible, so that our forces could withdraw quickly."[168] Eisenhower was hesitant to use force at all and wanted any action to involve a minimal footprint inside Lebanon. Despite these tensions, by early July the Lebanese crisis actually eased somewhat and appeared to be resolvable.[169]

Iraq: Uneasy Quiet

Meanwhile, during the period of the Lebanese crisis, the U.S. focus was decidedly not on Iraq's domestic affairs. The Nuri regime (now at least nominally joined with Jordan in the Arab Union) appeared stable, though the administration was aware of simmering domestic tensions. The State Department, over the objections of the Pentagon and the JCS, continued to deflect Iraqi requests for aid, emphasizing British primacy in Iraq.[170]

Considering that it was Dulles who had encouraged Iraqi membership in the "Northern tier" scheme to begin with, however, and given Iraq's considerable assets as compared with Lebanon, the U.S. neglect is somewhat puzzling. The JCS took a different view, requesting on June 11 contingency plans for defending Iraq "in view of the strategic importance of Iraq and its stature as a pro-Western influence in the Middle East."[171] But as late as July 3, a CIA analysis concluded that if the United States and Britain intervened in Lebanon, the Iraqi government would probably be able to control any popular reaction, noting that the opposition "lacks the immediate capacity to overthrow the regime."[172] Just eleven days later, this estimate would prove dramatically wrong. U.S. policy in the first half of 1958 thus reflected a continued preference for the status quo in

Iraq and inattention to Iraqi internal problems, leaving the United States without good intelligence about the domestic situation there.

THE IRAQ COUP AND EISENHOWER'S DECISION MAKING: JULY 1958

On July 14, General Abdul Karim Qasim led Iraqi troops into Baghdad, quickly overtaking the palace and killing King Faisal II and Crown Prince Abdel Ilah. Nuri tried to flee the city disguised as a woman but was caught and killed, his body dragged through the streets. The coup unleashed mob violence as thousands of residents showed their anger at the old regime and their support for the new republic. Two American businessmen were killed. Almost immediately on hearing word of the coup, Chamoun cashed in his intervention check, calling on the United States to land troops in Lebanon to shore up his regime. But McClintock cabled Washington, "As for hard evidence of an increased military threat to Lebanon, it is difficult to find this morning. . . . We feel decision on military intervention can only be taken in light of broader intelligence and political and strategic considerations affecting the entire Middle East. So far as Lebanon alone is concerned, we cannot as of midday discern need for so portent[ous] a step."[173]

In Washington, Eisenhower learned of the coup and Chamoun's request first thing in the morning on July 14. The reports from Baghdad were initially very sketchy, and the fate of the royal family was still in doubt during the first decision-making meetings. John Foster Dulles met with his brother Allen (the CIA director), JCS chairman Nathan Twining, and other State Department officials at 9:30 a.m.; Twining argued that "we had no alternative but to go in." Someone in the meeting (the memorandum is vague) argued that the United States "would have to be prepared to go into the whole area; this might involve a 'division of labor' with the British (going into Iraq and Kuwait)."[174]

At 10:50 a.m., Eisenhower met with his top advisers. Eisenhower's national security adviser, Robert Cutler, described the president as "the most relaxed man in the room . . . [who] knew exactly what he meant to do."[175] Indeed, as Eisenhower himself put it in his memoirs, "Because of my long study of the problem, this was one meeting in which my mind was practically made up regarding the general line of action we should take, even before we met. The time was rapidly approaching, I believed, when we had to move into the Middle East, and specifically into Lebanon, to stop the trend toward chaos."[176] The memorandum of conversation does not indicate that Eisenhower himself mentioned Iraq, instead concentrating on Lebanon.[177]

After meeting with congressional leaders, Eisenhower again met with his top advisers to finalize decisions and plans. Here Eisenhower suggested that "it might be better to put our troops into Lebanon unilaterally," despite the long-standing plans for joint U.S.-U.K. intervention. By this time, King Hussein of Jordan was indicating a desire for British help (a formal request for Western intervention would come two days later). Dulles warned that the British would want U.S. help with operations in Jordan and Iraq, but Eisenhower replied that he "did not see how we could commit ourselves quickly to do more" than logistical support, "since this would exceed his constitutional authority without legislative action."[178] In the congressional meeting, however, the president indicated that he planned to act first and go to Congress later.[179] The discussion quickly moved on to final decisions on the timing of the Lebanese landings, which were set for the next afternoon. Eisenhower said that he "thought that our best course is to put our forces ashore in Lebanon, with the United Kingdom holding its force ready for Iraq or Jordan."[180]

Thus by the afternoon of July 14, with the whereabouts of King Faisal and Nuri still not confirmed, U.S. intervention in Lebanon was set and the prospect of a U.S. rollback in Iraq was off the table. These decisions would stick, despite pressure from many important quarters, including Saudi Arabia, Israel, and the other Baghdad Pact countries, especially Turkey.[181] Additionally, Nixon spoke to Foster Dulles by telephone on July 15, urging that there be "no hesitation on our part on the Jordan-Iraqi thing."[182] But nowhere was the pressure greater than from Britain. In repeated communications on the evening of July 14, Macmillan frantically urged Eisenhower to commit both to intervention in Lebanon and to rollback in Iraq. Eisenhower told Macmillan that the British troops should be held in reserve, perhaps a tacit indication that the United States would look favorably on British rollback plans. But on the question of U.S. action beyond Lebanon, Eisenhower responded firmly, "Well, now, I will tell you of course I would not want to go further."[183]

Eisenhower's mind was made up. Accordingly, U.S. Marines landed—alone—in Beirut on the afternoon of July 15 and ultimately never fired a shot. As several historians of the crisis have noted, this outcome owed much to good luck and diplomatic skill: the Lebanese Army, not informed of the landings in advance, was furious, and McClintock and Shihab had to maneuver to avert bloodshed.[184] Jon Western notes that there was more risk involved than many observers realized: intelligence estimates had predicted significant local resistance, and Eisenhower was concerned about it.[185] But such concern about Lebanese domestic affairs did not deter Eisenhower or indeed even significantly affect how he managed the crisis.

Eisenhower did not talk about intervening in Lebanon in transformative terms, and the intervention itself involved a nontransformative demonstration of force. U.S. policy coalesced around a defensive deployment.[186] Robert Murphy—a colleague of Eisenhower's from the North African campaign in World War II who was called in to help resolve the crisis—cabled Washington on July 19 that the intervention was successful in military terms, but the "local political result is dubious" and the "mere presence of [U.S.] forces in a small coastal portion of the country seems to have brought no fundamental change in the local political climate." The intervention did not seek to effect institutional change militarily, at either the national or local level, nor did U.S. troops seek to interact with the local population. On the contrary, as Murphy described, the hope was that U.S. forces "would relieve the pressure on the Lebanese security personnel thus giving them a free hand in suppressing the insurrection." Since this Lebanese-led "clean up" of Beirut was not forthcoming, Murphy instead advocated focusing on electing a new president, which would "bring about relaxation in the country." But Murphy frankly acknowledged that there remained the problem of "what to do with [U.S.] forces" and that the larger regional problem would not have been solved.[187] Though the United States brokered a political compromise, allowing General Shihab to succeed Chamoun, it did not get deeply involved in building or altering Lebanese institutions. An integrated political-military solution was not part of the intervention strategy. Instead, the operation aimed at a short-term demonstration of force and ultimately replaced one leader with another. As Eisenhower wrote to his former treasury secretary, George Humphrey (by then retired), on July 22, "The fact is that we will take any honorable and practicable solution to the Lebanese problem, so that we can remove our troops."[188] By October 1958, the last Marines left Lebanon.

Meanwhile, in Iraq, in the days after the July 14 coup, information from Baghdad would show that the rebels were in control; that there was no clear faction for the West to support; and that the new regime had pledged to honor its international commitments and not to nationalize the oil fields. But these facts simply confirmed Eisenhower's existing inclination not to undertake rollback, a contingency (and indeed an intervention strategy) for which he had not prepared. In a telephone call with Eisenhower early in the morning on July 15, John Foster Dulles said of the Iraq situation that to "intervene militarily would introduce problems that we have not even considered." Eisenhower asserted that "we all agreed what we should do in Lebanon—we have studied that carefully."[189] Eisenhower and Twining did discuss making additional U.S. forces ready without attracting attention.[190] This discussion may have prompted a subsequent JCS request, on July 18, for a plan "covering a U.S.-British occupation of Iraq, with and without Turkish assistance from the North into the Mosul and Kirkuk area, with the main objective of controlling Iraqi oil. . . . The time frame for the plan is now, taking into consideration present U.S. and British deployments."[191]

Despite these planning steps, Eisenhower did not seriously entertain rollback. In reporting the Iraq situation to Humphrey on July 22, Eisenhower concentrated on international factors and the pro-Western inclination of the new government: "So far Iraq has not taken some of the mob-like actions that normally we could expect. They have not destroyed any of the pipe lines or attempted to interfere with production of oil in the region. There is some slight indication that they may want to remain on good business relationships with the West."[192] As long as Iraq's international behavior remained satisfactory, Eisenhower continued to avoid delving deeply into the Iraqi domestic situation.

Given Iraq's considerable oil resources, its pro-Western orientation before the coup, and its membership in the Baghdad Pact, why would Eisenhower have written off rollback? As discussed at the outset, most analyses of the period argue that Eisenhower intervened in Lebanon to shore up U.S. credibility. The evidence supports such an argument, but there remains the question why Eisenhower chose to demonstrate U.S. credibility in Lebanon and not in Iraq.

The answer is rooted in Eisenhower's belief that he could achieve an internationally successful outcome in Lebanon by stabilizing existing institutions with a show of force. An intervention in Lebanon could be kept limited and would at least appear to support a friendly government. The initial reports from Baghdad indicated strong popular support for the coup. To be sure, there were strategic interests at stake in Iraq: in a diary entry one day after the coup, Eisenhower openly acknowledged that the "true issue in the Middle East is whether or not the Western world can maintain its rightful opportunity to purchase vitally needed oil supplies peaceably and without hindrance or payment of blackmail."[193] But in July 1958, merely ensuring an internationally successful outcome— a pro-Western Iraq with secure oil supplies—might well have required an intervention that would take on a transformative character. Unwilling to intervene where he would have to fight the tide of popular opinion, take over institutions, and possibly rebuild them, Eisenhower chose the far simpler (but also unpopular) course of intervening in Lebanon, where he would not have to get deeply involved in local institutions. Furthermore, Eisenhower did not see additional benefits to building new Iraqi institutions that might be more stable and secure than those in place at the time of the coup. A rollback operation in Iraq also would have smacked of backing up a colonial power, given long-standing British interests. Eisenhower did not seriously consider seizing the short window of opportunity to reverse the coup.

Eisenhower's views on the use of force came out strongly in a July 20 White House meeting, in a discussion about whether or not to back the British in some sort of military action to protect Kuwait or other Persian Gulf countries. Although Dulles stated that "he had thought it agreed that force would be used to preserve access to Middle East oil" and noted that the "terrain is such that the situation could easily be held there," Eisenhower firmly asserted that "even if we put in large military forces we cannot see what to do beyond that point. He was sure that we would not wish to use military force as the medium for trying to settle this problem. . . . [The] use of force will outrage the Arabs. Accordingly, the best chance may be to make a deal with Iraq and Kuwait." The president even suggested that the United States might have to "adjust" to the "new Arab groups."[194] Eisenhower seemed to grasp that deploying even "large military forces" in a nontransformative way would be difficult and possibly unproductive in terms of achieving an internationally favorable outcome—securing the flow of oil—and risked drawing the United States into the domestic affairs of Arab states. Despite his frequent concerns about revolutionary governments in the Third World, in this case Eisenhower was fairly quickly willing to make a "deal." As long as the new government would make such a deal, he saw few additional benefits to transforming Iraq or other Arab states, relative to the high costs. Thus by July 23, both the United States and Britain had moved on to the question of recognizing the new regime. Although there were concerns that Iraqi professions of friendship might be a sham,[195] many within both the U.S. and British governments argued that recognition might keep Iraq out of the communist orbit. Accordingly, the United States recognized the new regime on August 2.

Once the coup leaders signaled their pro-Western intentions, Eisenhower paid little further attention to Iraq's domestic issues. It is interesting to note that in the months after the coup, the new Iraqi regime *did* begin to drift further under the influence of Iraqi communists. An internally focused leader might have seen the nature of Iraqi institutions as a potential source of such influence and sought more sway over the postcoup institutions, but Eisenhower's lack of attention to Iraqi domestic politics meant that the administration once again considered this development from an international perspective. As concerns about communists in Iraq mounted, Eisenhower reverted to old habits and U.S. officials considered both overt and covert options for Iraq.[196] But Eisenhower ultimately decided against intervention. Finally, Qasim put down a communist uprising in Kirkuk in July 1959.

Thus Eisenhower consistently avoided a large-scale commitment to the Middle East, despite declaring a doctrine. His external focus led him to act where he could avoid significant interference in local affairs and to concentrate on the international facets of the Iraq coup, such as securing the flow of oil and keeping Iraq in the Western camp. If these benefits could be secured without force, he saw no need to get involved in Iraq's domestic affairs. Eisenhower hoped to avoid force altogether, and when the time came to draw a line, he was careful to go no farther than Beirut, in an operation arguably only one notch in intensity above gunboat diplomacy.

Eisenhower consistently focused on the international dimensions of crises and channeled his responses toward limited U.S. involvement in the domestic affairs of Third World states. In Indochina, he chose not to intervene in a crisis that could be seen as an international threat but where even a nontransformative intervention to secure an internationally favorable outcome risked drawing the United States into local affairs. His subsequent policy toward South Vietnam took a primarily nontransformative approach. Faced with simultaneous crises in Iraq and Lebanon, he selected the intervention target that allowed him to achieve an internationally successful outcome with the strategy for which he was better prepared. He therefore intervened with a nontransformative strategy in his only overt military intervention, in Lebanon. While he was concerned with maintaining U.S. credibility—as all Cold War presidents were—he managed the perception of U.S. credibility so that it was most visibly at stake where he was comfortable defending it.

Alternative Hypotheses

Eisenhower's causal beliefs influenced his intervention decisions even in the face of other important factors, as is especially evident in his reaction to the 1958 crises. Consider first the hypothesis that structural and material factors drove his decisions. The anticipated Soviet reaction, for example, might have guided U.S. action in 1958. But the Soviet reaction was not expected to be significant in either Lebanon or Iraq.[197] Another consideration is the military feasibility of the two operations. The Lebanese operation was certainly far simpler (though not without its own risks) and, as discussed, had been planned for extensively with presidential involvement, whereas Iraqi contingency plans were requested only on June 11 by the JCS. In a sense, this point reinforces the argument that Eisenhower was less likely to pursue rollback in Iraq because it would be so costly, but his policies also left the administration less prepared to deal with such a contingency. And although an operation in Iraq would have been more difficult than the one in Lebanon, in April 1959, as Iraq slid toward communism, General Twining told the NSC, "We could easily take over Iraq by military force if the appropriate preparations were made in advance."[198]

One might expect that the United States would have played a more prominent role in Iraq before the coup, given its potential as a counterweight to Nasser, its oil supplies, and the potential for base rights. Lebanon was important as a center of oil transportation (and regional transportation generally), but Iraq was a major oil source. In the end, there was no interruption in Iraqi oil production, but this did not become clear for several days. Of course, Eisenhower had shown no restraint in helping to reinstall the Shah of Iran after the nationalization of Iranian oil. But that operation had involved, as Bowie and Immerman put it, the "surgical" removal of a regime rather than a full-scale overt military intervention. Although Iraqi oil mainly went to Western Europe and the Suez crisis had shown that the United States could help Europe weather shortages, Eisenhower had called oil the "true issue in the Middle East," and U.S. officials were clearly concerned about oil security in the long term.[199]

Credibility, the argument most frequently invoked for the U.S. intervention in Lebanon, was a major factor, but here again Eisenhower's beliefs played an important role. Eisenhower's desire to do *something* in the Middle East but to keep that something as limited and nontransformative as possible led him to set his sights on Lebanon. The May 13 commitment, in which Washington told Chamoun that the United States would respond to a call for intervention in Lebanon under certain conditions, explicitly put U.S. credibility on the line in Lebanon, where Eisenhower was willing to defend the U.S. reputation for resolve.

Eisenhower's policy investments were also an important factor. His constraints on conventional forces left few options for operations beyond Lebanon, and the lack of planning for transformative strategies made rollback in Iraq even more daunting. Thus the argument that capabilities drive decisions must be considered in light of Eisenhower's underlying beliefs, which helped determine what capabilities were available. More generally, the issue of available capabilities is especially relevant here because of Eisenhower's emphasis on fiscal restraint. Cost was undoubtedly a frequent consideration when Eisenhower evaluated intervention options. It is even possible that his cost consciousness was one source of his externally focused beliefs. But his fiscal conservatism encompassed defense issues generally. Although it is true that transformative strategies had little place in Eisenhower's overall defense policy, neither did nontransformative, conventional wars. Given the evidence that Eisenhower was relatively unconcerned with domestic institutions as a source of threat, his threat perception can thus be considered an independent source of his aversion to transformative strategies even in light of his fiscal conservatism. Furthermore, while Eisenhower may have seen transformative strategies as particularly costly, this view is not the only way to assess cost. Nontransformative strategies can be highly costly, depending on the size of the intervention, for example. Additionally, an internally focused leader might look at the limited and nontransformative actions Eisenhower took in Indochina and the Middle East as penny wise but pound foolish, in that they did not address what such a leader would see as underlying institutional problems. As discussed in the next chapter, Kennedy often criticized Eisenhower's policies in this way. And as chapter 5 illustrates, the far more fiscally liberal Johnson was also disinclined toward transformative strategies, illustrating that a concern with cost need not necessarily correlate with the choice of strategy. Thus the structural and material conditions hypothesis does not receive much support in the context of Eisenhower's decisions in 1958.

Next we turn to the domestic competition hypothesis. Eisenhower was firmly in control in all three crises considered in this chapter. He dominated his advisers and the bureaucracy, which if anything was pushing for more action in the Middle East. In terms of American domestic politics, although Eisenhower was near the end of his second term when the Middle East crises erupted and was not subject to reelection pressures, there were domestic political factors that might have been expected to contribute to his decision making. Eisenhower repeatedly emphasized congressional reluctance as a reason for not pursuing rollback in Iraq, especially in his exchanges with Macmillan. Many in Congress were skeptical about U.S. intervention in Lebanon, questioning the outside interference theory. But Eisenhower also had critics in Congress (as well as within the administration) who deplored his reliance on nuclear weapons and advocated a more muscular U.S. policy in limited wars. Congressional displeasure was probably a constraint on Eisenhower's decision making, though arguably Eisenhower had the standing to make a case for going further. American corporate interests might also have been a factor, particularly given the role of oil in the Middle East and the fierce debate over whether other Eisenhower actions, such as the covert operation in Guatemala, were designed to protect American business interests. But there is little evidence that corporate interests played a significant role in the Middle East crises.[200]

There are other potential alternative explanations worth considering. In terms of normative and international legal arguments, Eisenhower and Dulles, though committed internationalists, were quite willing to bend norms and laws to suit their purposes. Their post hoc search for a justification to intervene led them to rely on the portion of the Eisenhower Doctrine known as the Mansfield Amendment, which they had previously opposed. Though Eisenhower made much of the Lebanese invitation for U.S. intervention, most observers saw the Lebanese situation as a domestic matter precipitated by Chamoun, the very person who issued the invitation. Furthermore, Eisenhower himself had inserted the invitation formula into the doctrine, over Dulles's objection that those who might call for intervention could be swept away by a coup—exactly what happened in Iraq. Similarly, Eisenhower and Dulles were also willing to go around the UN if necessary. They discussed intervention while the United Nations Observation Group in Lebanon (UNOGIL), set up to monitor cross-border infiltration, was still operating in Lebanon. Eisenhower and Dulles agreed that it would be better to land troops in Lebanon before calling an emergency UN Security Council session, since Article 51 justified stabilizing the situation before the UN could act.[201] The administration wanted, but was not willing to wait for, the legitimacy provided by the UN.

One might also argue that Eisenhower's anticolonial beliefs naturally led to an aversion to transformative operations. But while Eisenhower was extremely sensitive to any hint of colonialism, anticolonial views need not have inevitably led him to reject transformative strategies. Kennedy was also firmly opposed to colonialism, but he believed the United States had to actively guide the development of newly free states.

Given Lebanon's unique demographics, we might also consider whether cultural or religious factors played a role in the 1958 crises. But the administration recognized that there were risks in appearing to intervene on the side of Christians and that many Christians might oppose the intervention, especially since the Lebanese opposition contained many prominent Christians.[202] The documents do not suggest an overtly religious motive, and by May 1958, Eisenhower was under no illusions about Chamoun. Yaqub also points out that it is difficult to separate "anti-Arab sentiment from the blanket condescension with which top administration officials regarded Others in general, be they Arabs, Jews, Europeans, or U.S. congressmen."[203]

Finally, it is important to consider what evidence would show that Eisenhower was not an externally focused leader or that his beliefs did not correlate with his intervention choices. His strong antistatist beliefs, expressed in his fear of the "military-industrial complex," suggest a concern with domestic institutions at least within the United States. But he channeled this concern into limiting defense spending. Eisenhower was politically conservative, of course, which made him particularly suspicious of left-leaning governments. But somewhat paradoxically, his causal beliefs about the origin of threats led him to avoid interventions or to intervene in a nontransformative way against such regimes. His frequent use of covert operations when he perceived communist encroachment in the Third World might also seem to be contradictory evidence. But as I have discussed, Eisenhower undertook these operations where he believed they provided quick and relatively inexpensive fixes requiring a small U.S. footprint. His use of covert operations for such change does not in itself provide evidence of an internal focus; indeed, the form of these operations was often in keeping with a nontransformative strategy. His preference for stability might also represent an affirmative preference for autocrats. But in keeping with his distaste for local politics stretching back to World War II, he usually saw dictators as a convenient way to secure U.S. interests while otherwise paying little attention to the domestic politics of the Third World.

Eisenhower's causal beliefs about the origin of threats, developed in his long career in the military, emphasized international factors and downplayed domestic conditions within other states. As a result, Eisenhower concentrated on the international dimensions of crises and largely ignored domestic politics and institutions. In Latin America, Indochina, and the Middle East, Eisenhower consistently sought to resolve conflicts so that the foreign and security policies of Third World states were favorable to the United States, and he paid little attention to the internal aspects of crises. His beliefs also informed his policy investments, which in turn affected his assessment of preparedness when he considered intervening.

Eisenhower's only overt military intervention, though nominally triggered by domestic unrest in Lebanon, in fact had little to do with Lebanese domestic politics and instead, as Yaqub puts it, "had everything to do with the Eisenhower Doctrine" and international politics.[204] Indeed, Lebanon's public embrace of the doctrine contributed to Chamoun's increasing unpopularity at home and forged the link between Lebanon and U.S. credibility, a link that ultimately attracted U.S. intervention. Eisenhower saw Lebanon as a way to refute criticism that his defense policy could not meet threats in the Third World: in his memoirs Eisenhower claimed that "the Lebanon operation demonstrated the ability of the United States to react swiftly with conventional armed forces to meet small-scale, or 'brush fire' situations."[205] Far from hasty decisions resulting from the Iraq coup, the intervention in Lebanon and the nonintervention in Iraq reflected his long-held beliefs. Consistent with these beliefs, Eisenhower chose the most limited "brush fire" he could find, and avoided, as he did so often, large-scale transformative operations. His successor, John F. Kennedy, would take a different approach.

4

John F. Kennedy

John F. Kennedy's presidency was marked by many forms of political, economic, and military intervention. Kennedy's interventions—including his only overt military intervention, the counterinsurgency effort in Vietnam—stand out among those of Cold War presidents for their transformative character: from Latin America to Southeast Asia, Kennedy sought to influence the domestic institutions of Third World states on a large scale. But this pattern of interference did not result from international pressure, political expedience, or idealism. Kennedy came to office with a transformative agenda already in place, the product of a consistent and unusual focus on the Third World's domestic problems throughout his congressional career.

This chapter argues that in sharp contrast to Dwight Eisenhower—and, more surprisingly, to Lyndon Johnson—Kennedy held strong beliefs that located the source of threats in the internal institutions of other states. These beliefs were reflected in his speeches and writings in Congress. Even before reaching the Oval Office, Kennedy saw not only communist regimes but also repressive anticommunist dictatorships as potentially threatening. As president, Kennedy immediately began to invest forcefully in transformative strategies.

As with other presidents, however, the path from beliefs to decisions is not linear. Many commentators have pointed out that Kennedy had a strong pragmatist, even realist, streak.[1] His transformative agenda did not stem merely from idealism: Kennedy believed that U.S. national security was bound up with the internal conditions of Third World states. Furthermore, though more tolerant of neutralism and "diversity" within the international system than Eisenhower,[2]

Kennedy was not above resorting to the knee-jerk anticommunism so common in the 1950s and 1960s. But while his decisions reflect a careful weighing of circumstances, capabilities, credibility, and, of course, politics, Kennedy also paid significant attention to the domestic characteristics of other states.

I begin by establishing Kennedy's beliefs about the origin of threats and then turn to his policy investments as president. Kennedy invested significant effort in transformative strategies, including a foreign aid program that focused far more on economic development and political reform than had Eisenhower's aid efforts. But among Kennedy's policy investments, his very personal effort to develop a counterinsurgency capability is especially notable. Kennedy was interested in an approach to counterinsurgency that contained transformative elements and called for deep involvement in local institutions.

In the remainder of the chapter, I discuss Kennedy's major intervention decisions. I briefly describe his Latin America policies, which included some reflexive anticommunist actions but also contained overtones of political reform and economic development. This discussion of Kennedy's transformative agenda sets up a contrast with Johnson's approach to Latin America. I then turn to Kennedy's decisions in Laos and Vietnam. His focus on domestic characteristics made him a discriminating intervener. He accepted a neutralist settlement in Laos but initiated a counterinsurgency war in Vietnam. Kennedy's concern with domestic reform and the political nature of the war culminated in his consideration of and effective acquiescence in a coup against South Vietnamese president Ngo Dinh Diem.

Kennedy provides an illuminating contrast to both Eisenhower and Johnson. Both Kennedy and Johnson were Democratic senators with their eyes on the presidency, and both reacted to many of the same Eisenhower administration policies and decisions. Johnson served as Kennedy's vice president and, after Kennedy's assassination, inherited Kennedy's foreign policy and national security programs and personnel. Yet while their threat perceptions and foreign and defense policies are often discussed as a unit or in terms of continuity,[3] I argue that despite some continuity, Kennedy and Johnson viewed threats, particularly in the Third World, through very different lenses.

The Kennedy period also allows me to evaluate several alternative explanations. In terms of structural and material conditions, neither international pressure nor military capabilities are sufficient to account for Kennedy's decision making. The Kennedy era illustrates that threat perception leads to investments in particular kinds of capabilities. In terms of domestic competition, Kennedy's decision making also helps to illustrate the primacy of the executive's causal beliefs over other domestic actors. Like Eisenhower, Kennedy clearly led, rather than followed, his advisers. Although many scholars have noted the influence of development economists and modernization theorists in Kennedy's advisory circle, Kennedy held his causal beliefs about the origin of threats before coming into regular contact with this group, and as president, he recruited a community of advisers who reinforced his preexisting views.[4] Once in office, he frequently rejected both military and civilian advice and pursued some aspects of the modernization agenda even more faithfully than the advisers who initially embraced it. Kennedy's assassination means that hypotheses about learning cannot be examined in this chapter. Nevertheless, his brief tenure provides a useful window on how leaders' beliefs shape military interventions.

Kennedy's Beliefs

Commentators often note that Kennedy came to office with a foreign policy strategy largely in place.[5] The record from the pre-presidential period reveals that in his years in Congress, Kennedy developed the views that would inform his presidency.[6] He did not ignore the problem of Soviet aggression and conventional preparedness to meet such threats. But most notable is the attention he paid to domestic problems affecting Third World states. Kennedy believed that the condition of Third World domestic institutions—not only their stability but also their content and vitality—was an important risk factor for communist takeovers. These years also reveal his early and sustained interest in guerrilla warfare. Building his foreign policy credentials was certainly a smart strategy for a future presidential candidate, but the *form* of Kennedy's beliefs was hardly the most politically beneficial. After Korea, U.S. involvement in Third World political and economic institutions was not the easiest project to sell to the public despite Kennedy's belief that it was necessary for national security. In the fall of 1951, Kennedy embarked (with his brother Robert, among others) on a seven-week tour of the Middle East and Asia, a trip that both reinforced and shaped his views on the nature of threats and responses. But his interest in the Third World was not particularly popular: as Robert Dallek notes, Kennedy's "enthusiasm was largely self-generated; back home and among Americans abroad, his journey of discovery evoked more indifference and hostility than encouragement or praise."[7] Yet Kennedy devoted a significant portion of his foreign policy effort on the House and Senate floor to the Third World.

The Nature of Threats

Kennedy's view of threats consistently focused on the domestic institutions of other states, whether the Soviet Union or countries in the Third World. For example, Kennedy talked about the Soviet Union in internal terms even earlier than Eisenhower. During his first congressional campaign in 1946, Kennedy delivered several versions of a speech taking a hard line with the Soviets, extensively detailing Soviet internal repression. As Dallek notes, the speeches appealed to his constituents,[8] but they nonetheless provide an early illustration of how he approached the coming Cold War. Kennedy explicitly aligned himself with those like Secretary of State James F. Byrnes, who saw the Soviets as aggressive and advocated containment, rather than the view espoused by former vice president Henry Wallace that cooperation was still possible. According to Kennedy, Wallace saw Soviet behavior as a "natural" reaction to years of security threats, and thus in Wallace's view, Russia's "efforts to control the countries surrounding her are merely to build buffers against invasion from the East [and] West." Byrnes's view, which Kennedy endorsed, argued that the Soviets doubted the world was "big enough for both Western Democracy and Communism," and instead posited that "Russia's policy seems predicated on the assumption that the Soviet conception of Soviet security means a Communistic world for as long as there are capitalistic states Russia has no security." Kennedy noted that "internally Soviet Russia is a ruthless dictatorship, and externally is on the march." In the same month that Eisenhower argued publicly that there was "room in the world for different philosophies of government," Kennedy told a Massachusetts audience that the "problem of peace is a hard one, for the two most powerful nations of the world—the United States and Russia—do not have a common philosophy and a common morality."[9]

Although he displayed an early interest in Europe, by mid-1951 Kennedy was talking about the Third World as a locus of new threats, and his concern focused on the risk that Third World states would "go communist" from within. In a speech to the Massachusetts Federation of Taxpayers in April 1951 (before he set out on his seven-week trip), he argued that "while the threat to our security in both Western Europe and the Far East is primarily military, the political struggle for power has assumed increasing importance in recent months in other and equally vital areas." In describing the crisis in Iran over the Iranian seizure of British oil interests, he displayed an early tendency to diagnose internationally oriented crises and threats in terms of domestic problems, arguing, "The crisis in Iran is not over oil alone. . . . The exploitation by [f]oreign countries of the resources and manpower of backward nations, the widespread illiteracy, misery and starvation, the domination by venal and corrupt politicians, and a massive and inefficient bureaucracy, a new and self-conscious proletariat, all compound to divide the [n]ations by turmoil and discontent." Kennedy asserted that to respond to these problems, "Of equal importance to military action is the development of techniques by which we might adjust the internal instability that creates a special threat to the security of the [M]iddle East, and which can result in action such as the [nationalization] of the oil of Iran. We must recognize that by indirection, the Soviets can take control over areas without the use of military force."[10] This prescription contrasts with that of Eisenhower, who had declared himself "almost solely" focused on simply keeping Iranian oil "flowing to the westward."[11]

Kennedy sounded a note of pragmatism—perhaps in a nod to his taxpayer audience—in urging that the United States "avoid the suspicion of attempting to dominate the internal affairs of these nations" and acknowledging that "the economy of the United States is already strained." But he pressed the case that U.S. policy had to become more active: "We have been anti-communist. We have been 'Pro' nothing. . . . That puts us in partnership with the corrupt and reactionary groups whose policies breed the discontent on which Soviet Communism feeds and prospers. . . . In short we even support and sustain corruption and tyranny to maintain a status-quo wherever we find existing regimes anti-communistic."[12] Stability, in Kennedy's view, was not an end in itself but could actually nurture future threats. These early views would lead Kennedy to see repressive dictatorships that might be prone to communist revolution as potential sources of threat.

Kennedy's travel journal from his 1951 tour of the Middle East and Asia also reflects an internally focused view of threats. His journal entries frequently discuss local economic and political conditions. While most of his meetings were with elites, he attempted to grasp how the forces of nationalism, colonialism, and poverty would affect the international landscape. During his stay in Malaya, for example, he wrote that the "reason for [the] spread of Communism is [the] failure of those who believe a different . . . and as they feel superior theory of life to explain this theory in terms intelligible to the ordinary man and to make its ameliorating effect on his life apparent."[13] Among his many stops on the trip was Tehran, where he wrote extensively in his journal about the Iranian oil crisis. He noted that in Tehran, the "Communist Party has grown to 25,000 . . . due to poverty and maldistribution of wealth."[14]

Kennedy continued to emphasize the internal nature of the Soviet threat to the Third World in the remainder of his career in Congress. Of course, he usually framed this threat in terms of the calculated advance of worldwide communism. Like most politicians at the time, however, Kennedy believed in such a conspiracy. But whereas some worried only about outright communist aggression or subversion through a small group of elites, Kennedy diagnosed widespread domestic vulnerabilities in Third World states that made them ripe targets for communism. In a fascinating 1955 speech draft, Kennedy worried that the Soviets would use peace itself as a weapon. "This containment of communism was infinitely difficult in the days of Stalin," he lamented, "but at least he personified to the world a bitter and implacable enemy on the make and in a hurry. Now with his passing and the substitution of the new policy of conquest by peace, with the resulting relaxation of external pressures, the task has become nearly insuperable."[15] The Soviets had turned Clausewitz on his head, making peace "simply 'the continuation of war by other means.' . . . Peace has never been used with such effectiveness as a tactic in a strategy of world conquest. And the central problem for us now is to develop techniques that will checkmate this new advance."[16] By 1958, he noted to John Kenneth Galbraith that the Democrats had "tended to magnify the military challenge to the point where equally legitimate economic and political programs have been obscured."[17]

In terms of how the United States should respond to this internally oriented threat, Kennedy reported after his 1951 trip that "Communism cannot be met effectively by merely the force of arms. It is the peoples themselves that must be led to reject it, and it is to those peoples that our policies must be directed."[18] But in a 1951 speech, Kennedy also sounded an emphatic note of caution that informed his later decisions, warning: "We cannot reform the world. We cannot and should not impose upon this Eastern world our values, our institutions or our customs. True, there is a basic sameness in all men, the desire to be free from want, from illness, from tyranny. But, however much we may value our conceptions of suffrage, our mechanical well-being, even our bathtubs, the East may think little or nothing of them."[19] Thus Kennedy took a cautious approach to reform. But he saw the internal institutions of other states, particularly in the Third World, as an important dimension of the threat to U.S. national security.

ALLIANCES AND AMERICA'S SPHERE OF INFLUENCE

Kennedy also displayed an internal focus in his approach to the problem of building and maintaining America's network of alliances and sphere of influence, even at the expense of short-term successes in forming or maintaining alliances or other friendly ties. An early and consistent Kennedy theme was the recognition of nationalism as a powerful trend that was both futile to resist and crucial to harness, even if it meant gaining fewer formal allies in the short term or disagreements with those already allied with the United States. For example, following his Middle East trip, he told a radio audience, "To check the southern drive of Communism makes sense but not only through reliance on the force of arms. The task is rather to build strong native non-Communist sentiment within these areas and rely on that as a spearhead of defense. . . . To do this apart from and in defiance of innately nationalistic aims spells foredoomed failure. To the rising drive of nationalism, we have unfortunately become a friend of its enemy and as such its enemy and not its friend."[20] Insofar as nationalism was an expression of popular sentiment in developing nations, suppressing it might bolster the kind of corrupt, weak, or autocratic institutions that Kennedy saw as potentially damaging to Western objectives in the Cold War.

Kennedy extended this view of nationalism by arguing that the United States should support independence movements and resist foreign domination of Third World states even at the risk of conflict with existing allies. He would become an outspoken critic of U.S. support for continued French and British colonial aims. As discussed below, like Eisenhower, he was unwilling merely to prop up the French position in Indochina, but he went further than Eisenhower (or Johnson) in focusing on the domestic dimension of the crisis. In 1957, he also made a forceful speech in Congress advocating U.S. support for Algerian independence, arguing that "the single most important test of American foreign policy today is how we meet the challenge of imperialism, what we do to further man's desire to be free. . . . If we fail to meet the challenge of either Soviet or Western imperialism, then no amount of foreign aid, no aggrandizement of armaments, no new pacts or doctrines or high-level conferences can prevent further setbacks to our course and to our security."[21]

Another extension of Kennedy's views on the newly independent nations was his willingness to accept neutralism, rather than requiring new nations to pick sides in the superpower contest, or as he put it, "voting the Western ticket."[22] On his 1951 tour, he talked with Indian prime minister Jawaharlal Nehru and his advisers about nonalignment and the problems of newly independent nations, and came away with a more sympathetic view of neutralism. Though he admitted ongoing doubts, he saw "the enormous domestic problems that faced [India] and how she would necessarily have to concentrate her energies on these for many years."[23] To capitalize on divisions within the Eastern bloc, he also introduced legislation to amend the Battle Act to allow aid to bloc countries that showed independence from Moscow. In a speech introducing the legislation, he lamented the Battle Act's division of the world into only two categories: Soviet-dominated and friendly nations. Focusing on recent domestic changes within Poland, he argued, "We must be very careful not to miss the internal realities of the Polish scene while looking at the outward and legal forms." Recognizing that there were "shades of gray" in the world, Kennedy showed a willingness to tolerate less than perfect foreign and domestic policies from states that showed tendencies toward internal reform.[24] Simply demanding that states align with one superpower or the other could be counterproductive, but if countries could begin to get their political and economic houses in order, foreign policy might follow. Such tolerance of different forms of internal politics was, however, in tension with his view that the United States must be ready to defend against communist aggression by providing a strong political alternative. But in Congress, Kennedy was free to criticize without the pressure of resolving these contradictions.

In terms of the Middle East, while Yaqub notes that Democrats generally registered a partisan reaction to the 1957 Eisenhower Doctrine,[25] Kennedy's response, recorded just after he joined the Senate Foreign Relations Committee, nonetheless underscores his internally focused view. Kennedy criticized the proposed legislation as unnecessary and incomplete in terms of the "real problems" of the Middle East, though he said he would vote for it anyway for the sake of presidential credibility in the eyes of the world.[26] In a speech draft, he acknowledged the "legitimate objective" of blocking Soviet domination of the Middle East but again argued that the "threat of aggressive communism cannot be separated from our assessment of and reaction to the political problems of the area; nor in turn can our methods in dealing with political difficulties be divorced from a reasonable approach to the problems of the underdeveloped economies of the area."[27] In another speech draft, he asserted that the administration's attempt to deal with the whole region all at once would not work, because "today, no two nations in that area justify the same considerations. The Jewish State of Israel, the strong nationalism of Egypt, the deterioration in Jordan, the dangers of an overthrow in Iraq, the Communist penetration of Syria, the separate alliances to which Turkey, Iran and Pakistan belong—these are all individual considerations which make it difficult to provide a single remedy for these widely varying problems of all of these nations in one blanket resolution."[28] Kennedy thus recognized the possibility of a coup in Iraq at a time when the Eisenhower administration was largely ignoring Iraqi domestic issues.

Kennedy also criticized Eisenhower and Dulles's drive to build military alliances in the Third World and thus took a dim view of the Baghdad Pact. A few months before the 1958 crises in Lebanon and Iraq, he wrote to an Arizona voter that Dulles's "Northern Tier" concept was "dubious," and he noted that "the danger of external aggression is not the chief one in the Middle East at the present time." "Unless we can develop an economic program which embraces the Middle East regionally and which stimulates multilateral assistance in the area," he wrote, "the Baghdad Pact will have little effective influence."[29] To a constituent (with whom he disagreed on an upcoming vote), Kennedy wrote of "the delusion of the Baghdad Pact which represents a belief that military alliances can provide stability and which has encouraged inter-Arab cleavages through its emphasis on the 'Northern Tier.'"[30] These statements fit with his long-standing view that addressing the military and international dimensions of Third World problems would not be enough, and could even be harmful if it caused intraregional or domestic strife, as the Baghdad Pact had done in Iraq. In a major Senate speech on India in 1958, he called a "purely military response to the tides in the Middle East and Asia" an "illusory breakwater," since "military pacts and arms shipments . . . are themselves new divisive forces in those areas shot through with national and regional rivalries and often lacking historic boundaries and allegiances."[31] Alliances and pacts were insufficient, in Kennedy's view, if they did not account for the domestic health and needs of potential members.

Foreign Aid

Another particularly interesting way to measure Kennedy's beliefs is to examine his views on foreign aid. In contrast to Eisenhower, and later Johnson, Kennedy persistently emphasized the *form* aid should take; the connections among political factors, economic aid, and military aid; and the necessity of responding to each country's needs.[32] Though his constituent mail reflected much hostility to aid, Kennedy consistently defended it as a vital tool not only for gaining military allies but also "for the prevention of limited wars," to "protect against Democratic failure in some underdeveloped areas," and to prevent other states from "accept[ing] the Russian model of economic modernization."[33] In 1959, he made a major speech titled "The Economic Gap," which he called an "equally clear and present danger to our security" as the "missile gap."[34] Thus his view of aid was not simply idealistic; he saw it as an important tool for defending American interests.

Here again Kennedy's travels influenced the evolution of his thinking. In 1951, before embarking on his trip to the Middle and Far East, Kennedy argued for a reduction in proposed aid to Africa and the Middle East, saying, "I do not think that we can afford in this country to raise the standard of living of all the people all over the globe who might be subject to the lure of communism because of a low standard of living."[35] A year later, admitting he had changed his mind, he said that in the wake of his trip, he felt cutting nonmilitary aid would be a "tremendous mistake."[36] Kennedy also criticized programs that blindly shipped military aid to countries without regard to the recipients' needs or capacity.[37] By 1957, in a speech draft on the Eisenhower Doctrine, he took particular aim at military aid that went beyond supporting "modest forces capable of maintaining internal security. To build forces beyond this level has various effects none of which are conducive to the attainment of long run stability or vibrant economic or social strength." Since soldiers in the Third World tended to "enjoy amenities unknown to [the] masses," he continued, "such security as we may attain" through military aid "could be wiped out overnight by popular discontent with the effects of overemphasis on military preparedness." While allowing for the occasional utility of military aid, Kennedy stressed that "larger and larger forces do not necessarily add measurably to the security of the Free

World and may have serious political, economic and social implications."[38] Thus a document (presumably for public consumption) highlighting his foreign policy activities noted that Kennedy had been "especially concerned to achieve a better balance between our economic and military programs and to make certain that our large commitment in military assistance . . . is used constructively and not merely for political blackmail or prestige buildups."[39] In Kennedy's view, building up conventional armies to meet external threats, as Eisenhower had emphasized, would not be enough and might even increase the danger of internal threats. He also advocated shifting military aid toward local economic and social programs, including "village development." Noting that in such regions as Southeast Asia "future wars will likely be limited in nature and depend on guerilla-type action" and that in "such wars much depends upon the morale and disposition of the peasants," he pointed out that if the military became involved in local development, "our military assistance can leave a permanently good social impress."[40]

Kennedy also stressed the need to be proactive with aid and urged patient, long-term investment rather than responding on a crisis-by-crisis basis to Soviet moves.[41] In emphasizing the "quality" of aid, he noted in a 1958 speech to a development conference that short-term credit was less effective than "longer-term 'seed' capital."[42] In March 1958, Kennedy used some political capital to cosponsor, with Senate Republican John Sherman Cooper of Kentucky, a concurrent resolution calling for the United States to join a multilateral effort to aid economic development in India as it attempted to navigate its second Five-Year Plan. Kennedy also made a major speech on aid to India.[43] Though this effort helped Kennedy score points with liberals, aid to India—and indeed foreign aid generally, much less aid to a neutral country—was not particularly popular (the resolution passed the Senate but failed in the House).[44] Yet in his India speech, Kennedy argued that only through "programs of real economic improvement" could Third World states "find the political balance and social stability which provide the true defense against Communist penetration." He also addressed the question of Third World neutralism, arguing, "Our friendships should not be equated with military alliances or 'voting the Western ticket.' To do so only drives these countries closer to totalitarianism or polarizes the world."[45] Importantly, the domestic trajectory of potential recipients influenced how Kennedy viewed their eligibility for U.S. help. He singled out India as one of the few countries with the necessary " 'ground rules' of economic performance and political freedom" to make good use of U.S. aid.[46]

It was also during the development of the India resolution and speech that Kennedy made contact with and began to employ the help of development economist Walt Rostow. Kennedy and Rostow met for lunch on the day before Rostow testified before the Senate Foreign Relations Committee in February

1958.[47] While Rostow undoubtedly influenced Kennedy, Kennedy was primed to be receptive to Rostow's ideas.

As he did in other areas, Kennedy displayed a pragmatic, cautionary streak in his thinking on foreign aid. He acknowledged the politically difficult task of selling aid to India to the American people.[48] Even in 1951, he urged caution. "There is just not enough money in the world to relieve the poverty of all the millions of this world who may be threatened by Communism," he warned. Later he added, "Uncle Sugar is as dangerous a role for us to play as Uncle Shylock."[49] Instead, his view of foreign aid reflected a belief that healthy domestic institutions in other states could enhance U.S. security interests.

STRATEGY AND POLICY INVESTMENTS: PRE-PRESIDENTIAL EVIDENCE

We can also examine Kennedy's views on strategy, the use of force, and U.S. defense policy in his pre-presidential years. These views show how his internal diagnosis of threats translated into policy prescriptions in these years, and provide evidence that his early policy investments as president were not simply a response to outside pressures or proximate crises.

One of the most striking and well-documented aspects of Kennedy's pre-presidential views on strategy was his deep interest in guerrilla warfare and his resulting interest in counterinsurgency. Counterinsurgency does not necessarily have to take a transformative form: for example, brutal, scorched-earth tactics are a destructive approach that does not involve institution building. But Kennedy was drawn to the kind of counterinsurgency that emphasized transformative elements such as modernization and institution building. As discussed in chapter 2, this approach sees counterinsurgency as an inherently political enterprise requiring deep involvement in the local institutions of target states. Guerrilla fighters are themselves fighting a political battle for control of the local population, on whom they depend for support (in the form of food and supplies, recruits, and intelligence). To counter this threat, counterinsurgency theorists such as Sir Robert Thompson, a leader of the British effort to defeat the insurgency in Malaya, emphasized the rule of law and an effective civil service as particularly critical.[50] The integration of political and military efforts is also seen as a key to successful counterinsurgency operations of this type.

On his 1951 trip, Kennedy witnessed the British approach in Malaya. Known as the "Briggs Plan," this strategy, as Kennedy noted in his diary, involved a large-scale resettlement program designed to move the population into areas that counterinsurgency forces could more readily control and to cut the insurgents off from their base of support among the people.[51] Such resettlement programs built up villages, often from scratch—an inherently transformative, political enterprise, regardless of its ultimate efficacy.[52] The Briggs Plan involved resettling more than 400,000 mainly Chinese squatters into so-called New Villages designed to cut the population off from the insurgents, who were mainly ethnic Chinese. Though at the time Kennedy visited Malaya he recorded in his diary that the "Briggs plan [was] not a success" and was behind schedule, he seemed to understand the local nature of the conflict.[53] He observed that much of the Chinese population was "sitting on [the] fence as [they] don't want to pick [the] wrong side," and was "subject to threats and intimidation" by guerrillas.[54] Although as president he would ignore some important differences between the Malayan and Vietnamese conflicts, on his 1951 trip he explicitly noted in his diary a "contrast" in the nature of the guerrilla movement in Malaya as compared with Indochina, especially that the insurgents in Malaya, mostly Chinese "aliens," did not have "nationalist backing."[55]

Kennedy took his impression that counterinsurgency was a distinctive type of war back to the United States. During the debate over whether to intervene to save the French position at Dien Bien Phu in 1954, he cautioned, "We must remember that the type of aggression which is going on in Indochina is not comparable to that which occurred in Korea."[56] He frequently criticized the Eisenhower administration's "New Look" strategy for its reliance on nuclear retaliation, saying as early as February 1954 that "we must ask how the new Dulles policy and its dependence upon the threat of atomic retaliation will fare in these areas of guerilla warfare."[57]

Of course, Kennedy was not only concerned with counterinsurgency but also believed the United States had to build up conventional forces generally to deal with "brush fire" or limited wars, which he accused the Eisenhower administration of ignoring. After the 1958 Middle East crises, he hammered the theme of a "lag in conventional forces." He was particularly critical of the lack of "airlift and sealift capacity necessary to give [conventional] forces the swift mobility they need to protect our commitments around the world."[58] Kennedy's presidential policy investments in conventional capabilities were thus based on long-standing views, though because Eisenhower had deemphasized conventional war, Kennedy began from a baseline he considered inadequate and had more catching up to do. His interest in conventional preparedness does not detract from his emphasis on counterinsurgency; indeed, unlike many of his fellow Democrats, including Johnson, Kennedy focused on preparedness for *both* regular and unconventional warfare.

Kennedy also wrote and spoke specifically about the struggle in Indochina, providing a baseline look at how his internal focus informed his view of the conflict before he took office. He connected the nature of the communist threat to domestic issues in Indochina. He visited Saigon on his 1951 trip, recording in his

travel journal that the communists were "preaching" issues such as independence, reform, and development, and thus "[the communists] preach against [the]
status quo—we will lose if all we offer is merely a defense of [the] status quo."[59]
He also talked with Edmund Gullion, a U.S. Foreign Service officer in Saigon,
who bucked the official U.S. position in support of France and argued against
both continued French domination of Indochina and military plans calling for
conventional warfare.[60] Kennedy would echo both positions.[61] Kennedy's diary
reflects his deep skepticism of the French position in Vietnam, as well as his concern about the implications for the military effort of continued French control.
According to Kennedy's notes, Gullion "believes that we should go into this
thing skeptically [and] [i]nsist that political conditions here match the military
effort. Make sure that people are given sufficient independence so that they will
fight." Kennedy observed that the United States was "more and more becoming
identified in the minds of the people with the French [and] [w]e must do what
we can as our aid gets more important to force [the] French to liberalize political
conditions."[62] These views would appear in his 1954 speeches on U.S. involvement in Indochina.

Of course, as discussed in chapter 3, Eisenhower would also complain in
1954 that the French used "weasel words in promising independence."[63] But as
early as 1951, Kennedy displayed greater concern about the domestic conditions
of Indochina, even at the expense of relations with key allies. In his travel diary,
he concluded that "our policy must be true" to issues such as land reform and
independence "regardless of ties to France" and Britain.[64] He would begin making speeches that talked tough to the allies as soon as he got home. In his post-
trip radio address, he bluntly asserted that in "Indo-China we have allied ourselves to the desperate effort of a French regime to hang on to the remnants of
empire," predicting "foredoomed failure" if the United States pursued the effort
in opposition to nationalism.[65] Kennedy called for pressure on France, knowing
it might cost him some French Catholic votes.[66] He also kept up his fact-finding
after the 1951 trip. In April 1953, he asked his staff for a report on French economic aid to Indochina and on the question whether "the US should insist on
reforms being made . . . before aid is given" to the French effort.[67] In May 1953,
he wrote to Secretary of State John Foster Dulles, again calling for pressure on
France to grant independence.[68]

On several occasions, Kennedy also explicitly rejected an externally driven
view of the Indochina conflict. Publicly, in a strongly worded speech on the Senate floor, Kennedy called on France to grant Cambodia, Laos, and Vietnam full
independence as a way to strengthen the military campaign against the communists.[69] In April 1954, amid the crisis at Dien Bien Phu, he argued that American
intervention would be useless without independence and reform.[70] In a draft of
a speech to a group of Democrats, he asserted that "the war in Indo-China is an

internal one" and that "the assistance given to the Communist forces within the country by the Chinese is substantially less than what we are giving the French Union forces." Thus "military guarantees of assistance from surrounding countries in case of outright aggression by the Chinese will be of little value in a war that is primarily civil."[71] After the fall of Dien Bien Phu, he expressed skepticism about Eisenhower's push for the SEATO alliance, consistent with his dim view of military pacts as a solution to regional conflicts.[72]

Later, in a speech to the American Friends of Vietnam in 1956, Kennedy embraced a domino-like view of Vietnam as "the cornerstone of the Free World in Southeast Asia, the keystone in the arch, the finger in the dike." But he also called the independence of Vietnam "crucial to the free world in fields other than the military," because it was "an inspiration to those seeking to obtain or maintain their liberty," and thus Vietnam was "a proving ground of democracy in Asia." A major element of America's stake in Vietnam, he concluded, was the U.S. role in the "democratic experiment" within the "laboratory" of Vietnam. Though military alliances, the development of the Vietnamese army, and direct aid were important, Kennedy warned that they were "not enough" and that the United States must offer a "revolution—a political, economic and social revolution far superior to anything the Communists can offer."[73] Thus he saw defending the domino of Vietnam as bound up with the fate of Vietnam's domestic institutions. While recognizing the importance of states like Indochina in terms of the ubiquitous domino theory, Kennedy believed that aiding an ally like France would be worthwhile only if the United States gained a domestically strong, independent, and stable Vietnamese ally in the process.

On the specific issue of sending combat troops, however, Kennedy was cautious. In handwritten notes before a 1957 speech in New York, he wrote, "Fighting thousands of miles from home in a jungle war in the most difficult terrain in the world—man to man—with the majority of the population hostile and sullen—or fighting guerilla warfare. . . . It will be another Korea. . . . The U.S. is willing to make any sacrifice on behalf of freedom but can American servicemen be the fighters for the whole free world, fighting every battle, in every part of the world[?]"[74]

The evidence of Kennedy's reactions to Eisenhower's other intervention decisions is instructive, though it is somewhat limited in quantity and must be taken with a grain of salt given Kennedy's status as a Democratic presidential hopeful. For example, just days before the 1958 Iraq coup, while the Lebanese crisis simmered, Kennedy wrote that the "Lebanese situation is by no means entirely an 'internal' one but neither is it a clear case of outside aggression."[75] This statement contrasts with Johnson's view of the crisis in decidedly external terms, as discussed in chapter 5. After the Marines landed in Beirut, Kennedy wrote that he was "opposed to this intervention and did not feel that it made much sense . . . in terms of the evidence about the internal situation in Lebanon and Iraq." While he acknowledged that "it was a calculated risk and the decision was not wholly implausible in that light," he also concluded that "the intervention has obscured as many problems . . . as it has helped to solve."[76] Kennedy seems to have recognized the credibility issues in Lebanon, but whereas Eisenhower chose to intervene in Lebanon largely because he would not have to deal with its internal issues, Kennedy concluded that the intervention was inappropriate because of those same issues. One could also speculate that he would not have intervened to restore the status quo in Iraq, though for different reasons than Eisenhower. While Eisenhower would have preferred the stability of the status quo but was unwilling to pay the high, overt price of intervening in a revolution, it is unlikely that Kennedy—who had recognized the danger of a coup in Iraq—would have been eager to restore a repressive regime in Iraq, given his stated views that supporting dictatorships and the status quo could be a source of threat (especially in the context of the Middle East and oil, as discussed above).

Along similar lines, Kennedy took an initially tolerant view of revolutionary Cuba in 1959. Eisenhower had also harbored early hopes that the United States could work with the new regime, but Kennedy's initial optimism toward and subsequent disillusionment with the Castro regime stemmed from a different, internally oriented view. Noting that the previous Batista regime was also "cruel and oppressive,"[77] Kennedy connected the revolution to Cuba's internal situation. He argued that there "are genuine elements in the revolutionary situation which arise from the dictatorship and from the [supp]ression of popular rights by the Batista regime." "Although the Castro movement is a radical movement," he wrote, "it is not Communist—and it will probably remain so if the regime is able to come to grips with Cuba's social and economic problems . . . there is a good chance that it can become a stable, popular regime."[78] He agreed with two constituents that "in Latin America there is a good and sound case to be made for granting recognized preferences to governments of a genuinely democratic nature. . . . Both the British and Americans followed a very curious policy of 'non-intervention' in Cuba."[79] Kennedy could tolerate Castro's radicalism as long as it appeared to be on the path of reform.

Thus Kennedy's pre-presidential views on strategy and defense policy emphasized the importance of local domestic conditions. Kennedy wanted the United States not only to confront crises but also to prevent them. In his speech to the American Friends of Vietnam in 1956, he likened the United States to a "volunteer fire department" whose volunteers "rush in, wheeling up all their heavy equipment, and resorting to every known method of containing and extinguishing the blaze . . . and then the firemen rush off to the next conflagration, leaving the grateful but still stunned inhabitants to clean up the rubble, pick up the pieces and rebuild their homes with whatever resources are available. . . . A volunteer fire department halts, but rarely prevents, fires. It repels but rarely rebuilds; it meets the problems of the present but not of the future."[80] If aid and peaceful reform efforts were not enough, then the military could be used as a tool of transformation to advance U.S. interests and prevent future "fires" from starting. But using force without attention to domestic institutions might bring only fragile, short-lived victories.

In sum, Kennedy believed that threats stemmed not simply from other states' foreign and security policies but also from their domestic order, and thus he placed a strong emphasis on local conditions in the Third World. To maintain an effective sphere of influence and network of alliances, the United States had to promote independence and domestic institutional stability among its friends, even if it meant tolerating nationalism or neutralism. Kennedy saw the need for balance between military and economic aid, and he emphasized that aid could help promote institutional development. He opposed several of Eisenhower's nontransformative actions and his overall strategy and defense posture. For Kennedy, fighting communists on the battlefield and in Third World institutions went hand in hand. He carried these views directly to the White House.

Kennedy as President: Strategy and Policy Investments

STAFFING DECISIONS

As president, Kennedy eschewed the formal planning embraced by Eisenhower, but his policy investments were nonetheless quite deliberate.[81] Significantly, he recruited many advisers who, like Rostow, were academic theorists of development or modernization. As we have seen, such advisers appealed to his preexisting views.[82] There were numerous influential advisers from outside this tradition, however, including Defense Secretary Robert McNamara and General Maxwell Taylor, a military adviser who would later become chairman of the Joint Chiefs of Staff. Yet the collective expertise on the developing world was still a marked change from the previous administration.

STRATEGY, DEFENSE POSTURE, AND THE USE OF FORCE

A major assumption underlying the Kennedy strategy was that the Third World would be a crucial battleground, an assumption long held by Kennedy himself. As Gaddis argues, many of Kennedy's policies represented "nothing less than a determination to alter the internal structures of foreign societies to enable them to withstand unavoidable pressures for revolutionary change without resorting to communist solutions."[83] Kennedy's "Flexible Response" strategy also maintained a strong nuclear force and strengthened conventional forces in Europe. But here I concentrate on policy investments related to the Third World, which played a comparatively large role in the Kennedy strategy and provided most of the venues for potential interventions.

Since Eisenhower relied so heavily on nuclear weapons, achieving the flexibility Kennedy demanded required an increase in non-nuclear capabilities. As Lawrence Freedman observes, however, almost immediately after taking office Kennedy made it clear that where he "really wanted flexible response was not at the nuclear or conventional levels, but with counterinsurgency."[84] Many commentators note that while the United States had some limited experience with guerrilla warfare in Greece and the Philippines, the Kennedy period marked the first real emphasis on counterinsurgency.[85] Furthermore, Kennedy personally oversaw the drive for increased counterinsurgency capabilities.

When Soviet leader Nikita Khrushchev's "Wars of National Liberation" speech reached Kennedy just before the inaugural, it was the incoming president who sent it to members of the NSC staff with a memo instructing them to "read, mark, learn and inwardly digest. . . . Our actions, our steps should be tailored to meet these kinds of problems."[86] The pre-presidential evidence shows that the speech confirmed, rather than drove, Kennedy's perception of threats.[87] At his first National Security Council meeting, Kennedy asked McNamara to examine means of increasing counterguerrilla forces, a request immediately enshrined in the administration's second "National Security Action Memorandum" (NSAM).[88]

Closely tied to this focus on guerrilla and internal threats was an emphasis on economic development and foreign aid, which also had a central role in Kennedy's strategy. As Gaddis notes, Rostow viewed economic development "not as a traditionally liberal end in itself, but as a means of stabilizing the world balance of power," a view Kennedy shared, as we have seen.[89] Rostow's "Basic National Security Policy" draft (never officially approved by Kennedy, who was averse to the constraints of formal planning documents) included policy for the underdeveloped world as one of its five "dimensions" of strategy, on equal footing with policy toward communist states.[90] In a special message to Congress in May 1961, Kennedy declared that the strength of underdeveloped countries "depends on the strength of their economic and their social progress," and that the United States "would be badly mistaken to consider their problems in military terms alone." He called for the Military Assistance Program to be given a "new emphasis," saying that military aid "cannot be extended without regard to the social, political and military reforms essential to internal respect and stability."[91]

The Kennedy counterinsurgency programs had an explicitly transformative bent, attempting to merge the low-level use of force with economic development and the management of local societies. As Michael Latham notes, "modernization theory profoundly influenced the Kennedy administration's understanding of counterinsurgency."[92] Counterinsurgency was closely linked to nation building; the United States aimed, as the Kennedy-approved "U.S. Overseas Internal Defense Policy" put it, to ensure the "immunization of vulnerable societies not yet seriously threatened by communist subversion or insurgency."[93] Just as Kennedy saw development as a security tool, he saw the military as a tool of development. In December 1961, for example, he issued NSAM 119, pushing for more attention to "civic action," defined as "using military forces on projects useful to the populace at all levels in such fields as training, public works, agriculture, transportation, communication, health, sanitation, and others helpful to economic development."[94] Local military forces would be strengthened, to be sure, but Kennedy also reoriented U.S. military aid to the Third World toward "internal security," issuing several NSAMs related to the training of "friendly police and armed forces" in methods of riot control and counterinsurgency.[95] Many of these programs represented deeply intrusive interference in local affairs. Some, especially the internal security programs, would strengthen unsavory regimes. But what is interesting is the extent to which Kennedy tried to keep this theoretical linkage between the military and the political at the forefront of U.S. policy.

BUDGETS

The Kennedy administration's strategy translated into budgetary increases for conventional and counterinsurgency forces. As Gaddis notes, Kennedy disagreed strongly with the Eisenhower approach of holding down budgets, instead arguing that the nation had to pay whatever costs were necessary to provide adequate security.[96] In late March 1961, after McNamara provided a sweeping review of the Pentagon strategy and budget that called for an increase in spending on limited war capabilities of $806 million beyond what Eisenhower had proposed for 1962, Kennedy delivered a special message to Congress that strongly emphasized both limited and unconventional war.[97] In his message, Kennedy asked for $650 million in additional spending (for all categories). He also discussed increases and upgrades in nuclear capabilities, but he argued that limited war preparedness "should constitute the primary mission of our overseas forces." He recommended an increase in the size of the army and Marine Corps, in part to "expand guerilla warfare units and round out other existing units," for a total of 13,000 new personnel.[98] In another special message to Congress, in May,

Kennedy said he would direct McNamara "to expand rapidly and substantially . . . the orientation of existing forces for the conduct of nonnuclear war, para-military operations and sub-limited or unconventional wars," with further requests for equipment ($100 million) and Marine Corps strength ($60 million).[99]

Kennedy did not neglect other capabilities: despite the postinaugural confirmation that there was, in fact, no "missile gap," the administration also increased the nuclear stockpile, as well as conventional forces aimed at a major land confrontation with the Soviets.[100] Overall, as the total U.S. budget increased by 6.02 percent in 1962, Pentagon personnel costs increased by 6.71 percent and operation and maintenance costs by 8.65 percent, before declining slightly the following year.[101] Budget data are not sufficiently fine-grained to indicate precisely how much of this additional spending went to programs specific to countering guerrilla warfare, but, as mentioned, Kennedy increased the budgetary emphasis on counterinsurgency. Similarly, international development and humanitarian assistance saw a 46 percent increase in the 1962 budget while international security assistance declined by 21 percent.[102]

INSTITUTIONAL CREATION AND CHANGE

Kennedy also worked to institutionalize his strategy within the bureaucracy, both by creating new institutions and by shifting existing ones. It was in the latter attempts, however, where his plans most often ran aground. On counterinsurgency, he recognized that sustained White House attention was crucial to shifting the bureaucracy's priorities. Kennedy significantly expanded counterinsurgency training. He took particular interest in the Special Forces, rapidly increasing their number and ordering them to wear the Green Beret, over the objection of the military leadership.[103] But by January 1962, an unhappy Kennedy wrote McNamara: "I am not satisfied that the Department of Defense, and in particular the Army, is according the necessary degree of attention and effort to the threat of Communist-directed subversive insurgency and guerrilla warfare, although it is clear that these constitute a major form of politico-military conflict for which we must carefully prepare. The effort devoted to this challenge should be comparable in importance to preparations for conventional warfare. . . . The Army has a particularly important role to play, and I would like to find recognition of this importance in Army organization and training."[104] Just one week later, Kennedy issued another NSAM establishing an interagency group, chaired by Maxwell Taylor, to "assure unity of effort and the use of all available resources."[105] This new group, the "Special Group (Counterinsurgency)" or "Special Group (CI)," included the secretaries of state and defense, the chairman of the JCS, the CIA director, and, crucially, Attorney General Robert Kennedy, a signal of the president's seriousness.[106] But while this institutionalization of oversight was a signal of Kennedy's intentions, in practice the Special Group (CI) had serious limitations. As Douglas Blaufarb notes, the participants were actually *too* senior to delve deeply into and monitor the problems they were asked to confront.[107]

On the economic development side, Kennedy made the new Agency for International Development the center of development assistance and created the Peace Corps as an outlet for American youth to help the development process. In March 1961, he also launched the Alliance for Progress, a major aid program for Latin America. As Michael Latham notes, all these initiatives had an explicitly transformative character that fit into a larger modernization agenda, although Kennedy was not always faithful to the principles of reform that these programs supposedly represented.[108]

Many of the programs, including the Alliance for Progress, suffered significant problems, but the investments in counterinsurgency were the most heavily resisted, particularly by the military.[109] Army doctrine was organized around the expectation of a regular ground engagement with enemy forces, with little emphasis on domestic issues or counterinsurgency. Furthermore, as Richard Betts argues, counterinsurgency and nation building had little appeal for the army because these missions required "a delicate interweaving of political and military functions—the kind of fusion that irritated so many of the military elite who preferred a clear line of demarcation between the two spheres."[110] Counterinsurgency required a light footprint, without heavy equipment, yet the army was pushing to modernize its forces. The army also had budgetary and institutional reasons to resist a change in its mission, as Deborah Avant details.[111] But though he kept up the pressure—even personally inspecting new equipment for counterinsurgency, such as sneakers to replace heavy boots[112]—Kennedy did not engage in the high-level personnel confrontations or changes in promotion policy that might have forced the army to evolve along the lines he preferred.[113] Instead, Kennedy ended up with a military still largely unprepared for the counterinsurgency task he would put before it.

Kennedy attempted to redistribute intervention capabilities to deal with a wide range of threats, many of them related to domestic conditions in the Third World. He thus invested heavily in programs designed to shape the domestic order within other states, notably a transformative form of counterinsurgency and a foreign aid program with a strong emphasis on political and economic development. To do this, Kennedy increased military and other capabilities, both to overcome the reduced size of the military after the Eisenhower years and to take on these additional goals. Given that all Cold War presidents had to manage and maintain a nuclear arsenal and a conventional army of at least a certain size,

Kennedy's policy investments were remarkable for their attempts to elevate internal threats to a high priority.

Kennedy's vision was not enthusiastically shared by all segments of government. Moreover, there were fundamental problems with his counterinsurgency approach. Blaufarb stresses that one crucial problem concerned the assumption that regimes under threat from insurgencies could reform themselves in the midst of crisis.[114] As the State Department's U. Alexis Johnson put it, radical reforms "may strike at the very foundations of those aspects of a country's social structure and domestic economy on which rests the basis of a government's control."[115] Furthermore, despite his beliefs about the root causes of conflicts, Kennedy still talked about guerrilla warfare as directed by communists. In a memorandum to McNamara, for example, he referenced the problem of "Communist-directed subversive insurgency and guerrilla warfare" and "related forms of indirect aggression";[116] in a message to Congress, he referred to "small externally supported bands of men."[117] Even Rostow would later go on to advocate a bombing campaign in Vietnam, abandoning hope that domestic political processes could be harnessed.[118] Thus a combination of flawed or incomplete thinking, unsuitable "agents" carrying out the wishes of the president as "principal," and clashes with military doctrine left Kennedy's policy investments on shaky ground. For my purposes, however, it is important to note that while Kennedy's policy investments were nowhere near completely successful, they increased the intellectual, bureaucratic, and material resources available for transformative strategies.

Intervention Choices: Latin America

Kennedy's administration was brief but did not lack for intervention opportunities. Aside from the major crisis in Berlin in 1961 and the Cuban Missile Crisis of 1962, both of which were directly overshadowed by the risk of nuclear escalation, there were numerous crises in the Third World. His choice of conflicts and of strategies, however, shows that his beliefs exerted a strong influence on how he viewed the costs and benefits of particular intervention opportunities even given credibility concerns, the availability of capabilities, and other considerations highlighted by existing theories. Because he saw additional benefits to transforming domestic institutions, Kennedy was not willing to intervene unless he could secure a domestically successful outcome within the target state.

Although Kennedy did not undertake overt intervention in the region, Latin America was in some respects a showcase for his transformative programs. In

March 1961, he initiated the Alliance for Progress, a major economic and political development program designed to prevent radical communist revolution. As discussed in chapter 3, Eisenhower had laid the foundation for the Alliance late in his second term, but Kennedy had been pushing for a more transformative approach to the Third World for many years. In line with his belief that defending the status quo in the face of change could itself represent a threat to U.S. interests, Kennedy also repudiated Eisenhower's tendency (at least until late in his presidency) to give medals to Latin American dictators. Instead, Kennedy pressured dictators such as "Papa Doc" Duvalier in Haiti and supported elected reformers in Venezuela, Chile, and Peru.[119]

But Kennedy also succumbed to Cold War "hyperactivity." Many progressive leaders in Latin America got support in part because they were reliably anticommunist. In tiny British Guiana, by contrast, Kennedy expended remarkable covert energy undermining the elected leader Cheddi Jagan.[120] The dilemmas of Kennedy's policy—to encourage reform within the overarching goal of preventing another communist regime in the region—are illustrated by his approach to the Dominican Republic. Kennedy began by denouncing the right-wing dictator Rafael Trujillo and gave covert support to anti-Trujillo factions. When Trujillo was assassinated in May 1961, Kennedy made a famous statement of preferences, arguing that there were "three possibilities . . . in descending order of preference: a decent democratic regime, a continuation of the Trujillo regime or a Castro regime. We ought to aim at the first, but we really can't renounce the second until we are sure that we can avoid the third."[121] Though there were Kennedy-approved contingency plans in place for U.S. intervention in the wake of any assassination, Kennedy first resigned himself to working with Trujillo's son. But when popular demonstrations against the younger Trujillo grew stronger, Kennedy employed gunboat diplomacy not to preserve stability but rather to persuade the remaining Trujillo family members to leave the country. Yet despite initial hopes, Kennedy soured on newly elected president Juan Bosch as, ironically, both insufficiently transformative and insufficiently anticommunist.[122] Still, Kennedy's actions in the Dominican Republic illustrate his belief that repressive dictators were not always the best defense against communism. His actions also contrast with Johnson's 1965 intervention, discussed in chapter 5, to restore a reliably anticommunist regime on the island.

Even closer to home, as Kennedy confronted Cuba's strengthening ties to Moscow, his early tolerance toward Castro quickly shifted. Yet Kennedy did not authorize overt operations to support the covert Bay of Pigs invasion in 1961. As Freedman details, Kennedy had inherited "an advanced plan that had momentum behind it."[123] Interestingly, the initial plans called for a traditional invasion with guerrilla operations as a fallback, but Kennedy pushed for guerrilla operations to play the central role so that the force would take "shape as a Cuban force within Cuba, not as an invasion force sent by the Yankees."[124] Caught between pressure not to look weak and a feeling of high political risk if things went wrong, Kennedy allowed the plan to go forward only with no trace of U.S. involvement. Of course, "deniability" was unrealistic, and the operation failed miserably.

As Rabe concludes, Kennedy's "remark about the descending order of possibilities in the post-Trujillo Dominican Republic proved to be a reliable guide" to his choices.[125] Notably, Kennedy himself framed this list as a preference ordering. He would aim at his first choice, a "decent democratic regime," but would take circumstances, costs, and benefits into account, as the theory predicts. Sometimes this consideration of costs and benefits led him to choose less desirable outcomes on the list. By November 1963, just before his death, he was announcing the Kennedy Doctrine: the United States would not allow another communist regime in the hemisphere, an open repudiation of the principle of nonintervention.[126] Thus Kennedy's Latin America policy aimed at transformation, but within the overarching framework of the Cold War.

Intervention Choices in Southeast Asia: Laos

It was in Southeast Asia, however, where Kennedy would face intervention decisions that put his beliefs and policy investments to their most difficult test. The remainder of this chapter discusses his decisions in Laos, where he decided against intervention, and in Vietnam, where he initiated a counterinsurgency war. The discussion by no means represents a full archival history. Rather, I highlight the decision-making process as it relates to the two causal mechanisms posed by the theory and to alternative explanations, notably that his decisions were driven primarily by structural and material conditions or by competition among domestic actors.

When President-Elect Kennedy met with Eisenhower on the day before the inauguration in January 1961, the most pressing issue on the agenda was the crisis in Laos, a poor, landlocked country with no obvious strategic importance other than its position in the middle of the Southeast Asian geopolitical storm. Kennedy nonetheless faced significant pressure during his first two years in office to intervene in Laos to demonstrate credibility and to improve the general situation in Southeast Asia. His beliefs informed his decision making in Laos in two ways. He did not see Laos, with its weak central government and apathetic local troops, as a good candidate for the kind of domestically successful outcome that would make intervention worthwhile. He also did not believe that his policy investments were ripe enough for an early intervention in Laos. Rather than apply what he saw as an inappropriate conventional strategy or try a transformative strategy too soon, Kennedy accepted a negotiated settlement.

Eisenhower had struggled with Laos in the latter stages of his presidency, approaching it as he did many other Third World crises.[127] The 1954 Geneva Accords, under which Laos gained independence, did not provide a detailed domestic political settlement, leaving unresolved the issue of how to deal with the communist Pathet Lao movement. Eisenhower took a dim view of Souvanna Phouma, who became prime minister in 1956 and immediately tried to incorporate the Pathet Lao into the government. For this, Souvanna received a lecture in Washington on the evils of communism.[128] Despite U.S. interference in the May 1958 elections, the Pathet Lao won some assembly seats. Eisenhower strongly backed the right-wing Phoumi Nosavan, who took control of the government in a CIA-assisted coup in 1959. Souvanna, backed by the Pathet Lao guerrillas and many communist nations, then fought with Phoumi for control of the country. Eisenhower gave significant military aid to Laos but concentrated on conventional assistance such as "jeeps, trucks and a Transportation Corps" even though "Laos had no all-weather roads."[129] Training assistance focused on preparation for conventional warfare.[130]

Eisenhower and Kennedy met at the White House on January 19, 1961, in a meeting that was "Rashomonesque," as Fred Greenstein and Richard Immerman detail.[131] Eisenhower's statements, interpreted in different ways by the participants, can be read as a strong recommendation of intervention or simply a willingness to consider it. But Eisenhower clearly saw intervention through the SEATO alliance—his own creation—justified in terms of North Vietnamese aggression, as preferable to a neutralist settlement.[132]

In the ensuing months, Kennedy was caught between competing imperatives in dealing with Laos: on the one hand, to avoid another fiasco like the Bay of Pigs, but on the other hand, to avoid looking weak personally and to maintain U.S. credibility.[133] The new president immediately confronted both a weak domestic political situation in Laos and a lack of U.S. counterinsurgency capabilities, a legacy of army culture and Eisenhower's failure to invest in such capabilities. Over the inaugural weekend, Kennedy's Laos Task Force prepared a report that listed as an "adverse factor" the "internal situation in Laos which makes the general populace and even large segments of the army apathetic toward the course of events there. The only real determination appears to reside in the Pathet Lao."[134] At the January 23 meeting to discuss the report, Kennedy "expressed concern at the weakness of the local situation in Laos coupled with the weakness of allied support for our position."[135] Meanwhile, he had begun to push for an increased emphasis on counterinsurgency. In a February 6 meeting, Kennedy "mentioned guerrilla activities in Laos, the Congo and Viet-Nam and asked what we are doing in each of the Services on this type of training." Kennedy also "asked how the special forces in Laos are doing with the tribesmen," and "if we should do more about bringing more Laotians out of Laos, training them and sending them back in. Are we doing enough in this field?"[136]

Kennedy soon signaled that he saw little benefit in a nontransformative intervention that might demonstrate U.S. firmness internationally but lacked a successful postconflict plan for Laos's domestic affairs. On March 3, he authorized JCS planning for a Royal Laotian Army offensive to retake the crucial Plain of Jars.[137] When Kennedy met with his advisers on March 9 to discuss the plan, however, he expressed concern about the political dimensions of any intervention, both because the plan lacked a postconflict political vision and because of concerns about the viability of the domestic situation in Laos. He repeatedly asked about political questions, specifically inquiring about what the U.S. "political plan" would be "if the military action . . . is successful." When the State Department responded that "we would then hope to continue about where we were in the Geneva Accord," Kennedy was dissatisfied, responding that "as a political objective, it was limited and did leave us open to continued torture in this situation." Kennedy told his advisers he "wanted to make sure that if there is a military offensive in this area, we have some capability of holding things together in Laos." He was also concerned about the "lack of morale and the lack of leadership" in Laos itself.[138]

Kennedy had reason to be concerned about the prospects that the Laotians would be able to fight successfully, let alone achieve a firm domestic settlement in Laos. Indeed, just two days before the March 9 meeting, Rostow had reported to Kennedy that Phoumi's men did not show "much fight" against a communist probe.[139] In May 1961, John Kenneth Galbraith, who had been working on the diplomatic side from his post as ambassador to India, observed in a letter to the president, "As a military ally the entire Laos nation is clearly inferior to a battalion of conscientious objectors from World War I." He identified Laos as one of the "jungle regimes . . . where the writ of government runs only as far as the airport."[140] In several meetings, including one with the U.S. ambassador to Laos, Winthrop Brown, Kennedy asked probing questions about the political figures in Laos. He understood that most U.S. allies, such as Britain and France, believed Souvanna to be the best option for unifying the country and preserving some form of Laotian neutrality, despite his willingness to embrace the Pathet Lao.[141] Whereas Eisenhower had seen intervention as a more viable option because he aimed only at a show of force that would keep the communists out of power, Kennedy wanted a stable internal settlement, and thus, as Freedman puts it, Laos's internal weakness disqualified it "as a candidate for backbone-stiffening American intervention."[142]

Kennedy recognized early in the crisis that the chances of a successful domestic outcome in Laos were not high and that his own policy investments were
still unripe. He therefore stalled and began to develop a diplomatic alternative
that would involve a neutral government incorporating all the parties, including
the Pathet Lao. Neutralism had been unacceptable to Eisenhower, but Kennedy
was willing to accept it as the soundest domestic solution that would avoid involvement in a civil war with little prospect of an internally successful outcome,
while preserving hope of keeping the communist role in the government minimal. Still, even as he began to turn his attention to negotiations with Moscow,
some of his advisers insisted that the United States had to make a stand in Southeast Asia sooner rather than later, and that not intervening in Laos would make
any future move in Vietnam more difficult.[143] Rostow proposed that a small
U.S. force seize some Mekong Valley territory as a bargaining chip, to which the
JCS objected because the force would be too limited, and only full-scale intervention with air cover would suffice.[144] Kennedy resisted both moves, and negotiations with Moscow over Laos began.

The pressure to intervene continued, especially from the military, which
pushed particularly hard for intervention in a meeting on April 29.[145] On the
domestic front, Kennedy feared looking weak and had openly pledged to support Laos. But he also felt the public would not relish another entanglement
when he had just passed up a serious effort close to home in Cuba. In the face of
these pressures, Kennedy pursued the neutralist option even as the military situation deteriorated and the U.S. military kept pushing for intervention. In addition to Laotian apathy, the rushed military planning was an important factor.
Kennedy adviser Arthur Schlesinger reports that Kennedy was "appalled at the
sketchy nature of American military planning for Laos—the lack of detail and
the unanswered questions."[146] Intervening in Laos would be risky enough without the extra danger stemming from a lack of preparedness or poor planning.

As Freedman puts it, "In the end procrastination turned out to be the best
policy."[147] After joint missions to Moscow, Beijing, and Hanoi, Souvanna and the
Pathet Lao announced a cease-fire in early May. When Kennedy met Charles de
Gaulle in Paris at the end of May, de Gaulle pressed the neutralist option as
the best course in Laos and Southeast Asia generally, arguing that the area was
"not a good terrain for the West to fight on."[148] Finally, when Kennedy met
Khrushchev at the otherwise disastrous summit in Vienna in June 1961, the two
agreed on goals for maintaining the cease-fire.[149]

Kennedy thus decided against intervention in Laos, over the more bellicose
recommendations of some of his advisers, particularly in the military. Kennedy
did not see Laos as a good place to try reform because its domestic situation
provided so little basis for defeating the Pathet Lao, especially with his policy

investments still at an embryonic stage. In the absence of a viable domestic option, the benefits of a nontransformative intervention—for example, a show of force along the lines contemplated by Eisenhower—did not outweigh the costs. Kennedy accepted that U.S. credibility and his own reputation for firmness might take a hit, but he also felt that the available means of intervention and the target environment were inadequate to demonstrate credibility through a successful domestic outcome. Of course, Kennedy also had an alternative place to stand firm. Amid the frustration of the Vienna summit, he told James Reston of the *New York Times*, "We have to see what we can do that will restore a feeling in Moscow that we will defend our national interest. . . . And we have to confront them. The only place we can do that is in Vietnam."[150]

Intervention Choices in Southeast Asia: Vietnam

Kennedy's Vietnam decisions have been and will be endlessly debated. It is impossible to provide a full account here. But what is notable about his approach to Vietnam is the tight link Kennedy saw between the political situation within South Vietnam and the war effort. Given this view, Kennedy devoted considerable attention to not only *whether* to intervene but also *how* to intervene. As Leslie Gelb and Richard Betts argue, there was "a sort of two-dimensional hawks versus doves division" within the Kennedy administration, but the debate "was not whether one was for or against force, but rather what *form* force should take," conventional operations or counterinsurgency.[151] As the arbiter of this debate, Kennedy chose a limited but transformative counterinsurgency strategy, partly as a middle path between all-out intervention and backing down in Vietnam. But the population-centered counterinsurgency approach, designed to address what Kennedy saw as a fundamentally political war, also fit squarely with his long-held beliefs. Although the Kennedy administration claimed to send only military "advisers" to Vietnam, given the advisers' role in combat operations and the public's access to information through media reports, the intervention can be treated as overt.

Kennedy's preference for a domestically successful outcome led him to reject repeated recommendations to intervene using a conventional, nontransformative strategy that he felt was ill-suited to combating an insurgency with domestic roots. Although as mentioned, he often referred to the problem of insurgency as "Communist-directed" or a form of "indirect aggression," Kennedy located the source of the conflict within Vietnam. Kennedy's policies in Vietnam were not successful, for a variety of reasons. But the theory aims to explain his intended intervention strategy. This discussion highlights the connections Kennedy saw between the domestic conditions within Vietnam and the military and international aspects of the war, connections that influenced his policy choices.

KENNEDY'S EARLY VIETNAM POLICY

As discussed in chapter 3, the Eisenhower administration's approach in Vietnam, as in Laos, did not concentrate significant attention on domestic affairs. Only in March 1960, after the North Vietnamese insurgents stepped up their campaign, did the United States begin to develop a counterinsurgency plan. But even this plan remained largely conventional. Kennedy inherited a commitment in South Vietnam of 1,500 U.S. advisers and an economic aid program, but the commitment was not massive, and Kennedy had shown a willingness to resist Eisenhower's recommendations in Laos.

From the earliest days of his administration, Kennedy rejected the separation of the problem into military and political subsets and was already focused on the political nature of the crisis. He backed away from conventional recommendations for Vietnam and urged his advisers to provide him with counterinsurgency options that would address underlying internal issues. When Kennedy discussed the belated Eisenhower counterinsurgency plan with advisers on January 28, 1961, he "asked whether the situation was not basically one of politics and morale."[152] On February 6, Kennedy also directly queried JCS chairman Lyman Lemnitzer whether troops in South Vietnam could be redistributed for "anti-guerilla activities," even if it meant taking troops away from defending the border.[153]

In response to Kennedy's push, bureaucratic factions wrangled among themselves over how to proceed in Vietnam, but the options they considered were almost all conventional. In May 1961, Kennedy resisted a JCS recommendation for a deployment intended, among other purposes, to deter a potential invasion from North Vietnam or China and to signal "firmness."[154] The president authorized the additional deployment of only four hundred Special Forces troops. He approved the objectives stated in the Vietnam Task Force Report: "to prevent Communist domination of South Vietnam; to create in that country a viable and increasingly democratic society, and to initiate, on an accelerated basis, a series of mutually supporting actions of a military, political, economic, psychological and covert character designed to achieve this objective."[155] Meanwhile, he sent a very reluctant Vice President Johnson on a trip to Southeast Asia (including a stop in Saigon), in part to boost Diem's morale. This trip is discussed in further detail in the next chapter since it is a revealing episode in Johnson's pre-presidential involvement in Vietnam. Here it is sufficient to note that Johnson's statement lauding Diem as "the Winston Churchill of today"—a statement made largely because Johnson saw Diem as the only viable alternative in South Vietnam—left Kennedy "stuck with Diem."[156]

The pressure on Kennedy to send a conventional deployment to Vietnam would only increase. On July 27, 1961, Taylor and Rostow presented Kennedy with a memo titled "A Choice of Strategy." The first option was to "disengage from the area as gracefully as possible"; the second, "to find as soon as possible a convenient political pretext and attack with American military force the regional source of aggression in Hanoi"; and the third, "to build as much indigenous military, political and economic strength as we can in the area, in order to contain the thrust from Hanoi while preparing to intervene with U.S. military force if the Chinese Communists come in or the situation otherwise gets out of hand." They wrote that they assumed that the last of these was the official policy but proceeded to call for thinking about pressure on Hanoi and contingency plans for border protection.[157] Taylor and Rostow guessed correctly that Kennedy would prefer the combination of military, political, and economic action. The day after the Taylor-Rostow memo, in a meeting with top advisers to consider action on Laos and options for Vietnam, Kennedy asked questions that revealed the military planning for air and naval operations in Vietnam to be underdeveloped. To aid in planning, Alexis Johnson pressed Kennedy to make it "understood that the President would at some future time have a willingness to decide to intervene if the situation seemed to him to require it." Kennedy responded by expressing reluctance to go into Laos. He also asserted that "nothing would be worse than an unsuccessful intervention in this area, and that he did not yet have confidence in the military practicability of the proposal which had been put before him; though he was eager to have it studied more carefully."[158]

In the fall of 1961, Kennedy sent Rostow and Taylor to Vietnam, specifically instructing Taylor to examine political, social, and economic issues, which were "equally significant" to military considerations.[159] Yet two of Taylor's "Eyes Only for the President" dispatches from the trip recommended a troop deployment to provide flood relief in the Mekong Delta but also to help deal with the Viet Cong. He added that "this force is not proposed to clear the jungles and forests of Viet Cong guerillas," a task to be left to the Vietnamese.[160] The author of the *Pentagon Papers*, the Pentagon's history of the Vietnam decisions, notes that the cables were "rather sharply focused on the insurgency as a problem reducible to fairly conventional military technique and tactics."[161]

But the November 1961 debate over the Taylor-Rostow report turned into no debate at all: despite repeated recommendations to send troops, Kennedy would not agree to a conventional deployment and pushed for a counterinsurgency alternative. He expressed not only skepticism about the wisdom of intervening at all but also his displeasure with his advisers' strategy for intervention.

Kennedy told Schlesinger, "They want a force of American troops. . . . They say it's necessary in order to restore confidence and maintain morale. But it will be just like Berlin. The troops will march in; the bands will play; the crowds will cheer; and in four days everyone will have forgotten. Then we will be told we have to send in more troops. It's like taking a drink. The effect wears off, and you have to take another."[162] On the day before a major NSC meeting to discuss Vietnam, Kennedy wrote to McNamara and Secretary of State Dean Rusk to "get our ducks in a row," specifically asking "to have someone look into what we did in Greece. How much money and men were involved. How much money was used for guerrilla warfare? Should we have not done it at the company level rather than at the battalion level?" He thought "there should be a group specially trained for guerrilla warfare. I understand that the guns that have been used have been too heavy. Would carbines be better? Wonder if someone could make sure we are moving ahead to improve this."[163] Indeed, Yuen Foong Khong notes that Kennedy saw analogies to the unconventional conflicts in Malaya, the Philippines, and Greece as far more relevant than the analogy to the conventional war in Korea, in contrast to Johnson's extensive use of the Korean analogy.[164]

Instead of follow-up from his advisers, however, Kennedy received more recommendations for a conventional, nontransformative deployment. But when the NSC met on November 15, as adviser after adviser recommended action, Kennedy emphasized the political nature of the conflict. In the meeting, he

> noted that Korea was a case of clear aggression which was opposed by the United States and other members of the U.N. The conflict in Viet Nam is more obscure and less flagrant. The President then expressed his strong feeling that in such a situation the United States needs even more the support of allies in such an endeavor as Viet Nam in order to avoid sharp domestic partisan criticism as well as strong objections from other nations of the world. The President said that he could even make a rather strong case against intervening in an area 10,000 miles away against 16,000 guerrillas with a native army of 200,000, where millions have been spent for years with no success.

Kennedy added that in "Viet Nam the issue is vague and action is by guerrillas, sometimes in a phantom-like fashion." Though he encouraged discussion of how to get North Vietnam to break the Geneva Accords to provide an excuse for the United States to act, he "implied doubts because of the pitfalls of the particular type of war in Viet Nam. He described it as being more a political issue, of different magnitude and (again) less defined than the Korean War."[165]

Kennedy thus highlighted the political nature of the conflict and explicitly rejected the Korea analogy. He authorized an increase in the U.S. advisory role with expanded rules of engagement, including "operational collaboration."[166] But he also continued to press for an alternative strategy to address the underlying political issues. It was his focus on the political dimension of the war that suggests Kennedy believed a transformative form of counterinsurgency was necessary rather than simply any counterguerrilla approach. In 1962, he even said of the Special Forces training efforts he had pushed for, "What they're doing at Fort Bragg is really good, but, in the final analysis, what is needed is a political effort."[167]

The Strategic Hamlet Program

Finally, in early 1962, a strategy Kennedy deemed acceptable began to come together. Passing over many of his top advisers, Kennedy relied instead on the State Department's Roger Hilsman, who had experience in guerrilla warfare. In a conversation that Hilsman recalls as "spirited," Kennedy repeated "his own conviction that the most likely and immediate threat from the Communists was neither nuclear war nor large-scale conventional wars . . . but the more subtle, ambiguous threat of the guerilla."[168] After going to Vietnam at Kennedy's request, Hilsman wrote a report drawing on the ideas of Robert Thompson, leader of the British advisory group in Vietnam, who had worked on the Briggs Plan in Malaya. The report, "A Strategic Concept for South Vietnam," combined with Thompson's "Delta Plan," became the basis for U.S. policy in South Vietnam by March 1962.[169] As in the Briggs Plan in Malaya, the idea was to separate the population from the insurgents (via resettlement if necessary) and provide village-level security. During the Eisenhower administration, Diem himself had initiated the "agroville" program along these lines, though the United States had been on the sidelines and the program had been unsuccessful; the Saigon regime had already moved toward a new version of the program at the time Thompson drew up his plans.[170]

At the heart of the new policy was the "Strategic Hamlet Program," which, on paper at least, aimed at local-level transformation through civic action designed to change the national government's relationship to its people. The Hilsman report, for example, explicitly focused on the internal dynamics of South Vietnam, noting that the "struggle cannot be won merely by attempting to seal off South Vietnam from the North. It must be won by cutting the Viet Cong off from their local sources of strength, i.e., by denying them access to the villages and the people." The report's "Strategic Concept" section listed as its first principle that the "problem presented by the Viet Cong is a political and not a military problem—or, more accurately, it is a problem in civic action." In addition to the physical creation of strategic hamlets for the purpose of providing security to the population (a key to the counterinsurgency approach promoted by Hilsman and Thompson), the plan called for civic action teams "to assist locals in the construction of strategic villages and to build the essential socio-political base. . . . The public administration members will set up village government and tie it into the district and national levels assuring the flow of information on village needs and problems upward and the flow of government services downward."[171] As Latham notes, despite abuses in the program, supporters of the hamlet program "continued to believe that civic action and the organization of a new political culture could provide the institutional framework and activist values to win the allegiance of a dislocated population" and even create "local democracies among a previously static, politically isolated, and generally ignorant population."[172] It is important to note that while officially the U.S. commitment remained "advisory," the "operational collaboration" with the South Vietnamese made it an overt military intervention (which the public could follow through media coverage).[173] The Kennedy commitments peaked at 16,000 U.S. military advisers in South Vietnam.

Thus the intended American strategy—which is of primary interest here—was transformative, in the sense that the aim was to build local-level institutions, interact with the population, and integrate nonmilitary issues with the overall military strategy. Many scholars have seen the Kennedy approach in Vietnam in terms that can be described as "transformative," or as Douglas Macdonald puts it, "reformist."[174] In a history of state building in Vietnam, James Carter notes that the United States "pursued an ambitious program aimed ostensibly at developing a political, economic, and social infrastructure in the countryside and bringing it into direct contact with the regime in Saigon." He argues that the "strategic hamlets . . . became the vehicle for this transformation" and the "embodiment of the administration's combination of military and developmental solutions for Vietnam."[175] Although it is true that counterinsurgency and transformation do not necessarily go together, in this case the intention—albeit one that never came close to being fulfilled—was to build up South Vietnam's local institutions as a direct war-fighting strategy designed to separate the population from the insurgents. Thus Kennedy, who was no dove, showed a willingness to intervene in South Vietnam with force, but only if the intervention strategy was transformative and could address what he saw as the underlying political nature of the war. Rather than deploy a deterrent force or air strikes, he chose deep—and damaging—interference in the domestic affairs of South Vietnam to create a stable, "immunized" noncommunist bulwark.

The Strategic Hamlet Program, however, was ultimately a failure, for complex reasons. In its implementation, the program did not serve the actual needs of the peasants. As Frances Fitzgerald describes, the rural population suffered terrible social and economic dislocation, further diminishing support for the government.[176] Diem also used the program to attack opposition groups and increase his own power. And as Khong notes, Kennedy ignored critical differences between the situation in South Vietnam and the British effort in Malaya.[177] On the U.S. side, the military still did not shift its emphasis away from conventional operations enough to enact the program as its designers intended.[178] Even more critically, however, the program depended on Diem to reform his regime by broadening its base of support. Galbraith had noticed this problem in November 1961 on a visit to Saigon, warning Kennedy that it was "politically naïve" to expect Diem to reform: "He senses that he cannot let power go because he would be thrown out."[179] Diem was no less subject to the "logic of political survival" than the U.S. presidents urging him to reform.[180]

The Coup against Diem

By 1963, Kennedy had to confront Diem's increasingly weak popular support. Matters came to a head in August, when Diem cracked down on Buddhists in a move that highlighted the dangers of his repressive regime to the overall counterinsurgency effort. In the fall of 1963, Kennedy's linking of the political and military aspects of the war led him to consider removing Diem, whom he perceived as an obstacle to reform, even as he was concerned about the added instability such a move might bring to South Vietnam. The consideration of the coup was part of an ongoing debate over how much and how best to push Diem to reform in order to improve the war effort, and thus the debate over the coup can be considered part of the overall debate over intervention strategy.[181] Kennedy vacillated on the question of a coup—to a large extent out of concern that the coup itself might fail—but as Freedman notes, while he "did not really choose to overthrow Diem . . . his indecision had the same effect as an anti-Diem choice."[182]

The complex decision making surrounding the coup partly reflected a lack of consensus within the administration about the nature of the threat. As Robert Gallucci summarizes, within the administration, "those who believed the struggle in Viet-Nam was basically a political problem were unhappy with Diem's inept, despotic regime" and wanted a coup, whereas those "who admitted that there was a political component to the conflict but considered the insurgency principally a military problem" opposed it.[183] A notable member of the anticoup group was Lyndon Johnson.

Although he vacillated on the coup itself, Kennedy sympathized with the view that the problem was political in nature and that Diem was an obstacle to military progress. On August 24, 1963, Kennedy approved a cable to Ambassador Henry Cabot Lodge in Saigon that raised the possibility of a coup, arguing that "we must face the possibility that Diem himself cannot be preserved," and that the "Ambassador and country team should urgently examine all possible alternative leadership and make detailed plans as to how we might bring about Diem's replacement if this should become necessary."[184]

Kennedy later had misgivings about this cable, which was drafted by Hilsman and put through the clearance process while key figures such as McNamara were away from Washington, rendering it almost immediately controversial within the bureaucracy. Yet despite his anger at the bureaucratic maneuvering by coup proponents within the administration, as well as his own doubts about the feasibility and consequences of a coup, Kennedy remained remarkably consistent in his diagnosis of the problem. In a discussion a few days after the August 24 cable, for example, he asked about the impact of the "civil disturbances" and Diem's actions against the Buddhists on the war effort against the Viet Cong.[185] In instructions to McNamara before a mission to Saigon in September 1963, Kennedy wrote that "events in South Vietnam since May have now raised serious questions both about the present prospects for success against the Viet Cong and still more about the future effectiveness of this effort unless there can be important political improvement in the country." Kennedy further argued, "It is obvious that the overall political situation and the military and paramilitary effort are closely interconnected in all sorts of ways, and in executing your responsibility for appraisal of the military and paramilitary problem I expect that you will consult fully with Ambassador Lodge on related political and social questions."[186] At the meeting to discuss McNamara and Taylor's report—which did not endorse the view that the political situation was affecting the war, much less endorse a coup—Kennedy stated, "We are agreed to try to find effective means of changing the political atmosphere in Saigon. We are agreed that we should not cut off all U.S. aid to Vietnam, but are agreed on the necessity of trying to improve the situation in Vietnam by bringing about changes there."[187]

Kennedy was under no illusions that there was a logical, much less desirable, successor to Diem, making the president's willingness to entertain a change in government in South Vietnam in the face of such potential uncertainty and instability all the more surprising. At a meeting on October 29, Robert Kennedy weighed in against a coup, arguing that to "support a coup would be putting the future of Vietnam and in fact all of Southeast Asia in the hands of one man not now known to us."[188] As Freedman observes, it was certainly true that "there had been a stunning lack of political analysis on the consequences of a coup," but many who supported a coup "acknowledged that the logic of the situation would be to draw the United States even more deeply into responsibility for the government of the country and the prosecution of the war."[189]

Another major concern that had a significant impact on the decision making—or rather, the lack of a firm decision either way—was the fear that the coup itself would fail, or even lead to civil war. For example, as late as October 29, 1963, just days before the actual coup, Kennedy pressed his advisers for evidence that the coup would be successful, and he worried about how to instruct Ambassador Lodge in Saigon so that a coup could be stopped in time if the United States deemed its prospects dim. While the original instructions to Lodge included discussion of "post-Diem government matters," Kennedy argued that this should be "dropped," going as far as to say that "he was not so concerned now about the kind of a government which would exist after the coup as he was about the correlation of pro- and anti-Diem forces," which would determine the coup's success or failure.[190] Kennedy's concerns directly influenced the next instructions for Lodge, who replied that although worries about the probability of success were valid, there was little the United States could do to stop the coup.[191]

Ultimately, scholars such as David Kaiser and Lawrence Freedman come to the sensible conclusion that Kennedy was amenable to a change in government but never actually decided one way or the other on a coup, in part because he preferred to defer decisions and keep options open as long as possible.[192] But administration officials, including Kennedy, frequently discussed U.S. policy as if there would be a coup and at several junctures decided affirmatively not to discourage a coup, even if they were not sure they wanted to actively encourage it. McGeorge Bundy's message to Lodge on October 30, while instructing that the United States should not take sides in any coup, nonetheless concluded that "once a coup under responsible leadership has begun, and within these restrictions, it is in the interest of the U.S. Government that it should succeed."[193]

The move against Diem was motivated by neither moral outrage against his repressive policies nor the impulse to democratize Vietnam for its own sake, but rather the link many in the administration saw between the political situation and the war effort. The goal was not necessarily a democratic government in South Vietnam but rather a government that at least had a broader base of support. Indeed, at the NSC meeting on October 2, Kennedy explicitly argued that U.S. policy should be based "on the harm which Diem's political actions are causing to the effort against the Viet Cong rather than on our moral opposition to the kind of government Diem is running."[194] One need not assume, therefore, that Kennedy was motivated by an idealist impulse to conclude that he connected military success with some form of political change.[195]

Kennedy and his administration placed the objective of winning the war against communism above democratizing South Vietnam, as many commentators have noted.[196] But there remained disagreement about *how* to go about winning the war, and for some in the administration—a group with which Kennedy sympathized, and Johnson did not—domestic reform went hand in hand with the goal of winning the war. On November 4, 1963, Kennedy dictated thoughts about the coup, concluding that the "question now is whether the generals can stay together and build a stable government or whether . . . public opinion in Saigon, the intellectuals, students, etc., will turn on this government as repressive and undemocratic in the not too distant future."[197] For its proponents, at least, the coup was part of a transformative strategy rather than an operation that would simply swap one leader for another. Despite his awareness of the hazards of removing Diem, Kennedy was willing to risk destabilizing Vietnam to transform it. Ironically, the fears of those who opposed the coup proved correct: removing Diem left internal instability in South Vietnam that would preoccupy Johnson.

Diem was killed on November 2, 1963, just three weeks before Kennedy himself was assassinated. Although the murder of Diem came as a surprise to Kennedy, who thought the South Vietnamese leader would go into exile, the coup was remarkable even in the context of U.S. covert operations against foreign dictators: Diem, a U.S. ally, was removed because he was not transformative enough, whereas other U.S.-supported coups had been directed against leaders the United States perceived as dangerous reformers with possible communist sympathies (such as Arbenz in Guatemala and Mossadegh in Iran). Most U.S. government officials, including both Kennedy and Johnson, recognized that there was no single, logical alternative to Diem. But despite having his eyes open to this lack of an obvious candidate to succeed Diem, Kennedy was willing to take the risk of instability to secure domestic reform in South Vietnam. His consideration of the coup can be seen as part of the overall pattern of his decision making in Vietnam: he diagnosed the nature of the threat in terms of domestic issues within Vietnam and therefore sought a solution that would address those issues, keeping the military and nonmilitary aspects of the war connected as he chose his intervention strategy.

This discussion of Kennedy's decision making is by no means complete.[198] But summarizing his decisions, we see that Kennedy did not let opportunities drive his decision making, and he exploited multiple opportunities in Southeast Asia that allowed him to choose what he perceived to be the most suitable target. He consistently rejected the application of nontransformative strategies to conflicts in Laos and Vietnam. He was concerned about international credibility and electoral consequences but resisted pressure to demonstrate strength just anywhere. He pushed to improve the capabilities he saw as most useful for domestic transformation. Finally, he chose a politically oriented counterinsurgency strategy in Vietnam. His diagnosis of the threat centered on Vietnam's domestic institutions, and thus he paid significant attention to the domestic dimension of the conflict, just as he had when he visited Saigon in 1951. He treated the military and nonmilitary aspects of the war as intertwined. In Kennedy's view, there were potential security benefits from transforming South Vietnam into a stable state with strong domestic institutions. Resistance to his policy investments, as well as flaws in the strategy itself, severely hampered the effectiveness of his approach. But Kennedy's investments raised the probability that the U.S. strategy would involve a transformative counterinsurgency approach, even if it was not ultimately successful.

Alternative Hypotheses

The discussion of Kennedy's decisions on Laos and Vietnam illustrates that while other factors clearly played a role, they were not decisive. In terms of structural and material factors, pressure to compete with Moscow in the Third World weighed on Kennedy in both Laos and Vietnam, but he was willing to wait for what he perceived as the more favorable confrontation, despite advice that backing down in Laos would only make standing firm in Vietnam harder. Kennedy was concerned about credibility, as well as losing territory within the U.S. sphere of influence. But these considerations are insufficient to explain why he passed up opportunities to demonstrate strength conventionally in Laos and in Vietnam, courses his advisers advocated.

There is also the argument that Kennedy's expansion of military capabilities led him to perceive more threats around the world and thus left him more likely to use force.[199] Indeed, one of the clearest incarnations of this argument is Rostow's 1961 lament about counterinsurgency forces: "It is somehow wrong to be developing these capabilities but not applying them in a crucially active theater. In Knute Rockne's old phrase, we are not saving them for the Junior Prom."[200] But the argument that capabilities drive decisions also falls short. The *lack* of capabilities—in part a legacy of Eisenhower's dearth of investments in transformative capabilities and the military's bias against transformative strategies—played a role in the early decisions Kennedy faced. But overall, Kennedy pushed to increase the capabilities he wanted to use rather than being guided by existing capabilities. Other material factors, such as terrain, no doubt played a role. Landlocked Laos was more inaccessible, though both Laos and Vietnam had difficult terrain. But Kennedy did not make a simple calculation about terrain; he also considered local domestic politics and the fighting will of the population. Though Kennedy was concerned about fighting in the inhospitable jungles of Southeast Asia, he was willing to do so with the right strategy.

Another argument related to the circumstances of the war is that a strong counterinsurgency effort may have been, as Freedman argues, a "logical answer" to Kennedy's search for a middle way between withdrawal and full-scale war.[201] But there was pressure from his top-level civilian and military advisers to take a different middle way, namely, to send a conventional, nontransformative deployment to fight the insurgency. As discussed in chapter 5, Johnson would also try to seek a middle course (admittedly under more difficult circumstances as the security situation in Vietnam deteriorated), but he did not seriously consider a transformative approach. Leaving aside debates about what strategy might or might not have worked, from the perspective of the participants at the time it is not clear that there was only one middle way.

In terms of domestic competition, Kennedy was more than just one actor among many, imposing his beliefs over the objections of many other domestic players. Bureaucratic politics played a constraining rather than a driving role. Kennedy repeatedly overruled his civilian advisers and the military and seemed at times to be single-handedly keeping counterinsurgency on the agenda. The military's preference, however, was a formidable intervening factor in the implementation of Kennedy's chosen strategy. Electoral politics played a more ambiguous role. Fear of looking weak seems to have weighed on Kennedy; as he reportedly told journalist Charles Bartlett, "We don't have a prayer of staying in Vietnam. Those people hate us. . . . But I can't give up a piece of territory like that to the Communists and get the American people to reelect me."[202] On the other hand, what he perceived as the public's intolerance for a protracted battle was a countervailing pressure. In the end, the two imperatives may have neutralized each other. Kennedy's actions in the Third World, and especially the move against Diem in South Vietnam, also counter the argument made by Bruce Bueno de Mesquita and George Downs that democratic interveners dislike imposing democratic institutions abroad because the target state's future foreign policies will be too uncertain.[203] Kennedy viewed transforming local institutions as a security benefit that would enhance the military effort and thus U.S. interests, and he was even willing to remove a U.S. ally and risk instability in the process of undertaking such a transformation (even if a full-fledged democracy was not necessarily his goal).

Neither international norms nor shared ideas within the government seem to have significantly influenced Kennedy's decisions. Even in his pre-presidential years, Kennedy complained that nonintervention principles hampered U.S. policy (for example, in Cuba before the revolution). While shared ideas among his advisers, particularly those steeped in modernization theory and development economics, played a role in his policy choices, his early embrace of these ideas long before he came into contact with this group, as well as his actions as president, indicate that he set the modernization agenda. Thus the executive's ideas, rather than a consensus of shared ideas, dominated the decision-making process.

Finally, we might consider what evidence would show that Kennedy was *not* an internally focused leader whose beliefs tracked with his intervention choices. It is true that he worried a great deal about Soviet moves in Europe and, of course, the missile provocation in Cuba. In addition to his deviations from a transformative agenda, especially in Latin America (where he announced the Kennedy Doctrine), in private Kennedy could be scornful of idealist rhetoric. In discussing a draft paper that may have been an earlier version of the document titled "U.S. Overseas Internal Defense Policy" (discussed above), Kennedy read aloud the portion of the text calling for the United States "to insure that modernization of the local society evolves in directions which will afford a congenial world environment for fruitful international cooperation and . . . for our way of life." The president added, "That's a lot of crap." After reading another section that called for "promoting the adoption of economic institutions and practices by the target country modeled along free-world lines of planning activity and the acceptance of free-world capital investment for economic development," Kennedy commented, "We're not really fighting for the private enterprise system."[204] Kennedy was not interested in exporting the American system for its own sake (or promoting a free market ideology for the sake of American business interests).

But the evidence in this chapter suggests that Kennedy's concerns had more to do with his distinction between a universalist commitment to democratic institutions, on the one hand, and securing U.S. interests through interference in local societies, on the other. Kennedy believed that local domestic institutions mattered, but this belief was consistent with a view of a world full of threats. He was well aware that he could not pursue transformative aims everywhere, nor could he remake the world in America's image.

This chapter has argued that John F. Kennedy perceived threats based on a causal belief that the internal conditions of other states represented possible threats to U.S. national security; that he formed this belief early in his political career and, on becoming president, invested in capabilities to meet these threats; and that this belief shaped his intervention decisions, especially in Southeast Asia. Kennedy's experience with counterinsurgency remains a cautionary tale: even when the president presses for investments in a certain strategy, a gap between ends and means may still result, especially from bureaucratic resistance. Transformative strategies, which entail deep local involvement, can be especially risky endeavors that require patient and sustained implementation, as well as local support. Kennedy's threat perception and policy investments raised his estimate of the probability of success enough to persuade him to intervene transformatively, but it does not necessarily follow that these factors raised the probability of success high enough to ensure victory. Nevertheless, although his was a "revolution that failed,"[205] Kennedy's long-standing interest in counterinsurgency and his view of the nature of the conflict in Vietnam brought transformative strategies to the bureaucratic and decision-making table in a significant way. And while his strategy did not successfully transform Vietnam in the way Kennedy intended, explaining his intended policy choice—the goal of this chapter—is still important because his chosen strategy had consequences for the conduct of the war during and after his tenure.

Historians continue to debate whether Kennedy would have escalated in Vietnam. As George Herring has put it, the question has become "tired and unanswerable."[206] While historians are divided on this question,[207] many agree on Kennedy's role in actively squelching repeated proposals for a conventional deployment and his consistent search for a counterinsurgency strategy. Johnson would face difficulties in Vietnam with which Kennedy never had to grapple—chief among them the instability left by the coup against Diem. In the next chapter, I show that Johnson held a very different set of beliefs and did not share Kennedy's focus either on domestic political and economic development or on counterinsurgency. Thus Johnson provides an interesting contrast to Kennedy, and together their intervention decisions highlight the importance of leaders in shaping military interventions.

5

Lyndon B. Johnson

Lyndon Johnson assumed the presidency with far less interest in or experience with foreign policy than his predecessor. But his record on national security and foreign policy issues is more complex and multifaceted than previously understood, as a wave of scholarship has shown.[1] His long career in the House and Senate brought him into contact with many of the same national security and foreign policy issues with which Eisenhower and Kennedy grappled.

Johnson is a particularly difficult figure to classify. The theory developed in this book identifies ideal types, which by definition cannot perfectly reflect reality. But his pre-presidential record indicates that he is best characterized as externally focused.[2] Johnson would seem to be an unlikely case for an externally focused leader, given his support of transformative domestic policies in the United States such as the New Deal and the Great Society, and the similarities between Kennedy's administration and his own. But Johnson tended to keep track of how strongly other states supported the United States in the bipolar struggle with the Soviet Union and otherwise largely ignored what went on inside those states. Moreover, unlike Kennedy, Johnson focused on the international aspects of Cold War issues such as maintaining credibility and countering aggression, and he rarely connected these issues to the domestic institutions of other states. To be sure, as with Eisenhower and Kennedy, there are complicating factors in compiling a portrait of Johnson's beliefs. Johnson expressed genuine sympathy for the plight of the poor in other countries and showed some interest in economic development programs. But he often viewed these domestic issues as largely parallel to, rather than intertwined with, U.S. national security.

Following the pattern of the previous two chapters, I begin by tracing Johnson's beliefs about the origin of threats from his years in Congress through the vice presidency, using the indicators discussed in chapter 2. The documentary record from Johnson's pre-presidential years is vast, but unfortunately does not contain the same rich collection of private documents and diaries that are available for the Eisenhower and Kennedy eras.[3] Nevertheless, the evidence from Johnson's career in Congress, where he served on several defense-related committees, as well as his time as vice president, reveal him to be externally focused. Since Johnson took over from Kennedy abruptly, he did not have an initial period in which to make significant policy investments. But his choices during the transition are still illuminating. Most importantly, Johnson did not continue Kennedy's top-down pressure to build transformative capabilities.

I then turn to Johnson's intervention decisions. Johnson was certainly concerned about communist takeovers. But his concern fell closer to that of Eisenhower: Johnson worried principally about externally driven takeovers by small, elite groups rather than the internal, popularly driven path to communism that often concerned Kennedy. I examine the decisions Johnson made in Latin America, where he first handled the relatively minor Panama crisis of 1964 without intervention but later intervened using military force in the Dominican Republic in 1965. Johnson's policies in Latin America contrasted with Kennedy's emphasis on political and economic reform, a contrast that culminated in Johnson's nontransformative intervention in the Dominican Republic. In sharp contrast to Kennedy's statement of preferences ranging from a "decent democratic regime" to a "Castro regime," Johnson would articulate his own statement of preferences during the 1965 crisis, stating, "We will have one of 3 dictators: 1) U.S., 2) Moderate dictator, 3) Castro dictator."[4] Finally, I consider how Johnson handled Vietnam, where he employed a nontransformative strategy for the initial escalation. Examining his choices in Vietnam is difficult because Johnson faced a very different situation in South Vietnam than Kennedy, thanks in part to the coup against Diem (an action Johnson had opposed) and because he sought to show continuity with Kennedy's policies. Nevertheless, I argue that changing conditions within Vietnam are not sufficient to explain the differences between the Kennedy and Johnson approaches.

Methodologically, Johnson's service in Congress alongside Kennedy during the Eisenhower presidency provides an important window of comparison among the three leaders as they faced similar and ongoing challenges. Johnson often supported Eisenhower's policies to such an extent that he drew the ire of fellow Democrats, suggesting that he was not entirely constrained by his party.[5] It is also particularly useful to examine his vice presidential term, during which he took issue with many of Kennedy's policies, including those related to foreign aid, Latin America, and Vietnam. When Johnson assumed the presidency, there were important elements of policy continuity; to find otherwise would be surprising. But given that Johnson inherited many Kennedy advisers and programs and felt a strong need to emphasize the stability of U.S. policy to the public, his differences with Kennedy and his shifts in policy after taking office are all the more remarkable.

Johnson's presidency also provides an opportunity to assess alternative explanations, from structural and material conditions such as credibility concerns to the role of other domestic actors. Johnson retained many Kennedy advisers and interacted with many of the same military figures, allowing me to assess how he dealt with a similar cast of characters and the relatively consistent preferences of the military. But Johnson was not a prisoner of others' ideas.

The evolution of Johnson's policies in Vietnam also allows me to examine arguments about learning, although it is difficult to assess whether a leader's beliefs truly changed in the middle of an ongoing intervention. His reemphasis on pacification operations represented a policy shift, but Johnson never fully integrated pacification into the overall strategy for Vietnam. Thus Lyndon Johnson's career, during which he dealt with many of the same issues and crises as his predecessors, provides leverage in understanding how leaders shape military interventions.

Johnson's Beliefs

Many portraits of Johnson highlight his inexperience with and lack of interest in foreign policy.[6] But to dismiss Johnson as lacking experience with or convictions about national security and foreign policy would be to gloss over a more complex record, especially in the pre-presidential period.[7] For Johnson, as for Kennedy, building up his foreign policy and national security credentials while in Congress was a politically advantageous move, and Johnson enthusiastically exploited issues for his own political benefit. Even given the electoral motive, however, Dallek argues for greater attention to Johnson's substantive record. Dallek highlights Johnson's "role in the rise of the national security state," particularly his sustained advocacy of greater defense spending and his role in shaping foreign and defense policies.[8] As Thomas Gaskin notes, foreign and defense issues were central in the extremely close race that sent Johnson to the Senate in 1948.[9] In Congress, he served on the House Naval Affairs and Armed Services Committees, the Joint Committee on Atomic Energy, and the Senate Armed Services Committee, and he chaired the Senate Preparedness Subcommittee. As the Democratic leader in the Senate beginning in 1953, Johnson fought several foreign policy battles alongside Eisenhower.[10] Political gain mattered, but politics alone cannot explain the *form* that Johnson's focus on national security took.

THE NATURE OF THREATS

Johnson's view of threats in the international environment focused with remarkable consistency on the risk that the Soviets or their allies would engage in outright aggression against Third World states, either directly through an attack or through subversion directed from the outside, to which all states were susceptible regardless of their institutions. Occasionally, he discussed the importance of raising living standards as part of the Cold War struggle, but he concentrated more frequently on externally driven aggression directed at small states, or externally driven subversion that aimed at a small group of elites within these countries. In this sense, like Eisenhower, he was concerned about keeping other states' domestic institutions out of communist hands, but he saw the danger resting with a Soviet-directed elite takeover of these institutions rather than arising from the nature of the institutions themselves. Most importantly, he did not connect the nature of other states' political institutions to the threat that the states would fall under communist control and thus harm U.S. interests. Admittedly, it is the relative dearth of statements about other states' domestic institutions that provides the best evidence for his lack of attention to domestic issues. But this relative inattention, combined with his strong public and private statements about aggression and the evidence on other dimensions, forms a coherent picture of an externally focused leader. As Doris Kearns Goodwin argues, World War II impressed on Johnson a worldview centered on deterring aggression. This focus on aggression came at the expense of an understanding of the internal dynamics of conflicts. As Goodwin puts it, "In every war, Johnson believed, the enemy is an alien force that 'invades' the allies' house. Such a view does not facilitate an understanding of civil war."[11]

Johnson tended to see other states, particularly in the Third World, in external terms, as relatively undifferentiated targets of potential communist attack. In October 1953, for example, he told the Pan American Round Table in El Paso, Texas, that the "communists are eager to obtain a beachhead on the American continents. Once it is gained, it will gradually be extended and widened in preparation for a major assault." Echoing Eisenhower, he argued, "Good neighbors are independent neighbors who live in friendship but who keep their own yards tidy. . . . Each holds himself responsible for his own homestead." He asserted that there was little danger of a communist takeover "through the voluntary desire of our neighbors. But a neighborhood divided is easy prey for burglars."[12] Nearly five years later, after Vice President Nixon's disastrous trip to Latin America, Johnson asserted on the Senate floor, "We are faced by a common peril—an unthinking force directed by coldly thinking men in Moscow and Peiping. . . . It is not mere coincidence that the dispatches from Latin America, from Lebanon and from North Africa should all be bleak. . . . Those areas of the world are widely separated in terms of geography. But they are not widely separated in terms of plans for world domination." While blaming communists was politically expedient—as most politicians, including Kennedy, were well aware—Johnson still provided a distinct and externally driven diagnosis of the problem. Arguing that the world had entered an "era of 'brush fires' which can spring out at unexpected points in the world," he asserted that the attacks on Nixon were "manifestations of temporary conditions which are being exploited," and that the "bad economic conditions in Latin America are a direct reflection of the recession in this country."[13] Johnson made no mention of the repressive regimes—and U.S. policies supporting them—against which many of the demonstrations aimed. Instead, he argued that "there must have been some antagonism against the United States for the hysteria to generate the way it did."[14]

A recurring manifestation of this focus on external aggression was Johnson's tendency to emphasize drawing lines against aggressors and maintaining U.S. credibility, without much attention to exactly where the lines were drawn. Johnson did not focus on whether the domestic characteristics of the front-line states might make them more or less vulnerable to communism, or whether successful line-drawing might require shoring up the target state's domestic institutions. As discussed in chapter 4, Kennedy had also seen the need to draw lines but was far more concerned with the internal conditions within states that might serve as test cases for U.S. firmness. For Johnson, line-drawing had few, if any, internal criteria.

An early example of Johnson's focus on line-drawing came in correspondence with former Texas state senator and Austin attorney Alvin J. Wirtz, a Johnson mentor. In April 1947, amid the debate on the Truman Doctrine, Wirtz sent Johnson a copy of a letter in which he argued that if Franklin Roosevelt confronted the situation, he would first work on "quarantining the aggressors," knowing that "you cannot appease a bully." Second, if Roosevelt wanted to stop aggression, and "if he decided that the place to stop it is Greece . . . he would announce a firm policy to the effect that the United States proposes to go into Greece and do whatever the situation requires." And third, Roosevelt "would see that the Greek economy is rebuilt."[15] In his reply, Johnson wrote, "I think, although the President did not spell it out so bluntly, that he should say, and the people should support him in saying, 'This is it. We will not tolerate prima donna, high-handed, sulking, thieving forces who seek to gobble up help-less peoples in order to become the dominant power and rule the world.' As you well said, Truman chose to say that the place is Greece, the time is now."[16] John-son's reply did not mention economic reconstruction.

In his subsequent House floor speech on the Truman Doctrine, Johnson played up the theme of standing up against aggression. "Human experience teaches me," Johnson asserted, "that if I let a bully of my community make me travel back streets to avoid a fight, I merely postpone the evil day. Soon he will try to chase me out of my house." The bully metaphor would recur throughout his career. Johnson's analysis did not pay much attention to Greece or Turkey, except to note that they were far from American soil. "Whenever security of this country is involved," Johnson said, "we are willing to draw the quarantine line—and we would rather have it on the shores of the Mediterranean than on the shores of the Chesapeake Bay or the Gulf of Mexico."[17] Truman's own speech, in contrast, placed significant emphasis on the internal problems in Greece and Turkey and the necessity of economic reconstruction to U.S. secu-rity interests.[18] Kennedy's remarks on the Truman Doctrine also emphasized line-drawing and invoked Munich but devoted several paragraphs to Greece and Turkey.[19] For Johnson, it seemed to matter only that a line be drawn; precisely where the line fell or whether domestic institution building might help the line hold was of little consequence.

Johnson continued to emphasize drawing lines against aggression into the 1950s. For example, in the 1954 Guatemala crisis, while Eisenhower was using the CIA to oust Arbenz from power, Johnson introduced a resolution support-ing action to reaffirm the Monroe Doctrine and to stop external interference in the Western Hemisphere.[20] The resolution passed 69 to 1—and Kennedy voted for it—but Johnson was its main sponsor. Johnson pressed ahead with the reso-lution, despite a warning from aide George Reedy in late May that "as a practical matter, the Monroe Doctrine simply does not apply." Reedy also pointed out that "the native government of Guatemala has bought the arms. There is not the slightest evidence that Soviet forces have moved into the nation and taken over by strength of arms."[21]

Nevertheless, Johnson persisted in his view of the crisis as an externally driven takeover by a small cadre of communists and having little to do with Gua-temala itself. On the Senate floor, he described the "blueprint for Communist conquest": first, "the victim nation is infiltrated by small groups which struggle for a base of political power," then "Communist advisers in the Kremlin decide it is time for a show of force," and finally "the victim nation becomes another member of the terrorized 'family' behind the Iron Curtain."[22] A day after Arbenz resigned, Johnson even continued to push for the House to pass his resolution. In a telephone call with Secretary of State Dulles, Johnson argued, "If we can really nail down this principle of the Monroe Doctrine applying to communism here . . . if we can begin to show it in deeds and not words, a lot of these boys won't be so keen about accepting communist support for leadership in these South American countries."[23] In letters, Johnson called the situation in Guatemala "the first overt attempt of world communism to establish a military beachhead in the Western Hemisphere."[24] He argued on the Senate floor that his resolution would provide bipartisan support for drawing "a line into which the Communists cannot penetrate." He also pledged that the United States had "no intentions whatsoever of interfering in [Latin America's] internal affairs. The force of this resolution is directed solely against external aggression."[25] He exhibited little interest in the problems and issues inside Guatemala itself, writing to a constituent that he did not "know the names and the characters of the rebels in Guatemala," which was significant primarily "as an entering wedge of communist penetration."[26] While there is little direct evidence of Kennedy's particular stance on the Guatemala issue apart from his vote supporting Johnson's resolution, Kennedy was generally more inclined to look at whether the conditions inside a country made it ripe for communist penetration and whether transformative policies might be required to address these conditions. Johnson's focus on stopping beachheads required no such attention to internal details.

On a few occasions, Johnson expressed concern that domestic problems, particularly economic conditions, could be a threat to the United States. There were early hints in Johnson's rhetoric that his concern for poverty, hunger, and other domestic issues might carry over into his threat perception. In a speech in Austin in 1947, for example, he used the language of stopping aggression but later urged the United States to "act the role of the good samaritan" lest it "fan the flames of envy and [jealousy] in the hearts and minds of the 94 per cent" of people outside America.[27] Over a decade later, in the spring of 1958, he argued, "We have preached freedom but patted the foes of freedom on the back. We have accorded our friendship to leaders of other governments who stood in those lands for what we oppose at home. We have trafficked in expediency and sold ourselves down the river for doing so."[28] And in a somewhat uncharacteristic public statement, in the form of a column in the *Dallas Times Herald*, Johnson argued,

It seems rather strange that the destiny of our country can depend upon street mobs in Baghdad and Beirut and upon burnoosed Arabs in Saudi Arabia and Kuwait, but there is the stark and simple fact. The people of the Middle East have been hungry and ragged for several centuries. . . . They are angry and they are resentful at what they consider unjustified treatment by other powers. . . . They are insisting on a better way of life which can come about only through modern methods of agriculture and through industrialization. We must help them—not with gifts but with loans and with technical assistance. If we do not, they will follow the Communist road because they will feel there is no place else to turn.[29]

But these statements are less frequent in Johnson's pre-presidential record than his focus on outside aggression. Furthermore, the emphasis Johnson placed on better economic conditions was hardly ever accompanied by calls for political or institutional reform, and he was somewhat skeptical of foreign aid, as discussed below. More frequently, Johnson tended to limit the connections between his genuine concern for the world's poor and his view of international threats. In his speech announcing his Senate candidacy in May 1948, he again came close to calling poverty a threat, asserting, "War thrives on squalor and poverty, hunger and disease. The nations of the World can overcome these war-breeding conditions only by restoring their internal prosperity." But echoing Eisenhower, he immediately argued that the situation "demands a free flow of goods in the channels of international trade."[30] World poverty might be an important issue, but responsibility for it rested with poor countries themselves rather than with U.S. national security institutions. He continued the speech by reemphasizing the need to meet aggression: "Firmness with international bullies is an essential ingredient of the peace. . . . Always we must stand up to war-makers and say, This far and no farther."[31]

ALLIANCES AND AMERICA'S SPHERE OF INFLUENCE

Johnson weighed in on a variety of foreign policy crises and controversies during his years in Congress. But although his comments on alliance issues are rare, there is little evidence that his views on relationships with allies and the American sphere of influence were influenced by domestic considerations within the states in question. In 1951, he echoed Eisenhower's sentiments about taking any available allies, defending aid to Yugoslavia and Spain to a constituent critical of U.S. policy. "Both governments have indicated a strong desire to resist Communist aggression," Johnson wrote. "Our only real enemy in the world is Communism, and it seems to me that we should utilize and befriend any and all anti-Communist nations that we can."[32] Johnson was also far less interested in or sympathetic to the question of nationalism, although Reedy warned him of the "rising tide of nationalism in Asia."[33] While Johnson condemned imperialism, in general there was little in his writing or rhetoric to parallel Kennedy's view of nationalism as an unstoppable domestic force with which the United States had to align. In July 1957, as Kennedy spoke out forcefully against the continued French effort to maintain control of Algeria, Johnson did not comment (despite receiving an advance copy of the speech).[34] In one of his very few direct references on the subject, Johnson warned in May 1958 that the "Middle East is aflame with the bright fires of nationalism," but as discussed below, he would soon couch the crises in Lebanon and Iraq in terms of aggression.[35]

On the question of neutralism, there is little direct evidence with which to assess Johnson's views. But (as discussed in more detail below) some of his letters on foreign aid indicate that his primary concern was with winning the Cold War competition for allies by getting Third World states to sign up with the West rather than ensuring their long-term internal sustainability. As discussed in chapter 4, Kennedy believed that U.S. interests might not be particularly well served by forcing Third World states to "vote the Western ticket" and concentrated instead on the domestic health of these states, potentially rendering them more valuable allies later. In his approach to allies and America's sphere of influence, Johnson was mainly focused on keeping Third World states solidly in the U.S. camp and standing firm in the face of challenges to the pro-Western orientation of these states. Beyond this, he showed little interest in the domestic politics of the Third World. Johnson's approach to foreign aid would follow a similar pattern.

FOREIGN AID

Johnson's views on foreign aid are somewhat complex. On the one hand, there is the image of Johnson attempting to export the New Deal (and later the Great Society) to the Third World.[36] On the other hand, there is his discomfort with foreigners and his relative inattention to Third World politics and institutions. The key was that for Johnson, economic and social issues such as poverty and underdevelopment, in which he had a long-standing interest within the United States, were problems with only a limited connection to national security threats. Burton Kaufman makes a similar argument, noting that Johnson "had a real interest in eliminating hunger and in providing adequate nourishment worldwide" but that "many of Johnson's own views on the foreign-aid program were narrowly circumscribed."[37] Johnson's preferred forms of aid—such as aid for infrastructure, following the example of the rural electrification program he supported in the United States—constituted clearly delineated projects to help the world's poor and improve living standards rather than reform institutions. This view contrasts with that of Kennedy, for whom significant investment in the domestic institutions of states he deemed promising candidates for reform was an essential dimension of U.S. national security.

Johnson certainly saw a connection between foreign aid and the Cold War. But he focused on aid as an instrument to induce countries to align themselves with U.S. interests rather than a tool to build or reform their institutions. In a speech on the Marshall Plan in April 1948, he said that hunger and poverty fed a "sinister and ruthless evil" moving across Europe, and that aid would help "contest with the evil in a battle for peace."[38] Johnson used similar language in a March 1958 letter, arguing that foreign aid might help "as a means of battling for the cooperation of the one-third of the world's population that is not at present committed to the United States or Russia."[39] He frequently justified his support for aid in these terms, targeting those who "live in parts of the world that are backward and poorly developed, [and] are trying to make up their minds as to which course offers them the brightest future—democratic capitalism or dictatorial communism."[40] In a 1957 speech in which he sounded skeptical notes on foreign aid generally, Johnson argued,

> The United States can maintain its security in a world in which the individual nations are free. We need fear only the situation in which the other nations are tightly controlled by an enemy. . . . We cannot "create" freedom for another country nor can we "buy" its friendship. The people must create their own freedom and must be at liberty to decide for themselves their friendships and their enmities. . . . We can, however, help other people to help themselves. We can supply them with technical knowledge, with loans, and with other forms of aid that will release their own productive energies and enable them to determine their own destinies.

Johnson went on to warn, "We cannot—by 'sharing' our prosperity—keep the rest of the world on standards of living to which they would like to become accustomed." He cited technical assistance such as showing "a farmer in India how to improve his productivity" or "set[ting] forth for the people of arid regions the techniques of soil and water conservation. . . . And when they are self-supporting, we need not fear communism. They will not succumb."[41]

Thus, though he warned against trying to "buy" the friendship of other countries, Johnson's version of a "hearts and minds" campaign did not have much depth in terms of its long-term commitment to the development of other states' institutions. In 1951, in the context of Asia and aid to India, Johnson wrote to a constituent of "the hazards which would face any effort on our part to improve the world situation along the lines of our own beliefs. . . . In our efforts to overcome the threats of would-be world conquerors, we must be realistic in appraising our own limitations as well as the difficulties confronting us."[42] He defended his votes for aid and called it beneficial to U.S. interests, but he often highlighted the loan-based nature of the programs he supported or what the United States would receive in return. In a 1953 letter, for example, he argued that he had "stressed . . . the need for insisting that these countries regard the aid program as truly mutual in character. In accepting assistance from us, it seems to me they take on certain responsibilities toward us. In some cases, I think, they have not been meeting those responsibilities."[43] This approach contrasts with Kennedy's willingness to aid countries even if they had not "voted the Western ticket."

More generally, aid to the Third World did not have nearly the significance for Johnson that it did for Kennedy. In Congress, in keeping with his "watchdog" image, Johnson pushed to cut costs. He was a consistent supporter of military assistance, and only in his last few years in the Senate did he begin to talk more frequently about poverty and underdevelopment.[44] As the leader of the Senate Democrats, he often helped marshal support for Eisenhower's foreign aid bills in an increasingly skeptical climate. But he also displayed ambivalence and even his own skepticism about foreign aid, writing in March 1958 that he sometimes "felt that we should eliminate foreign aid completely."[45] In the late 1950s, Johnson began to speak more about the need to help underdeveloped nations. But Kaufman concludes that "in a number of respects, Johnson was more in sympathy with the [aid] program's critics than with its defenders."[46]

Johnson frequently emphasized a more externally oriented solution for economic growth abroad: increased trade. He was sympathetic to Eisenhower's notion of "trade not aid," specifically urging that the United States "should seek to translate the slogan 'trade, not aid' into a meaningful program" and should "encourage the economic health of free nations through sound trade policies from which we would all profit." "It is only by unfettered exchange of goods and services," Johnson asserted, "that the free world can be built up into a healthy economic unit."[47] In the late 1950s, as Eisenhower began to increase aid, Johnson was still arguing for the United States to "try to shift the emphasis away from 'aid' to 'trade.'"[48] In 1959, maintaining that "economic warfare" was a "vital front" in the Cold War, Johnson called for "bold, imaginative programs to open new markets" as well as "new patterns of distribution" in trade.[49] His approach— viewing economic warfare in external terms and thus seizing on an externally oriented solution like trade—contrasts with Kennedy's tolerance of neutralism and emphasis on the domestic restructuring of aid recipients in the interest of promoting long-term stability and prosperity.

As vice president, Johnson took issue with Kennedy's foreign aid policies, not because Johnson opposed aid in general, but because he disagreed with the form of Kennedy's program. Although Johnson sympathized with the world's poor, he did not support the emphasis on political reform that undergirded the

Alliance for Progress, deeming the program a "thoroughgoing mess."[50] In 1960, given what he saw as his extensive knowledge of the hemisphere, Johnson identified Latin America as an area where he might contribute. But as Philip Geyelin summarizes, "Lyndon Johnson could not have been John F. Kennedy's man for Latin America."[51]

All this is not to suggest that Johnson opposed aid entirely or was unsympathetic to Third World problems. He simply viewed these problems as largely separate from the ongoing Cold War struggle. On his 1961 tour of Asia as vice president, Johnson talked publicly about the benefits of aid, though he was also under instructions to carry that message on Kennedy's behalf. He also spent considerable time mingling with ordinary people on his foreign travels, and he continued to show interest in improving infrastructure.[52] Yet going directly to the people and focusing on discrete local development projects suited Johnson's genuine, but limited, interest in Third World development. While Kennedy was pushing for far more invasive forms of economic aid as a preventive tool for building up the domestic strength of other states, Johnson saw aid as useful for humanitarian purposes or as a security tool only insofar as it won over the uncommitted or helped the United States exert leverage.

Strategy and Policy Investments: Pre-presidential Evidence

Johnson's externally oriented beliefs about the nature of threats translated into a nontransformative view of strategy in his pre-presidential years. To deal with aggression, Johnson concentrated his efforts in Congress on conventional (i.e., nontransformative) military preparedness. In April 1948, he wrote Truman that his "shoulder always has been and always will be at the wheel of preparedness."[53] Staff memos to Johnson in 1948 show him making inquiries on many issues that would later become themes in his Preparedness Subcommittee work, such as manpower strength, stockpiling, and particularly air power.[54] Dallek notes the "advantages to Texas and himself" in the air power push, but also Johnson's "genuine anxiety about the communist threat."[55]

Once in the Senate, Johnson continued to promote preparedness while reaping its considerable political advantages. He pushed air force expansion and preparedness in 1949 and 1950.[56] In July 1950, shortly after Truman's commitment of troops to Korea, Johnson persuaded his colleagues to set up a watchdog subcommittee for preparedness and to make him chairman.[57] Although many, including Truman, viewed his enthusiasm as political showmanship (since Truman himself had made his name in the Senate during World War II through work on a similar watchdog committee), Johnson nonetheless had what Dallek describes as "a genuine commitment to advancing the war effort with little regard for partisan considerations."[58] Johnson's Preparedness Subcommittee issued a series of unanimous reports on topics such as manpower, air power, stockpiling of critical raw materials, and conditions at military facilities, with no discernible interest in unconventional warfare.[59]

Johnson's preparedness work undoubtedly had political motivations and was inconsistent in its intensity. But it dovetailed with his belief that apart from nuclear war, external aggression was the major threat facing the noncommunist world. Furthermore, the Preparedness Subcommittee gave Johnson significant pre-presidential exposure to important security issues. Thus in the period when Kennedy began to focus on the Third World's domestic problems as a source of threat and called for investments in capabilities to address these problems, Johnson simply saw territory that might be grabbed by the Soviets and prepared to defend it accordingly. Kennedy by no means discounted the importance of conventional preparedness. But Kennedy called for *both* conventional and unconventional preparedness whereas Johnson's work on military affairs did not take up the problem of countering unconventional threats that emerged from within other states.

Johnson's externally focused views also informed his response to the intervention decisions of his predecessors, providing a baseline for measuring how his beliefs translated into policy preferences in the pre-presidential period. In the 1954 Indochina crisis, as the French faced defeat at Dien Bien Phu, Johnson was well informed through high-level briefings.[60] John Prados notes that Johnson is often credited with helping to prevent a U.S. intervention in Indochina in 1954 because in a key meeting with Dulles and other congressional leaders, Johnson asked which allies supported the intervention (to which Dulles had to reply that none did).[61] But Prados concludes that Johnson was sympathetic to intervention and merely asked his question in a "pro forma" way, "doing exactly what the Eisenhower administration expected of him." Indeed, Prados notes that "Johnson had acquired a stance on Vietnam at the time of Dien Bien Phu."[62]

By this time, as Jon Western argues, there were competing strands of opinion on Indochina. In this context, Western categorizes Kennedy as a "liberal": an anticommunist, but one who believed that "instability in the Third World was the product of internal inequalities, perpetual poverty, and social and political forces."[63] Johnson arguably falls closer to what Western calls a "selective engager," a category in which he places Eisenhower. In a letter to a constituent on May 18, 1954, Johnson argued that it would be a mistake to "fight alone," implying that he opposed *unilateral* U.S. intervention in Indochina, without the backing of allies.[64] But he saw a need to stand firm, writing a constituent that the "real question involved here, of course, is where, when and how to take a stand."[65] He repeatedly wrote constituents—the overwhelming majority of whom opposed intervention, as Prados notes—that America had been "caught bluffing," and that the "only language [communists] understand and respect is the language of strength."[66]

Aside from expressions of anticolonialism, Johnson did not seem especially concerned with the domestic affairs or conditions of Indochina.[67] As Prados observes, in the absence of diaries, notes, or interviews, Johnson's newsletters to constituents are the most "authoritative sources" on his position on Indochina, and they "consistently and repeatedly make the case for U.S. intervention."[68] In the April 24, 1954, newsletter, for example, he invoked the domino theory, arguing that "if [Indochina] should be captured by the communists, they would be in a commanding position to take over the entire continent of Asia." Johnson's only discussion of the internal situation in Indochina was to note that the "French have refused to grant full independence."[69] His letters on Indochina vacillated between the need to stand firm and the hope of avoiding intervention. In a letter to a friend on April 23, Johnson wrote that the threat to Indochina was "very grave" and that it was "a threat we must resist."[70] After the fall of Dien Bien Phu, he called the defeat a "stunning reversal" for the United States, saying "we have been caught bluffing by our enemies," but arguing that sending U.S. troops "would be a tragedy of great magnitude."[71] In another letter, he explicitly wrote that he was "opposed" to sending U.S. troops.[72] But in other letters, Johnson continued to emphasize the language of toughness and avoiding appeasement.[73] Publicly, in a speech on May 6, 1954—the day before Dien Bien Phu fell—Johnson painted a "picture of our country needlessly weakened in the world."[74] Prados concludes that Johnson favored intervention and only softened his stance when Dien Bien Phu was "on its last legs."[75]

Johnson's vice-presidential years, in which he suffered diminished power but had access to high-level information, illustrate both the continuity of his views on the conflict in Southeast Asia and his differences with Kennedy. This record is very helpful in establishing that Kennedy and Johnson approached Vietnam differently under similar circumstances. In 1961, Kennedy persuaded a very reluctant Johnson to go on a goodwill trip to Asia with the particular aim of demonstrating support for South Vietnamese president Diem.[76] Parsing Johnson's views on the trip is somewhat difficult because he was Kennedy's agent and spokesman. Johnson's pretrip briefing included material on U.S. economic aid and hopes for internal reform.[77]

Although his discussion with Diem in Saigon covered military, economic, and social issues, Johnson's primary message was the need to stand up to communist aggression rather than a focus on domestic strength and reform. In his speech at the farewell dinner in Saigon, Johnson used a familiar formulation, asserting, "If a bully is loose in the world, and can come in and run you off your lawn today, he'll be back tomorrow to drive you from your porch." He saw Diem as someone who would say, "Don't cross this line."[78] Johnson's private reports on his return placed the most emphasis on shoring up U.S. credibility and holding the line in Southeast Asia. His classified report to Kennedy opened with the damage to U.S. credibility inflicted by the Laos crisis. "If these men I saw at your request were bankers," Johnson wrote, "I would know—without bothering to ask—that there would be no further extensions on my note."[79] Only after a discussion of the regional implications of the crisis, the potential need for U.S. troops, and the need for any help to be mutual, did Johnson add, "In large measure, the greatest danger Southeast Asia offers to nations like the United States is not the momentary threat of Communism itself, rather that danger stems from hunger, ignorance, poverty and disease."[80] He then immediately returned to discussing credibility in primarily international terms, arguing that the United States "must decide whether to help these countries to the best of our ability or throw in the towel in the area and pull back our defenses to San Francisco and a 'Fortress America' concept. More important, we would say to the world in this case that we don't live up to treaties and don't stand by our friends."[81]

There were other elements to Johnson's report. For example, a paper that may have been an annex or even a draft version of the report called for a "simultaneous, vigorous and integrated attack on the economic, social and other ills of the Vietnamese peoples." But there was little sense that such an effort was a prerequisite for securing Vietnam—in fact, Johnson argued only that Viet Minh "terrorism" was disrupting development.[82] In terms of Asia more broadly, his report to the House Foreign Affairs Committee went so far as to note that "such military strength as we can provide can be only a shield behind which free governments provide the economic and social progress that the masses of people are demanding passionately. Either these economic and social reforms are pushed or we shall find that our military men have built iron fortresses on foundations of quicksand."[83] Another report on the trip, attributed to Johnson but with no drafting information available, argued that in Vietnam, the "new aid commitment plunges us very deeply into the Vietnamese internal situation. The attitude of our mission people must begin immediately to reflect that depth." The United States "must attempt to strengthen the National Assembly and other democratic institutions in Viet Nam," in part to ensure continuity in case something happened to Diem.[84] In large part, however, Johnson was uncritical of Diem. In his farewell dinner speech in Saigon, Johnson compared Diem to George Washington, Andrew Jackson, Woodrow Wilson, and Franklin Roosevelt, and publicly, Johnson hailed Diem as another "Winston Churchill," thereby deepening the U.S. commitment to Diem, whom Johnson later called "the only boy we got out there."[85] In his statement to the House Foreign Affairs Committee, Johnson was clear: "This certainly is no time for nit-picking where Diem is concerned," he argued. "We either decide that we are going to support him and support him zealously or that we are going to let South Vietnam fall."[86] Just two years later, Kennedy would do far more than "nit-pick."

In terms of the other crises and interventions that occurred during his predecessors' tenures, Johnson was usually a staunch supporter of presidential action to stop what he perceived to be external aggression. For example, despite his wrangling with the administration over the legislation related to the Eisenhower Doctrine in 1957 (during which he secured some limitations on the aid provisions, among other moves), Johnson supported Eisenhower's intervention in Lebanon in 1958.[87] His view of the crisis was predictably focused on aggression. In a speech on the Senate floor on July 15, 1958, he declared that the United States would "make it clear to the aggressors that this country is determined to maintain freedom in this world, at whatever the cost." As the *New York Times* noted, Johnson "did not specify what 'aggressors' he was referring to."[88] And while Kennedy wrote a constituent that the Lebanese crisis was *not* "a clear case of outside aggression," Johnson diagnosed the crisis in external terms, writing that the United States had "not become involved in a country which is engaged in civil strife in the ordinary sense" because "all of the evidence seems to indicate strongly that external influences, as well as military assistance, have provoked the uprisings in Lebanon."[89]

But perhaps Johnson's most interesting statements—and omissions—came on the subject of guerrilla warfare and counterinsurgency. As Lawrence Freedman observes, "Johnson was less inclined to the political theory behind counterinsurgency strategy."[90] During his years as vice president, Johnson had exposure to the Kennedy administration's counterinsurgency program (with its links to modernization theory) but largely ignored it. Johnson attended several NSC meetings dealing with strategy, including the first postinaugural Vietnam meeting, at which the new counterinsurgency plan was discussed.[91] In his report to the House Foreign Affairs Committee following his 1961 trip to Asia, Johnson paid lip service to the special nature of guerrilla warfare, calling the Viet Cong onslaught a "new kind of assault which never involves direct attack but whose stock gambit is treachery by night."[92] In his reports to Kennedy and to the House, however, Johnson argued that the "most important thing is imaginative, creative, American management of our military aid program."[93]

While Johnson put forward Kennedy's proposals as a loyal lieutenant on the 1961 trip, his rare but forceful comments in the meetings on managing the ongoing Laos and Vietnam crises found him falling back on the framework of outside aggression. During the Laos crisis, he was a frequent, if mostly silent, participant in both NSC meetings and small group meetings with Kennedy. Johnson attended the March 9, 1961 meeting, discussed in chapter 4, in which Kennedy demanded to know what the political dimension of any military campaign in Laos would look like.[94] At the NSC meeting on May 1, 1961, around the peak of pressure from the military to intervene in Laos, Johnson spoke up when Kennedy asked for "current thinking" on whether or not the United States should intervene. Johnson "suggested that a more careful analysis be made of the impact of going into Laos. He suggested consideration be given to more immediate action if movement into the area were contemplated at a later date." At the end of the meeting, Johnson "suggested that the JCS, while considering involvement of U.S. forces, also evaluate the effects of [a] pull-out of forces with the possible creation of greater chances for war eventually."[95] The effects of pulling out, as well as domestic and congressional opinion, were at the forefront of Johnson's concerns. These concerns continued into 1963, when Johnson made handwritten notes on a memorandum detailing diplomatic and political efforts to boost noncommunist forces in Laos and to prevent the fall of neutralist forces in the Plain of Jars, a critical test of the Geneva Agreement on Laos. Next to these recommendations, Johnson wrote comments such as "ineffective," "Effect NIL," and "Wholly inadequate & ineffective. Plays directly into hands of Commie obstructionists."[96]

Thus Johnson's pre-presidential statements on strategy and policy investments reflect his emphasis on standing firm against conventional aggression and his tendency to separate military and international considerations from the domestic conditions within target states. Johnson's views of Kennedy's decision making on Vietnam, discussed below, are consistent with these general tendencies.

In sum, Johnson saw threats primarily in terms of outside aggression, with domestic concerns largely separate. He focused on the international dimension of alliances and the U.S. sphere of influence. Although he sympathized with the poor in the Third World, he viewed foreign aid not as an investment in local institutions but rather as a short-term way to sway the uncommitted. And he saw strategy in conventional terms, largely ignoring the issue of guerrilla warfare and preparedness for transformative strategies. Johnson would bring these views with him to the presidency.

Johnson as President: Strategy and Policy Investments

The unique circumstances of Kennedy's assassination meant that Johnson had less flexibility than most new presidents in making policy investments at the outset of his administration; indeed, he went to great lengths to emphasize continuity with Kennedy's policies at home and abroad.[97] A direct comparison with the policy investments of Kennedy or Eisenhower is therefore difficult. This section does not discuss budgets because in the early Johnson administration they largely reflected Kennedy's priorities. Nevertheless, Johnson's staffing decisions, strategy and defense posture, and institutional creation and change are useful to examine.

STAFFING DECISIONS

There was both continuity and change in personnel. Johnson deliberately tried to retain Kennedy personnel, yet as Freedman notes, there were subtle but critical shifts.[98] The top level remained largely intact: Rusk at State, McNamara at Defense, Bundy as national security adviser. There would be important changes below this group, however. Notably, midlevel officials who favored a politically oriented approach to Third World conflicts became increasingly peripheral.

STRATEGY, DEFENSE POSTURE, AND THE USE OF FORCE

Johnson did not officially alter Kennedy's strategy of "Flexible Response." But there were shifts in emphasis that would be magnified in Johnson's intervention choices. Johnson did not continue the top-down presidential pressure to build up counterinsurgency forces, for example. In February 1964, a National Security Action Memorandum (NSAM) dealing with counterinsurgency training programs superseded two related Kennedy NSAMs. It was worded as a presidential directive, but a memo from the NSC's Michael Forrestal—one of those who pushed for a politically oriented approach in Vietnam and supported Kennedy's efforts to expand counterinsurgency—makes clear that the impetus for the NSAM came from the bureaucracy and that Johnson may never have read it.[99]

Johnson also differed from Kennedy in the role he saw for foreign aid. Johnson counted among his favorite books economist Barbara Ward's *The Rich Nations and the Poor Nations* (published in 1962), which argued for helping the world's "havenots."[100] Nonetheless, Robert Packenham notes that despite much continuity with Kennedy's aid program, Johnson "never spent a large share of his political capital for development-oriented aid" and demanded something in return for it, usually "support for his anti-Communist objectives."[101] Johnson "would hope for economic development," but whereas Kennedy had employed a mixture of what Packenham calls the "economic approach," the "Cold War approach," and the "explicit democratic approach" to political development, Johnson prioritized the Cold War approach "over any other."[102] Kaufman goes further, calling "Johnson's approach to economic development . . . a throwback to the early years of the Eisenhower administration" and the "trade not aid" policy.[103] For

Johnson, the Cold War came first and separately, whereas for Kennedy, economic and political development had been a way to fight the Cold War itself.

INSTITUTIONAL CREATION AND CHANGE

Johnson was an institution builder at home, but he was far less active in building institutions for foreign and security policy, and he allowed some of Kennedy's policy investments to lapse. The Special Group (CI) continued to exist at first, but as CIA director John McCone noted in a meeting with Rusk in March 1965, "its position had eroded away," and McCone argued vigorously that it should be "revitalized."[104] In March 1966, after a review of U.S. counterinsurgency activities led by Maxwell Taylor, the Special Group was abolished and its functions subsumed into a new State Department–based group with much wider-ranging responsibilities, including general foreign policy and intelligence matters.[105] Bundy's deputy, Robert Komer, wrote Bundy to say he was not impressed with Taylor's report and that "putting this new machinery in State will not result in greater attention to the problem, but probably less."[106] The timing of this debate is somewhat odd given that at nearly the same time, as discussed in more detail below, the White House was searching for a way to give civil projects in Vietnam special priority. Just a few weeks and two NSAMs after the abolition of the Special Group (CI), Komer himself was appointed to coordinate "peaceful construction" in Vietnam, perpetuating the separation of military and civil action in the war.[107]

But perhaps Johnson's most controversial moves with respect to a Kennedy institution came with the Alliance for Progress. Historians continue to debate whether Johnson's policy toward Latin America and the Alliance was merely a continuation of trends already under way before Kennedy's death or a sharp break with the Kennedy philosophy. On the one hand, by 1963 Kennedy himself recognized the significant problems and contradictions plaguing the Alliance.[108] In October 1963 Kennedy approved a statement by Assistant Secretary of State Edwin Martin lamenting that democracy might be unattainable in certain Latin American countries and recognizing the important role of the military in Latin American society.[109] Kennedy went so far as to proclaim the Kennedy Doctrine, stating that the United States would not tolerate another communist regime in the region. Johnson's policies in Latin America, in this view, should be seen as an extension of Kennedy's.[110] On the other hand, several scholars see Johnson's moves as a departure from the principles underpinning the Alliance.[111]

The change in approach to the Alliance was significant. Although Johnson pledged support for the Alliance and continued to press for Alliance-related funds, he also moved quickly to change its underlying philosophy. He appointed Thomas C. Mann, who had "little enthusiasm" for the Alliance, to serve simultaneously as assistant secretary for inter-American affairs, special assistant to the president, and coordinator of the Alliance.[112] Stephen Rabe asserts that Kennedy "would not have named Thomas Mann his 'Mr. Latin America.'"[113] In a familiar formulation, Johnson remarked to a group of reporters, "I know these Latin Americans. . . . They'll come right into your yard and take it over if you let them. And the next day they'll be right up on your porch. . . . But if you say to 'em right at the start, 'hold on, just wait a minute,' they'll know they're dealing with somebody who'll stand up. And after that you can get along fine."[114]

The Mann—and Johnson—approach to the Alliance differed significantly from that of Kennedy. Gone was the idea of gradual domestic transformation to stave off a communist takeover. Instead, the Alliance was to emphasize the role of private investment, cooperation with the U.S. business community, and the pursuit of stability.[115] During a March 1964 conference in Washington, this shift would become awkwardly public when Mann's private comments to a group of U.S. diplomats in Latin America appeared in the *New York Times*. According to the *Times*, Mann said that the United States would no longer distinguish between "good guys or bad guys," and he stressed four main purposes for U.S. policy in Latin America: fostering economic growth, protecting U.S. investments, nonintervention in Latin American internal affairs, and opposing communism.[116] The elements of the speech quickly became known as the Mann Doctrine. While Kennedy recognized the need for pragmatism and even occasional Cold War cynicism in the hemisphere, the Mann Doctrine illustrated that the two presidents held different preference orderings. As Joseph Tulchin argues, democracy did not disappear from the U.S. agenda under Johnson, but it was a lower-priority goal.[117] Johnson favored internationally successful outcomes—stable, anticommunist regimes.

The precise extent to which Johnson departed from Kennedy's approach is still a matter of debate. Furthermore, Johnson and Mann were arguably far more realistic in their assessment of what the Alliance could and could not accomplish. But given how much Kennedy had emphasized reform in Latin America and the congruence between Johnson's policy and his earlier beliefs, it seems that the shift in emphasis in the Alliance's goals and strategies can be attributed at least partly to presidential leadership.

Summarizing Johnson's policy investments (adjusting for the circumstances surrounding the transition), we can see elements of continuity and change. While many Kennedy advisers stayed on after the assassination, Johnson made important shifts. Johnson emphasized countering threats and combating aggression. He placed much less weight on capabilities to address threats from within other states, lessening the pressure on the military and civilian bureaucracy to build up counterinsurgency forces, for example. He shifted the goals of Kennedy programs such as the Alliance for Progress so that they prioritized stability and internationally favorable outcomes. At the same time, however, he inherited the commitments Kennedy made and pledged that America would honor those commitments.

Intervention Choices in Latin America: Panama

Johnson may not have enjoyed dealing with foreign policy as much as domestic affairs, but the international environment did not provide him the luxury of avoiding engagement. Johnson inherited the ongoing crisis in Vietnam and faced several new crises, including one in Panama just weeks after Kennedy's assassination. Johnson's choices during these crises reflected his long-standing beliefs. The theory posits that all leaders are concerned with international imperatives such as the need to demonstrate credibility, but differ on the extent to which they connect these issues to the domestic institutions of other states. Johnson's consideration of the costs and benefits of intervention was usually confined to international factors such as the effect on U.S. credibility or potential U.S. gains in the long-term struggle with the Soviet Union. He saw far fewer potential security benefits from successfully transforming other states' domestic institutions. Though the blame for the shortfall in transformative capabilities by no means rests with Johnson alone, his inattention to building such capabilities left him at a deficit when he tried to emphasize nonmilitary aspects of strategy, for example late in the Vietnam escalation. Thus Johnson's beliefs informed his intervention decisions and left their mark on the interventions themselves.

In January 1964, Johnson faced a crisis in Panama, where long-simmering hostility over the treaty governing the Panama Canal and the U.S.-controlled Canal Zone flared. The crisis never quite developed into a full-blown decision over whether to deploy troops, but Johnson's handling of it is nonetheless illuminating as a case of nonintervention. Johnson made clear throughout the crisis that his overriding concern was U.S. credibility and the appearance of standing firm. Despite some prodding, he expressed little interest in strengthening Panama's domestic institutions or addressing the long-standing political and economic tensions between Panamanians and Americans living in the Canal Zone.

Several historians have argued that Johnson handled the episode in nontransformative terms that are consistent with his actions in other Third World crises. For example, Michael Latham, who traces the roots of the crisis to the U.S. imperial legacy in Panama and the pattern of political and economic inequality stemming from the Zone arrangement, concludes that Johnson saw the crisis as a "symbolic struggle" that challenged American credibility, but he did not understand "the roots of Panama's economic or political structure" and "never recognized the deeper, historical sources of the conflict."[118] Johnson's strategy for demonstrating credibility did not include addressing the underlying problems that triggered the crisis in the first place. Furthermore, according to Mark Lawrence, in the end Johnson compromised in Panama only because of a "peculiar set of circumstances," namely, that he could manage the political risks, that conceding some rights in the Canal Zone might actually strengthen the ruling oligarchy in Panama, and that the bureaucracy would not stand in the way of concessions. Thus Johnson's willingness to compromise was "the exception that proves the rule," since his actions were "rooted in the same caution and conservatism that characterized Johnson era policymaking toward the third world more generally."[119]

Kennedy had negotiated an agreement with Panamanian president Roberto Chiari over how U.S. and Panamanian flags would be flown in the Canal Zone, a sensitive issue given resentment over the continued U.S. presence in the area. But on January 7, 1964, American students raised the U.S. flag outside a high school in the Zone, in violation of the agreement, leading to rioting that killed four U.S. soldiers and twenty-one Panamanians.[120] Johnson and his aides quickly assumed that although the provocation had come from the United States, communists had started the riots.[121] Chiari called for an end to the violence but also suspended diplomatic relations with the United States, insisting on "a complete revision of all treaties which affect Panama-U.S. relations."[122]

In the ensuing weeks, Johnson and his advisers worked to achieve some sort of diplomatic agreement. But negotiations stalled when the two sides haggled over the wording of a communiqué: the United States asserted that the parties "have agreed to begin discussions" on matters relating to U.S.-Panamanian relations while Chiari insisted that the text meant there would be negotiations rather than simply "discussions."[123] Johnson balked at any suggestion that he was committing to a renegotiation of the treaty, and the deal collapsed. The crisis dragged on for the next few months, and Johnson ordered contingency plans for U.S. military intervention in Panama if the Chiari government came under threat from, or was overthrown by, communists. The request for plans called for "minimum force" to "establish sufficient control . . . to permit a non-Communist government to exercise power," with "the earliest possible withdrawal of U.S. forces."[124] Finally, after the parties had exchanged draft after draft and haggled over virtually every word, the United States and Panama reached an agreement on April 3. The United States agreed only to "discussions," a formula that Chiari, under pressure to settle the crisis, accepted. In December 1964, Johnson announced that he was prepared to negotiate a new treaty.

Two features characterized the way Johnson managed the crisis. First, he consistently focused on the international aspects of issues that affected U.S. interests, paying much less attention to domestic Panamanian affairs and treating them as separate from resolving the crisis itself. While he was willing to acknowledge the necessity of discussing the underlying treaty issues, he repeatedly refused to accept draft language that included any hint of "negotiations" and consistently invoked the need to stand firm with the Panamanians. On the treaty revision, Johnson told his Senate mentor Richard Russell in a telephone conversation, "It seems to me that we're kinda givin' in there and respondin' at the point of a pistol."[125] Johnson then called Bundy and said he would instruct Mann that "under appropriate circumstances, we'll be very happy to discuss any trouble-some problems with them, but we're not goin' to do it at the point of a gun. We've got the rest of the world to live with."[126] While expressing some sympathy for Zone issues, he did not connect them to the crisis itself. Johnson saw the riots as a Panamanian attempt to renegotiate the canal treaty rather than viewing all the issues as intertwined. In a conversation with Mann and Ralph Dungan of the NSC on January 14, in one of his few references to the underlying social and economic disparities between Panamanians and American citizens in the Zone, Johnson said, "I want to be fair and want to be reasonable and want to be just to these people, and if we've got problems with wage scales or arrogant military people or Zonites that cause these troubles, or any improvement or changes we can make, we're anxious to do it—wage scales, or whatever it is. But if they think that all they gotta do is to burn a USIS and shoot four or five soldiers and then we come runnin' in and—hat in hand—well, that's a different proposition."[127] At several points during the ensuing months, Johnson haggled with aides over the wording of draft language. In March 1964 he called Mann and objected to the words "negotiations," "Panama Canal," and "international" in the latest draft, adding, "I want to resist somebody somewhere, some time."[128]

As Latham notes, Johnson's diagnosis of the problem centered on the idea that "the violence remained Chiari's sole creation and personal bargaining tool" rather than an expression of institutional problems. The "dynamics of Panamanian politics . . . largely were lost on a Johnson administration unfamiliar with the local context."[129] Thus while Johnson expressed some willingness to talk about "issues" within Panama, his diagnosis of the problem meant that standing firm internationally was paramount, with discussion of domestic issues at best a secondary concern to be dealt with later and not a principal means of solving the crisis. Indeed, after the crisis had passed, Johnson wondered in a telephone conversation with Mann whether "we could make some adjustment in wages and show a little social consciousness" to help the postcrisis talks along.[130] Yet others urged Johnson to connect the crisis to domestic conditions within Panama even as it was still unfolding. On January 31, Senate Majority Leader Mike Mansfield wrote Johnson that the United States had only one "fundamental national interest to protect": the canal. But he also asserted that the "pressure for social change is just short of violent revolution in Panama and in much of the rest of Latin America. The pressure comes primarily from the inside, from the decay and antiquation of the social structures of various Latin American countries. . . . We may have something constructive to contribute to the form and pace·of the change if we play our cards carefully and wisely."[131]

But though he was quick to react to any hint of communist encroachment, Johnson saw the crisis almost solely in terms of credibility and did not pay much attention to the domestic dynamics within Panama, apart from a general willingness to talk about issues and a few references to wage disparities. Indeed, Johnson used an Alliance for Progress anniversary event to reiterate his willingness to discuss issues with Panama but with no commitment to renegotiating the treaty.[132] If he could achieve his international (and electoral) goals, Johnson saw little additional benefit to peering beneath the surface of Panama's domestic problems, though an internally focused leader might have seen these problems as a potential threat to U.S. interests such as the canal.

A second feature of the Panama crisis was Johnson's repeated overruling of aides. At the end of February, Johnson told Russell that he was under tremendous pressure from his top advisers—including Rusk, McNamara, and Bundy—to accept a new draft agreement but "overrode all of them" and stuck to the same position he had held from the beginning.[133] In March, Mann brought another agreement to Johnson, who again rejected it, telling Russell on March 9 that he told Mann, "No I won't sign that; I just won't do it," despite the urging of Rusk, McNamara, and Bundy.[134] A few days later, Johnson lost patience with Mann. Bundy told Johnson that the Organization of American States (OAS) had proposed yet another draft, and Mann was "very eager" to get Johnson's approval. Declining to accept the draft, Johnson said, "Tom [Mann] capitulates easier than I thought. He was the strongest guy you ever saw when he started."[135] Later in March, Johnson took the initiative himself, proposing to Rusk that he make a presidential statement emphasizing the positive aspects of U.S.-Panamanian relations and his willingness to talk about—but not "negotiate" over—the issues between the two countries.[136] The statement helped break the deadlock, and the crisis was resolved in early April. Though Johnson was still very early in his presidency, he was willing to stand up to his advisers and take control of the crisis.

Panama never reached the urgency of other crises Johnson faced—military intervention was on the table only briefly—and throughout the crisis, Johnson showed a willingness to compromise. And as Dallek notes, the crisis "would probably have frustrated Kennedy as well."[137] But the episode is significant because it illustrates many of the principles Johnson employed in other conflicts: an external focus and a willingness to become personally involved and to overrule his own advisers. As Lawrence notes, American domestic politics (particularly pressure from the right to stand firm) and Johnson's need to build a reputation for toughness also played important roles.[138] The unique circumstances of the case allowed Johnson to choose compromise, once he was satisfied he had made his firm stance known. The outcome would not be as favorable in his next Latin American test.

Intervention Choices in Latin America: The Dominican Republic

In April 1965, with the Vietnam escalation already effectively in progress, Johnson faced a crisis in the Dominican Republic that would culminate in a U.S. military intervention involving 24,000 troops and a year-long occupation.[139] The democratically elected regime of Juan Bosch had been overthrown in a military coup in September 1963. On April 24, 1965, "constitutionalist" rebels, including some in the army, staged a countercoup that overthrew the military-backed regime of Donald Reid Cabral. The countercoup quickly evolved into a civil war between the constitutionalist rebels and "loyalists," who backed the military regime. Although hoping to avoid direct military involvement, the Johnson administration almost immediately began to worry about "another Cuba." On April 28, at the embassy's request, Johnson ordered more than four hundred Marines to land in Santo Domingo to evacuate U.S. citizens. The next day, the embassy requested full-scale military intervention. Over the next few days, Johnson authorized steady increases in the number of U.S. troops deployed in support of the junta, stabilizing Santo Domingo. After tense negotiations over several months, the crisis finally concluded with the installation of a provisional government and, ultimately, elections that returned Joaquín Balaguer, the former puppet president under Rafael Trujillo, to power. Despite the electoral outcome and an American military presence that lasted more than a year, however, the intervention was nontransformative, using the smallest footprint possible to replace one acceptably anticommunist, military-backed government with another.[140] In the end, the intervention in 1965 had more in common with Eisenhower's intervention in Lebanon than with Kennedy's actions in Latin America or Southeast Asia.[141]

Some commentators argue that Johnson's options in the crisis were limited.[142] But Johnson's handling of the crisis was consistent with his own causal beliefs. Like both Eisenhower and Kennedy, Johnson worried about communist encroachment in Latin America and maintaining U.S. credibility. But unlike Kennedy, Johnson did not connect the nature of the crisis to the Dominican Republic's institutions to any significant degree. Johnson also pushed beyond what even his own advisers recommended and was clearly the man in charge: George Ball remembers that Johnson "assumed the direction of day-to-day policy and became, in effect, the Dominican desk officer."[143]

As discussed in chapter 4, Kennedy also had confronted instability and change in the Dominican Republic. After the assassination of longtime dictator Rafael Trujillo, Kennedy used U.S. power to try to facilitate a transition to a more democratic regime. Although we lack evidence as to what Kennedy might have done in the 1965 crisis, his policy toward the Dominican Republic—a policy no less influenced by fears of "another Cuba"—involved a wider range of options than Johnson considered and, at least for a time, prioritized a domestically successful outcome. When Juan Bosch was elected president in 1962, Kennedy sent Vice President Johnson to Santo Domingo for the inauguration, to express the administration's support and to tell Bosch that Johnson and Kennedy were "keenly interested in the success of your campaign to build democratic institutions, to foster economic stability and prosperity and to secure social justice for the Dominican people."[144]

When Bosch was overthrown, the United States protested but did little else, at a time when Kennedy was increasingly frustrated with the Alliance for Progress. Indeed, the Kennedy administration was moving toward recognizing the new Dominican regime, a step Johnson took shortly after taking office.[145] Thus many observers see Johnson's handling of the 1965 Dominican Republic crisis as a continuation of Kennedy's policy toward Santo Domingo. Notably, Kennedy's support for internal security and counterinsurgency efforts within Latin American countries bolstered local armies, prompting historian Piero Gleijeses to lay a large share of the blame for the events of 1965 at Kennedy's door.[146]

But within his decidedly anticommunist framework, Kennedy made clear that his first preference was for reform and democracy, not simply for the sake of idealism but also because he saw danger in *both* a communist takeover in Santo Domingo *and* a return to a repressive Trujillo-type dictatorship, which he feared would lead to a communist revolt anyway. In the wake of Trujillo's assassination, Kennedy argued that the crucial element was "the emergence of . . . a liberal figure who can command popular support as against the military and who will carry out social and economic reform. . . . The great danger in the next six months is a take-over by the army, which could lead straight to Castro."[147] In October 1963, a cable sent to the embassy in Santo Domingo transmitting guidance on U.S. objectives referred to controlling "communist and Trujillo threats."[148] Kennedy thus saw danger from the left and from the right. Within the limits of feasibility and the overriding concern to prevent "another Cuba," he did not want just any anticommunist government—the form that anticommunism took mattered.

When Johnson confronted a sudden countercoup aiming to restore the exiled Bosch to power in April 1965, he began from a very different starting point that placed far less emphasis on Dominican institutions. Johnson had paid less attention to Latin America generally. Nonetheless, the new U.S. ambassador to the Dominican Republic, W. Tapley Bennett, cabled shortly after his arrival in Santo Domingo in May 1964 that "economic misery" was a major problem and that he recommended "getting under way with [a] full-scale Alliance for Progress program."[149] Despite Bennett's warning, Washington was caught largely by surprise when military officers sympathetic to Bosch moved against the Reid regime on April 24, 1965.

On the morning of April 26, Johnson spoke by phone with Mann. He immediately made clear his opposition to Bosch's return and his instinct to stabilize the country. "We are going to have to really set up that government down there, run it and stabilize it some way or another," Johnson told Mann. "This Bosch is no good. I was down there."[150] The following day, as it became clearer that the rebels would not be easily defeated, the State Department cabled the embassy in Santo Domingo that the "primary objectives are restoration of law and order, prevention of possible Communist takeover, and protection of American lives." The embassy staff was instructed to try to contact both sides and work toward the establishment of a military junta to reestablish law and order.[151]

But while the administration hoped to avoid overt intervention, Johnson made it clear, as he told Mann on April 28, that he "[didn't] want the rebels to win."[152] Shortly thereafter, Bennett cabled to say the situation had deteriorated further and that a newly declared loyalist junta reported "that without help they would 'have to quit.'" Switching to the statement that "American lives are in danger," he recommended an "immediate landing."[153] Johnson authorized more than four hundred Marines from ships offshore to land and evacuate American citizens. The hope, as expressed by Mann, was that the mere presence of U.S. troops would "strengthen the will" of the loyalist forces and perhaps lead to a negotiated settlement.[154] Later that evening, Bennett cabled again with more bad news. Invoking the specter of "another Cuba," he recommended that "serious thought be given in Washington to armed intervention which would go beyond the mere protection of Americans and seek to establish order in this strife-ridden country."[155]

In the next few days, Johnson would home in on the alleged communist dimension of the conflict, working to ensure a loyalist victory. He was concerned above all that the island not go communist, but beyond that, he was not particularly interested in the details of how the domestic situation in the Dominican Republic evolved. The result was a decision to deploy troops without a clear plan for how to use them. Johnson also pushed for more action than his advisers recommended. On the morning of April 29, Johnson spoke to Bundy, telling him, "We want to be very, very careful not to sit here and let them augment their forces. . . . I sure don't want to wake up a few hours later and say we're awaiting developments and find out Castro's in charge." Johnson still hoped to avoid taking sides overtly, but he worried there was not enough force on the ground. "Why did [Bennett] just want 400?" he asked. "It looks like to me that that's the only weakness thing."[156] Finally, late that night, Rusk cabled Bennett that Washington was considering putting American troops between the two sides, to help the junta forces win. "This is consistent with our primary purpose," wrote Rusk, "which is to protect American lives, and with our general policy of opposing the spread of communist controlled governments in this hemisphere."[157] Johnson approved the landing of thousands more Marines, who began to arrive overnight on April 29–30. Within ten days, there would be almost 23,000 American troops in the Dominican Republic.

To be sure, Johnson preferred a junta victory and was willing to employ military force to achieve it. But his strategy did not involve significant institutional interference; rather, the landing aimed to maintain the status quo. As Abraham Lowenthal and Peter Felten point out and the documentary record makes clear, despite the landing of thousands of troops, Johnson did not yet have a clear idea of what the troops would do on the ground beyond staving off a communist takeover.[158] On April 30, Johnson met with his senior advisers and clarified his focus on the international dimension of the crisis and his inattention to Dominican domestic issues. According to notes recorded by White House aide Jack Valenti, Johnson told the group: "I am not willing to let this island go to Castro. OAS is a phantom—they are taking a siesta while this is on fire. How can we send troops 10,000 miles away and let Castro take over right under our nose. Let's just analyze—we have resisted Communists all over the world: Vietnam, Lebanon, and Greece. What are we doing under our doorstep. We know the rebel leaders are Communist, and we are sitting here waiting on OAS. We know Castro will hate us. We got rid of the dictator and we will now get a real dictator." Rusk pressed Johnson to work through the OAS, but Johnson instead told McNamara, "Why don't you first find out what we need to take that island. Rusk, why don't you determine what it takes to make this take on the right color." Johnson was also out in front of his advisers, as the following discussion makes clear:

> BUNDY: We have done a great deal. We are talking about a division going in and we couldn't do that several days ago.
> LBJ: I think enough leaders are there to make it Castro. . . . I am ashamed of the little we have done.

BALL: But we have done considerable; we have put men ashore without real angry response.

LBJ: I want McNamara to get ready so that Castro cannot take over.

McNamara himself urged that real evidence of a communist takeover be shown and that the United States "must have some government to get behind." Johnson concluded, "I want us to feverishly try to cloak this with legitimacy. We cannot stand with our hand in our pocket and let Castro win. Military get ducks in a row. Diplomats see if we can do anything to get observers in here or troops from other Latin American countries. We are willing to do whatever is necessary to put the pistols down. We will have one of 3 dictators: 1) U.S., 2) Moderate dictator, 3) Castro dictator."[159] Johnson had made his own statement of preferences: any dictator would do as long as it was not Castro. He expressed none of Kennedy's concern that a dictator might also lead to communism.

Meanwhile, on the ground in Santo Domingo, there remained the question of how to deploy the troops. Initial hopes that the mere presence of the troops would stiffen the junta and cause the constitutionalists to collapse proved unfounded. After the two sides agreed to a cease-fire on April 30, the United States still provided support to the junta while maintaining a veneer of impartiality.[160] The JCS ordered Lieutenant General Bruce Palmer Jr. to take command of U.S. ground forces in the Dominican Republic. "Your announced mission is to save US lives," JCS Chairman Earle Wheeler's orders to Palmer read. "Your unannounced mission is to prevent the Dominican Republic from going Communist. The President has stated that he will not allow another Cuba—you are to take all necessary measures to accomplish this mission. You will be given sufficient forces to do the job."[161]

But the Johnson administration sought to ensure a loyalist victory using the smallest footprint possible. When he arrived in Santo Domingo, Palmer found U.S. forces deployed on different sides of the city with no link between them; U.S. military officers wanted to join up the troops and even sought authorization to move into the rebel areas to quash the rebellion.[162] In a cable to the embassy drafted by Mann on April 30, Washington expressed alarm that the junta might think U.S. intentions were to attack and defeat the rebels directly, but added that U.S. "tactics will be designed to support Junta in the achievement of this objective."[163] At a May 2 meeting of a newly formed Dominican Task Force, Johnson's advisers, including McNamara, Bundy, and Mann, discussed three possible options for deploying U.S. forces to ensure a constitutionalist defeat with minimal involvement. The group chose the option to cordon off the rebels—but not to the tightest extent possible, arguing that their chosen option was "quick, militarily the soundest, and, in fact, could be accomplished by less than a division." The group also discussed political solutions, including distancing the United States from the increasingly unpopular junta and possible names to lead a new government. But there was little discussion of doing anything more in terms of domestic Dominican institutions, apart from a relief effort, which would "make it clear that our soldiers do other things besides fire weapons at Dominicans."[164]

In the next few days, the administration's attention shifted to the political situation, where Johnson again focused on the communist angle—amid the increasing skepticism and frustration of his advisers—to the exclusion of other internal considerations. Rival governments formed on both sides, and the White House covertly aided the junta-led Government of National Reconstruction (GNR). But the only aspect of the potential new government that captured Johnson's attention was the participation (or even the hint of participation) of alleged communists, even as his closest aides expressed increasing doubts about the degree of communist infiltration. In a tense telephone conversation with McNamara on May 12, Johnson asked if the military had contingency plans in place for any possible scenario. He felt that "the time is going to come before very long when we have to kind of make up our choice to either let Castro have it, or take it." Telling Johnson that the United States had to get a political solution, McNamara said that waiting a few days would not reduce U.S. military capabilities. Johnson disagreed: "I believe everyday you lose it. . . . I think they get a good deal stronger. . . . Do we know they aren't shipping them stuff?" McNamara insisted that the military balance was not changing and that a political solution was necessary. "Well," said Johnson, "if they are controlled by the Castroites, they are not going to give it to you." Finally, McNamara grew impatient, retorting, "I don't think they are. . . . I just don't believe the story that Bosch and [rebel leader Francisco] Caamaño are controlled by the Castroites."[165] Johnson was so focused on Castro and U.S. strength that he brushed past the political reality on the ground.

From here the crisis proceeded along both military and political fronts. On May 13, the GNR began an offensive against the constitutionalists. As Felten states bluntly, "Washington was not neutral. . . . The Johnson administration continued to use armed force to destroy the rebellion."[166] On the political front, however, Johnson expressed willingness to negotiate with Bosch through a back channel. In late May, the United States very nearly accepted a deal to allow Bosch's preferred man for the presidency, Antonio Guzmán, to lead the new government. In one of the back-channel conversations, Johnson referred to the need to "deal with" both communists and "Trujilloistas," a rare reference to potential problems with the Dominican right.[167]

But his need to be tough on communists, and to be seen doing it, ultimately led Johnson to reject the "Guzmán formula" and to focus more closely on the participation of alleged communists in the new government than any other aspect of the settlement. The sticking point was the U.S. demand that Caamaño and the rebels leave the country. Johnson's domestic political concern with appearing tough on communists (particularly to right-wing Republicans) was evident in a telephone call with his advisers on May 18. Johnson asked, "Now, we're not getting into any position where the people can truthfully or effectively say that we sold out and turned it over to the Commies? . . . What can we say to the right-wingers, up to the end that we have insured against their running the government?"[168] The internal Dominican situation was an afterthought. As the two sides reached an impasse on the question of the rebels leaving the country, Johnson cabled the embassy to say that the United States "will insist upon an anti-Communist government in [the] Dominican Republic and will take all necessary measures to secure this objective."[169]

As Felten points out, the White House was more interested in the negotiations on the communists than in the "institutional act" that would establish basic law under the provisional government.[170] Johnson was concerned about the Dominican government, but only in the negative sense that he wanted to block even the appearance of a communist regime. Finally, in August 1965, after several more months of negotiations, Johnson approved Héctor García Godoy, who had been a diplomat in both the Trujillo and Bosch governments and had the backing of moderates on both sides, as provisional president. OAS ambassador Ellsworth Bunker vouched for García Godoy and said he planned to send the communists "to a rocky island off the coast."[171] In June 1966, Balaguer defeated Bosch in national elections. Johnson ordered the CIA to ensure that Balaguer would win. The election was decisive and observers found it to be fair.[172]

Thus Johnson used massive military force to forestall "another Cuba," despite conflicting evidence from his advisers as to whether there actually was a communist threat to the island. Given the scant evidence and his advisers' skepticism, Johnson may simply have wanted to avoid the *perception* of another Cuba, as his concerns about hard-liners in the United States illustrate. The public backed the intervention, although important fissures emerged, especially when Senator J. William Fulbright, a longtime Johnson ally, openly criticized Johnson's handling of the crisis, calling for noncommunist reform in Latin America and accusing Johnson of misrepresenting the facts.[173]

Overall, the striking element in Johnson's decision making was his overwhelming focus on keeping communists, real or imagined, out of the Dominican Republic, to the exclusion of most other domestic Dominican concerns. As Tulchin notes, "Once it became clear that Bosch was not going to return to power, Johnson lost interest in the Dominican Republic and instructed his foreign policy people to get the OAS involved as a cover for the U.S. intervention and to get

U.S. troops out as fast as they could."[174] Johnson simply wanted an anticommunist to stabilize the situation and seemed far less interested in exactly who would fulfill that role and what might happen after a settlement was reached. There is little evidence that Johnson saw a dual threat from the left and the right. Furthermore, military and domestic political issues were, as usual, largely separate for Johnson, in the sense that he ordered troops to land without a clear idea of exactly what he would do with them or what the final political goal might be, beyond a noncommunist government like the military-backed regime that had ruled before the outbreak of the crisis.

Of course, the intervention was political in the sense that it opposed the constitutionalists, and certainly its *effect* was a massive intrusion into Dominican internal affairs. In the end, however, the United States effectively reinstalled a military-backed regime without significant intended institutional change. Furthermore, there was no clear link between domestic institutional aims and military action, and little evidence that the intervention strategy was deliberately transformative. U.S. troops stayed on the island for months, first alone and then as part of a new Inter-American Peace Force, and engaged in some civic action programs and "peacekeeping" activities designed to win hearts and minds.[175] But beyond humanitarian relief and fixing power, water, and garbage services, the military action was aimed mainly at keeping order until a political settlement took hold.

Many commentators on the Dominican Republic intervention argue that the episode represented a continuation of, rather than a break from, Kennedy's policies, or that the intervention was the logical outgrowth of Kennedy's approach.[176] As discussed above, there was indeed some continuity between the two administrations' policies in Latin America. Johnson continued Kennedy's obsession with preventing a second Cuba. In explaining his actions to the American people on May 2, 1965, Johnson even invoked the Kennedy Doctrine as a justification for a U.S. policy to prevent "another Communist government in the Western Hemisphere."[177]

Where Johnson differed from his predecessor was in the far smaller degree to which he perceived the internal structure of the Dominican Republic to be a source of threat in itself. Kennedy had seen danger both from communists and from the dictatorial and repressive status quo, and had at least initially aimed at reforming the structure of the Dominican state. Johnson worried almost exclusively about communists; reform was not a precondition for a successful outcome. Kennedy's late, pragmatic shift in policy notwithstanding, Johnson's actions constituted a significant change both in threat perception and in the nature of the U.S. response. Ironically, some observers deem the Dominican intervention a success, in the sense that it achieved Johnson's goals at a relatively low cost in

American lives and money.[178] In this sense, Johnson may have been more realistic than Kennedy. An externally focused threat perception, combined with pressure to look tough, shaped how Johnson considered the benefits of intervening and the costs of staying out and led him to choose a nontransformative intervention strategy.

Intervention Choices in Southeast Asia: Vietnam

No discussion of Johnson's intervention decisions would be complete without considering his escalation of the intervention in Vietnam. It is impossible to describe the escalation decisions in full detail here.[179] Comparing Johnson's actions in Vietnam with those of Eisenhower and Kennedy is perhaps unfair. Eisenhower dealt principally with the problem of the French defeat and withdrawal, under the arguably different circumstance of deciding whether to intervene on the side of a colonial power. Full-scale formation of the insurgency occurred toward the end of his presidency. Kennedy struggled with the increasingly difficult problem of how to manage Diem, whose government had little popular support and undermined its own attempts to defeat the insurgency. Diem's death left Johnson with a politically unstable and volatile South Vietnam. Historians continue to debate the differences—if any—between the Kennedy and Johnson approaches, as well as whether Johnson was a prisoner of inherited circumstance or instead had considerable freedom to maneuver, ultimately rendering Vietnam a war of choice.[180] Fredrik Logevall concludes that Johnson himself was the most important factor in "choosing war."[181] As Dallek, biographer of both Kennedy and Johnson, summarizes, Johnson was a "different man facing different circumstances" and "charted his own course."[182]

As discussed in chapter 1, Johnson's escalation in Vietnam is a difficult case for the theory. Not only did all U.S. presidents who dealt with Vietnam care, at some level, about the nature of its government, but Johnson also felt pressure to continue Kennedy's commitment to an ongoing conflict in which the United States was already involved. Given that Vietnam is a difficult case for the theory, and that the theory identifies only ideal types, I therefore make a limited claim here. I argue that Kennedy and Johnson viewed the conflict in Vietnam through different prisms that reflected their causal beliefs, and that these different approaches left a discernible imprint on their choices.

Recalling the theory's predictions for a case like Vietnam, we would expect an internally focused leader to identify Vietnam's domestic institutions as an important source of vulnerability to a communist takeover—either because the government might fall from within or because fragile or corrupt institutions would weaken the country's ability to stave off a military attack—and thus aim to shore up or build those institutions as a means to prevent the loss of the country. In contrast, an externally focused leader would be expected to focus less attention on domestic institutions, accepting any noncommunist government and perhaps concentrating more on the international or outside sources of vulnerability (such as the risk of aggression). Although both leader types worry about maintaining credibility, internally focused leaders are more likely to associate a successful demonstration of credibility with a favorable domestic outcome that would allow a victory to last, whereas externally focused leaders are less concerned about exactly where and how they make a stand as long as they do so. For Kennedy, helping South Vietnam resist communism meant countering the insurgency in such a way as to help reform South Vietnam's domestic institutions because he saw the political and military dimensions as intertwined. For Johnson, the emphasis was on the threat of outside aggression from the North and the need to stand firm. Though Johnson made some effort to bolster South Vietnam internally, he paid generally less attention to the domestic dimension of the crisis within South Vietnam than to the international dimension.

This focus on the international dimension of the conflict led Johnson to choose what can be considered a nontransformative strategy. Although he struggled with the instability in South Vietnam in the wake of the Diem coup, he did not connect the domestic aspects of the war to the international and military dimensions to the same degree as Kennedy. Furthermore, Johnson saw the conflict in terms of aggression from North Vietnam. He focused on fighting conventionally, aiming only to deny the North a victory, and did not see extra benefits from successfully transforming the South. Though I address the shift in U.S. policy toward an increased emphasis on pacification operations as the war dragged on, the argument applies most clearly to Johnson's early decisions and choice of strategy.

I discuss how other factors influenced the Vietnam decisions at the end of the chapter, but one alternative explanation deserves mention here. The structural/material conditions hypothesis would expect different leaders facing an ongoing conflict to make similar calculations depending on available capabilities and the situation on the ground. Thus a simple explanation for Johnson's choice of a conventional, nontransformative strategy is that by governing later in time, he confronted different circumstances (another reason why Vietnam is a difficult case to explore). In this view, Kennedy had the luxury of trying a transformative counterinsurgency strategy because the situation in South Vietnam was not as bad as it would become during Johnson's tenure. By the time Johnson considered escalation, he had only one possible strategy: a nontransformative, conventional war.[183]

The theory developed in this book does not predict that leaders ignore the logic of the situation (or the views of other domestic actors); rather, it argues that these factors are not sufficient to explain the choice of strategy. Both Kennedy and Johnson confronted proposals from within their administrations to try alternatives to their favored strategy: Kennedy faced repeated calls for a conventional, nontransformative deployment whereas several Johnson administration officials pushed for a renewed emphasis on a transformative form of counterinsurgency even well after Kennedy's death. Thus both presidents had to consider both options. Furthermore, though we do not know what Kennedy might have done in 1964 and 1965, we have the record of Johnson's vice presidency, when Johnson had access to information about Kennedy's counterinsurgency program and decision making. Johnson's statements and decisions on Vietnam in the immediate aftermath of Kennedy's assassination also illustrate the differences in his approach when the circumstances were still close to those Kennedy confronted and at a time when many within the administration still advocated continuing aspects of Kennedy's policies. Thus even with all the differences of circumstance and the elements of continuity between the two administrations, Johnson displayed a distinctive focus on the external dimensions of the war in Vietnam and accordingly escalated with a nontransformative strategy.

Johnson as Vice President

One way to disentangle the effect of the two presidents' threat perceptions from that of the evolving circumstances within Vietnam is to look at how Kennedy and Johnson approached the problem when they confronted the same or still relatively similar circumstances, such as in Johnson's years as vice president. As discussed, Johnson sat in on many key meetings (including those on Vietnam) during the Kennedy presidency and had exposure to debates about the nature of the war and Kennedy's counterinsurgency approach. Air Force colonel Howard Burris, a Johnson aide covering the NSC, wrote frequent memos for Johnson on both Laos and Vietnam, including a March 1962 memo outlining the plan of British counterinsurgency expert Robert Thompson to cut off local support for the Viet Cong by focusing on the village level rather than regular conventional operations.[184] Yet Johnson fit more naturally with those who placed less emphasis on the political aspects of the war and thus opposed a coup against Diem or even pushing Diem to reform. Johnson had warned Congress after his 1961 trip to Asia that the United States could not "nit-pick" with Diem.

Johnson's comments during the late 1963 discussion of how to deal with Diem were remarkably forthright. On August 31, 1963, amid the debate over a coup against Diem, Johnson attended a high-level meeting at the State Department. As discussed in chapter 4, the Kennedy administration was split between those who saw the conflict in Vietnam as political and thus favored a coup, and those who saw it in military terms and thus opposed the coup. At the August 31 meeting, Johnson, who had attended several meetings at which the coup had been debated, came down in the latter camp. One State Department Vietnam expert, Paul Kattenburg, pointed to popular discontent in South Vietnam, which "made the people the unwilling allies of the Viet Cong," while Diem had become "a petty dictator." Kattenburg therefore felt that "it would be better to withdraw in a dignified way."[185]

But Johnson rejected Kattenburg's proposal, saying he "recognized the evils of Diem but has seen no alternative to him. Certainly we can't pull out. We must reestablish ourselves and stop playing cops and robbers."[186] Another account of the meeting notes that Johnson said he "had never been sympathetic with our proposal to produce a change of government in Vietnam by means of plotting with Vietnamese generals. . . . He thought that we ought to reestablish ties to the Diem government as quickly as possible and get forward with the war against the Viet Cong."[187] For Johnson, internal reform was distinct from moving "forward with the war," whereas for Kennedy they were closely interconnected, despite the lack of a clear alternative to Diem.

JOHNSON'S EARLY VIETNAM POLICY

In the wake of the coup against Diem and the assassination of Kennedy, Johnson, as he did in other areas, moved to reassure the public that he was committed to Kennedy's policies. But behind the scenes he quickly demonstrated a key difference: he was less interested in domestic issues within Vietnam or in nation building. According to notes prepared by CIA director John McCone, in the new president's first group meeting with advisers on Vietnam, on November 24, 1963, Johnson said that he "was not at all sure we took the right course in upsetting the Diem regime. . . . He said now that it was done, we have to see that our objectives are accomplished." In response to McNamara's assessment of the economic picture and recommendation to be generous with aid, Johnson "said that he supported this, but at the same time he wanted to make it abundantly clear that he did not think we had to reform every Asian into our own image. He said that he felt all too often when we engaged in the affairs of a foreign country we wanted to immediately transform that country into our image and this, in his opinion, was a mistake. He was anxious to get along, win the war—he didn't want as much effort placed on so-called social reforms." McCone commented in his notes that he "received in this meeting the first 'President Johnson tone' for action as contrasted with the 'Kennedy tone.' Johnson definitely feels that we place too much emphasis on social reforms; he has very little tolerance with our spending so much time being 'do-gooders.' "[188] Johnson did, however, embrace the commitment to standing firm in Vietnam itself. According to another account of the November 24 meeting, Johnson declared, "I am not going to lose Vietnam. I am not going to be the President who saw Southeast Asia go the way China went."[189] Thus almost immediately after taking office, Johnson made clear both his determination to stand firm and his aversion to a transformative strategy.

Johnson made a point, however, of at least appearing to support Kennedy's approach. On November 26, in the wake of Kennedy's assassination, the White House issued NSAM 273, which reaffirmed Johnson's commitment to Kennedy's policies.[190] But U.S. officials would soon learn that the situation in the hamlets was far grimmer than previously known.

Yet there remained important voices, inside and outside the administration, that favored sticking with something like the Strategic Hamlet Program or at least retaining a transformative strategy that would focus on connecting the population to the South Vietnamese government. As Bundy put it early on the morning of November 22, 1963, even after Diem's death "everyone recognized that the strategic hamlets . . . had to remain the center of the war effort."[191] On December 7, Senator Mansfield wrote Johnson, "What is called for are political and social acts of popular benefit by the Vietnamese authorities . . . even if it means curtailing the present elusive and so far unsuccessful chase of the Viet Cong all over the land."[192] In a memo on December 11, Forrestal argued that the "principal difficulty remains what it has always been, i.e. bringing the government effectively to the villages in such a way as to win the peasants' confidence and support."[193] In March 1964, McCone called for the hamlet program to be "revitalized and attacked as the top priority."[194]

In late 1964 and early 1965, Johnson wrestled with internal governance problems in South Vietnam and showed a persistent interest in finding stability. On the one hand, he did not want to make a major move on Vietnam until after the 1964 election.[195] On the other hand, the administration grappled behind the scenes with growing instability in South Vietnam and a deteriorating military situation that made the measures taken to this point seem increasingly untenable. During this period, Johnson, like Kennedy before him, rejected several military proposals for escalating the U.S. response in Vietnam using a conventional, nontransformative strategy, including options to take the war to the North.[196] Furthermore, he gave some significant attention to bolstering South Vietnam's domestic institutions. For example, in a May 1964 telephone conversation with Bundy, Johnson asserted, "I think that if we can furnish the military government people that are trained in civil administration, the mayors, and the councilmen, and folks of that type . . . get enough of them where one good

American can run a hamlet . . . I think that'll improve that situation a good deal."[197] The following week, Robert Kennedy told Johnson in a telephone call that the war could be won only through "the political war" and emphasized the need to take "political action . . . concurrently." Johnson agreed, telling Kennedy, "that's not any different from the way that I have felt about it." Given Johnson's tense relationship with Robert Kennedy in this period, however, such conversations must be taken with a grain of salt.[198]

Still, in a December 30, 1964, cable to Maxwell Taylor (then serving as ambassador in Saigon), Johnson seemed to reference Kennedy's buildup of counterinsurgency forces:

> I have never felt that this war will be won from the air, and it seems to me that what is much more needed and would be more effective is a larger and stronger use of Rangers and Special Forces and Marines, or other appropriate military strength on the ground and on the scene. I am ready to look with great favor on that kind of increased American effort, directed at the guerrillas and aimed to stiffen the aggressiveness of Vietnamese military units up and down the line. . . . We have been building our strength to fight this kind of war ever since 1961, and I myself am ready to substantially increase the number of Americans in Vietnam if it is necessary to provide this kind of fighting force against the Viet Cong.[199]

Additionally, even as he considered escalation in March 1965, Johnson "expressed concern and understandable frustration" about the pacification effort, and "[kept] wondering if we are doing all we can."[200] As McNamara noted in a cable to Taylor, Johnson "is continuing to support such action against [the] North as is now in progress but does not consider such actions a substitute for additional action within South Vietnam. The President wants us to examine all possible additional actions—political, military, and economic—to see what more can be done in South Vietnam."[201] In mid-March, Johnson directed several units (including State and USAID) to craft "a program designed to match and even out-match the military efforts outlined above," including "close control of the population," "land reform operations," and "intensified housing and agricultural programs"; by April, the president had approved a forty-one-point program of nonmilitary measures.[202]

This attention to South Vietnam's domestic affairs, however, must be seen in light of several considerations, as well as the larger sweep of the evidence. First, as mentioned, Johnson hoped to keep Vietnam on the back burner until after the 1964 election, especially in terms of major military decisions. Furthermore, arguably any U.S. president taking over from Kennedy and pledging to maintain the commitment to Vietnam would have had to confront the internal instability within South Vietnam after the coup against Diem.

More significantly, in this same period, even as Johnson discussed political and other nonmilitary measures to shore up the South, his analysis of the problem in Vietnam and his discussion of solutions for it were consistent with an external focus. The source of South Vietnam's vulnerability to a communist takeover, in Johnson's diagnosis, was aggression from the North. Indeed, Khong finds that Johnson was a firm believer in the analogy to the Korean War, which defined the problem in terms of external aggression, a premise Johnson did not question.[203] On November 2, 1964, the day before his landslide general election victory, Johnson ordered a new NSC Working Group to study options in Vietnam, setting the escalation in motion in earnest. U.S. policymakers ultimately embraced the so-called Option C, a limited bombing campaign against the North (and rejected Option A, to "continue on present lines").[204] Khong argues that Johnson found the Korean analogy persuasive and thus a diagnosis of external aggression was crucial to his choice of Option C.[205] The salience of the Korean analogy in Johnson's thinking, in turn, may have resonated with his causal beliefs. In contrast, as Khong notes, Kennedy had been far more inclined to draw on the Greek and Malayan analogies (and had rejected the Korean analogy), although both Kennedy and Johnson had lived through all three crises.

A second manifestation of Johnson's external focus, even in the period in which he considered nonmilitary efforts in South Vietnam, was his concentration on the credibility implications of Vietnam without connecting the threat to its domestic institutions. In a May 1964 conversation with Richard Russell, for example, Johnson said that Vietnam was important because the United States was "party to a treaty." Johnson also feared appearing soft on communism, asking Russell, "Well, they'd impeach a President though that would run out, wouldn't they?"[206] Later that same day, in a long conversation with Bundy, Johnson mused, "What the hell is Vietnam worth to me? . . . What is it worth to this country?" Then, reviving a long-standing theme, he said, "Of course if you start running from the Communists, they may just chase you right into your own kitchen."[207] Johnson's fear of looking weak, abroad and at home, was a significant factor in his perception that he had to do something in Vietnam, even if he did not perceive it as a direct threat.

Consistent with this pattern, in this period Johnson also displayed a tendency to separate the political and military aspects of the war. For example, on the same day he approved the forty-one-point nonmilitary program in April 1965, Johnson was, according to Bundy's notes, "full of determination—we have set our hand to wheel. . . . We got to find em & kill em."[208] And as early as the late winter and early spring of 1964, before the election and the NSC

Working Group debate over options, Johnson's focus began to shift to North Vietnam, even as Washington received increasingly pessimistic assessments of the situation in the South.[209] At the NSC meeting on February 20, 1964, Johnson ordered that contingency planning for "pressures against North Vietnam should be speeded up."[210] On May 13, in a call with Bundy, he argued that "we've got to have some program out there from the Joint Chiefs, to start stepping that thing up and do some winning and do a little stuff up in the North some way or other. We just can't sit idly by and do nothing there."[211] As Logevall points out, there was "a kind of logic" to the shift to an emphasis on the North, given how badly the war in the South was going, and yet Johnson's own intelligence analysts predicted that bombing the North would not work since "the problems were political and in the South, not military and in the North."[212] As Freedman notes, Kennedy had shown interest in covert operations against North Vietnam, consistent with "his fascination with guerrilla warfare," but he "had always resisted American involvement" in more intense operations in the North.[213]

U.S. policy increasingly reflected Johnson's external focus. In mid-March 1964, Johnson approved a major expansion of U.S. involvement in the conflict, in a report that was adopted as NSAM 288. The United States sought an "independent, non-Communist Vietnam," without which "almost all of Southeast Asia will probably fall under Communist dominance." Globally, "the South Vietnam conflict is regarded as a test case of U.S. capacity to help a nation meet a Communist 'war of liberation.'" The report discussed at length increasing efforts to strengthen the pacification program.[214] The *Pentagon Papers* analyst notes, however, that the document "came close to calling for war *à outrance*—not the centrally political war, with severe restriction upon violent means, following counter-guerilla warfare theory." Furthermore, "pacification was to receive less comparative emphasis, in fact, in the next year or so than it had before."[215] Even as momentum built for going to the North, however, Forrestal tried at the end of March to revive concerns about the need for a different kind of military strategy, stating in a White House staff meeting that "search and clear," the military's favored operations, "are not the type of actions that will be most effective in achieving US objectives."[216]

Yet even in public, Johnson treated domestic issues within Vietnam separately from the war effort. On April 7, 1965, he made a highly publicized speech at Johns Hopkins University in which he offered to invest $1 billion in a program to develop the Mekong Delta region, "on a scale to dwarf even our own TVA." North Vietnam was invited to participate. He concluded the speech by evoking his own childhood, when electricity came to his hometown.[217] As Lloyd Gardner details, Johnson himself pushed for the inclusion of the Mekong plan in the speech, and for more about economic development. More broadly, Gardner sees a link between the intervention in Vietnam and the Great Society and the War on Poverty.[218] Johnson had a genuine desire to help the people of Vietnam, as he had after his 1961 trip as vice president.

But consistent with the separation of military and civil issues in his pre-presidential thinking, Johnson's development initiative appeared suddenly, disappeared quickly (after the North Vietnamese emphatically rejected it), and was not well integrated with his overall approach to Vietnam. Many analysts dismiss the speech as an effort to placate critics. Logevall notes that in a meeting with the JCS the day after the Johns Hopkins speech, Johnson "again emphasized the need to kill more Vietcong."[219] The speech itself did not suggest that Johnson saw reform as central to the U.S. effort to win the war. The offer of $1 billion for development came in its own section, after an opening section that addressed head-on the question, "Why are we in South Viet-Nam?" Johnson answered, "We are there because we have a promise to keep. . . . We are also there to strengthen world order. . . . We are also there because there are great stakes in the balance. . . . The central lesson of our time is that the appetite of aggression is never satisfied." Echoing the language of the speech launching his Senate campaign nearly twenty years earlier, he told the American people, watching on television at home, "We must say in southeast Asia—as we did in Europe—in the words of the Bible: 'Hitherto shalt thou come, but no further.' "[220]

Thus while Johnson paid significant attention to shoring up South Vietnam in the run-up to the escalation, we cannot look at this behavior in isolation. Many other actions he took in this period were consistent with a nontransformative approach. Furthermore, the dual imperatives he felt—to continue his slain predecessor's commitment to Vietnam while keeping the war relatively quiet until after the 1964 election—made some of his concern with South Vietnam's domestic institutions logical.

Late 1964: Is a Stable South Vietnam Required?

In the latter half of 1964, after the Tonkin Gulf incident and U.S. retaliatory air strikes, there were indications that Johnson might not necessarily insist on a stable government as a prerequisite for escalating. By the end of August, instability in South Vietnam had once again given way to crisis. In a meeting on September 9, Johnson addressed the proposal to go to the North immediately, arguing that "we should not do this until our side could defend itself in the streets of Saigon." Johnson then approved the recommendations of Taylor, by this time installed as the new ambassador in Saigon and still an advocate for nonmilitary measures to shore up the South. Johnson said he "did not wish to enter the patient in a 10-round bout, when he was in no shape to hold out for one round. We should get him ready to face 3 or 5 rounds at least."[221] This was not a ringing endorsement of a stability-first approach, however, much less a plan to transform South Vietnam's institutions.

As the election drew near, another rationale for escalation emerged. In an October 1964 draft titled "Aims and Options in Southeast Asia," Assistant Secretary of State John McNaughton argued that it was "essential—however badly [Southeast Asia] may go over the next 2–4 years—that [the] US emerge as a 'good doctor.' We must have kept promises, been tough, taken risks, gotten bloodied, and hurt the enemy very badly."[222] The United States had to do *something*—what happened in Vietnam itself was secondary. Though Logevall argues that this idea resonated less with Johnson himself than with his advisers, his conversation with Russell (noted above) suggests Johnson thought along these lines.[223]

When the administration debated the options that emerged from the November NSC Working Group, the deliberations further signaled a gap between the aim of a stable South and the decision to take the war to the North. Option A—continuing the present course, including the counterinsurgency effort—had important advocates, but when the working group met on November 24, the consensus ran against this option.[224] Ultimately, the group recommended a short period of Option A (perhaps as brief as thirty days) and then "Phase II," which would escalate to Option C, the limited bombing campaign against the North.

When the group met with Johnson on December 1 to discuss the recommendations, the president again expressed concern for stability in the South, but with a focus on finding a strong leader and demonstrating to the world that the United States had tried its best, rather than Kennedy's emphasis on increasing the government's base of support. Johnson at first expressed a strong sense that "basic to anything is stability. . . . No point in hitting North if South not together." When the discussion turned to international views, Johnson said the United States must try everything to shore up the government, but seemed to imply this effort was intended to demonstrate to other countries that the United States had done everything it could. "Hesitant to sock neighbor if fever 104," he said. "Want to get well first. . . . We want to be prepared to answer the questions." Johnson even argued, "If need be, create a new Diem."[225] Johnson was not concerned, as the internally focused Kennedy had been, about increasing the base of support for the government in the South, concentrating instead on the narrower question of regime stability. The domestic problems Diem himself had fostered were not a prominent feature of Johnson's thinking, and he even sought a return to rule under a Diem-like figure. At one point in the same meeting, Johnson asked McNamara whether he "shared [the] view that it's [a] downhill slide in [South Vietnam] no matter what we do in country." Johnson thought U.S. action would be "better if allies with us, dependents out, done all we can," with "conditions as favorable as we can get them." He wanted to give Taylor "one last chance." But he summed up, turning to Wheeler: "If more of the same, I'll be talking to you, General."[226]

Logevall interprets this meeting as a major presidential decision to "fundamentally alter the American involvement in Vietnam" by agreeing to strike the North, albeit reluctantly, regardless of the situation in the South.[227] Johnson cemented the go-without-stability rationale in a meeting on January 27, 1965, after Bundy and McNamara presented him with a paper that became known as the "fork in the road" memo. In the meeting, according to Bundy's handwritten notes, Johnson stated that "stable govt or no stable govt," "we'll do what we oughta do. I'm prepared to do that. We will move strongly."[228]

To be sure, the idea behind going to the North included the hope that such action would stiffen morale in the South and thus enhance stability. But Logevall cautions against seeing the option to attack the North as inevitable. Indeed, Logevall notes that most foreign and domestic audiences, including American allies and even communist adversaries, felt that America's stake in Vietnam depended on the situation in the South, leaving Johnson "considerable freedom to maneuver in the months following his election."[229] Though Johnson aimed for stability in South Vietnam, Logevall concludes that the "documentary record leaves no doubt as to Johnson's determination. His seeming insistence on securing a stable Saigon government before proceeding to escalation pales in importance next to his insistence on preventing defeat."[230]

The 1965 Decisions

In the fateful escalation decisions from February through July 1965, Johnson focused primarily on hurting the North and stopping the Viet Cong with conventional force, and there were few connections between the military strategy and changing the internal situation in the South. In February 1965, following a Viet Cong attack on U.S. advisers based at Pleiku, Johnson authorized the beginning of the air campaign, Rolling Thunder, over which he kept tight personal control.[231] But resolve only increased in the North, while the situation continued to erode in the South. In March, two Marine battalions arrived to guard the U.S. base at Da Nang, at General William Westmoreland's request.[232] From this point, the escalation took on what Logevall calls an "inexorable" quality; Gelb and Betts note that Johnson was the "driving force in eliciting and approving the troop commitment."[233]

There remained a debate over exactly how the troops would be deployed. Westmoreland's most recent estimate had already concluded that the war had moved from the "purely guerilla phase" into "more formalized military conflict"—

also known as the "third phase" of guerrilla warfare, when guerrillas shift to engaging enemy forces directly in regular, organized military units.[234] By 1965, there were some North Vietnamese main-force units operating in South Vietnam, threatening to deal a fatal blow to the South Vietnamese army.[235]

For my purposes, however, it is important to note that from the perspective of 1965, there were multiple possibilities for the intervention strategy. Analysts have long debated whether a conventional attrition strategy aimed at main-force units or a population-centered counterinsurgency strategy could have won the war, particularly in the later stages, or whether any U.S. strategy could have worked at all.[236] This discussion does not address that debate but rather highlights the fact that policymakers at the time, as well as subsequent analysts, saw several possibilities for the ground strategy. As some of Johnson's advisers recognized before the escalation, even if the conflict had entered the "third phase" of guerrilla warfare (which several of them doubted) and the United States successfully engaged enemy main-force units, the Viet Cong could simply revert to guerrilla tactics.[237] As Andrew Krepinevich notes, "winning the big battles is not decisive unless you can proceed to defeat the enemy at the lower levels of insurgency operations as well."[238] As Guenter Lewy argues, the North's main-force units meant that some large-unit fighting was perhaps inevitable and necessary, but it could have served to "provide a shield behind which pacification . . . could proceed" rather than becoming an end in itself.[239] The United States thus faced both a conventional and unconventional challenge, leaving the question of intervention strategy open to debate.

The U.S. military's preference was for conventional, main-force fighting, a preference that reflected long-standing doctrine. Johnson was hardly responsible for this tendency, which Eisenhower and Kennedy also faced. But unlike Kennedy, who had at least tried to shift the emphasis to counterinsurgency, Johnson showed little inclination to challenge the conventional approach. Indeed, in a March 15 meeting with the JCS, Johnson said he wanted "the killing of Viet Cong intensified."[240]

In the Johnson administration's debate over how to deploy the troops, there were two alternative strategies. The first option was to deploy troops along the coast in "enclaves," with a primary focus on defense. As Gelb and Betts note, the adoption of this "defensive enclave concept would have represented a last cleaving to the pacification-oriented counterinsurgency strategy that had been favored by Hilsman, Thompson, and Lansdale."[241] The other alternative was to place U.S. troops in the highlands of Vietnam, in what would become the "search and destroy" strategy. The army favored search and destroy from the beginning, in line with its preference for conventional war. Furthermore, the enclave strategy required U.S. forces to interact with the Vietnamese population whereas under search and destroy the Vietnamese troops were to take care of population security while U.S. forces chased the enemy. Search and destroy, then, sought to avoid the kind of institution building and interaction with the population associated with a transformative, population-centered counterinsurgency. Although the military favored search and destroy, the enclave strategy sought stalemate by denying the insurgents access to the population, whereas search and destroy was intended to punish the enemy enough to bring him to the negotiating table.[242] The enclave strategy had its backers, however, especially Taylor.

Amid this tension between the two strategies, the final decisions to escalate arrived in June and July 1965. Westmoreland wanted to deploy U.S. forces inland, away from the population. Yet as the *Pentagon Papers* analyst notes, "enclave thinking was still very much alive."[243] Much of the ensuing debate centered on a proposal from McNamara developed in late June and submitted to Johnson on July 1. McNamara accepted Westmoreland's premise that the Viet Cong were entering the "third phase" of guerrilla warfare and thus recommended a conventional escalation. His proposal explicitly noted that the troop increase was "too small to make a significant difference in the traditional 10–1 government-guerrilla formula" but would be enough for "the kind of war which seems to be evolving in Vietnam—a 'Third Stage' or conventional war in which it is easier to identify, locate and attack the enemy."[244] As Larry Berman details, however, other top advisers took issue with McNamara's proposal and specifically criticized the assumption that the Viet Cong had entered the "third phase"; they highlighted the ineffectiveness of a conventional strategy and argued instead for either withdrawal (in George Ball's case) or some sort of concentration on guerrilla warfare.[245]

The final debate over escalation culminated in a series of lengthy meetings beginning on July 21 (though as Berman notes, there is some question as to whether the decision had already been made, and thus whether these meetings represented a real "debate" at all).[246] According to Valenti's notes, at the morning meeting on July 21, the issue of strategy came up quickly. McNamara stated that the U.S. "mission would be to seek out the VC in large scale units." When Ball questioned the nature of the Viet Cong threat, Johnson showed little interest in the ensuing debate, saying, "Right now I feel it would be more dangerous for us to lose this now, than endanger a greater number of troops." When the weakness of the South Vietnamese government came up, Johnson again brushed past the issue, letting stand Henry Cabot Lodge's statement that "I don't think we ought to take this government seriously. . . . We have to do what we think we ought to do regardless of what the Saigon government does." In the afternoon meeting, Johnson asked whether other countries would "say Uncle Sam is a paper tiger—wouldn't we lose credibility breaking the word of three presidents. . . . It would seem to be an irreparable blow." The only mention of non-military measures for Vietnam came at the very end of the meeting, when Johnson asked about getting information out about "our economic and health projects" and the need to "constantly remind the people that we are doing other things besides bombing."[247] Johnson showed little interest in integrating these measures with the military program he had just spent most of the day debating.

Even after this meeting, a few voices still raised the question of how best to fight the war, urging a more transformative emphasis. In a memo to Bundy following the meeting, for example, the NSC's Chester Cooper argued that if the Viet Cong avoided direct confrontation with U.S. units, or if U.S. strategy forced the Viet Cong back to guerrilla tactics, either way the insurgency would have to be tackled head-on eventually, and thus the military plan might not lead to a "favorable outcome" without "a political-economic-psychwar program as carefully developed and as massive in its way as the military effort envisaged in the McNamara proposal."[248] In a list of suggested topics for another meeting on July 22, Bundy listed the problem of getting a "political and social effort within Vietnam that is equal in strength to the military effort," but there was no talk of this in the meeting itself, according to Valenti's notes.[249] Even among Johnson's military advisers, General Wallace Greene, commandant of the Marine Corps, stated that the "enclave concept will work." Greene wanted *more* troops than Westmoreland requested, presumably in line with the high ratio of counterinsurgency troops to guerrillas traditionally thought to be necessary to combat an insurgency. But Johnson again showed little interest in the strategic question.[250]

Finally, on July 28, Johnson announced the escalation—effectively under way for months—to the public. The main thrust of U.S. strategy, far from being sensitive to the needs of the population, damaged and even destroyed villages. On one level, such a strategy was deeply and destructively transformative, disrupting Vietnamese life at every level. Putting 500,000 troops in a small country could hardly be otherwise. As Frances Fitzgerald summarizes, by 1967 the "Americans were in control of South Vietnam."[251] But in the sense that the strategy did not involve the kind of local institution building called for in population-centered counterinsurgency, it can be considered nontransformative. U.S. soldiers would clear out insurgents from an area, but rarely did they stay to provide security and protection and thus build the population's loyalty to the government. James Carter details how the increasingly militarized U.S. effort after 1965 physically transformed Vietnam as the Americans built infrastructure to support the war effort, but the "kind of infrastructure being put in place was explicitly military and did not aid in the development of an independent southern state."[252] While bureaucratic tendencies were partly to blame, the strategy was not inevitable.

The Marines, as Deborah Avant shows, developed effective counterinsurgency techniques in Vietnam.[253]

In arguing that Johnson "was indeed exposed to dissenting views" and that "the president and not his advisors must accept most of the blame," Berman concludes that the United States "sought no military victory of its own, no territory, nothing except the goal of convincing Hanoi it could not unify Vietnam by force."[254] Scholars have also noted that Johnson understood that a conventional escalation would most likely fail to achieve a victory over the insurgency but that he chose to fight anyway, further suggesting that transforming South Vietnam's institutions was not the intended strategy.[255] But as Krepinevich puts it, the "tragedy is that the nature of the war required that emphasis be placed . . . on the internal threat to the stability and legitimacy of the South Vietnamese government. Indeed, one could argue that the external, conventional threat was formidable because of the internal strife within South Vietnam."[256]

Such a prescription suggests a diagnosis of the threat that is different from the way Johnson perceived the conflict. Johnson applied a nontransformative strategy to a conflict with domestic roots, soon miring the United States in what can be considered a "mismatched" intervention. Despite some attention to South Vietnam's domestic problems in the wake of Kennedy's death, Johnson's decisions during the escalation fit more naturally with the pattern of his pre-presidential beliefs, the way those beliefs translated into views about strategy in his pre-presidential career, and his early pronouncements about "do-gooding" in the immediate aftermath of Kennedy's assassination.

In highlighting those who raised objections to the escalation strategy, I do not claim that Johnson bears sole—or even most—responsibility for actively choosing the search and destroy strategy, although many studies note the dominance of Johnson himself, rather than his advisers, in the deliberations.[257] The key point is that he was exposed to arguments for an alternative, transformative strategy yet did not question the nature of the war. The administration officials who pushed Johnson to consider concentrating on reforming South Vietnam or on pacification illustrate the alternative strand of thinking on precisely *how* to escalate in Vietnam. As Gelb and Betts point out, members of the "reformer group" were not doves; if anything, the "evidence suggests that they were actually hawks who wanted to do it a different way by pressuring for reforms before deepening the American involvement."[258]

Johnson's approval of the search and destroy strategy may well have been the passive acceptance of a man with little understanding of military tactics, although we have seen that he had significant experience with defense issues by this point. Moreover, he was willing to overrule advisers and micromanage aspects of the war, famously boasting that "they can't even bomb an outhouse without my approval."[259] Johnson also saw his policy choice as a relatively limited one, designed to be a gradual escalation, and resisted those (including counterinsurgency enthusiasts) who urged an even bigger troop buildup. But it is important to note that Johnson had access to contrary advice, and his exhortation to "kill more VC" suggests that he did not see the need to question the strategy.

My purpose is not to assess the debate over which strategy might or might not have worked in Vietnam, but rather to highlight that others within the administration (and subsequent analysts) identified alternative strategies. It is true that a large-scale population-centered counterinsurgency strategy might have required even more troops than Johnson ultimately committed, a move with potentially prohibitive political consequences.[260] The theory does not make predictions about the size of the intervention, however; it predicts only the effect of leaders' causal beliefs on the cost-benefit calculation they make at a given time. But regardless of whether a transformative counterinsurgency strategy would have worked with the (still significant) troop levels Johnson deployed, one can ask why he was so much less interested in using such a strategy, given Kennedy's willingness to try this strategy at even lower troop levels, the calls for considering such a strategy within Johnson's administration, and Johnson's own knowledge that the escalation strategy he embraced was unlikely to work. Admittedly, Johnson faced different circumstances on the ground in Vietnam when he decided to escalate, but he had also been dismissive of transformative strategies during the Kennedy years.

Johnson and the "Other War"

A final consideration concerns the effort, from late 1965, to reemphasize nonmilitary programs and pacification in what came to be known as the "other war." Although Johnson lavished significant personal attention on this effort, he continued to treat military and nonmilitary aspects of the war as separate, perpetuating pacification's status as the "other war" even as he elevated its importance. Though it is difficult to assess learning, in the sense of a true change in beliefs, in the middle of an ongoing intervention, the increased emphasis on pacification nonetheless presents an opportunity to examine how Johnson's thinking evolved.

In late 1965, the Johnson administration made a push to increase nonmilitary activities, telling the embassy in Saigon in an October 1965 cable that there is "continuing concern at the highest levels here regarding need to emphasize our non-military programs and give them maximum possible public exposure both in U.S. and abroad."[261] Whereas the *Pentagon Papers* and others hint that the effort was largely a response to domestic war critics, Herring argues that for Johnson, "the one aspect of the war that excited him was the possibility of improving the lot of the South Vietnamese people."[262] Such concern for the welfare of the Vietnamese even as he sent thousands of troops to Vietnam was consistent with his pre-presidential years, when he showed concern for the world's poor even as he approached national security through an externally focused lens.

But this genuine presidential concern with and renewed emphasis on pacification masked a continuing tendency to keep the civil and military aspects of the war separate. In early February 1966, Washington hastily convened a conference at Honolulu, with little staff work in advance, at which Johnson personally and publicly pushed for a renewed focus on pacification. In a telephone call with Rusk just two days before the conference, however, Johnson referred to "military matters" on the one hand and "non-military matters" and "pacification" on the other, treating them as separate issues for discussion.[263] Out of Honolulu came a series of reorganizations of the pacification effort, including the choice of Robert Komer as coordinator of the "other war." But while this move appeared to elevate nonmilitary aspects of the conflict, it was also consistent with the existing pattern of Johnson's conduct of the war. Komer had responsibility only for nonmilitary programs; Johnson rejected a recommendation to create a White House–based "Mr. Vietnam" who would integrate all elements of the war, including military, economic, and political issues.[264] As mentioned, Komer's appointment occurred at nearly the same time that the Special Group (CI) was abolished. Furthermore, the lack of policy investments in transformative capabilities made shifting strategy even harder.

Johnson continued to demand improved pacification, however. In October 1966, after a high-level debate about how to reorganize the pacification effort yet again, he decided to give the civilians ninety days to improve the program. But in 1967 he moved pacification into the military structure, with Komer as the top civilian.[265] The result was the Civil Operations and Revolutionary Development Support (CORDS) program. Although the effectiveness of the CORDS program is controversial, it melded military and civilian pacification operations; even Westmoreland accepted it "with good grace."[266]

But within the overall U.S. military structure in Vietnam, CORDS—and thus pacification—still remained separate. It did not represent a switch to a pacification strategy, or even the integration of pacification into the overall strategy. As Herring concludes, "counterinsurgency doctrine emphasized the essentiality of integration of effort," but CORDS merely continued to illustrate that pacification was the "other war" rather than a central aspect of the overall war effort.[267] Indeed, Avant observes that CORDS "succeeded bureaucratically because it operated within the . . . military structure without questioning the Army's military operations."[268] On pacification, Herring notes that Johnson attempted to "build up pacification activities and forces without choosing between the conflicting approaches or integrating them in any effective way."[269] Thus CORDS could operate only as a limited, "other" operation, just as for Johnson, internal and external issues were largely separate.

Analysts of the U.S. involvement in Vietnam disagree over the precise reasons why Johnson escalated in 1965. This is not the place to adjudicate the debate. But what does seem clear is that Johnson's motivation for intervening in Vietnam had far less to do with Vietnam itself and more to do with the costs, as he perceived them, of *not* intervening, in terms of both American domestic politics and international politics. As Bundy recalled decades later, "LBJ isn't deeply concerned about who governs Laos, or who governs South Vietnam—he's deeply concerned with what the average American voter is going to think about how he did in the ball game of the Cold War."[270] His language in public and private meetings and conversations stressed following through on the commitment to Vietnam. To be sure, Kennedy had considered the costs of nonintervention as well. But in making a cost-benefit calculation about fighting in Vietnam, Johnson did not see additional benefits from transforming South Vietnam's domestic institutions. If he had to intervene, his externally focused threat perception led him to concentrate on the international dimension of the conflict.

The two presidents faced very different circumstances, of course, and Kennedy was not dovish on Vietnam. But one point of contrast lies in the primarily internally focused view Kennedy took of the conflict. Indeed, in considering differences between Kennedy and Johnson, Logevall—who gives Kennedy low marks for his rejection of neutralization proposals and negotiations in Vietnam—concludes that Kennedy still had a better understanding, even before his own aides, of the internal nature of the conflict and the "problems this might cause for American intervention," as well as an appreciation of the "need for genuine political reforms in South Vietnam if there were to be long-term success in the war effort."[271] Kennedy was unwilling to use what he perceived to be a wrongly conventional strategy in Vietnam that would not address underlying political problems. Furthermore, his attempts to invest in transformative capabilities—admittedly not as successful as he might have believed—left him ready to question his military advisers when they advocated conventional strategies and to push for a more integrated politico-military strategy. Johnson, in contrast, placed far less emphasis on reform from the very first days of his presidency through the escalation decisions, when he spoke of trying to "create a new Diem." Even when he emphasized economic development and pacification, he did not consider them central aspects of the war effort, as illustrated by his speech on the Mekong development project and his treatment of nonmilitary matters as the "other war." Johnson's lack of investments left him less prepared to undertake a transformative strategy, even when he finally focused on pacification issues. Thus under difficult circumstances for the theory—a case in which Johnson felt pressure to continue Kennedy's policies and expressed some concern about the nature of the South Vietnamese government—Johnson's approach to Vietnam revealed a different emphasis that had consequences for the way the Vietnam intervention unfolded.

Overall, the intervention decisions Johnson made reflected the influence of his causal beliefs. He approached the conflicts in Panama, the Dominican Republic, and to a large extent Vietnam through an externally focused lens, and he viewed domestic considerations within these states as a parallel rather than an integrated concern. In his view, transformative approaches would provide few additional benefits for U.S. national security. He did not make significant policy investments in transformative strategies and struggled to shift the U.S. effort toward pacification in Vietnam.

Alternative Hypotheses

As with his predecessors, Johnson made his decisions in the shadow of many other considerations that played a role but did not ultimately overwhelm his beliefs. In terms of structural and material conditions, Johnson was arguably more susceptible to outside pressures than Eisenhower or Kennedy, perhaps a reflection of his more limited foreign policy experience before taking office. But although such pressures may have provided the short-term impetus to act, they are not entirely sufficient to explain *how* Johnson intervened. Both Kennedy and Johnson felt the Soviet challenge in the Third World, but they chose different strategies to meet that challenge. The need to maintain U.S. credibility weighed heavily on Johnson in both the Dominican Republic and Vietnam. At a general structural level, Gareth Porter concludes that it was the global and regional balance of power, which favored the United States in the period of the Vietnam decisions, that "gave the United States such complete freedom of action to intervene militarily."[272] Yet this argument does not fully explain the evolution of U.S. strategy over time, and even Porter falls back on the argument that bureaucratic pressures, and especially Johnson's inability to resist those pressures (where Kennedy had been more successful), ultimately led the United States into war.[273]

One might argue that domestic and international politics shaped the form of intervention, particularly in the Vietnam case, since Johnson consistently chose a middle course that would neither overwhelm the American people nor invite Russian or Chinese counterintervention. A classic population-centered counterinsurgency strategy called for a high ratio of troops to guerrillas, requiring far more troops than the United States had in Vietnam. Even Kennedy, who chose a more limited counterinsurgency effort, might have balked at such troop levels. But Kennedy also sought a middle course in Vietnam, and he rejected conventional deployments while making the consistent argument that they were ill-suited to the political nature of the war; he embraced counterinsurgency with a lower level of troops as his middle course. Johnson showed little interest in even limited counterinsurgency or transformative strategies as vice president (viewing the same circumstances Kennedy confronted) and only marginal interest as president, suggesting that even if both presidents sought to fight while minimizing their political risks at home and abroad, there was no single, obvious middle way to do so.

As we might naturally expect, in the case of Vietnam the evolving circumstances of the conflict undoubtedly affected the decision making, but they are not sufficient to explain the evolution of U.S. strategy. The circumstances were most comparable in the late stages of the Kennedy administration and the early months of the Johnson administration. Thanks to Johnson's service as vice president, we have a record of his views of Kennedy's transformative policies; as discussed, these views were not favorable. Additionally, even as the circumstances evolved, many of the debates over how to fight the war remained similar. Leaving aside the debate over precisely when the Viet Cong formed main-force units, it is interesting to note that the issue of the "third phase" of guerrilla warfare concerned both the Kennedy and Johnson administrations. For example, Hilsman's original report in February 1962 advocating the Strategic Hamlet Program nonetheless noted that "the Viet Cong forces are in a transitional stage from a guerrilla to a conventional type of warfare."[274]

In terms of material capabilities and costs, as Gaddis argues, both Kennedy and Johnson were willing to spend whatever they deemed necessary, and Johnson kept steadily increasing the troop commitment to levels that had significant political consequences.[275] He imposed certain limits on the military, but beyond those limits he answered demands for more resources. His externally oriented view of the war led him to ignore most of the calls to examine alternative strategies. As Gaddis notes, Kennedy and Johnson spent liberally on defense, and the increased capabilities may have made them more willing to use force. But despite their shared commitment to high levels of defense spending, their choices in terms of resource allocation and intervention strategy differed. Johnson allowed Kennedy's investments in counterinsurgency to lapse. Later, he tried to shift the strategy in Vietnam without an underlying stock of transformative capabilities on which to draw, or even the modest increases of the Kennedy era.

The interaction among various domestic actors has received significant scrutiny in scholarship on Johnson. Domestic politics undoubtedly played a role, though there is disagreement about precisely how and to what extent. But it seems safe to say that electoral concerns, particularly through the 1964 election, as well as the fear of damage to his cherished Great Society program, influenced the Vietnam decisions.[276] Johnson's personal credibility was also an issue in both the Dominican Republic and Vietnam. Johnson feared looking weak almost more than he feared public intolerance of war. But these factors again are insufficient to explain how Johnson intervened.

The bureaucracy also influenced the intervention decisions, but Johnson was a decisive factor. He pushed his advisers and frequently overruled them in all three crises. He deferred to the military's preference for conventional war in Vietnam, but his willingness to overrule the military in other instances suggests that he was not cowed into accepting its proposals. Kennedy was perhaps more distrustful of the military and of military solutions generally,[277] but both men shut down or altered military proposals at key points. In terms of partisanship, while Johnson's decision making was influenced by domestic politics, it was not driven by the Democratic Party. From his career in Congress through the presidency, Johnson's positions often put him at odds with his fellow Democrats.

Like his predecessors, Johnson did not show much respect for international norms or institutions. He worked through international institutions to some extent in the Dominican crisis, but only after initially dismissing the OAS as a "phantom" and manipulating it to serve as a cover for the intervention.

Finally, I have tried to highlight evidence that would show that Johnson was not an externally focused leader. Much of this evidence consists of his real concern for the plight of the poor in the Third World and the connections he saw between bringing improvements to poor, often rural areas in the United States and similar programs overseas. But Johnson rarely integrated these concerns into his view of national security. Instead, he framed his approach to national security and foreign policy questions in terms of resisting aggression and confronting bullies. He also acted in significant ways to limit U.S. transformative actions in the Third World.

I have argued in this chapter that Lyndon Johnson's causal beliefs about the origin of threats differed from Kennedy's and were closer in substance to Eisenhower's. Johnson saw threats to the United States and its clients as originating in the external actions of other states. He viewed the internal conditions of other states as a largely separate issue, though he sometimes tried to better those conditions. Johnson was deeply concerned about sweeping domestic changes within United States but was less interested in transforming other countries, and in some cases, skeptical of the consequences of more participatory or democratic outcomes abroad. Perhaps Johnson felt he had to make a choice about where to push for transformation, and chose to focus his efforts at home. As he wrote in a newsletter for constituents in 1958, "We must rekindle those fires of liberty within ourselves before we can warm the hearts of other men in other lands to a new trust in America."[278]

Johnson's interventions had long-lasting effects. Though the Dominican intervention was relatively small in scale, it damaged U.S.-Latin American relations because it was, of course, an intrusion into internal Dominican affairs. Vietnam underscored the tragedy of a mismatched intervention, in which the United States employed a strategy ill-suited to the conflict at hand. Johnson was perhaps an unlikely figure to preside over a war that had devastating effects on a poor, Third World country. But his long-standing beliefs contributed, at least in part, to the decisions that shaped the longest active U.S. military intervention of the Cold War.

6

Before and After the Cold War

This book has concentrated, for theoretical and methodological reasons, on the Cold War. To show how leaders' causal beliefs about the origin of threats exert an independent and systematic effect on decisions to intervene—beyond arguments that decisions are merely contingent events that hinge on the role of individuals—I restricted my empirical investigation to one country within one international system and focused on three leaders who confronted a relatively stable part of the Cold War as well as some of the same ongoing challenges.

The analytical leverage afforded by this narrow window, however, comes at the price of demonstrating the argument across a wider temporal range, at least within the United States. This chapter extends the argument beyond the Cold War, illustrating that the pattern holds under different international circum- stances and during periods when intervention meant something different, as Finnemore argues. I discuss how the theory applies to U.S. interventions both before and after the Cold War, from the early twentieth century to what Derek Chollet and James Goldgeier have called the "modern interwar years," between the fall of the Berlin Wall and September 11, 2001.[1] I compare two additional pairs of leaders and their intervention choices in the same countries: Theodore Roosevelt and Woodrow Wilson in the Dominican Republic, and George H. W. Bush and Bill Clinton in Somalia. The post–Cold War cases must be considered speculative since they rely on publicly available sources and secondary accounts. I also discuss how the argument applies to the Iraq War. While there remains debate about whether George W. Bush's beliefs evolved in the wake of the Sep- tember 11 attacks, I highlight the theory's implications for our understanding of the Iraq War based on the evidence available to date. Though the empirical evidence is still incomplete, together these cases illustrate that the theory can do much to illuminate other historical and contemporary interventions.

Before the Cold War: Theodore Roosevelt and Woodrow Wilson in the Dominican Republic

Presidential leadership left an imprint on the military interventions of the early twentieth century. Although the United States was still evolving into a great power in this period, the presidencies of Theodore Roosevelt and Woodrow Wilson provide a useful contrast.[2] Roosevelt and Wilson are often invoked as exemplars of realism and idealism, respectively.[3] But as John Milton Cooper notes, "each man was both an idealist and a realist, albeit of different stripes."[4] Roosevelt and Wilson represent, for my purposes, two contrasting approaches to both threat perception and military intervention, particularly in Latin America. Where Roosevelt preferred using American naval power and limited armed intervention to assert U.S. power in the region and on the world stage, Wilson attempted to restructure the domestic order of the Latin American states in which he intervened.

Roosevelt, as Howard Beale notes, brought "definite ideas and interests" to office.[5] He served as assistant secretary of the navy in the first McKinley administration and was a strong advocate of building up American naval power. In his pre-presidential years, during the debate at the turn of the century over whether the United States should become a colonial power, Roosevelt was a strong proponent of expansion, and he usually framed his arguments in externally focused terms. His expansionism was based in part on national pride—a sense that the United States should demonstrate its power and take its place as a strong nation. On the question of annexing Hawaii, for example, he was primarily concerned with beating out other great powers in the imperialist race, arguing that "if we don't take Hawaii it will pass into the hands of some strong nation, and the chance of taking it will be gone forever."[6] Similarly, his desire to hold the Philippines stemmed from his "wish to see the United States the dominant power on the shores of the Pacific Ocean."[7] His interest in Cuba was driven by a desire, as he put it, to "put Spain out of the western hemisphere."[8] He was aware that acquiring territory would mean imposing U.S. rule on potentially hostile populations, but he seemed more interested in the effects on U.S. power and prestige. In 1899, he wrote that good men must rule in the new territories in order to avoid a "series of disasters at the very beginning of our colonial policy." Such disasters "might produce the most serious and far-reaching effects upon the nation as a whole" because they "might mean the definite abandonment of the course upon which we have embarked—the only course I think fit for a really great nation."[9]

Roosevelt's expansionism was also based on a belief that the United States would spread "civilization" to new areas of the world. But as Beale notes, Roosevelt "never really defined what he meant by 'civilization.' "[10] In practice, Roosevelt, who advocated some government intervention in U.S. domestic affairs if it would maintain internal harmony, seemed genuinely to believe in spreading order and prosperity and ultimately granting the new territories independence. He was less interested, however, in the precise form of political or economic order within a particular state or territory. Any part of the world could become "civilized," which in turn would promote peace once "each part of the world" became "prosperous and well-policed."[11] In his study of Roosevelt's policies in the Caribbean, Richard Collin argues that Roosevelt actually "opposed colonial rule" and "rejected territorial, political, or economic domination as a means of achieving national progress."[12] Roosevelt lamented what he saw as the "weakness" and "inability" of Latin Americans to "rule themselves effectively," as Beale notes.[13] What made small countries like those in Latin America of primary interest to Roosevelt, then, was their role in helping the United States demonstrate its strength in the hemisphere and their ability to maintain internal equilibrium so that they could play this role effectively.

These beliefs translated into a strongly interventionist policy when Roosevelt became president on McKinley's death in 1901, but it was a policy that placed distinct limits on the degree to which the United States would interfere in the domestic politics of target states. Roosevelt's policy in the Dominican Republic is illustrative. At the turn of the century, the Dominican Republic experienced significant internal turmoil, which spilled over into its dealings with Americans and Europeans who held its debt.[14] In 1903, the country plunged into civil war. By January 1904, small contingents of U.S. Marines were landing on the island. But Roosevelt worked to keep the intervention limited. As Lester Langley argues, Roosevelt's response is "instructive . . . not only for the choices taken but for the alternatives Roosevelt rejected," such as a full-scale military intervention of the transformative type that Wilson would later undertake. Such a course "was not seriously considered." Roosevelt was mainly concerned with keeping some other power, such as Britain, from intervening, and thus he aimed only for "the creation of a system whereby the republic could pay its foreign obligations" (i.e., an internationally successful outcome) rather than a full transformation of Dominican institutions.[15] As Roosevelt himself put it, "I have been hoping and praying for three months that the Santo Domingans would behave so that I would not have to act in any way. I want to do nothing but what a policeman has to do in Santo Domingo. As for annexing the island, I have about the same desire to annex it as a gorged boa constrictor might have to swallow a porcupine wrong-end-to. . . . If I possibly can, I want to do nothing to them. If it is absolutely necessary to do something, then I want to do as little as possible."[16]

Over the course of a year, the American navy patrolled the Dominican coast and even intervened in a few internal battles. But Roosevelt still hoped to keep U.S. intervention limited to ensuring that debt could be collected. Finally, in 1904, amid debate on how far the United States should go in dealing with the Dominican crisis, he promulgated the Roosevelt Corollary to the Monroe Doctrine. According to Roosevelt's corollary, "chronic wrongdoing" might "require intervention by some civilized nation," and in the Western Hemisphere might lead "the United States, however reluctantly, in flagrant cases of such wrongdoing or impotence, to the exercise of an international police power."[17] As Collin puts it, Roosevelt's position represented a "middle ground that . . . allowed the United States to clean up the mess, appear to solve the underlying problem, and get out."[18] Accordingly, the United States assumed control of the Dominican customhouses, removing them as a target for the revolutionaries and ensuring that creditors would be paid. "All we desire," Roosevelt wrote, "is to see all neighboring countries, stable, orderly, and prosperous. . . . If a nation shows that it knows how to act with decency in industrial and political matters, if it keeps order and pays its obligations, then it need fear no interference from the United States."[19] Roosevelt suggested that domestic turmoil might trigger the interest of the United States, but he increased American involvement when the fighting began to directly affect American lives and property.[20] A "civilizing" mission to provide order also underpinned the intervention. But as Langley summarizes, Roosevelt "had established strict limitations on what he believed the United States should and should not do in the republic. . . . We would collect the customs. . . . We would protect the customhouses from the perils of insurrection. After that, if their political house was in disorder—and it usually was—it was *their* house."[21]

Woodrow Wilson, who was elected to the presidency in 1912, would take a much more intrusive approach to Latin America in general and the Dominican Republic in particular. The nature of his beliefs is complex and remains a subject of debate. They evolved significantly in his pre-presidential years, when he was a political scientist, president of Princeton University, and governor of New Jersey.[22] Although he began as a conservative, by the time of his Princeton presidency he was known as a reformer. The pre-presidential Wilson supported imperialism, viewing it as part of America's growth as a world power. In 1901, he wrote that the "impulse of expansion is the natural and wholesome impulse which comes with a consciousness of matured strength."[23] But his belief in expansion was also connected to his reforming impulse, and thus he went beyond Roosevelt's notion of spreading "civilization."[24] For Wilson, an "ardent Anglophile," imperialism meant spreading not just "civilization" but Anglo-American values, including democracy.[25] Thus, as John Mulder argues, "moral imperialism became a political imperialism as well."[26] In a speech in 1904, Wilson argued that the United States was "a sort of pure air blowing in world politics, destroying illusions and cleaning places of morbid miasmatic gases."[27] In 1909, he insisted, "Every nation of the world needs to be drawn into the tutelage of America to learn how to spend money for the liberty of mankind."[28]

During his presidency, this impulse to export political and moral ideals would fuse with Wilson's pursuit of U.S. national security. In Latin America, Wilson was initially restrained, but ultimately he became a frequent employer of military intervention, which involved an unprecedented—and long-resented—degree of interference in local affairs. The early promises Wilson made of a Pan-American pact and fair dealings in hemisphere relations foundered as he deemed them insufficient to ensure U.S. national security—for example, in maintaining access to the Panama Canal. This security imperative, which Wilson did not ignore, became coupled to his impulse to promote political change.[29] In analyzing Wilson's Latin America policy in the context of American democracy promotion, Tony Smith notes that "the focus of Wilson's policy was on changing the internal structure of the states in Central America and the Caribbean, in the expectation that this would provide the enduring political stability the United States needed of them." Wilson saw internal reform as the best way to achieve a "lasting solution to regional instability damaging to American security."[30] For Wilson, security in the hemisphere was closely linked to the domestic institutions of Latin American states. This confluence would result in several major U.S. military interventions, including operations in Mexico, the Dominican Republic, and Haiti.

In the Dominican Republic, Wilson went beyond Roosevelt's intervention. American troops occupied the country from 1916 until 1924.[31] In 1916, after a period of civil war and political turmoil, the U.S. intervention force occupied the Dominican capital but could not "get a Dominican government to do its bidding."[32] Facing the choice between withdrawal and deepening involvement, Wilson approved a proclamation that removed the existing regime and declared an American military government. The U.S. occupation sought to remake Dominican institutions, in areas such as agriculture, transportation, communication, and of course, government bureaucracies. To promote domestic order, the Americans attempted to disarm the population and create a new "modern, national police force," the Dominican national guard.[33] One product of the new system for training the guard was Rafael Trujillo, whose ascent to power in

1930 and repressive rule until his assassination in 1961—leaving Kennedy and Johnson to deal with his legacy—symbolized the failure of Wilson's democratic project in the Dominican Republic.

Thus Roosevelt and Wilson took very different approaches to securing U.S. interests in the hemisphere, based on their differing views of the ultimate source of threats. Where Roosevelt saw Latin American states in terms of a basic standard of domestic stability and order and concentrated on their international behavior, Wilson believed their domestic characteristics were crucial. Though both men intervened in Latin American internal affairs, Wilson's policies, as illustrated by his intervention in the Dominican Republic, were far more transformative.

After the Cold War: George H. W. Bush and Bill Clinton in Somalia

The early post–Cold War period is a difficult time in which to assess the impact of leaders because, as many commentators have pointed out, with the Soviet threat removed, the United States lacked an animating principle behind its foreign policy and national security strategy, or as George H. W. Bush put it, the "vision thing."[34] Bush was left to grapple with a massive shift in the international environment during his presidency. We lack available archival evidence with which to examine this period and thus must rely to a much higher degree on public statements and contemporaneous accounts. Many of Bill Clinton's pre-presidential statements in particular come from the 1992 campaign and must be taken with the appropriate grains of salt. Nonetheless, in light of research showing that elite beliefs are stable even in the face of major changes in the international system (including the end of the Cold War), it is useful to briefly examine how Bush and his Democratic challenger in 1992, Bill Clinton, approached the new era and the crises it presented, such as the collapse of state institutions in Somalia.[35] As Finnemore argues, the end of the Cold War produced a shift in collective understandings of the purpose of intervention, from the Cold War emphasis on maintaining stability to the post–Cold War era of humanitarian intervention.[36] Yet there is evidence that the same basic distinction between transformative and nontransformative operations applies within this different context of intervention.

Both Bush and Clinton were committed internationalists, prompting the *Washington Post*'s Don Oberdorfer to note a high degree of similarity in their foreign policy positions during the 1992 campaign.[37] Nonetheless, differences in their approaches became apparent. Bush had a far stronger and clearer record on foreign and defense issues, having served as envoy to China, ambassador to the

United Nations, and CIA director during the Cold War. David Halberstam notes that Bush's service in World War II and his "instinct to resist overt aggression" resulted in hawkish views on the Vietnam War and Saddam Hussein's invasion of Kuwait in 1990.[38] Jon Western classifies Bush as a "selective engager" who did not see regional conflicts after the Cold War as engaging U.S. interests, beyond the further spread of instability.[39]

Clinton, on the other hand, ran for office with very little foreign policy experience. His views as expressed during the campaign must be seen in light of the political contest. He ran on an economy-first message and devoted little time to foreign policy; indeed, foreign policy did not play a central role in the campaign.[40] But when Clinton did bring up foreign policy, despite his apparent experience deficit, he attacked Bush for his lack of leadership in the emerging new order and for his handling of specific issues such as the ongoing crises in Bosnia and Somalia. Clinton's views coalesced around the Democratic tradition of liberal internationalism, along with some more muscular elements.

In his first foreign policy speech, in December 1991, Clinton called for reducing overall forces while maintaining a strong military, and for a greater role for the UN. He also argued for foreign aid to help build up institutions within the former Soviet Republics, and criticized Bush for continuing China's most-favored-nation status without demanding concessions on human rights.[41] In April 1992, Clinton attacked Bush and called for "a global alliance for democracy as united and steadfast as the global alliance that defeated Communism."[42] In a speech to the Los Angeles World Affairs Council in August, he specifically criticized Bush for embracing stability. "Time after time," Clinton argued, "this President has sided with the status quo against democratic change, with familiar tyrants rather than those who would overthrow them, and with the old geography of repression rather than a new map of freedom." In keeping with a liberal internationalist approach coupled to the promise of a "peace dividend" after the Cold War, Clinton maintained that in "Bosnia, Somalia, Cambodia, and other torn areas of the world, multilateral action holds promise as never before, and the U.N. deserves full and appropriate contributions from all the major powers. It is time for our friends to bear more of the burden."[43] And in a speech in early October 1992, Clinton called for a renewed commitment to democracy abroad, in the name of the long-term national interest.[44] As Chollet and Goldgeier note, Clinton's emphasis on democracy promotion fit with his overtures to neoconservatives, who had broken with liberals after Vietnam and many of whom had become Reagan Democrats.[45] While Clinton shared many of Bush's realist and internationalist instincts, therefore, he articulated a sense that the domestic conditions of states in the post–Cold War era would present challenges to U.S. national security.

Somalia was an early test of how both Bush and Clinton would approach internal conflicts in the post–Cold War world.[46] From Bush's vantage point, the collapse of state institutions and the resulting famine in Somalia unfolded along with the crisis in Bosnia. As Western argues, the Bush administration opposed intervention in either Somalia or Bosnia, on the grounds that U.S. strategic interests were not involved. Despite months of pressure from liberals both inside and outside the government, only after Bush lost the 1992 election did the administration finally decide it had to do *something*. In the face of the two ongoing crises, Bush was concerned about his legacy and feared that an incoming administration that was likely to be dominated by liberals might choose intervention in Bosnia. Bush and his JCS chairman, Colin Powell, decided to intervene in Somalia, and not Bosnia, because Somalia would be an easier mission and could be kept limited.[47]

The Bush administration's intervention in Somalia was thus grounded in a fundamental caution about how much domestic conditions within Somalia affected U.S. interests, and thus how deeply involved the United States would get in internal Somali affairs. Bush and Powell took pains to keep the intervention's goals limited to protecting the existing UN relief effort, known as UNOSOM I. In December 1992, the UN Security Council authorized the Unified Task Force, or UNITAF, to be led by the United States; the idea was to quickly return control to the UN, in accordance with the overall goal of getting out quickly. The United States insisted that the mandate for UNITAF be limited to security for the relief effort and not involve other goals such as disarming factions.[48] In an address to the nation, Bush said that while the United States would "not tolerate armed gangs ripping off their own people," the Americans "[did] not plan to dictate political outcomes."[49] The U.S. representative in Somalia, Robert Oakley, pursued a strategy of accommodating existing factions, including that of Mohamed Farah Aideed. The United States took pains not to appear to be taking sides.[50] But as Walter Clarke and Jeffrey Herbst point out, despite the administration's desire to keep the operation limited, once U.S. forces became involved in the relief effort, "they disrupted the political economy and stepped deep into the muck of Somali politics."[51] The intervention's limited aims were at odds with the nature of the problem and would complicate later U.S. and UN efforts, although in the short term UNITAF itself was considered a success. From the Bush administration's perspective, however, the intention was to undertake a nontransformative intervention.

The degree to which the change in presidential leadership from Bush to Clinton in January 1993 was responsible for a policy shift in Somalia remains to be fully assessed. The story of what happened when UNITAF handed control back to the UN (in the form of UNOSOM II) in the spring of 1993 is complex. What is clear is that the mission of UNOSOM II was far broader than that of either the U.S.-led UNITAF or UNOSOM I. UNOSOM II, as authorized by UN Security Council Resolution (UNSCR) 814 in March 1993, involved nation building.[52] UNOSOM II had ambitions to build or rebuild many Somali political and civil institutions at both the national and local level, from democratic institutions to a new police force. UNSCR 814 envisioned the use of coercive force to achieve these goals, including the disarmament of factions within Somalia; UNSCR 837, adopted on June 6, 1993, explicitly authorized bringing Aideed's militia to justice.[53] Ironically, however, the wider and more intrusive mandate of UNOSOM II was backed up with a smaller force than the more limited UNITAF. UNOSOM II had an authorized strength of 28,000 but never achieved a strength of more than 16,000. Additionally, U.S. military participation declined significantly between UNITAF, which involved 28,000 U.S. forces, and UNOSOM II, in which just over 4,000 U.S. troops remained. Of these, 1,200 formed a rapid reaction force (which remained under separate U.S. operational control).[54] In August 1993, amid worsening violence, the Pentagon deployed a further contingent of U.S. Army Rangers and Delta Force commandos as the United States became more committed to capturing Aideed, an effort that would culminate in the downing of two Black Hawk helicopters and the deaths of eighteen American soldiers in Mogadishu in early October 1993.

The incoming Clinton administration was preoccupied with U.S. domestic issues and not well prepared to deal with Somalia, and thus did not take a hard look at the policy when it assumed the reins of power. As Halberstam describes, the shift toward the more assertive nation-building policy took place without significant presidential attention to the problem.[55] But as Clarke and Herbst point out, the shift in policy cannot be blamed entirely on the UN, despite the increased emphasis on nation building that came from the UN secretary general, Boutros Boutros-Ghali. Clarke and Herbst note that "all the major Security Council resolutions on Somalia, including the 'nation-building' resolution, were written by U.S. officials, mainly in the Pentagon, and handed to the United Nations as faits accomplis."[56] John Hirsch and Robert Oakley also note that "policy directions taken initially by the departing Bush administration were changed by the Clinton administration," and that the UN expanded the mandate "with full U.S. support."[57]

Furthermore, Clinton administration officials—and sometimes Clinton himself—discussed the mission in Somalia in transformative terms, invoking "nation building" and the need to confront the root causes of the conflict, with force if necessary. The U.S. ambassador to the UN, Madeleine Albright, called the UN resolution "an unprecedented enterprise aimed at nothing less than the restoration of an entire country."[58] In a speech in February 1993, barely a month after taking office, Clinton spoke of the need "to update our definition of national security and to promote it and to protect it and to foster democracy and human rights around the world."[59] In a radio address in June, after U.S. forces attacked Aideed's positions, Clinton noted that "crops are growing, starvation has ended, refugees are beginning to return, schools and hospitals are reopening, a civil police force has been recreated, and Somalia has begun a process of national reconciliation with the goal of creating the institutions of democracy."[60] In an interview with foreign journalists in July, Clinton said he thought the United States was "on the right path in Somalia, but we have to have patience in nation-building."[61] And in August, Albright published an op-ed in the *New York Times* explicitly referring to the UN effort in the context of "international nation-building operations that include a military component." She wrote of the importance of disarming the factions in Somalia, "because humanitarian and political goals cannot be assured unless a secure environment is created." She warned that pulling out would "allow Somalia to fall back into the abyss" whereas staying would "help lift the country and its people from the category of a failed state into that of an emerging democracy."[62]

Even after the Black Hawk incident in October 1993, Clinton told reporters, "We didn't want to go there, pull out, and have chaos, anarchy, starvation return."[63] Clinton also frequently invoked burden sharing with the UN and other states, as well as the need for Somalis to take the lead in reconstruction, leaving his view of how far the United States itself should go in nation building unclear. But U.S. forces were still playing a significant role in the UN mission at the time, and Clinton seemed clear on the UN's mandate.

The degree of presidential influence may not have been high in this case, and as Halberstam notes, in general the Clinton administration, especially during its first term, tended to deal with foreign policy "issue by issue, with no guidelines" beyond the shadow of domestic politics.[64] Furthermore, the number of U.S. forces involved in UNOSOM II was relatively small. But the shift to a broader mission fit with the Clinton administration's early ambitions to work through the UN and promote democracy abroad. Thus the new administration may have provided a permissive environment for the United States to play a significant if limited role in a more expansive, transformative strategy than that envisioned by Bush. When the policy failed—symbolized by the Black Hawk incident— Clinton backed away from the nation-building mission. But in his first few months in office, there was little indication that Clinton viewed the move toward nation building as problematic.

For my purposes, although the details of the decision making, particularly after January 1993, remain somewhat murky, there were discernible differences in the Bush and Clinton administrations' goals for Somalia. The elder Bush might have preferred to stay out of crises such as Somalia altogether; once he decided to intervene, he aimed to do so in the most limited way possible. His attempt at a "surgical" intervention did little to address the country's underlying problems (leading to a reversion to chaos once U.S. forces pulled out). But there were short-term successes for UNITAF in terms of saving lives, and the expansion of the mission in 1993 without proper preparation had its own tragic results. Though a difficult case given the changing international environment and relative inattention by the Clinton administration, the Somalia intervention illuminates the enduring relevance of leadership in the post–Cold War world.

The contrast between Bush and Clinton also manifested itself in other intervention choices, notably in Haiti. After a coup overthrew the elected government of Jean-Bertrand Aristide in 1990, the Bush administration "limited itself to ineffectual protests" and "showed no interest in reinstalling Aristide to power through the use of force."[65] Philippe Girard argues that it was the election of Clinton in 1992 that "made a change in Haitian policy possible," leading to the 1994 intervention to restore Aristide and reform Haiti's domestic institutions, including the government and the police.[66] Like so many other attempts at transformation, the 1994 intervention in Haiti was not particularly successful in terms of long-term democratization. But Clinton's policy was markedly different from that of both George H. W. Bush and his son, who criticized Clinton's intervention in Haiti during the 2000 campaign.

The Iraq War

Given the centrality of the Iraq War to American foreign policy in the post–September 11 world, it is natural to ask how the theory applies to the Iraq case. On one level, the answer is unsatisfying. With the conflict so recent and without access to the relevant private papers and internal administration documents, we lack sufficient evidence to fully assess either George W. Bush's threat perception or the true goals and intended strategy for the intervention. Analysts and policymakers have put forth many explanations for the intervention and its aftermath, and it will take careful examination of all the evidence, when it becomes available, to make a complete assessment.

Nevertheless, in this section I highlight what the theory can say about the Iraq case given the publicly available evidence, though this discussion must be considered speculative. At first glance, the 2003 invasion of Iraq and the removal of Saddam Hussein from power stand in stark contrast to the first Gulf War in 1991, when the United States reversed Iraq's invasion of Kuwait and explicitly rejected an opportunity to change Iraq's regime and transform its domestic institutions. But while the 2003 invasion resulted in regime change in Iraq, one of the most puzzling aspects of the war is why the administration was so unprepared to deal with the postwar phase. The initial war plan apparently did not call for the United States to engage in extensive institution building.

Significant evidence suggests that before taking office, George W. Bush was averse to strategies such as nation building, and in the early, pre–September 11 phase of his tenure, the administration downgraded the priority of peacekeeping and stability operations. Two important questions, then, are whether Bush's beliefs changed after September 11 and whether the goal of the Iraq War was to thoroughly transform Iraq or was instead to make a more limited demonstration of American strength by removing Saddam Hussein's regime while leaving other Iraqi institutions in place. As this book has stressed, an intervention that results in regime change is not necessarily transformative, if it does not also seek to transform the domestic institutions of the target state. These questions are not yet fully answerable. But regardless of the war's true goal, the available evidence suggests that the initial U.S. intervention strategy may have been effectively nontransformative. Furthermore, the Bush administration's lack of initial policy investments in transformative strategies reduced U.S. preparedness for combatting the insurgency that eventually developed in Iraq and the United States' ability to adjust course even when the administration shifted to a more transformative approach.

The Pre-presidential George W. Bush

Like Bill Clinton, Bush campaigned for the presidency as a governor with little direct foreign policy experience. We must therefore rely on his campaign statements to assess his pre-presidential views, and as in the case of Clinton, these statements must be taken with a grain of salt. By the time he took office, however, Bush had articulated a relatively clear stance on certain aspects of intervention, namely, a firm opposition to nation building and getting deeply involved in other states' domestic affairs. In his first major foreign policy speech of the campaign, in November 1999, Bush was critical of American involvement in peacekeeping missions, a critique that became a campaign theme. Bush also sounded an externally focused note, arguing, "We value the elegant structures of our own democracy but realize that, in other societies, the architecture will vary. We propose our principles but we must not impose our culture."[67] As the campaign proceeded, Bush became more critical of specific Clinton interventions. In late November 1999, when asked by Tim Russert on NBC's *Meet the Press* whether he would send troops to "a place like Haiti or Somalia," Bush replied, "I strongly doubt it. I strongly doubt it."[68]

By the time of the October 2000 debates with Vice President Al Gore, Bush had honed his stance against nation building. In the first debate, in response to moderator Jim Lehrer's question about when it would be in the national interest to use force, Bush replied, "I think we've got to be very careful when we commit our troops. The vice president and I have a disagreement about the use of troops. He believes in nation building. I would be very careful about using our troops as nation builders. I believe the role of the military is to fight and win war and therefore prevent war from happening in the first place."[69] In the second debate, Lehrer asked each candidate about specific interventions. On Somalia, Bush answered that it "started off as a humanitarian mission and it changed into a nation-building mission, and that's where the mission went wrong. The mission was changed. And as a result, our nation paid a price. And so I don't think our troops ought to be used for what's called nation-building. I think our troops ought to be used to fight and win war. I think our troops ought to be used to help overthrow the dictator when it's in our best interests. But in this case it was a nation-building exercise, and same with Haiti. I wouldn't have supported either." Thus Bush even drew a distinction between overthrowing dictators and nation building. When Lehrer asked whether, as an alternative to using the military for civil functions, the United States should create "a civil force of some kind that comes in after the military," Bush responded, "I don't think so. I think what we need to do is convince people who live in the lands they live in to build the nations. Maybe I'm missing something here. I mean, we're going to have kind of a nation building core from America? Absolutely not. Our military is meant to fight and win war. That's what it's meant to do." And in response to a question about financial and economic obligations, Bush replied, "I'm not so sure the role of the United States is to go around the world and say this is the way it's got to be. We can help. . . . I want to help people help themselves, not have government tell people what to do. I just don't think it's the role of the United States to walk into a country and say, we do it this way, so should you."[70]

Thus the role of the military, according to Bush, was to fight conventional wars and not to get involved in building institutions within other states. Bush's lead foreign policy adviser, Condoleezza Rice, put it even more bluntly in an October 2000 interview, asserting, "We don't need to have the 82nd Airborne escorting kids to kindergarten."[71] There was little evidence that Bush viewed the domestic politics of other states as important to the national interest or national security of the United States, and he took a dim view of transformative strategies.

Bush also made some pre-presidential statements about Iraq and the general class of "rogue" states. Again, we must rely on publicly available accounts, and Bush's statements are vague enough to suggest multiple interpretations. It is also important to remember that the official U.S. policy toward Iraq at the end of the Clinton administration was regime change, and Clinton gave some support to Iraqi opposition groups.[72] In general, Bush's statements about Iraq and other "rogues" seem to have focused on Saddam Hussein and on the threat of rogue states acquiring weapons of mass destruction (WMD). In several instances, either Bush or his advisers suggested he would support removing Saddam Hussein.[73] In a Republican debate during the primary season, in December 1999, Bush said he would not ease the sanctions on Saddam Hussein but he would "try to negotiate with him and I'd make darn sure that he lived up to the agreements that he signed back in the early 90's. I'd be helping the opposition groups." And if "in any way shape or form . . . he was developing any weapons of mass destruction, I'd take him out. I'm surprised he's still there."[74] In the October 2000 debates, Bush again linked U.S. action to Iraqi WMD development and mentioned Iraq as a reason for developing a ballistic missile defense system. In arguing for continued friendship with moderate Arab regimes such as Jordan, Egypt, Saudi Arabia, and Kuwait, Bush said of Saddam Hussein, "We don't know whether he's developing weapons of mass destruction. He better not be or there's going to be a consequence should I be the president. But it's important to have credibility. . . . One of the reasons why I think it's important for this nation to develop an anti-ballistic missile system that we can share with our allies in the Middle East if need be to keep the peace is to be able to say to the Saddam Husseins of the world or the Iranians, don't dare threaten our friends."[75]

When Bush took office, therefore, he did so with an expressed distaste for nation building and a view that Iraq was a threat. He had been vague on precisely why Iraq represented a threat, but he usually referred to Iraq along with other rogue states and in the context of the possible development of WMD. In mentioning the overthrow of dictators but disdaining nation building, he seemed to suggest that the two could be separated—that it was possible to replace the leadership of a target state without involving U.S. forces in the building or rebuilding of institutions.

Early Policy Investments

There is some evidence that in the first eight months of the Bush administration, before September 11, 2001, policy investments—and divestments—began to reflect Bush's approach. In terms of staffing decisions, many key members of Bush's national security team, including Rice and Secretary of State Colin Powell, held externally driven threat perceptions and shared the president's unfavorable view of nation building.[76] Others, such as Defense Secretary Donald Rumsfeld, were interested in making policy investments, but of a particular kind: Rumsfeld was focused on turning the U.S. military into a lighter, quicker, information-driven force that could fight wars with fewer men and less materiel. Though often termed a "transformation" of the military, it was a very different kind of transformation than I discuss in this book, having nothing to do with capabilities for reforming or rebuilding the domestic institutions of other states; indeed, Rumsfeld was dismissive of nation building and later, planning for post-war Iraq.[77]

In the early Bush administration, there was a corresponding shift away from investing in transformative capabilities. During Clinton's second term, following the difficulties the United States encountered in peacekeeping missions, Clinton issued Presidential Decision Directive (PDD) 56, "Managing Complex Contingency Operations." According to an administration White Paper, the PDD called "for all U.S. Government agencies to institutionalize what we have learned from our recent experiences" in peace operations. The PDD made clear the expectation that the "need for complex contingency operations is likely to recur in future years."[78] However late in the administration the PDD appeared, or however flawed its design or implementation might have been, it was an attempt to pull together lessons from recent peace operations, many of which had faced serious problems, and to improve planning and coordination in future operations.

The Bush administration, as George Packer notes, rescinded PDD 56 in a national security directive shortly after Bush's inauguration. The new directive "abolished Clinton's system of interagency working groups and downgraded the 'contingency operations' group to a bureaucratic level where it was bound to languish—and it did."[79] Work began on a replacement, but as James Fallows notes, "nothing was on hand as of September 11."[80] It was not until December 2005, with the insurgency in Iraq more than two years old, that the Bush administration issued National Security Presidential Directive 44, replacing Clinton's PDD 56 and tasking the State Department, through its Office of Reconstruction and Stabilization (created in 2004), to take the lead in interagency coordination of nonmilitary efforts.[81] Thus in the period before September 11, 2001, the Bush administration deemphasized investment in capabilities for nation building and other transformative strategies.

U.S. STRATEGY IN IRAQ

It is worth considering the subsequent decision to invade Iraq and the war's aftermath in light of these pre-presidential views and initial presidential policy investments. There are many questions about Iraq that remain unanswered. But if the evidence from Bush's pre-presidential statements and initial period in office before September 11, 2001, suggests that he was generally inclined not to connect internal conditions in other states to U.S. national security, then a basic question is whether Bush's beliefs changed after September 11. In terms of Iraq specifically, did Bush perceive the threat in Iraq to be Saddam Hussein's international behavior (with the risk that he might acquire WMD), or did he perceive the entire domestic structure of Iraq to be the threat? In other words, how deep did the threat from Iraq go? As Jervis points out, Bush talked about both the external threat and the democracy motive, and "both views could have been right, but either one would have been sufficient for the decision, and there is no logical reason why the two should have gone together."[82] This issue, in turn, suggests another set of questions about the goals of the intervention and the nature of the intervention strategy: in terms of its original goals, was the intervention intended to be a "decapitation" of the regime, leaving underlying institutions relatively intact, or was it intended to be a thorough remaking of Iraqi institutions and even Iraqi society? And thus was the strategy intended to be thoroughly transformative?

On the issue of Bush's beliefs, there are at least two possibilities. First, it is possible that Bush had a true change in beliefs after September 11 and became an internally focused leader. As discussed, although empirically I do not find much evidence of presidential learning, a direct attack such as that of September 11 might be the kind of moment that induces a change in beliefs.[83] This scenario would suggest that Bush perceived the entire domestic structure within Iraq as a threat and intended the invasion to fundamentally remake Iraq. Alternatively, he may have viewed the aftermath of September 11 through the framework of his existing beliefs and thus viewed Saddam Hussein and his foreign and security policies as the primary source of threat. Under this alternative, one might expect that the invasion was intended to be a decapitation. There are still other possibilities: for example, it is possible that the goal was transformation but with a limited strategy based on the assumption that removing Saddam would be enough to trigger democratization. Furthermore, given reports about significant differences among Bush administration officials, the Iraq War may have represented a logroll between some who had transformative aims for Iraq and others, such as Rumsfeld, who were interested in reforming the military and thus wanted to invade with the smallest U.S. force possible.

On the question whether Bush's beliefs changed, there is evidence on both sides. On the one hand, Bush himself suggested that his mindset changed after September 11. In August 2002, he told Bob Woodward in an interview, "I will seize the opportunity to achieve big goals. . . . Clearly there will be a strategic implication to a regime change in Iraq, if we go forward. But there's something beneath that, as far as I'm concerned, and that is, there is immense suffering. . . . As we think through Iraq, we may or may not attack. I have no idea, yet. But it will be for the objective of making the world more peaceful."[84] Two years after September 11, in another interview with Woodward, Bush said that the attacks on September 11 "obviously changed my thinking a lot about my responsibility as president. Because September the 11th made the security of the American people the priority . . . a sacred duty for the president."[85] The 2002 National Security Strategy outlined the goal of creating "a balance of power that favors human freedom" and employed some democracy promotion rhetoric.[86] In a speech to the American Enterprise Institute a few weeks before the Iraq War began, Bush outlined an internally focused vision of the problem and indicated that a transformed Iraq would eliminate the threat, arguing, "Acting against the danger will also contribute greatly to the long-term safety and stability of our world. The current Iraqi regime has shown the power of tyranny to spread discord and violence in the Middle East. A liberated Iraq can show the power of freedom to transform that vital region, by bringing hope and progress into the lives of millions. America's interests in security and America's belief in liberty both lead in the same direction, to a free and peaceful Iraq."[87] By the time of Bush's 2005 inaugural address, nearly two years into the war, the connection between freedom and national security was even more explicit. "For as long as whole regions of the world simmer in resentment and tyranny, prone to ideologies that feed hatred and excuse murder," Bush argued, "violence will gather and multiply in destructive power and cross the most defended borders and raise a mortal threat."[88]

Furthermore, some in the administration believed that Bush had undergone a change in beliefs after September 11 and was now committed to what might be termed a transformative course. Woodward notes that speechwriter Michael Gerson saw a "change in the president's thinking" to reflect new goals, including promoting democracy and reforming societies abroad.[89] Woodward also reports that Vice President Dick Cheney believed Bush's goal was to "not just get rid of Saddam but replace his regime with a democracy."[90]

Additionally, there was a contingent within the administration and among its outside supporters that focused on the internal conditions in Iraq even before the Bush administration took office. Many were neoconservatives, whose views on foreign policy explicitly incorporated an internal focus. Within the administration, perhaps the most notable of this group was Deputy Defense Secretary Paul Wolfowitz.[91] Wolfowitz had supported the Clinton-era interventions and pushed for more consideration of toppling Saddam Hussein early in the Bush administration, though as Thomas Ricks notes, Wolfowitz was "in a minority" in the early Bush administration.[92]

On the other hand, there is also evidence to support the idea that the intervention aimed at a much narrower threat from the international behavior of Saddam Hussein's regime. It is possible that under this scenario a democratic

Iraq was viewed as a welcome and positive bonus, though not a motivating goal sufficient in its own right to drive the decision to intervene or the choice of strategy. Bush's own rhetoric does not make clear which of his underlying beliefs may have changed. In some cases, Bush invoked September 11 as a moment of change in his thinking, but it was in terms of how imminent or proximate he viewed the threat from Saddam Hussein's Iraq rather than a change in how he viewed the nature of that threat. In a news conference just weeks before the war began, he said, "September the 11th changed the strategic thinking, at least, as far as I was concerned, for how to protect our country. My job is to protect the American people. It used to be that we could think that you could contain a person like Saddam Hussein, that oceans would protect us from his type of terror. September the 11th should say to the American people that we're now a battlefield, that weapons of mass destruction in the hands of a terrorist organization could be deployed here at home."[93]

It is also difficult to pinpoint the true motivation behind the democracy promotion rhetoric, which appeared in some early post–September 11 and prewar statements but was put forward as a motivation for the invasion well after the war itself began. As Packer observes, though there were those like Wolfowitz and some outside the government who embraced the transformative agenda, it "wasn't at all clear that Bush's inner circle shared the dreams and visions of war intellectuals outside government."[94] Instead, the basis for war was defined narrowly, in terms of WMD. Packer notes that the "idea of diminishing the threat to America from ideologies originating in the Middle East by moving the politics of the region toward democracy, beginning in Iraq, had occurred to the Bush administration before the [WMD] turned out not to exist," and it was a "serious" idea that deserved to be engaged, but the prewar emphasis was not on democracy promotion.[95]

Regardless of the war's true aim, there is also the issue of how the war was planned and executed. Here again there are several possibilities. The strategy may have been intended to be a decapitation, and thus postwar planning would have been considered largely unnecessary. Alternatively, the strategy may have been intended to result in a fully changed Iraqi state, but using a deliberately minimal footprint to remove Saddam and provide the catalyst for change, which would be largely undertaken by Iraqis. A third possibility is that the strategy may have been intended to be truly transformative, but with overly optimistic assumptions about the postwar phase and a failure to foresee how difficult transformation in Iraq would be.

There is evidence in the available accounts of the war planning, the war itself, and the response to the war's aftermath to suggest that the initial, intended U.S. strategy was effectively nontransformative, in the sense that it did not envision

American troops undertaking significant roles in Iraqi domestic institutions. Instead, the strategy built on the assumption that Iraqi institutions would be left largely intact and would not be rebuilt by a lengthy American occupation.[96] Such a strategy would be consistent with the first two scenarios outlined above: either a decapitation or a deliberately minimal footprint that left transformation up to the Iraqis. The third possibility, that the intention was transformation but with overly optimistic assumptions about the postwar phase, nonetheless highlights the lingering effect of the administration's early external focus and emphasis on nontransformative war fighting (in the sense of not transforming Iraqi institutions; of course, as mentioned, Rumsfeld had his own, very different agenda to "transform" the U.S. military). When the United States confronted the emerging insurgency, the lack of preparedness for transformative strategies hampered efforts to stabilize the situation quickly. The United States had catching up to do in terms of reorienting its strategy to deal with the postwar institutional vacuum and with the insurgency, exposing a gap between ends and means.

As Michael Gordon and Bernard Trainor note in their account of the war planning, the United States may have set "far-reaching goals," but "in keeping with the Bush administration's antipathy toward Clinton-style nation-building, the Bush team intended to carry out this project by relying heavily on Iraqi institutions like the military and the police to maintain order."[97] In an interview with Gordon and Trainor, Rice said that the "concept was that we would defeat the army, but the institutions would hold, everything from ministries to police forces. . . . You would be able to bring new leadership but we were going to keep the body in place."[98] The war plan itself, as available accounts make clear, was also focused on a nontransformative attack with the smallest U.S. footprint possible. As Ricks summarizes, in "military terms, there was a disconnect between the stated strategic goal of transforming the politics of Iraq and the Mideast and the plan's focus on the far more limited aim of simply removing Saddam Hussein's regime."[99] The plan, Cobra II, stated that the operation's purpose was "to force the collapse of the Iraqi regime and deny it the use of WMD to threaten its neighbors and U.S. interests," and defined the "endstate" of the operation as "regime change."[100] The focus of the operation, however, was a "very conventional campaign designed as an attack by one state's military on another's."[101] The administration's approach resembled its early strategy in Afghanistan in 2001, when arguably the initial aim was to remove the top leadership but the United States did little to directly transform underlying institutions.[102]

Much of the impetus to keep the U.S. force small came from Rumsfeld, who aimed to demonstrate a new kind of war fighting with a lighter, quicker, and more maneuverable force. In this sense, the plan was unconventional, but it did not contemplate the direct transformation of Iraqi institutions. Yet although the army continued to suffer from a deficit in terms of transformative capabilities (and counterinsurgency advocates were not a prominent part of the discussion at this stage), many in the army pushed for a larger force, which would improve the chances of securing postwar Iraq. This view was perhaps most famously expressed by Army Chief of Staff Eric Shinseki, who told the Senate Armed Services Committee in February 2003 that the postwar phase would require "something on the order of several hundred thousand troops," and was soon publicly contradicted by Wolfowitz, who called Shinseki's estimate "wildly off the mark."[103] The Shinseki view was based in part on the requirements for securing a country as large and complex as Iraq in light of experience with peacekeeping during the Clinton years.[104] The army's own study of the war, *On Point II*, acknowledges the military's long-standing resistance to transformative operations and the lack of training in operations such as counterinsurgency, but it also highlights the cumulative experience the army gained in stability operations during the 1990s.[105] Yet Rumsfeld continued to attack the concept of nation building, giving a speech titled "Beyond Nation Building" just over a month before the Iraq War began.[106]

While the record remains incomplete, Bush himself does not seem to have questioned this thinking. According to Woodward, in one meeting with CENTCOM commander Tommy Franks during the planning phase, Bush expressed a desire to have the operation "done as efficiently and in as short a time as possible," giving what Franks interpreted as a "presidential hint" that shorter was better.[107] Packer reports that when key Iraqi opposition figures met with Bush in January 2003, Bush seemed "unfocused on the key policy questions of the future of the Iraqi army, de-baathification, and an interim government."[108]

As has been well chronicled, the U.S. war plans emphasized the "kinetic" phase of the war—defeating Saddam's army and getting to Baghdad—at the expense of the postwar phase. In part, this omission may have been a deliberate decision: postwar planning in the run-up to the war might have seemed like putting the cart before the diplomatic horse and might have weakened the case for the war itself.[109] Other analysts stress that there was some postwar planning, but it was based on optimistic or inaccurate assumptions, resulting in hastily developed and inadequate plans.[110] Those who genuinely wanted to democratize Iraq and those who saw democratization as a positive by-product of removing Saddam seemed to agree that the American military would not actually do much institution building. Instead, perhaps these policymakers believed that merely removing the constraint of Saddam Hussein would be enough to allow democracy to grow in Iraq. But there was a deliberate assumption, at least for the *initial* U.S. effort, that direct U.S. involvement in Iraqi institutions would be minimal.

These overly optimistic assumptions were reflected in the postwar planning. The NSC spent a week in January 2003—two months before the war began—developing a document on postwar coordination for the president to sign, in what Woodward calls a "rush job." The result was the Office of Reconstruction and Humanitarian Assistance, or ORHA.[111] ORHA, headed by retired lieutenant general Jay Garner, had very little time and not nearly enough resources to deal with the postwar phase. As many accounts also point out, other groups, both inside and outside the government, had made efforts at postwar planning or at least conceptualizing the scope of the postwar problem, but they were ignored. While many of these efforts were not fully developed, implementable plans, they drew on experience in postconflict environments and many of them correctly predicted the problems that would arise in Iraq after the invasion. The range of planning included the State Department's "Future of Iraq" study, CIA war-gaming sessions, an Army War College study that focused on lessons from the American military past, and a Council on Foreign Relations working group.[112] Additionally, Franks's predecessor as CENTCOM commander, Anthony Zinni, had left behind a plan for dealing with Iraq should Saddam Hussein's regime collapse. Zinni's plan called for a far larger troop deployment—around 380,000—than would be used in the 2003 invasion, and it incorporated postwar operations.[113] Yet as Andrew Rathmell notes, "neither the ORHA nor the [Coalition Provisional Authority] deployed with either an integrated planning process or a set of strategic and operational plans."[114] As RAND analyst Nora Bensahel observes, in theory the Pentagon planning assumptions were "not unreasonable," but the "problem was that no planning occurred for scenarios where these assumptions might not hold."[115]

The role Bush played in the postwar planning remains to be fully examined, but the available record suggests, as Gordon and Trainor note, that when he turned to the postwar phase it was with "little of the attention and energy devoted for sixteen months to the invasion plan."[116] On March 4, 2003, the man in charge of postwar planning, Undersecretary of Defense for Policy Douglas Feith, began to give Bush a series of briefings on the postwar phase (known as Phase IV). In the March 4 briefing, Feith listed several objectives, including that "Iraq is seen to be moving toward democratic institutions and serves as a model for the region" and that the United States should accomplish its goals "urgently." He raised issues such as the postwar level of Baath Party participation in the bureaucracy. As Woodward reports, "It was a lot of abstract political science, and the president didn't have much to say other than to remark that he wanted to see information on how they would deal with the military and intelligence services."[117] On March 5, at Franks's final prewar briefing for the president, Bush asked about Phase IV. Franks responded that each city and town in Iraq would have a "lord mayor." Gordon and Trainor note that Franks's "response seemed to satisfy Bush and there was little follow-up."[118]

In the NSC meeting on March 10, after an NSC staffer briefed on the importance of keeping the Iraqi state running, including dealing with the bureaucracy and maintaining law and order in the postconflict environment, Bush said he wanted to gain the trust of the Iraqis and not choose their new leaders. He concluded, "We've got to hold our fire on getting the details set until we've learned more."[119] As Woodward notes, this decision killed the plan to install Iraqi exile Ahmed Chalabi in power and "defer[red] the notion of an early provisional government."[120] Chalabi was the Pentagon's preferred candidate and crucial to its hopes of allowing the United States to quickly stabilize Iraq and withdraw.[121] It remains unclear what Bush's refusal to endorse the Chalabi plan reveals about the administration's underlying goals. It is possible that the refusal to install Chalabi indicated a rejection of a plan that would simply replace one leader with another and stemmed from a desire to seek a more inclusive, democratic solution. But it may have also derived from Bush's view that the United States should stay out of the postwar Iraqi domestic political scene as much as possible. According to Woodward, Bush wanted to show trust in the Iraqis by turning over some ministries quickly and noted that the population "will have some resentment toward those Iraqis that were outside the country during Saddam's rule."[122] Bush did not indicate that avoiding the Chalabi plan would require the United States to undertake more significant military involvement in Iraqi institutions. Furthermore, in the 2001 intervention in Afghanistan, power had been transferred quickly to Hamid Karzai in a largely elite-driven process. Bush's wish to avoid choosing Iraq's leaders may have reflected a belief that removing Saddam Hussein was all that would be necessary to change Iraq, but such a belief still suggests Bush did not necessarily see U.S. forces undertaking a transformative postwar role.

Given the lack of detail surrounding the postwar phase, U.S. troops entering Iraq did not expect to significantly interfere in, much less take over, Iraqi domestic institutions. Of course, it remains an open question whether any strategy would have successfully secured—much less transformed—Iraq.[123] But here I am interested only in assessing whether the initial strategy was transformative. To be sure, regime change was the goal of the operation. But on the measures used to code interventions in this book, the initial strategy in Iraq scores closer to the nontransformative end of the spectrum. At the level of leadership change, planning focused on removing Saddam Hussein and the group surrounding him, with the number of senior Iraqis to be removed from power described as around fifty.[124] The planning also called for Iraqi institutions to remain intact. At the national level, as Bensahel notes, planning assumed that "no large-scale reconstruction would . . . be necessary" and that the "United States would only need to help the ministries continue their work for a short time during the transition of power." Indeed, Garner planned to leave Iraq in June 2003.[125] The only ministry defended by U.S. forces in the initial postinvasion period, when looting was rampant, was the oil ministry.[126] At the local level, as the army's study notes, initially U.S. forces did not have orders to halt the looting "or serve as a general police force."[127]

In terms of the intended integration of nonmilitary issues with the overall military strategy—an indicator for whether an intervention was intended to be transformative—the evidence points to a lack of cohesion between civilian and military planners that played out on the ground. Rathmell states that the coalition "failed to produce an integrated political-military plan for Iraq" before the war.[128] As Bensahel notes, the Pentagon took responsibility for the postwar mission, partly in the hope of ensuring unity of effort and command. But the military's lack of reconstruction experience, coupled with plans that did not call for ORHA even to enter Baghdad until 120 days after combat operations ended, meant that there was a disconnect between military and nonmilitary issues.[129] Furthermore, the Pentagon itself was led by officials committed to avoiding direct U.S. nation building. Even after L. Paul Bremer's arrival and the formation of the Coalition Provisional Authority (CPA) in May 2003, unity of command suffered from the lack of linkage between the CPA and the military command (CJTF-7).[130] Additionally, the initial U.S. plans did not call for extensive interaction with the Iraqi population.

The lack of postwar planning and capabilities became apparent in the slowness with which the Bush administration responded to the power vacuum in Iraq after the defeat of Saddam, as well as the emerging insurgency. U.S. policy in Iraq after the fall of Baghdad is often associated with the two major decisions taken by the newly arrived Bremer: to disband the Iraqi army and to undertake a sweeping removal of Baath Party members. But the initial U.S. plans called for significant reliance on the Iraqi army after the war; as the *On Point II* study notes, neither widespread debaathification nor the disbanding of the army was part of the original Pentagon plan for postwar Iraq (although the United States did plan a more limited removal of high-level Baath Party members).[131] Indeed, it is important to note that the installation of Bremer coincided with a significant change in the Bush administration's approach to Iraq. Whereas U.S. policy initially aimed to rely on existing Iraqi institutions, with Bremer's arrival, as Bensahel puts it, there was a "fundamental shift in US policy towards postwar Iraq."[132] Packer also notes that Bremer's arrival produced a "new vision of the American role in Iraq." Bremer now "began to plan in earnest," trying to "fill in all the blanks left empty back in Washington" to achieve "nothing short of an overhaul of Iraqi society from top to bottom."[133]

Yet the CPA "did not start with a clean slate," and thus the United States was slow to take on the responsibility for essential law-and-order functions.[134] Indeed, Washington was slow to recognize the emerging instability and ultimately the insurgency as a serious problem that required a large-scale, coordinated response. Even when Bremer arrived to take over from Garner with a mandate to transform Iraq, he had "only a rudimentary plan for the new Iraqi military and police forces and few resources to create those institutions."[135] In the case of the Iraqi army, as Fallows details, in the preoccupation with the insurgency no one seems to have devoted significant attention to creating a new army until it became perceived as a vital route to an exit strategy.[136] While Rathmell acknowledges that the postwar task in Iraq would not have been easy under the best of circumstances, he also concludes that the lack of postwar planning meant that the CPA "ended up creating nation-building institutions on the run" rather than benefiting from a "running start."[137] As Packer observes, "Even as Bremer and the CPA began to resurrect Iraq physically from its long decay and sudden collapse, the intellectual failures of the planning continued to haunt the occupation."[138]

On the military side, even when the insurgency began, the United States remained focused on offensive operations designed to kill insurgents rather than the kind of counterinsurgency operations intended to provide security and build up local institutions.[139] As Ricks details, some operations, particularly those undertaken by Army Special Forces, were carried out according to classic counterinsurgency doctrine and were successful; some army commanders also had success with population-centered counterinsurgency, with a focus on local institutions, in areas such as Tal Afar and northern Iraq.[140] But in terms of the overall U.S. strategy, such operations remained scattered, at least until the 2007 "surge" and the official shift to a counterinsurgency strategy. Though many individual American units began to develop contacts with the local Iraqi population and even to initiate reconstruction projects, such efforts remained ad hoc in the early postwar period. Military commanders in the field were often far ahead of higher headquarters and the CPA, which were slow to develop central guidance and standardize policies across Iraq.[141]

Regardless of whether the ultimate U.S. goal was a complete transformation of Iraq (from the beginning, rather than from the point at which Bremer arrived in Baghdad with a new mandate), what accounts for the apparently nontransformative strategy with which U.S. forces entered Iraq? The precise motivations of the decision makers in the Iraq War await further investigation. But irrespective of which threat perception (Saddam Hussein's international behavior or the Iraqi domestic structure) motivated the war, or which goal (decapitation, complete transformation, or transformation with a limited footprint) was intended, the theory developed in this book is relevant, for several reasons. Even if we assume that the goal was a true transformation of Iraq, the lack of policy investments in transformative strategies in the initial period of the Bush administration left U.S. forces shorthanded for the war. If the transformation was intended to occur with a small U.S. footprint, the United States still faced a gap between ends and means once the institutional vacuum and the insurgency emerged. And if the intention all along was simply a decapitation, we can still ask why the United States was so ill-prepared—materially, bureaucratically, and intellectually—to shift the strategy as the war evolved.

All three scenarios suggest that the lack of policy investments in transformative capabilities had important consequences. Furthermore, there is evidence that Bush's initial aversion to nation building left an imprint on the war plans. The Army's *On Point II* study notes that on "the level of strategic policy, the [Pentagon's] approach to Iraq was significantly shaped by the Bush administration's overall wary attitude toward . . . nation-building."[142] As Bensahel observes, the "interagency process reflects the preferences and style of the President," whose sustained leadership is necessary to force agencies to work together.[143]

It is difficult to assess learning in an ongoing case like Iraq, but the evolution of the war again raises the possibility that changes in intervention strategy occurred in response to events, with changes in beliefs slower to catch up. Policymakers in Washington were slow to recognize the magnitude of the problem inside Iraq; once they grasped that there was a serious problem, they were still slow to acknowledge it as a full-fledged insurgency. Even after U.S. strategy shifted in a more transformative direction with the arrival of Bremer in May 2003, the United States still lacked a comprehensive, Iraq-wide politico-military strategy to address Iraqi reconstruction and the insurgency in both military and nonmilitary terms. Only in 2006 and into 2007 did the "clear, hold, and build" strategy evolve into a more comprehensive counterinsurgency strategy, with an emphasis on nation building (as codified in the new Counterinsurgency Field Manual).[144] There remains significant debate over whether the new strategy and the accompanying "surge" were actually responsible for the subsequent reduction in violence. But leaving aside that debate, the relevant issue here is whether the shift in strategy reflected a true change in Bush's beliefs, or a response to events. It remains to be determined whether Bush's beliefs about the origin of threats evolved as the intervention progressed and the strategy shifted over time. Even if the new strategy was the result of learning, however, the administration's initial choices dramatically shaped the course of the war.

Furthermore, the war illustrates that even presidents who are averse to transformative strategies can find themselves facing conflicts where transformative capabilities may be deemed appropriate, such as insurgencies. Even if Bush was totally committed to the democratic transformation of Iraq, he still had to live with the effects of his pre–September 11 policies, which deemphasized capabilities that policymakers would later see as vital to turning the war around. Thus the president's beliefs and initial policy choices left their mark on an intervention whose origins and consequences will undoubtedly be debated for some time to come.

7

The Role of Leaders

CONCLUSIONS AND IMPLICATIONS

The decision to launch an overt military intervention, particularly in a democracy, can be highly complex. The international environment, domestic politics, and the bureaucracy all exert constraints on decision makers. International relations scholars have long shied away from incorporating leaders into their theories, either because they do not believe that leaders play an independent role in shaping state behavior or because they believe leaders are important but do not think it is possible to specify systematically *how* leaders matter. But this book has shown that leaders play an independent and systematic role in shaping decisions to intervene and the choice of intervention strategy. The role of leaders cannot be reduced to contingency, nor are leaders merely flawed misperceivers of otherwise objective cues from the international environment.

The framework developed here presents a simple typology of leaders. At least in terms of threat perception, leaders do not come in infinite varieties but rather can be usefully categorized into one of two ideal types. Leaders' causal beliefs about the origin of threats systematically influence decisions to intervene by altering the cost-benefit calculus of the intervention itself and by shaping the tools available to states when they undertake military interventions. Presidents from the early twentieth century—when the United States acquired the power to project its influence abroad and intervene militarily—to the post–Cold War era viewed the international environment they confronted through the lens of their beliefs and intervened accordingly.

I find that internally focused leaders are more likely to undertake transformative interventions whereas externally focused leaders are more likely to undertake nontransformative interventions. Leaders' causal beliefs about the origin of threats also affect their willingness to intervene at all. Furthermore, the leader's type influences preparedness for intervention, and preparedness in turn affects the estimated cost and risk of intervening. When other factors such as domestic political considerations overwhelm leaders' doubts about a given intervention, a "mismatched" intervention may result. Even if the leader chooses an apparently appropriate strategy, if he has not invested in the relevant capabilities, a gap between the ends and means of intervention may develop.

The primary alternative hypotheses addressed in this book—the structural/material conditions hypothesis and the domestic competition hypothesis—emphasize factors that while undoubtedly important, are not sufficient to account for the full range of intervention choices. Eisenhower, Kennedy, and Johnson were all willing to clash with their advisers and with the bureaucracy. They were sometimes constrained by existing capabilities and the situation on the ground, but these factors did not fully determine their intervention choices.

I began from the premise that demonstrating the systematic and independent role of leaders required holding domestic institutions and the structure of the international system constant, and thus the book focused on the United States during the Cold War. But the Cold War might seem an unlikely choice for exploring leaders' perceptions of how the domestic institutions of other states mattered for national security. After all, the Cold War was partly driven by a clash over how to organize domestic institutions, and many of its fiercest hot wars in the Third World were battles over domestic institutions.

The nature of the Cold War makes it a demanding test for the theory. Despite a shared anticommunist consensus, American presidents throughout the conflict held very different beliefs about just how much the inner workings of Third World states represented potential threats to or vulnerabilities for U.S. national security, and thus how deeply American concern with the domestic institutions of these states should extend. Was an anticommunist, pro-Western foreign policy enough, or should the United States worry about precisely what form these anticommunist governments took? Leaders' views on this question shaped U.S. intervention decisions during the Cold War.

Differing threat perceptions during the Cold War could also make for some strange bedfellows. Consider Eisenhower and Johnson, who had significant differences on questions such as the size of the defense budget and the American military. Eisenhower's restrained vision of defense spending and the scope of the military contrasted sharply with the far more expansive defense policies of both Kennedy and Johnson. These different visions affected the scale of these leaders' interventions: Eisenhower's only overt military intervention was far smaller in scope than Johnson's escalation in Vietnam, for example.

Yet on the question of how much the domestic politics of Third World states mattered for the national security of the United States, Eisenhower and Johnson were far more similar than Kennedy and Johnson. One of the advantages of the book's case selection is that the three leaders examined many of the same issues and crises: Kennedy and Johnson commented during their pre-presidential careers in Congress on several Eisenhower administration decisions. Consider the reactions to Eisenhower's nontransformative deployment of troops to Lebanon. As discussed in chapter 3, Eisenhower sent troops to Beirut despite indications from the U.S. ambassador that intervention was not needed in terms of Lebanon itself; the intervention had more to do with the coup in Iraq and the international situation. Johnson lauded the effort as a way to "make it clear to the aggressors that this country is determined to maintain freedom in this world, at whatever the cost," but the *New York Times* wondered which aggressors Johnson meant. Though Kennedy saw the intervention as "not wholly implausible," he wrote that he was "opposed to this intervention and did not feel that it made much sense . . . in terms of the evidence about the internal situation in Lebanon and Iraq." Even before the 1958 crises, he had called Dulles's effort to build the Baghdad Pact "dubious," saying it would be ineffective because economic development, rather than aggression, was the real problem in the Middle East.[1] Similarly, the three presidents' choices in Vietnam are illuminating. All three aimed to keep South Vietnam out of the communist camp. Yet Eisenhower and Johnson were content to accept the anticommunism of Diem (or in Johnson's case, a suitable successor) without paying much attention to what went on beneath the surface, whereas Kennedy saw Diem's repressive regime as part of Vietnam's vulnerability to communist encroachment. Thus even amid the Cold War consensus, important differences in threat perception led to divergent policy choices.

Although the book concentrated on the Cold War, chapter 6 shows that the argument applies in other settings. Each time period exerts constraints on how states wield intervention, as Finnemore shows,[2] and the Cold War is no exception—such constraints may have limited the total number of Cold War interventions and are perhaps one reason there were few transformative overt military interventions by the superpowers. But the typology of threat perception, and the correlation with intervention strategy, holds in other eras. During the post–Cold War period, when the loosening of international constraints led the United States to intervene at a more frequent rate, the contrast in intervention strategies remained striking. Although George H. W. Bush engaged in a somewhat transformative operation in Panama in 1989, in general he limited U.S. involvement in the building or rebuilding of domestic institutions within other states. In his largest intervention, he rolled back Saddam Hussein's aggression against Kuwait but declined to undertake regime change in Baghdad. An internal uprising that led to the removal of Saddam would have been welcome. But transforming Iraq itself was not worth the additional cost to Bush, who had defined American objectives in explicitly international terms—concentrating on reversing Iraqi aggression—and prosecuted the war accordingly.[3] His other intervention decisions, including the limited intervention in Somalia and the noninterventions in Bosnia and Haiti, were consistent with his external focus. Under Bill Clinton, however, U.S. interventions took on a decidedly transformative cast. Although he declined to intervene to stop the genocide in Rwanda—a case in which the shadow of Somalia, coupled with the intensity of the conflict and high estimated costs, led to inaction[4]—Clinton involved U.S. forces in nation building from Somalia and Haiti to the Balkans.

In the post–September 11 environment, the presidency of George W. Bush poses a challenge for the kind of analysis used in this book because of the possibility that September 11 may have prompted a shift in Bush's beliefs. Nevertheless, Bush's initial external focus on taking office affected his later decisions, including in Afghanistan and Iraq. Both interventions aimed at regime change but with small footprints and little initial attention to the rebuilding of domestic institutions; the lack of planning for transformative operations hindered efforts to shift strategy later on.

In the wake of the Iraq War, some commentators predicted that intrusive military interventions were a thing of the past,[5] but there is evidence that, even after Iraq, presidents still face many of the same basic choices outlined in this book. It is too early to assess the beliefs and policy investments of Barack Obama. As this book has stressed, what leaders actually say and do when they reach office may not be a reliable guide to their beliefs, and we do not want to infer his beliefs based on his early statements and decisions as president, especially since he inherited two ongoing wars. The available information on Obama's foreign policy beliefs before he took office remains relatively scant, and some of the evidence points in opposite directions.

The ambiguity of the available record makes even a preliminary categorization of Obama difficult. Perhaps his most famous foreign policy stance before his election was his opposition to the Iraq War. In his 2002 speech denouncing an invasion, he argued that Saddam Hussein was not an "imminent and direct threat" to the United States, suggesting an externally focused view of the threat posed by states like Iraq.[6] In his 2006 book *The Audacity of Hope* (published shortly before he announced his presidential candidacy), Obama argued that "there are few examples in history in which the freedom men and women crave is delivered through outside intervention," and that forcible democratization allows "oppressive regimes [to] paint democratic activists as tools of foreign powers and [retards] the possibility that genuine, home-grown democracy will ever emerge."[7]

On the other hand, one might imagine that Obama's work with local institutions as a community organizer, as chronicled in his memoir, would translate into an internally focused threat perception (although as the case of Johnson illustrates, experience and beliefs in the domestic context do not always translate into threat perceptions in the international sphere).[8] Furthermore, some of Obama's campaign statements—which, of course, must be read with appropriate caution—sounded more internally focused notes. In 2007, for example, he argued, "When narco-trafficking and corruption threaten democracy in Latin America, it's America's problem too. When poor villagers in Indonesia have no choice but to send chickens to market infected with avian flu, it cannot be seen as a distant concern. When religious schools in Pakistan teach hatred to young children, our children are threatened as well." He located the problem of terrorism in "the impoverished, weak and ungoverned states that have become the most fertile breeding grounds for transnational threats like terror and pandemic disease and the smuggling of deadly weapons."[9] It remains unclear whether Obama held an externally focused view or may instead have been dissuaded from supporting interventions such as the invasion of Iraq because he believed that transformation, while perhaps necessary to deal with the root of the threat, would be extremely difficult. In his 2002 speech on Iraq, he argued that "even a successful war against Iraq will require a U.S. occupation of undetermined length, at undetermined cost, with undetermined consequences."[10]

Despite the ambiguities about Obama's beliefs and subsequent decision making, it is possible to view the 2009 debate over whether and how to expand the war in Afghanistan as a choice between a transformative strategy and a nontransformative strategy. According to news accounts of the decision making, the lengthy debate in the summer and fall of 2009 centered on the overall U.S. objective: was it to defeat the Taliban and rebuild Afghanistan as the ultimate way to stop the threat of Al Qaeda terrorism or rather merely to contain Al Qaeda, a goal that might actually entail cutting deals with the Taliban and allowing them more of a role in the Afghan government? Some within the administration pushed for a more intrusive approach, but others, notably Vice President Joseph Biden, favored focusing on the counterterrorism dimension of the threat and limiting U.S. casualties and involvement in the corrupt world of Afghan institutions. While much of the media coverage focused on the level and timing of the troop "surge" that emerged from the debate, a key element of Obama's decision was to avoid a full-scale commitment to nation building and even to defeating the Taliban outright—indeed, the strategy involved reaching out to some Taliban who might be willing to work with the United States. As one senior White House aide put it, "The big moment when the mission became a narrower one was when we realized we're not going to kill every last member of the Taliban."[11]

There were elements of transformation—at least in terms of intentions—in the U.S. strategy, however, particularly the "clear, hold, and build" approach to counterinsurgency in the 2010 offensive to clear the Taliban stronghold of Marja. U.S. forces aimed to focus on local governance and building local institutions; at one point, Obama told General Stanley McChrystal, commander of U.S. and NATO forces in Afghanistan, "Do not clear and hold what you are not willing to build and transfer."[12] It remains unclear how effective this approach has been, but as in other cases the key question for my purposes is how transformative the president intended U.S. policy to be. The nature of the U.S. approach in Afghanistan remains murky and awaits an analysis that can draw on a more complete record.

The theory outlined in this book has limits. The theory identifies ideal types, which by definition do not capture all the inevitable nuances that differentiate individual leaders. Johnson is particularly difficult to categorize, for example, partly because he had such concern for the poor around the world and had genuine hopes that living standards and infrastructure in the Third World could be improved. Furthermore, the theory does not address many aspects of military intervention. As the contrast between the size of Eisenhower's and Johnson's interventions shows, the theory says little about the scale of interventions. One might predict that transformative interventions will be larger than nontransformative interventions, based on estimated force-level requirements for counterinsurgency or stability operations.[13] But leaders have also tried to undertake transformative interventions on smaller scales, as Clinton did in Somalia and Haiti, for example. Furthermore, nontransformative operations can involve large troop commitments, as Johnson's efforts in Vietnam and the large U.S. force employed in the first Gulf War illustrate. The theory also does not fully address the overall propensity for leaders to intervene or the long-term determinants of intervention success. While it acknowledges that factors such as bureaucratic resistance may affect how intended strategy translates into policy outcomes on the ground, it does not theorize these factors directly.

Additionally, to the extent I argue leaders' intended strategies are "mismatched," I mean a mismatch between intended strategy and the nature of the conflict at a general level, that is, whether the conflict required any sort of institution building. The theory does not address how leaders choose exactly where to target any attempted transformation (such as the local or national level, or the relative emphasis placed on political, economic, or security institutions) or on what dimensions they pursue transformation (for example, reshaping politics along ethnic or ideological lines). As our social-scientific knowledge of civil war and conflict has improved, scholars have, for example, criticized the new U.S. counterinsurgency strategy in Iraq as based on flawed assumptions about the nature of the conflict and the dynamics of the insurgency. These critiques see the United States as transforming the "wrong" institutions or going about transformation in the wrong way.[14] Such issues are beyond the scope of this theory, which is concerned with whether and how deeply states intend to transform domestic institutions at all. The theory could be extended to address these issues, however. Psychological biases and cognitive shortcuts may play a role in predicting how leaders will undertake transformation. Khong, for example, finds that Kennedy relied on the Malayan analogy when he approached the conflict in Vietnam. Yet as Khong notes, the analogy was in many ways inappropriate. For example, in Malaya the insurgents were a more readily identifiable ethnic Chinese minority, whereas in Vietnam they were part of the same ethnic group and thus could more easily disappear into the general population.[15]

Another limitation is that to ensure comparability across cases, this book examined only overt military interventions and did not directly address other forms of intervention, such as covert operations. Some might argue that this risks missing important variation in intervention choices since leaders might "substitute" alternative forms of intervention in place of an overt military commitment.[16] There are several reasons why it is nonetheless useful and important to study overt military intervention as a distinct phenomenon. First, as discussed in chapter 1, choosing overt military intervention means committing to a large-scale, visible deployment of force. Such a commitment brings public scrutiny and raises the potential costs—both material and political—that leaders must consider. The decision process that leads to an overt military intervention requires leaders to weigh a different set of factors and consider a different set of possibilities than the process that governs decisions to undertake covert forms of intervention. Lumping them together would risk comparing apples and oranges.

Second, since covert operations involve lower costs and could remain out of the public arena, it is likely that leaders will be tempted to use these tools more often. Indeed, one tendency shared by Eisenhower and Kennedy was a fondness for covert operations. Even after the disaster of the Bay of Pigs, Kennedy used covert operations to try to undermine or even decapitate left-leaning regimes, including in Latin America, where he remained publicly committed to transformative policies that aimed at institutional reform. But it is important to recall that the theory does not argue that leaders' threat perceptions perfectly correlate with their intervention choices. Rather, it outlines leaders' preference orderings for different intervention outcomes. Sometimes leaders will settle for a suboptimal outcome. Thus Kennedy's famous statement about the Dominican Republic was framed as a preference ordering: there were "three possibilities . . . in descending order of preference: a decent democratic regime, a continuation of the Trujillo regime or a Castro regime." He followed this list not with a definitive policy prescription but with a conditional argument: "We ought to aim at the first, but we really can't renounce the second until we are sure that we can avoid the third."[17] Sometimes Kennedy chose the second course—continuing reliance on "friendly dictators"—and even employed covert operations to secure such an outcome. But these cases do not undermine the validity of his statement of preferences. He also spent far more time trying to ensure a "decent democratic regime" than either Eisenhower or Johnson. Indeed, Johnson's own statement about the Dominican Republic yielded a different vision: "We will have one of 3 dictators: 1) U.S., 2) Moderate dictator, 3) Castro dictator."[18]

While there are good theoretical reasons to study overt military intervention separately, it is possible that the argument might be modified or extended to covert operations. As I have discussed, there are instances in which leaders' choices in covert operations track with their overt military intervention decisions. As many have argued, Eisenhower relied on covert operations because they seemed to provide a relatively cheap way to ensure reliably anticommunist regimes in the Third World with a minimal U.S. footprint. Despite their long-term internal consequences, the nature of the operations in Iran and Guatemala in the mid-1950s can be considered nontransformative, in the sense that they were more akin to palace coups that aimed to "surgically" remove leaders deemed too left-leaning. Eisenhower did not intend to transform Iranian or Guatemalan domestic institutions (at least in the short run, since of course his long-term overarching goal, as with all Cold War presidents, was a victory over communist institutions).

But we should be cautious in applying the theory to these kinds of decisions too readily. Covert operations seem to offer leaders the opportunity to pursue quick fixes that may make other overt policies more palatable, even as they appear to be contradictory. The attempts Kennedy made to undermine left-leaning figures in Latin America may have been an effort to prevent perceived losses to communism even as he pursued transformative policies through the Alliance for Progress. Future research might examine whether leaders' threat perceptions translate into intervention choices at the covert level in systematically different ways than they do for overt military intervention.

Implications for Scholarship

This book's findings have implications on a variety of levels. First, they have implications for international relations theory, which has not traditionally focused on the role of individuals (with the notable exception of studies drawing on psychological theories). But the book demonstrates that the attributes of individual leaders cannot be left out of explanations for how states use military force, and that it is possible to make arguments about leaders that yield generalizable predictions and rely on variables that are measurable *ex ante*. Leaders can be studied in a systematic, parsimonious way.

One area that bears further exploration is the origins of leaders' causal beliefs about the nature of threats and the extent to which such beliefs correlate with other beliefs, such as those governing the domestic political realm. I have highlighted the diverse pathways through which leaders can acquire these beliefs, pathways that help to show that the typology I identify is not merely a proxy for some other explanation. But it is also clear that however they acquire these beliefs, American leaders, at least, choose from a menu of beliefs that may be as old as the United States itself. Certain leaders are more likely to take an internally focused view of other states, a view perhaps traceable to Jefferson, whereas others focus on external behavior, an approach associated with Hamilton. These views have been associated at various times with particular political parties, but it remains an open question whether parties themselves are the source of these beliefs or whether individuals' beliefs transcend those of their party.[19] Based on the cases examined in this book, it seems less likely that leaders acquire beliefs through socialization into political parties as institutions. Rather, future leaders may tap into existing currents of thought and then either join the party that most closely corresponds to their beliefs or choose a party based on other factors.

The book also has implications for the study of military intervention. The argument opens up a broader range of intervention choices by distinguishing between transformative and nontransformative strategies. Following scholars such as John Owen, it also suggests that we should be precise about what we mean by "regime change," since not all interventions that change leaders necessarily transform domestic institutions.[20] Future scholarship on intervention should address nuances in how states use force within the boundaries of other states and how deeply intervention actually extends. Another direction for research would be to examine whether parties in civil or international conflicts who fight in the shadow of great-power intervention base their actions not only on their estimates of whether a great power will intervene, but also on whether the current leader of the great power is more likely to pursue a transformative or nontransformative strategy, or on the intervening state's policy investments, to the extent they are observable. The choice of strategy might also have implications for signaling credibility since transformative interventions are often more costly than nontransformative ones and thus might carry more signaling power. Yet since transformative interventions may be riskier, other actors may discount a great power's threat to intervene transformatively, making the credible signaling of such a threat more difficult.

The findings also show that leaders' threat perceptions are an important influence on the probability of intervention success through the mechanism of preparedness. In particular, choices made early in an administration, as well as early in the course of an intervention, can be crucial and difficult to change. While the book does not deal directly with the determinants of intervention success, it suggests that policy investments made early in a presidential administration are an important factor in the outcome of interventions on the ground.

Implications for Policy

This book does not endorse either intervention strategy in the abstract. It should be noted that both internally and externally focused leaders have faced problems and even failures in achieving their intervention goals, using both transformative and nontransformative strategies. But while it remains unclear whether one leader type or the other is more prone to intervene generally—since knowledge of the difficulty of intervening transformatively, for example, may restrain some internally focused leaders, but psychological pressures to believe their preferred strategy will work may propel others—it is nonetheless striking to note how frequently presidents who try to intervene transformatively find themselves falling short, either in the midst of the intervention or in its long-term effectiveness. Transformative capabilities, at least in the United States, can be particularly difficult to develop in a short time period. Both internally and externally focused presidents have confronted both kinds of intervention, and both leader types have found themselves short of transformative capabilities—including George W. Bush, who initially decried using military force to reshape other states' domestic institutions. Future presidents may want to consider whether transformative capabilities need special attention or whether the dearth of transformative capabilities should be a stronger constraint on the initiation of certain intervention strategies in the first place.

Given that interventions will recur, it is no great insight to say that careful calibrating of ends and means will be vital in future operations. Research has shown that ideas are a factor in shaping power-creation mechanisms within states,[21] but this book identifies a specific link between leaders and the nature and availability of material, bureaucratic, and intellectual resources for intervention. Presidents have a relatively brief window in which to influence the capabilities available for intervention, however, and must be willing to make the policy investments necessary to develop and institutionalize the tools they intend to use or believe will be required for ongoing or future interventions. Although presidents have limited time and must act with imperfect information, when they do make policy investments, it is important that they gather information about the success of those investments and in turn take that success—or failure—into account when making intervention decisions. The necessity of such follow-through is illustrated by Kennedy's failure to effectively monitor and implement his counterinsurgency investments while still choosing a counterinsurgency strategy. Of course, even successful policy investments may not be enough. Making policy investments may raise the probability of success for a given intervention strategy, but such an increase does not necessarily mean that for a given case the probability of intervention success is high in absolute terms.

Another important implication concerns changes in strategy as interventions unfold over time. I find that presidents seem to be slow learners with respect to threat perceptions. When they change strategy in an ongoing intervention, it can be difficult to assess whether the realities of the situation or a true change in beliefs drove their strategic adjustment. As in the case of the initial intervention strategy, we cannot simply observe a change in strategy and infer that a leader's beliefs have changed. The distinction between pragmatic adjustment and a change in strategy reflecting a change in beliefs is important, however, for two reasons. First, when decision makers reluctantly adjust policy without changing their fundamental beliefs about the origin of threats, they may tack on new policies or modify existing approaches without thoroughly changing the overall strategy. Thus Johnson's shift toward a renewed emphasis on pacification and counterinsurgency as the Vietnam War unfolded was not fully integrated into the overall politico-military strategy and merely perpetuated the status of nonmilitary programs as the "other war." Second, if leaders do not "learn" in the sense of changing their beliefs, they may employ their original beliefs when they confront later intervention decisions.

Even if leaders eventually change their beliefs, or if we adopt a looser definition of learning and consider changes in strategy to represent learning, leaders' causal beliefs about the origin of threats are still a crucial determinant of early intervention decisions that can have profound and enduring effects on the course of the intervention. Johnson's approach to Vietnam was difficult to change. Similarly, in Iraq, although the strategy shifted in a more transformative direction after the arrival of Bremer and then again after the "surge," the early decisions proved to have significant consequences for the conduct of the war for several years. Thus a leader's initial approach to an intervention can be critical even if that approach evolves over time.

Implications for Contemporary Issues

The book also has implications for contemporary policy debates. For example, Robert Litwak notes that the debate in the United States over how to confront ongoing and future challenges such as that posed by the Iranian nuclear program centers on whether to attempt to change either states' behavior or their regimes.[22] U.S. options in Iran undoubtedly will be severely constrained by developments in Iraq and Afghanistan, as well as the overall strain on U.S. forces. But variation in leaders' causal beliefs helps map the theoretical options for future U.S. policy toward Iran. An internally focused U.S. leader would be more likely to concentrate on Iran's internal structure, which would in turn be expected to shape future Iranian aggression or expansionist aims in the Middle East. Such a leader would be more likely to choose a transformative strategy for any future U.S. military intervention. Of course, the knowledge that such a strategy would involve enormous risk and potentially high costs—knowledge made all the more concrete by the U.S. experience in Iraq—might also restrain such a leader from intervening in Iran at all. In contrast, an externally focused U.S. leader would concentrate on Iranian power and behavior. If this leader confronted Iran militarily, he would be more likely to choose a nontransformative strategy, such as aiming only to destroy the nuclear program, without significant interference in Iran's domestic affairs.

Causal beliefs about the origin of threats might also affect how leaders approach potential power transitions, an issue that has returned to the fore as the United States considers how to manage its relationship with a rising China. Some theories posit that shared domestic characteristics, such as regime type or societal ties, dampen threat perceptions in both rising and dominant powers. For example, Stephen Rock argues that societal affinity between Great Britain and the United States was crucial to the peaceful power transition between the two countries in the late nineteenth century.[23] But it is possible that the degree to which shared characteristics influence threat perception depends on who leads. If the leader of the rising power is internally focused, for example, he may assess the dominant power's likely response based on the dominant power's domestic structure. In the case of shared democracy, the leader of the rising democracy may expect the dominant democracy to peacefully accommodate the rising power. If the rising power is an autocracy and its leader is internally focused, however, he may expect a democratic dominant power to take an aggressive stance. In contrast, an externally focused leader of the rising state would not base his threat assessment on the dominant power's regime type or domestic structure even if the two states share domestic characteristics. Similarly, leaders' threat perceptions may influence the dominant power's assessment of the rising power. Depending on who leads the dominant power, conflict may occur earlier or later than power transition theory expects. For example, an externally focused leader might see the rising state as unthreatening based on its current power. But at the same level of power, an internally focused leader may perceive a threat from the rising power's domestic order.

In the context of U.S.-China relations, Aaron Friedberg notes that U.S. observers vary considerably in whether they evaluate China's rise in terms of the country's internal structure. In the two most common views, "liberal optimists" point to the possibility of democratization in China as a pacifying force whereas "realist pessimists" focus on the distribution of material power and infer expansionist Chinese aims. Less commonly but still very plausibly, "liberal pessimists" point to the fundamental differences between the American and Chinese domestic systems whereas "realist optimists" highlight slowing Chinese growth and limited Chinese aims.[24] While military power and domestic trends within China will undoubtedly matter in future U.S.-China relations, the causal beliefs of leaders in both countries may play a role in determining how these two factors affect the relationship.

Future scholarship on military intervention and the use of force more generally must do more than pay lip service to the role of leaders. Leaders have fundamentally—and systematically—different views about the nature of threats. Through the beliefs they bring with them to office, as well as the choices they make at the outset of their tenure, leaders shape the way states define and confront threats and ultimately choose where and how to use force.

Abbreviations

DDEL	Dwight D. Eisenhower Library, Abilene, Kans.
PPP-PF	Pre-presidential Papers 1916–1952, Principal File
FRUS	*Foreign Relations of the United States* series, various volumes
	Most *FRUS* volumes through the 1952–1954 series do not include document numbers, and thus references to these early volumes refer to page numbers. All references to *FRUS* starting with the 1955–1957 series (and continuing into the Kennedy and Johnson years) are to the document number, as indicated by "Doc."
JFKL	John F. Kennedy Library, Boston, Mass.
PPP-HF	Pre-presidential Papers, House Files
PPP-SF	Pre-presidential Papers, Senate Files
LBJL	Lyndon B. Johnson Library, Austin, Tex.
NSF	National Security File
PPP-HRP	Pre-presidential Papers, House of Representatives Papers
PPP-LBJA	Pre-presidential Papers, Lyndon Baines Johnson Archive
PPP-SP	Pre-presidential Papers, Senate Papers
VPSF	Vice Presidential Security File
NARA	National Archives and Records Administration, College Park, Md.
NSAM	National Security Action Memorandum
Papers of DDE	*Papers of Dwight David Eisenhower*, various volumes

Notes

1. When and How States Intervene

1. On the debate over strategy in the summer and fall of 2009, see, for example, Rajiv Chandrasekaran, "Go All-In, or Fold," *Washington Post*, September 27, 2009; Peter Baker and Eric Schmitt, "Several Afghan Strategies, None a Clear Choice," *New York Times*, September 30, 2009.

2. See, for example, Thom Shanker, "Plan to Shift Military Spending Faces Skepticism," *New York Times*, May 10, 2009.

3. Haass 2009, 12. For a similar distinction in the context of military intervention, see Jentleson 1992.

4. Most, but not all, interventions are undertaken by great powers in smaller powers, since intervention involves deploying forces abroad and thus requires the ability to project power over a distance, and since the smaller power is usually too weak to repel the intervention. For a similar focus on great-power interventions, see Bull 1984, 1; Krasner 1999, 152. The debate has not been limited to the United States: historically, great-power military interventions have varied widely in the degree to which they interfere in the domestic institutions of target states. For discussions of how great powers have used military intervention over time, see, for example, Krasner 1999, chaps. 6–7; J. Owen 2002.

5. As discussed in chapter 2, many definitions assume that intervention means interfering in the domestic affairs of target states. See, for example, Rosenau 1969, 161.

6. On the distinction between wars of choice and wars of necessity, and the historical origins of the term "war of choice," see Haass 2009, 11. The definition I employ is somewhat looser than that of Haass: he argues that wars of necessity involve

self-defense as well as "the most important national interests," and that wars of choice involve "stakes or interests that are less clearly 'vital' " (ibid., 10). But part of my argument is that leaders may debate what constitutes a "vital" national interest.

7. Greenstein and Immerman 1992, 586; see also Rosenau 1969, 166–167. Examining leaders in the context of military intervention comes at the apparent price of moving to a level of analysis traditionally associated with lower-level foreign policy outcomes. But although they often take place in peripheral regions, interventions can have dramatic effects on both the intervening state and its target, as the shadow of the Vietnam War illustrates. Furthermore, leaders' beliefs can also influence larger-scale outcomes. For example, as Robert Jervis describes, individuals may differ in whether they view security in terms of the deterrence or the spiral model, with significant consequences for international politics. See Jervis 1976, chap. 3.

8. Waltz 1959.

9. For a discussion of these arguments, as well as a strong rebuttal, see Byman and Pollack 2001, 110–113.

10. In addition to Byman and Pollack's (2001) call for a return to studying leaders, see, for example, Samuels 2003; Horowitz, McDermott, and Stam 2005; Jones and Olken 2005; Goemans, Gleditsch, and Chiozza 2009.

11. As Alexander George notes, "the fact that any presidential decision has to be effectively implemented cannot be used to downgrade the importance of choices which the President makes." George 1972, 792; see also Art 1973, 478.

12. I draw on the definition of causal beliefs provided by Goldstein and Keohane 1993, 10.

13. Kissinger 1964; Walt 1996.

14. For a general statement of liberal theory, see Moravcsik 1997; on the effects of democracy and trade on conflict, see Russett and Oneal 2001.

15. For example, Michael Hunt identifies a consistent and coherent American foreign policy ideology since the late nineteenth century, but argues specifically that this ideology could accommodate a "diversity of views," pointing to the differing approaches of Theodore Roosevelt and Woodrow Wilson as examples. See Hunt 2009, 125–126.

16. For a discussion and critique of the "military conservatism" thesis, for example, see Sechser 2004.

17. Douglas Macdonald identifies a similar partisan pattern in examining when the United States takes a reformist stance in the Third World. See Macdonald 1992, 13.

18. Hamilton, *Federalist* No. 6, Rossiter 1961, 56. On the Jeffersonian and Hamiltonian views, see Hunt 2009, 21–28; on Jefferson's affinity for France and Hamilton's for Britain, see Combs 1970, chaps. 4–5, 7; see also Kagan 2006, 104–112. Robert Kagan rejects the characterization of Hamilton as a "realist" and Jefferson as an "idealist," however, arguing that they both viewed the domestic politics of Britain and France as crucial but had "two competing visions of American

liberalism." See ibid., 112. Walter Russell Mead also identifies the Jeffersonian and Hamiltonian traditions but adds two other traditions of American foreign policy: Jacksonianism and Wilsonianism. He argues that all four traditions—which cover a broader set of foreign policy issues than those addressed in this book—persist in U.S. foreign policy. See Mead 2001.

19. Smith 1994, xiii.
20. Westad 2005, chap. 1.
21. Kinzer 2006, 2.
22. Kagan 2006.
23. Finnemore 2003.
24. Quoted in Langley 2002, 81. On the contrast between Roosevelt and Wilson (discussed in more detail in chapter 6), particularly in their approaches to Latin America, see Smith 1994, 65–73; see also Kissinger 1994, chap. 2; Ninkovich 1994, chaps. 1–2.
25. Finnemore 2003, 78–83, 124–129.
26. Gaddis 2005.
27. There was significant debate, for example, over the meaning of Titoism: did Tito's break with Moscow mean that the United States should pursue other communist allies who were willing to break with the Soviets, or did the nature of allies' domestic institutions matter more? On the debate over Titoism, see Selverstone 2009, chaps. 5–6; see also Brands 1989, chaps. 4–5.
28. Khong 1992, 72–73; see also Gaddis 2005.
29. On the struggle to define threats in this period, see Chollet and Goldgeier 2008.
30. Byman and Pollack 2001, 140–141.
31. Krasner 1978, 11; Russett 1990, chap. 4.
32. J. Owen 2002, 391.
33. On patterns of Soviet interventionism, see Bennett 1999; Westad 2005.
34. Krasner 1993, 257.
35. Theorists of strategic and organizational culture have highlighted this aspect of measuring ideational variables: see, for example, Johnston 1995, chap. 1; Legro 1995, 30; Kier 1997, 33–34.
36. Others have used this approach to avoid explaining behavior in terms of outcomes: see, for example, Owen 1997, 18.
37. Jervis 1976, chap. 6; Khong 1992; Goldgeier 1994; Tetlock 1999.
38. Kissinger 1979, 54; see also Jervis 1976, 146–147; Gaddis 2005, viii–ix.
39. For presidents other than Eisenhower, Kennedy, and Johnson, these codings are based on secondary accounts.
40. Though still imperfect, the Kennedy-Johnson comparison goes some way toward Alexander George's ideal scenario for testing the effect of beliefs on behavior, in which "ideally, we would . . . identify two leaders who are matched in every important respect and differ only" in the relevant beliefs. George 1979, 114.
41. On the influence of opportunities to use force, see Meernik 1994; Bennett 1999, 16–17; Howell and Pevehouse 2007, chap. 4.

42. On the role of various conditions within target states, see Bennett 1999, 17; Regan 1998.
43. On this point, see Samuels 2003, 17–18.

2. Defining and Explaining Intervention

1. As Barry Posen notes in the context of great-power conflict, states must maximize security with scarce resources and thus must prioritize among threats. Posen 1984, 13.
2. Indeed, Stanley Hoffmann explicitly limits his definition of intervention to "acts which try to affect not the external activities, but the domestic affairs of a state." Hoffmann 1984, 10 (emphasis omitted). James Rosenau defines intervention as both "convention-breaking" and "authority-oriented," since it is "directed at changing or preserving the structure of political authority in the target society." Rosenau 1969, 161; see also Jentleson and Levite 1992, 5–8; Regan 2000a, 9–10. Others define intervention more broadly: see Bull 1984, 1; Tillema 1989, 181; Pearson, Baumann, and Pickering 1994, 209; Sullivan and Koch 2009, 709.
3. Finnemore 2003, 9–10.
4. In terms of James Mahoney and Gary Goertz's discussion of how to identify the universe of cases, this different causal process means that covert operations (as well as potential covert operations that did not occur) are beyond the scope of the theory. See Mahoney and Goertz 2004, 660–661.
5. Jentleson and Levite 1992, 17. Owen also excludes covert operations and focuses on forcible acts of institutional promotion. See J. Owen 2002, 406.
6. See, for example, Pickering and Peceny 2006, 546. Theoretically, air or naval power could be used in support of either a nontransformative or a transformative operation. For example, air power could be used to enforce no-fly zones in a peacemaking operation. Alternatively, leaders may choose air-only operations as part of an explicit decision to undertake a nontransformative strategy. But it is also possible that the decision to initiate an air-only operation is governed by a different causal process than the decision to deploy ground troops, since leaders may choose air-only operations in the hope of minimizing casualties or political debate.
7. On the "combat readiness" standard, see Tillema 1989, 181; Sullivan 2007, 510.
8. Other scholars have coded the 1991 Gulf War as an intervention: see, for example, Sullivan and Koch 2009; Kreps, forthcoming. On the difficulty of distinguishing between war and intervention, see Finnemore 2003, 9.
9. On this point, see Jentleson 1992, 53; Regan 2000a, 9.
10. On Wilson's intervention in the Dominican Republic (discussed further in chapter 6), see Langley 2002, chaps. 10–12; Smith 1994, 71–73.
11. J. Owen 2002, 405; see also Bueno de Mesquita et al. 2003, chap. 9.

12. Among the classic works on this form of counterinsurgency are Galula 2006 and Thompson 1966. For useful summaries of this approach to counterinsurgency, see Blaufarb 1977, chaps. 1–2; Krepinevich 1986, 7–16.

13. See *U.S. Army/Marine Corps Counterinsurgency Field Manual* 2007.

14. Of course, national-level reform may also be necessary for counterinsurgency or nation building to be successful, but this is an issue beyond the scope of the theory, since I aim only to explain whether the intended strategy was transformative rather than to identify the determinants of successful transformation.

15. On dichotomous versus continuous measures of concepts, see Collier and Adcock 1999.

16. Bruce Jentleson (1992) finds that the U.S. public makes a similar distinction.

17. This tendency spans a variety of theoretical and methodological approaches. See, for example, Brands 1987–1988; Smith 1996; Huth 1998; Taliaferro 2004.

18. See, for example, Walter 2002; Marten 2004; Paris 2004; Doyle and Sambanis 2006; Edelstein 2008; Fortna 2008.

19. Exceptions dealing with aspects of the depth of internal interference include Macdonald 1992; Peceny 1995; Watts 2007. Scholars have investigated other aspects of intervention strategy, such as the conditions under which states choose a multilateral intervention (e.g., Gent 2007; Kreps 2008) and the choice between diplomatic and military intervention (Regan 2000b). In addition, Khong (1992) directly addresses the choice of strategy in Vietnam.

20. Krasner 1999, 219. For a discussion of how realist theories can be applied to intervention, see Taliaferro 2004, 11–14.

21. See, for example, Kegley and Hermann 1996.

22. J. Owen 2002, 396. In the U.S. context, see Smith 1994; Westad 2005, chap. 1; Kinzer 2006. Colin Dueck (2006) argues that while there is a long-standing liberal tradition in American grand strategy, it often clashes with a reluctance to assume the full cost of the liberal vision, producing variation in outcomes. In contrast, Bruce Bueno de Mesquita and George Downs (2006) argue that democracies are more likely to promote autocracies in target states because autocrats will more reliably provide favorable foreign policies than democratic leaders.

23. See, for example, Betts 1977, 130–131; Krepinevich 1986, 4–7.

24. See Finnemore 2003, chap. 3.

25. In the context of U.S. interventions and U.S. counterinsurgency policy, respectively, see Tillema 1973, 22–29, and Shafer 1988, 34.

26. For example, Benjamin Miller (1998) and Sarah Kreps (2008) apply realist arguments to related questions, such as the size of the intervention effort and the choice between multilateral and unilateral intervention, respectively.

27. In the context of U.S. intervention policy, see Scott 1996; more generally, see also Allison and Zelikow 1999, chap. 5.

28. See Snyder 1991, chap. 7; Western 2005, 4–14. Similarly, Mark Peceny (1995) argues that a U.S. president's initial choice of a democracy promotion strategy in

interventions is driven primarily by security conditions but can be influenced by liberal internationalists in Congress. Additionally, so-called revisionist Cold War scholars have argued that the United States intervened in the Third World to protect American business interests. For example, there is a debate over whether the 1954 covert operation in Guatemala was designed to further the interests of the United Fruit Company (see Schlesinger and Kinzer 2005) or instead was motivated by fears of a communist takeover in Guatemala, albeit one that would threaten U.S. economic interests in the process (Immerman 1982, 123–124; Rabe 1988, 58–59). Finally, on the role of parties (in the European context), see Rathbun 2004.

29. See, for example, Morgenthau 1967, 430; Krasner 1978, 13–16; in the context of alliance decisions, see also Walt 1987, 21–26.

30. Doyle 1986, 1161. For an exception, see Farnham 2003. Additionally, John Owen's study of the liberal peace and how liberal states assess threats suggests that "liberals may have different visions for their own state—different strategies by which they believe individual autonomy is best secured," citing different perceptions among American elites. Owen acknowledges, however, that he leaves largely unexplored the puzzle of "how people sharing a basic worldview can have such divergent visions for their own polity." See Owen 1997, 40–41.

31. Hermann and Kegley 1995, 512–514.

32. Jervis 1976, 19–20.

33. In addition to the work of Jervis, past work on threat perception has highlighted cognitive and information-processing tendencies or biases. See, for example, Cohen 1979; Knorr 1976; for a more social approach, see Rousseau 2006. David Edelstein argues that states assess adversaries' intentions using indicators that include domestic characteristics and international behavior, although he posits that states rely on a portfolio of such indicators rather than privileging one or the other at a given time. Edelstein 2002, 9–11; on assessing intentions, see also Yarhi-Milo 2009.

34. See, for example, the Archigos dataset on leaders, described in Goemans, Gleditsch, and Chiozza 2009.

35. Bueno de Mesquita et al. 2003; Chiozza and Goemans 2004, 613–616.

36. See, respectively, Smith 1998; Guisinger and Smith 2002; Chiozza and Choi 2003.

37. Within this vast literature, see, for example, Jervis 1976; Larson 1985; Khong 1992.

38. On risk acceptance and aggression, see, for example, Vertzberger 1998; Talia-ferro 2004; Rosen 2005; on age, see Horowitz, McDermott, and Stam 2005; on personality, see Post 2004; on leadership style, see Goldgeier 1994; Greenstein 2004.

39. My argument is distinct, for example, from the "fundamental attribution error," or the general tendency for decision makers to attribute behavior to other actors' dispositions rather than situational pressures (see Tetlock 1998). In the frame-

work developed here, leaders diagnose behavior according to substantive beliefs rather than as a result of cognitive bias or an information-processing problem.

40. See Khong 1992, chaps. 4–5.

41. This research stretches back to pioneering work on belief systems and the operation code. See, for example, Holsti 1962; George 1969.

42. Goldstein and Keohane 1993, 10. Although Goldstein and Keohane's definition of causal beliefs adds that these beliefs "derive authority from the shared consensus of recognized elites," I do not make any assumptions about how widely beliefs are shared. For studies showing how other kinds of causal beliefs have affected conceptions of interest and thus preferences over outcomes, see McNamara 1998; Darden 2009.

43. For an example in the context of intervention, see Smith 1996.

44. On this point, see Reiter and Meek 1999, 368–369.

45. On the president's "preeminent position" in agenda setting, see Kingdon 1984, 25–28. On elite discourse and mass opinion, see Zaller 1992; Berinsky 2009, chap. 5. On the role of public opinion in war, see, among others, Mueller 1973; Western 2005.

46. Waltz 1959, chap. 4. Waltz, however, was searching for a single level of analysis at which to pitch his theory, and he rejected the second image in favor of the "third image," the international system.

47. Woodrow Wilson, "An Address to a Joint Session of Congress," April 2, 1917, Link 1983, 523–525.

48. As Bueno de Mesquita and Downs (2006) argue, for example. All leaders may not share this logic, however.

49. Walt 1996, chap. 2.

50. Werner 1996, 71–72; Haas 2005, 6–8 (focusing on ideological differences).

51. On the connection between domestic and foreign policy attitudes among elites, see, among others, Holsti and Rosenau 1988; Murray 1996.

52. Krasner specifically criticizes the bureaucratic politics approach for failing to account for the role of the president in "choos[ing] most of the important players," who "must share his values." Krasner 1972, 166.

53. Bennett 1999, 81 (emphasis omitted); see also Levy 1994, 297.

54. Jervis 1976, chap. 4; see also Murray 1996; Tetlock 1999; Goldgeier and Tetlock 2001, 72–73.

55. Roosevelt quoted (apocryphally, as Schmitz notes) in Schmitz 1999, 3–4.

56. Bueno de Mesquita and Downs (2006) argue that leaders of democratic intervening states generally prefer to install autocrats in target states to avoid this outcome, which could damage their political prospects. Bueno de Mesquita and Downs's theory assumes that all leaders share this logic, but another instrumental view is to regard democratizing the target state as providing direct security benefits, perhaps because the leader sees democracies as more stable and predictable in the long run.

57. Bunce 1981, 26.

58. An interesting avenue for future research would be to examine whether leaders are biased in their assessments of policy investments. If there has been strong bureaucratic resistance, or if "stickiness" means the changes have yet to take effect, then leaders may lack full information about exactly how well prepared they are. Leaders may or may not take this friction into account, possibly leading to perceptual bias in assessing preparedness. Leaders may ignore this aspect of preparedness and fail to incorporate it directly into their cost-benefit calculation.

59. Patrick Regan (1998) employs a similar decision-theoretic framework, although he examines only the decision to intervene.

60. See, for example, Western 2005, chap. 1.

61. On "latent public opinion" in the context of the Vietnam War, see Zaller 2003.

62. Fearon 1994; Smith 1998. Jessica Weeks (2008) argues that audience costs apply even in autocracies.

63. Western 2005, chap. 5.

64. Arreguín-Toft 2005; Lyall and Wilson 2009.

65. Critiques of the bureaucratic politics model note the importance of the president in structuring the bureaucratic environment and retaining the ability to ultimately overrule it. See, for example, Krasner 1972; Art 1973.

66. George and Bennett 2005, 86–87.

67. To identify interstate and intrastate crises, I consulted Regan's dataset on civil conflicts (see Regan 2000a, appendix) and the International Crisis Behavior dataset (Brecher and Wilkenfeld). Although he parses the data differently, Benjamin Fordham also consults these datasets to construct a universe of possible interventions. See Fordham 2008.

68. On this point, see Fordham 2008, 743.

69. Existing datasets do not adequately capture the variation I seek to study here. For example, the Military Intervention by Powerful States (MIPS) dataset (Sullivan and Koch 2009) codes the "political objectives" of interventions, from the defense of territory to the seizure or maintenance of political authority. But as I have stressed, such actions could vary in the depth of internal interference. While Owen's valuable study of institutional promotion has similar selection criteria to those I use here, he does not include cases of military force that did not involve institutional promotion, does not explore variation in the depth of institutional promotion, and focuses only on political institutions (see J. Owen 2002). Similarly, Macdonald (1992) examines only "reformist" interventions, partly because he explores the success or failure of such interventions.

70. On the debates over neutralism, see Brands 1989; Selverstone 2009, 139–142.

71. Institutional creation and change overlaps with the literature on structural choice and bureaucratic design. See, for example, Moe 1995, 140–142, on how presidents seek to shape the bureaucracy; see also Krasner 1972; Art 1973.

72. Gaddis, for example, argues that for U.S. policymakers during the Cold War, perceptions of available means influenced the perception of interests. Gaddis 2005; see also Fordham 2004.

73. This argument is similar to John Ruggie's assertion that "political authority represents a fusion of power with legitimate social purpose" and that power is not enough to predict the "content" of authority. Ruggie 1998, 64 (emphasis omitted). I focus on how individuals' beliefs, rather than social purpose, interact with power.

3. Dwight D. Eisenhower

1. Eveland 1980, 299.
2. Eisenhower's papers at the Dwight D. Eisenhower Library in Abilene, Kansas, contain an extensive record of private correspondence and diary entries from his pre-presidential years, as well as official records such as cables and reports from World War II and his postwar service as Army Chief of Staff and NATO Supreme Commander. Many Eisenhower papers, including his diaries, have been published in various collections cited in this chapter.
3. For a general critique of Eisenhower's Third World policies, see McMahon 1986. On the long history of covert operations in the Middle East, see Little 2004; on the Syrian operation, see Yaqub 2004, 149–158. On the covert operation in Indonesia, see Kahin and Kahin 1995. The literature on the covert intervention in Guatemala is also illuminating: see Immerman 1982; Gleijeses 1991.
4. On the conduct of the intervention, see Immerman 1982, 162–164. Gaddis refers to the operations in Iran and Guatemala as "palace coups." See Gaddis 2005, 179.
5. On the legacy of the Guatemalan operation, see Immerman 1982, chap. 8; Gleijeses 1991, 377–387; on Iran, see Bill 1988, 86–97.
6. Lehman 1997, 195–200; see also Rabe 1988, 77–83. For structured comparisons between Guatemala and Bolivia, where socialist tendencies were arguably far stronger and U.S. interests greater and yet no intervention took place, see Krasner 1978, 279–286; Lehman 1997.
7. Kahin and Kahin 1995, 18.
8. Gaddis 2005, 138.
9. Greenstein 1982; see also Immerman 1979, 1990; Divine 1981; Rabe 1993; Bowie and Immerman 1998.
10. Immerman 1990, 327. Studies that include extensive discussion of Eisenhower's pre-presidential years include Lyon 1974; Ambrose 1983; Bowie and Immerman 1998, chap. 2; Perret 1999. Holland 2001 is a full-length treatment of Eisenhower's interwar years.
11. Gaddis traces Eisenhower's "strong convictions . . . on the proper relationship of ends and means" to his study of Clausewitz under Fox Conner in Panama. Gaddis 2005, 133.
12. Dwight D. Eisenhower (hereafter DDE) diary entry, April 21, 1930, Holt and Leyerzapf 1998, 120.
13. DDE to Assistant Secretary of War, "Report of Inspection of Guayule Rubber Industry," June 6, 1930, Holt and Leyerzapf 1998, 133.

14. DDE diary entry, December 27, 1935, Holt and Leyerzapf 1998, 295; see also Ambrose 1983, 104–105.
15. DDE to MacArthur, June 15, 1936, Holt and Leyerzapf 1998, 312.
16. Perret 1999, 125; Holt and Leyerzapf 1998, 299–300, note 11. Eisenhower described the officers and enlisted men of the remaining constabulary as "completely detached" from the army. DDE to Gerow, September 22, 1938, Holt and Leyerzapf 1998, 402.
17. Lyon 1974, 77; see also DDE diary entry, February 6, 1936, Holt and Leyerzapf 1998, 305.
18. DDE to John Doud, April 29, 1937, Holt and Leyerzapf 1998, 333–334.
19. Ambrose 1970, 251. On the Darlan deal, see also Funk 1973.
20. Ambrose 1970, 107.
21. Funk 1973, 96.
22. DDE to Marshall, November 9, 1942, *Papers of DDE*, II, Doc. 594.
23. DDE to Clark, November 12, 1942, *Papers of DDE*, II, Doc. 613. See also DDE to Marshall, November 17, 1952, *Papers of DDE*, II, Doc. 639.
24. The minutes of the November 13 meeting in Algiers are in PPP-PF, Box 33, DDEL.
25. Ambrose 1970, 126. See also Atkinson 2002, 159.
26. Eisenhower wrote his brother Edgar in February 1943, "The only thing that made me a little peeved about the matter was that anyone should think I was so incredibly stupid as to fail to realize I was doing an unpopular thing, particularly with those who were concerned with things other than winning the war—which is my whole doctrine and reason for existence." DDE to Edgar Eisenhower, February 18, 1943, *Papers of DDE*, II, Doc. 825; see also Ambrose 1970, 126, note. For Eisenhower's message to Bedell Smith reporting the deal, see DDE to Smith, November 13, 1942, *Papers of DDE*, II, Doc. 621.
27. Churchill to FDR, November 17, 1942, *FRUS, 1942*, II, 445.
28. FDR statement quoted in *Papers of DDE*, II, Doc. 622, note 7.
29. FDR draft quoted in ibid. The draft may not actually have been sent to Eisenhower, however.
30. DDE to Bedell Smith, November 18, 1942, *Papers of DDE*, II, Doc. 642.
31. DDE to Marshall, November 30, 1942, *Papers of DDE*, II, Doc. 673.
32. Atkinson 2002, 198.
33. McCloy to DDE, March 1, 1943, PPP-PF, Box 75, DDEL.
34. JCS to DDE, December 11, 1942, PPP-PF, Box 63, DDEL.
35. Gaddis 2000, 75; see also 64–65, 75–80.
36. Quoted in Butcher 1946, 855.
37. Quoted in Ambrose 1983, 430. On the circumstances of Eisenhower's visit to Moscow, see also DDE to Marshall, June 15, 1945, *Papers of DDE*, VI, Doc. 158; see also ibid., notes 1 and 3.
38. Gaddis 2000, 312; see also Ambrose 1983, 447–452; Perret 1999, 368.

39. DDE, Speech to Richmond University, March 28, 1946, PPP-PF, Box 192, DDEL, 2–3.
40. DDE, Address before the Bureau of Advertising, American Newspaper Publishers Association, April 25, 1946, PPP-PF, Box 192, DDEL, 4.
41. DDE, Notes for Herald Tribune Forum, October 30, 1946, PPP-PF, Box 192, DDEL, 4. See also Address before the Economic Club of New York, November 20, 1946, PPP-PF, Box 192, DDEL, 2.
42. DDE, Notes for D-Day Address, Kansas City, June 6, 1947, PPP-PF, Box 192, DDEL, 5.
43. DDE, Speech to American Legion Convention, August 29, 1947, PPP-PF, Box 192, DDEL, 4 (emphasis in original).
44. Gaddis 2005, 30; Bowie and Immerman 1998, 47–48. On the strategy of "patience and firmness" that emerged in the wake of Kennan's Long Telegram, see Gaddis 2005, 21–23.
45. DDE to Hazlett, June 21, 1951, *Papers of DDE*, XII, Doc. 233.
46. DDE to Clement, January 9, 1952, *Papers of DDE*, XIII, Doc. 590 (emphasis in original).
47. On Eisenhower's concern about the threat to American institutions, see Bowie and Immerman 1998, chap. 6; Friedberg 2000, 127–129; Gaddis 2005, chap. 5.
48. DDE diary entry, May 26, 1946, Ferrell 1981, 136.
49. DDE diary entry, May 15, 1947, Ferrell 1981, 141.
50. DDE to Hazlett, September 12, 1950, *Papers of DDE*, XI, Doc. 981.
51. DDE press conference, January 20, 1951, quoted in Ambrose 1983, 503.
52. DDE to Clement, January 9, 1952.
53. DDE to Collins, August 25, 1951, PPP-PF, Box 25, DDEL (emphasis in original).
54. Ambrose 1983, 502–503.
55. DDE report to Truman, January 31, 1951, quoted in *Papers of DDE*, XII, Doc. 16, note 3.
56. DDE diary entry, January 6, 1953, *Papers of DDE*, XIII, Doc. 1034.
57. DDE diary entry, January 6, 1953, quoted in Gaddis 2005, 175, note.
58. Gaddis 2005, 174–181.
59. Brands 1989, 106.
60. DDE diary entry, May 15, 1947.
61. DDE to Patterson and Forrestal (on behalf of JCS), March 13, 1947, *Papers of DDE*, VIII, Doc. 1377.
62. DDE to JCS, May 10, 1947, *Papers of DDE*, VIII, Doc. 1482.
63. On the liberation of Paris, see Ambrose 1970, book 2, chap. 10, especially 482–486.
64. DDE to Montgomery, March 31, 1945, *Papers of DDE*, IV, Doc. 2378. On the Berlin question, see Ambrose 1967; Gaddis 2000, 207–209.
65. Ambrose 1967, 73–74; Ambrose 1970, book 2, chap. 19, especially 624-631.
66. Churchill to FDR, quoted in *Papers of DDE*, IV, Doc. 2374, note 2. On Roosevelt's desire to avoid postwar issues during the war, see Gaddis 2000, 206; see also 207–211.

67. DDE, Army Day Speech, April 6, 1946, PPP-PF, Box 192, DDEL, 2.
68. DDE, Notes for Address at National Press Club Luncheon, March 25, 1947, PPP-PF, Box 192, DDEL, 1–2.
69. DDE, Army Day Talk, April 7, 1947, PPP-PF, Box 192, DDEL, 3.
70. DDE to Hazlett, September 12, 1950.
71. Memorandum of Conversation, DDE, de Lattre et al., March 17, 1951, PPP-PF, Box 136, DDEL, 3.
72. DDE diary entry, March 17, 1951, *Papers of DDE*, XII, Doc. 88.
73. Memorandum of Conversation, DDE, de Lattre et al., March 17, 1951.
74. Gaddis 2005, 125.
75. DDE diary entry, January 27, 1949, *Papers of DDE*, X, Doc. 336. See also DDE to Edward Bermingham, February 28, 1951, *Papers of DDE*, XII, Doc. 51.
76. DDE diary entry, January 22, 1952, *Papers of DDE*, XIII, Doc. 614.
77. On Eisenhower's national security system, see Bose 1998, chap. 1; Bowie and Immerman 1998, chap. 5.
78. Gaddis 2005, 133.
79. Ibid., 135–136.
80. Macdonald 1992, 36.
81. Eisenhower's first major "restatement" of Basic National Security Policy, a document known as NSC 153/1, asserted at its outset that there were "two principal threats to the survival of fundamental values and institutions of the United States," the external threat from the USSR and the "serious weakening of the economy of the United States that may result from the cost of opposing the Soviet threat over a sustained period." NSC 153/1, Restatement of Basic National Security Policy, June 10, 1953, *FRUS, 1952–1954*, II, 379; see also Gaddis 2005, 132–134.
82. For the final version, see NSC 162/2, Basic National Security Policy, October 30, 1953, *FRUS, 1952–1954*, II, 578–597. On the drafting of NSC 162/2, see Bowie and Immerman 1998, chap. 9.
83. Quoted in Gaddis 2005, 164–165.
84. NSC 162/2, *FRUS, 1952–1954*, II, 587–588; see also Bowie and Immerman 1998, 214.
85. On Eisenhower's foreign economic policy and "trade not aid," see Kaufman 1982; see also Ekbladh 2010, 155–157.
86. NSC 162/2, *FRUS, 1952–1954*, II, 593.
87. Kaufman 1982, 14, 29.
88. Ibid., 35; see also Ekbladh 2010, 187.
89. Kaufman 1982, 49–50, 53–56.
90. DDE, Special Message to the Congress on the Mutual Security Program, April 20, 1955, *Public Papers of the Presidents of the United States: Dwight D. Eisenhower, 1955*, 406.
91. Kaufman 1982, 110.
92. Gaddis 2005, 154–155. On psychological warfare in the Eisenhower administration, see also Osgood 2006.

93. Bowie and Immerman 1998, 220.
94. Gaddis 2005, 162, appendix.
95. Data accessed through the Budget Trends Tool at the Policy Agendas Project website, http://www.policyagendas.org (Baumgartner, Jones, and Wilkerson).
96. Gaddis 2005, 169.
97. Data accessed through the Policy Agendas Project.
98. Kaufman 1982, 29–33.
99. Gaddis 2005, 151, 178.
100. Rabe 1988, 174.
101. Memorandum of Discussion at the 137th Meeting of the National Security Council, March 18, 1953, *FRUS, 1952–1954*, IV, 2.
102. Rabe 1988, 32; NSC 144/1, "United States Objectives and Courses of Action with Respect to Latin America," March 18, 1953, *FRUS, 1952–1954*, IV, 6–10.
103. Rabe 1988, 35–36.
104. Quoted in ibid., 146.
105. Ibid., 39.
106. Ibid., 113; see also 104–106. On the demonstrations during Nixon's trip, see ibid., chap. 6.
107. Quoted in ibid., 121. On the evolution of the administration's view of Castro, see ibid., chap. 7.
108. Ibid., 134.
109. Ibid., chap. 8. See also Kaufman 1982, 209.
110. Rabe 1988, 115.
111. Billings-Yun 1988, 92–95; see also Anderson 1991, 30–33. For other studies of Eisenhower's decision making in 1954, see Gravel 1971, 1:88–107; Spector 1983, chap. 11; Anderson 1991, chap. 2; Duiker 1994, chap. 5.
112. For the Truman administration position, see NSC 124/2, "United States Objectives and Courses of Action with Respect to Southeast Asia," June 25, 1952, *FRUS, 1952–1954*, XII, 127.
113. Memorandum of Conversation, DDE and Foster Dulles, March 24, 1954, *FRUS, 1952–1954*, XIII, 1150.
114. Billings-Yun 1988, 43–44.
115. Memorandum of Discussion at the 190th Meeting of the National Security Council, March 25, 1954, *FRUS, 1952–1954*, XIII, 1165, 1167–1168; Billings-Yun 1988, 54–55.
116. Gravel 1971, 1:101; Billings-Yun 1988, 99–100.
117. Memorandum of Discussion at the 192nd Meeting of the National Security Council, April 6, 1954, *FRUS, 1952–1954*, XIII, 1250–1265.
118. DDE to Hazlett, April 27, 1954, *Papers of DDE*, XV, Doc. 848.
119. Billings-Yun 1988, 147.
120. Ibid., 149.
121. Quoted in James Hagerty diary entry, April 26, 1954, *FRUS, 1952–1954*, XIII, 1411.

122. Minnich to DDE (summarizing April 26 meeting with legislators), undated, *FRUS, 1952–1954*, XIII, 1413. See also Anderson 1991, 37.

123. Herring 1996, 49.

124. Duiker 1994, 211.

125. Gravel 1971, 1:268; see also Spector 1983, 306–307; Herring 1996, 67.

126. Anderson 1991, 133.

127. Herring 1996, 51–52.

128. Memorandum of Discussion at the 210th Meeting of the National Security Council, August 12, 1954, *FRUS, 1952–1954*, XII, 730. Anderson notes that "the most revealing feature" of this NSC meeting "was the group's inability to agree on the wording" for the section on local subversion. The meeting, he notes, showed that "America's top policy makers were at a loss to deal with any situation outside of overt Soviet or Chinese action." Anderson 1991, 68–69.

129. Memorandum of Discussion at the 218th Meeting of the National Security Council, October 22, 1954, *FRUS, 1952–1954*, XIII, 2157–2158.

130. DDE to Diem, undated (but delivered October 23, 1954), *FRUS, 1952–1954*, XIII, 2166–2167.

131. Anderson 1991, 87.

132. See ibid., 106–108; Duiker 1994, 207–208.

133. Anderson 1991, 74, 204.

134. On state-building efforts in this period, see Carter 2008, chap. 3.

135. Spector 1983, 272–273, 298, 300, 320.

136. Ibid., 352–353.

137. Herring 1996, 64.

138. Spector 1983, 277–278.

139. On Diem's visit to Washington, see Anderson 1991, 160–164.

140. Spector 1983, 333–334.

141. Krepinevich 1986, 25–26.

142. Spector 1983, 372.

143. Duiker 1994, 245.

144. Anderson 1991, 180.

145. See, for example, Genco 1974, 338–355; Gerges 1994, 102–112; Little 1996; Yaqub 2004, chap. 7.

146. See, for example, the essays in Fernea and Louis 1991. U.S. and British officials reached this conclusion themselves a few days after the coup. See Memorandum of Conversation, Foster Dulles, Lloyd et al., July 17, 1958, *FRUS, 1958–1960*, XII, Doc. 122.

147. For an account of the Suez crisis, see Kyle 1991; on the economic pressure the United States placed on its allies, see Kunz 1991. For a discussion of the crisis in terms of the development of the Eisenhower Doctrine, see Yaqub 2004, chap. 1.

148. Gendzier 1997, 213–214.

149. For a highly detailed account of Iraq both before and after the 1958 revolution, see Batatu 1978. See also the essays in Fernea and Louis 1991, which are organized around Batatu's work.

150. Yaqub 2004, 38–39; see also 294, note 62.

151. Memorandum of Understanding between the Governments of the United States and the United Kingdom, February 26, 1954, *FRUS, 1952–1954*, IX, 2372.

152. Allen Dulles to Hoover, November 22, 1956, *FRUS, 1955–1957*, XII, Doc. 438.

153. State to Baghdad, November 24, 1956, *FRUS, 1955–1957*, XII, Doc. 439.

154. Axelgard 1991, 91; Gerges 1994, 115.

155. Special Message to the Congress by President Eisenhower on the Middle East, January 5, 1957, *Public Papers of the Presidents of the United States: Dwight D. Eisenhower, 1957*, 13.

156. On the difficulties in getting Arab governments to "stand up and be counted" on the side of the West, see Yaqub 2004, 3–5.

157. Quoted in Gaddis 2005, 152.

158. Dulles initially objected to this provision, since "a sudden coup might result in displacing the government which could make the request." Memorandum of a Conference with the President, December 20, 1956, *FRUS, 1955–1957*, XII, Doc. 175; see also Yaqub 2004, 83.

159. Yaqub 2004, 142; see also chap. 3 for a discussion of other reactions to the doctrine in the Arab world.

160. Eveland 1980, 252.

161. Yaqub 2004, 175–176. According to a State Department memo from February 1958, Dulles requested the plans on November 8, 1957. Irwin to Murphy, February 6, 1958, *FRUS, 1958–1960*, XI, Doc. 6.

162. Shihab's statement is reported in Beirut to State, May 11, 1958, *FRUS, 1958–1960*, XI, Doc. 23.

163. Memorandum of a Conversation, DDE, Foster Dulles et al., May 13, 1958, *FRUS, 1958–1960*, XI, Doc. 30. For the text of the Middle East Resolution, see Joint Resolution to Promote Peace and Stability in the Middle East, Public Law 85-7, March 9, 1957.

164. State to Beirut, May 13, 1958, *FRUS, 1958–1960*, XI, Doc. 31.

165. Yaqub 2004, 206.

166. Ibid., 211.

167. Eisenhower 1965, 268; Yaqub 2004, 215.

168. Memorandum of a Conversation, DDE, Foster Dulles et al., June 15, 1958, *FRUS, 1958–1960*, XI, Doc. 84.

169. See Yaqub 2004, 217–219.

170. The Pentagon and JCS objections are noted in Rountree to Dulles, January 18, 1958, *FRUS, 1958–1960*, XII, Doc. 96.

171. JCS to CINCNELM (Commander in Chief, U.S. Naval Forces, Eastern Atlantic and Mediterranean), June 11, 1958, Record Group 218, JCS Geographic File 1958, Box 3, NARA.

172. Wisner to Cumming, July 3, 1958, *FRUS, 1958–1960*, XII, Doc. 108.

173. Beirut to State, July 14, 1958, *FRUS, 1958–1960*, XI, Doc. 125.

174. Memorandum for the Record of a Meeting, Foster Dulles, Twining et al., July 14, 1958, *FRUS, 1958–1960*, XI, Doc. 123.

175. Cutler 1965, 363.

176. Eisenhower 1965, 270.

177. Memorandum of a Conference with the President, DDE, Nixon, Foster Dulles et al., July 14, 1958, *FRUS, 1958–1960*, XI, Doc. 124.

178. Memorandum of a Conference with the President, DDE, Foster Dulles et al., July 14, 1958, *FRUS, 1958–1960*, XI, Doc. 128.

179. Memorandum of a Conference with the President, DDE, Foster Dulles, Congressional Leaders et al., July 14, 1958, *FRUS, 1958–1960*, XI, Doc. 127.

180. Memorandum of a Conference with the President, DDE, Foster Dulles et al., July 14, 1958, *FRUS, 1958–1960*, XI, Doc. 128.

181. See Jidda to State, July 14, 1958, *FRUS, 1958–1960*, XI, Microfiche Supplement, Doc. 158; Tel Aviv to State, July 15, 1958, *FRUS, 1958–1960*, XII, Doc. 114; Yaqub 2004, 232–234. Yaqub cites the Turkish suggestion as a wake-up call that ultimately convinced even the British that rollback in Iraq was not feasible.

182. Memorandum of Telephone Conversation, Foster Dulles with Nixon, July 15, 1958, *FRUS, 1958–1960*, XII, Doc. 118.

183. Memorandum of a Telephone Conversation, DDE and Macmillan, July 14, 1958, *FRUS, 1958–1960*, XI, Doc. 131.

184. See Little 1996, 46–47; Gendzier 1997, 315–316; Yaqub 2004, 228–229.

185. Western 2005, 62–64.

186. Yaqub 2004, 239.

187. Beirut to State, July 19, 1958, *FRUS, 1958–1960*, XI, Doc. 197.

188. DDE to Humphrey, July 22, 1958, *Papers of DDE*, XIX, Doc. 784. On the resolution of the Lebanese political situation, see Yaqub 2004, chap. 8.

189. Memorandum of a Telephone Conversation, DDE and Foster Dulles, July 15, 1958, *FRUS, 1958–1960*, XI, Doc. 137.

190. Memorandum of a Conference with the President, DDE, Twining, and Goodpaster, July 15, 1958, *FRUS, 1958–1960*, XI, Doc. 140.

191. Memorandum for Deputy Director for Strategic Plans and Chairman, Joint Middle East Planning Group, July 18, 1958, Record Group 218, JCS Central Decimal File 1958, Box 64, NARA.

192. DDE to Humphrey, July 22, 1958.

193. DDE diary entry, July 15, 1958, *Papers of DDE*, XIX, Doc. 771.

194. Memorandum of Conference with President, DDE, Nixon, Foster Dulles et al., July 20, 1958, *FRUS, 1958–1960*, XII, Doc. 26.

195. Eisenhower himself said that he took the new government's friendly overtures "with reservation" in the July 20 meeting. See ibid.

196. For a discussion indicating that U.S. officials were working on both overt and covert options, see Memorandum of Discussion at the 402d Meeting

of the National Security Council, April 17, 1959, *FRUS, 1958–1960*, XII, Doc. 176; see also Little 2002, 202–203.

197. In Lebanon, the record indicates that Eisenhower and his advisers generally discounted the Soviet reaction. In terms of Iraq, a State Department intelligence estimate from July 20 concluded that invading Iraq entailed serious risks but that general war would be avoided. See Cumming to Reinhardt, July 20, 1958, *FRUS, 1958–1960*, XII, Doc. 126; on the "mainly symbolic" Soviet reaction to the Lebanon intervention itself, see Yaqub 2004, 230.

198. Memorandum of Discussion at the 402nd Meeting of the National Security Council, April 17, 1959.

199. In June 1958, U.S. and British officials submitted a report, in the works since early 1957, advocating ways to ensure oil supplies from the Middle East and elsewhere and characterizing a possible interruption of oil production in the Middle East as "a threat to Europe." See "Transport of Oil from the Middle East," May 12, 1958, *FRUS, 1958–1960*, XII, Attachment to Doc. 19. For a discussion of the oil situation following the July 1958 crises, see R. Owen 2002.

200. The oil companies were not clamoring for intervention. In Lebanon, Irene Gendzier notes that a Trans-Arabian Pipeline (TAPLINE) executive turned down U.S. military protection. Gendzier 2002, 117. In Iraq, three days after the coup, the president of Socony Mobil Oil Company asserted that the company had not and would not call for U.S. intervention. "Socony Forswears Any Aid Plea in Iraq," *New York Times*, July 17, 1958.

201. See, for example, Memorandum of a Conference with the President, DDE, Foster Dulles, Congressional Leaders et al., July 14, 1958.

202. In June 1958, Dulles cabled McClintock, "We have also noted growing indication that allied military intervention would be viewed with repugnance even by many Lebanese Christians." State to Beirut, June 19, 1958, Eisenhower Presidential Papers, Ann Whitman File, International Series, Box 37, DDEL, 3.

203. Yaqub 2004, 11–12. For a discussion of the cultural aspects of U.S. policy toward the Middle East, see Little 2002, chap. 1.

204. Yaqub 2004, 236.

205. Eisenhower 1965, 290.

4. John F. Kennedy

1. This line of argument can be found in many Kennedy biographies and is highlighted with respect to Latin America policy in Rabe 1999.

2. On Kennedy and "diversity," see Gaddis 2005, 200–201.

3. See, for example, Avant 1994, 71; Gaddis 2005, 200; see also the discussion later in this chapter of continuity between the Kennedy and Johnson approaches to Latin America. Those who see differences in the Kennedy and Johnson approaches to intervention include Macdonald 1992, 42; Logevall 1999.

4. On the influence of social scientists in the Kennedy administration, see Latham 2000; Marquis 2000.

5. See, for example, Bose 1998, 42–53; Freedman 2000, 32; Gaddis 2005, 197. Robert Dallek's biography also traces Kennedy's pre-presidential views extensively. See Dallek 2003.

6. The Pre-presidential Papers at the John F. Kennedy Library in Boston consist largely of legislative materials, speeches and speech drafts, and correspondence; the Personal Papers contain the travel journals from Kennedy's trips to Europe and the Middle East and Asia in 1951.

7. Dallek 2003, 167.

8. Ibid., 132–133.

9. These quotations are taken from a speech Kennedy gave in Lynn, Massachusetts; the latter portion of the speech was taken directly from a radio speech on Russia, which as Dallek notes, Kennedy used repeatedly toward the end of the 1946 campaign. John F. Kennedy (hereafter JFK), Speech to Professional & Business Women, October 21, 1946; and Radio Speech on Russia, both in PPP-HF, Box 94, JFKL; see also Dallek 2003, 133.

10. JFK, Speech to Massachusetts Federation of Taxpayers Associations, April 21, 1951, PPP-HF, Box 95, JFKL, 1–5.

11. DDE to Hazlett, June 21, 1951, *Papers of DDE*, XII, Doc. 233.

12. JFK, Speech to Massachusetts Federation of Taxpayers Associations, April 21, 1951, 6.

13. JFK Travel Journal, Personal Papers, Box 11, JFKL, 146.

14. Ibid., 42.

15. JFK, Speech Draft, 1955 (labeled "KS-9 1955" in the "Doodles" series organized by Evelyn Lincoln), Personal Papers, Box 40, JFKL, 7 (using Lincoln's page-numbering system).

16. Ibid., 6.

17. JFK to Galbraith, February 4, 1958, PPP-SF, Box 691, JFKL; see also Dallek 2003, 223.

18. JFK, Radio Speech reporting on Middle and Far East trip, November 14, 1951, PPP-HF, Box 95, JFKL, 3.

19. JFK, Speech to Boston Chamber of Commerce, November 19, 1951, Pre-presidential Papers, Campaign Files, Box 102, JFKL, 7.

20. JFK, Radio Speech reporting on Middle and Far East trip, November 14, 1951, 5.

21. JFK, "Imperialism—The Enemy of Freedom," July 2, 1957, Kennedy 1964, 511.

22. JFK, "The Choice in Asia—Democratic Development in India," March 25, 1958, Kennedy 1964, 607. On these themes, see also Kennedy 1957.

23. JFK, Speech to Boston Chamber of Commerce, November 19, 1951, 5.

24. JFK, "The Struggle against Imperialism, Part II—Poland and Eastern Europe," August 21, 1957, Kennedy 1964, 553, 559.

25. Yaqub 2004, 90–97.

26. JFK, "Promotion of Peace and Stability in the Middle East," March 1, 1957, Kennedy 1964, 470.

27. JFK, Speech Draft, undated (titled "Appropriate Introductory Remarks"), PPP-SF, Box 675, JFKL, 2.

28. JFK, Speech Draft, undated (titled "Congress Looks at the Eisenhower Middle East Doctrine"), PPP-SF, Box 675, JFKL, 6–7.

29. JFK to Maurice Mordka, March 18, 1958, PPP-SF, Box 691, JFKL. On the Baghdad Pact, see also JFK, "U.S. Membership in Baghdad Pact," March 25, 1957, Kennedy 1964, 479–481; Kennedy 1957, 46–47.

30. JFK to Frank Maria, August 18, 1958, PPP-SF, Box 693, JFKL.

31. JFK, "Choice in Asia," March 25, 1958, Kennedy 1964, 593.

32. On the latter point, see JFK to Dean Erwin N. Griswold of Harvard Law School, June 7, 1957, PPP-SF, Box 667, JFKL.

33. JFK, undated and untitled document that begins "There are many reasons why a drastic cut or abandonment of foreign aid . . . ," PPP-SF, Box 561, JFKL, 1.

34. JFK, "The Economic Gap," February 19, 1959, Kennedy 1964, 789.

35. JFK, "Mutual Security Act of 1951," August 17, 1951, Kennedy 1964, 99.

36. JFK, "Technical Assistance—Military Assistance: Appropriation Bill, Supplemental," June 28, 1952, Kennedy 1964, 120.

37. See, for example, JFK to Louis F. Medeiros, June 23, 1959, PPP-SF, Box 716, JFKL. See also the undated draft (which appears to be from 1958), titled "What about the Balance between Military and Economic Aid?" PPP-SF, Box 561, JFKL.

38. JFK, Speech Draft, undated (titled "Appropriate Introductory Remarks"), 4–5.

39. Memo, "Foreign Policy Activities" (unsigned and undated, but probably from September 1958), PPP-SF, Box 692, JFKL, 2.

40. JFK, Remarks to Fifth National Conference on International Economic and Social Development, February 26, 1958, PPP-SF, Box 561, JFKL, 5.

41. See ibid., 1.

42. Ibid., 4. The emphasis on long-term loans also appears in JFK's speech on India. See JFK, "Choice in Asia," March 25, 1958, Kennedy 1964, 599.

43. S. Con. Res. 74, 85th Congress, 2nd Session, copy in PPP-SF, Box 562, JFKL; the speech is "Choice in Asia," March 25, 1958.

44. Rostow 2003, 189–196, 204.

45. JFK, "Choice in Asia," March 25, 1958, Kennedy 1964, 607.

46. JFK to John Davenport, April 16, 1958, PPP-SF, Box 692, JFKL.

47. Rostow 2003, 205.

48. See JFK, "Choice in Asia," March 25, 1958, Kennedy 1964, 608.

49. JFK, Speech to Boston Chamber of Commerce, November 19, 1951, 7–8.

50. Thompson 1966, 50–55, chap. 6; similar thinking underpins Galula 2006.

51. JFK Travel Journal, 140. For a discussion of the Briggs Plan and the British approach in Malaya, see Blaufarb 1977, 40–51. See also Thompson 1966; Clutterbuck 1966.

52. On the state-building aspects of such rural resettlement programs, see Scott 1998, 185–191.
53. JFK Travel Journal, 137, 140.
54. Ibid., 139.
55. Ibid., 138, 142.
56. JFK, "The War in Indochina," April 14, 1954, Kennedy 1964, 295.
57. JFK, Remarks before the Cathedral Club, Brooklyn, N.Y., January 21, 1954, Kennedy 1964, 994.
58. JFK, "Our Lag in Conventional Forces," undated remarks (but from context, likely from 1959 or 1960), PPP-SF, Box 916, JFKL, 2.
59. JFK Travel Journal, 133–134.
60. Schlesinger 1965, 299–300; see also Halberstam 1972, 94.
61. Schlesinger reports that Kennedy "bridled under the routine embassy briefing and asked sharply why the Vietnamese should be expected to fight to keep their country part of France." Schlesinger 1965, 300.
62. JFK Travel Journal, 130–131.
63. DDE to Hazlett, April 27, 1954, *Papers of DDE*, XV, Doc. 848.
64. JFK Travel Journal, 123.
65. JFK, Radio Speech reporting on Middle and Far East trip, November 14, 1951, 5.
66. Halberstam 1972, 94.
67. L. P. Marvin to Priscilla Johnson, April 17, 1953, PPP-SF, Box 481, JFKL (emphasis in original). This episode is also discussed in Dallek 2003, 185.
68. JFK to Foster Dulles, May 7, 1953, PPP-SF, Box 481, JFKL. Kennedy also peppered Dulles with a list of forty-seven questions about Indochina, which appear in the same folder.
69. JFK, "Mutual Security Act of 1951, as Amended," June 30, 1953, Kennedy 1964, 262.
70. JFK, "The War in Indochina," April 6, 1954, Kennedy 1964, 284–294.
71. JFK, Speech Materials for Speech to Cook County Democrats, Chicago, April 20, 1954 (labeled "KS-3 1954" in the "Doodles" series), Personal Papers, Box 40, JFKL, 9.
72. See JFK to E. F. Baxter, July 16, 1954, PPP-SF, Box 647, JFKL.
73. JFK, Remarks to Conference on "America's Stake in Vietnam," June 1, 1956, PPP-SF, Box 895, JFKL, 3–6. This speech is also notable for Kennedy's ironic praise of South Vietnamese president Diem's ability to bring reform and stability to the country.
74. JFK, Notes, 1957 (labeled "KS-1 1957" in the "Doodles" series), Personal Papers, Box 40, JFKL, 2–3. Lincoln's cover note reads, "Notes made by Senator Kennedy prior to a speech to the Police Force in New York [in] the spring of 1957."
75. JFK to V. Veinmayr, July 11, 1958, PPP-SF, Box 693, JFKL.
76. JFK to Herbert J. Spiro, August 8, 1958, PPP-SF, Box 693, JFKL.
77. JFK to Paul Jameson, January 22, 1959, PPP-SF, Box 717, JFKL.
78. JFK to Douglas T. Barrett, January 20, 1959, PPP-SF, Box 717, JFKL.

79. JFK to Mr. and Mrs. Robert Ross, February 12, 1959, PPP-SF, Box 717, JFKL.

80. JFK, Remarks to Conference on "America's Stake in Vietnam," June 1, 1956, 2.

81. On the far less formal planning procedures in the Kennedy White House, see Bose 1998, chap. 2.

82. Latham 2000, 57–58; see also Rabe 1999, 22–27; Freedman 2000, chap. 3.

83. Gaddis 2005, 224.

84. Freedman 2000, 287.

85. See, for example, Blaufarb 1977, 52; Krepinevich 1986, 27; Rosen 1991, 100–101. For an analysis skeptical of the influence of presidents that nonetheless concurs on this point, see Shafer 1988, 20.

86. Quoted in Reeves 1993, 41.

87. On this point, see also Blaufarb 1977, 18; Krepinevich 1986, 29.

88. Record of Actions Taken at the 475th Meeting of the National Security Council, February 1, 1961, *FRUS, 1961–1963*, VIII, Doc. 8. See also NSAM 2, "Development of Counter-guerilla Forces," February 3, 1961, http://www.jfklibrary.org/Historical+Resources/Archives/Reference+Desk/NSAMs.htm.

89. Gaddis 2005, 216.

90. Rostow's draft of Basic National Security Policy is summarized in Editorial Note, *FRUS, 1961–1963*, VIII, Doc. 70.

91. JFK, Special Message to the Congress on Urgent National Needs, May 25, 1961, *Public Papers of the Presidents of the United States: John F. Kennedy, 1961*, 399–400.

92. Latham 2000, 167.

93. Summary of "U.S. Overseas Internal Defense Policy," Editorial Note, *FRUS, 1961–1963*, VIII, Doc. 106. The document was officially approved and distributed via NSAM 182, "Counterinsurgency Doctrine," August 24, 1962, *FRUS, 1961–1963*, VIII, Doc. 105. See also Gaddis 2005, 224.

94. NSAM 119, "Civic Action," December 18, 1961, *FRUS, 1961–1963*, VIII, Doc. 65.

95. See, for example, NSAM 114, "Training for Friendly Police and Armed Forces in Counter-insurgency, Counter-subversion, Riot Control and Related Matters," November 22, 1961, *FRUS, 1961–1963*, VIII, Doc. 59; NSAM 132, "Support of Local Police Forces for Internal Security and Counter-insurgency Purposes," February 19, 1962, *FRUS, 1961–1963*, VIII, Doc. 72.

96. Gaddis 2005, 224–226.

97. McNamara also recommended an increase of over $1 billion in resources for general nuclear war. His recommendations are in McNamara to JFK, February 20, 1961, *FRUS, 1961–1963*, VIII, Doc. 17.

98. JFK, Special Message to the Congress on the Defense Budget, March 28, 1961, *Public Papers of the Presidents of the United States: John F. Kennedy, 1961*, 231–237.

99. JFK, Special Message to the Congress on Urgent National Needs, May 25, 1961, *Public Papers of the Presidents of the United States: John F. Kennedy, 1961*, 399–401.

100. On the motives for the nuclear increases, see Gaddis 2005, 216–218.

101. Data accessed through the Policy Agendas Project. Actual spending on national security increased in the Kennedy years, but as Gaddis notes, since GDP increased during this period, the percentage of GDP devoted to defense declined, from 9.3 percent in 1960 to 8.9 percent by 1963. Gaddis 2005, 225, appendix.
102. Data accessed through the Policy Agendas Project.
103. Sorensen 1965, 632.
104. JFK to McNamara, January 11, 1962, *FRUS, 1961–1963*, VIII, Doc. 67.
105. NSAM 124, "Establishment of the Special Group (Counter-Insurgency)," January 18, 1962, *FRUS, 1961–1963*, VIII, Doc. 68.
106. Robert Kennedy reported to his brother after each meeting, as the participants knew. Blaufarb 1977, 69.
107. Ibid., 86.
108. Latham 2000. On the Alliance for Progress, see ibid., chap. 3; Rabe 1999, chaps. 1 and 7.
109. Krepinevich 1986, chap. 2, especially 36–38. Krepinevich provides a detailed account of the army's resistance; see also Rosen 1991, 101–104; Avant 1994, chap. 3. Harry Summers, in contrast, argues that counterinsurgency doctrine had a major impact on the army, with what Summers sees as unfortunate consequences for the conduct of the Vietnam War. Summers 1982, chap. 7.
110. Betts 1977, 130.
111. As Avant notes, the Marine Corps had institutional incentives to be much more receptive to the new approach. See Avant 1994, chaps. 3–4.
112. Sorensen 1965, 633.
113. On promotion policy and changes in doctrine in the context of Vietnam, see Rosen 1991, 103–104.
114. Blaufarb 1977, 65, 126–127.
115. Quoted in ibid., 65.
116. JFK to McNamara, January 11, 1962.
117. JFK, Special Message to the Congress on the Defense Budget, March 28, 1961, *Public Papers of the Presidents of the United States: John F. Kennedy, 1961*, 236.
118. On Rostow's abandonment of counterinsurgency as a strategy in Vietnam, see Preston 2006, 76–82.
119. Rabe 1999, chap. 5.
120. On the U.S. intervention in British Guiana, see Rabe 2005.
121. Quoted in Schlesinger 1965, 704–705.
122. Rabe 1999, 34–43, 44–46.
123. Freedman 2000, 127. On the Bay of Pigs generally, see ibid., chaps. 13–15.
124. Memorandum of Meeting with President Kennedy, February 8, 1961, *FRUS, 1961–1963*, X, Doc. 40. See also Freedman 2000, 127.
125. Rabe 1999, 197.
126. On the Kennedy Doctrine, see ibid., 97–98.
127. For a brief account of Eisenhower's decision making on Laos, see Kaiser 2000, chap. 1.

128. Ibid., 22.

129. Schlesinger 1965, 303.

130. Ibid., 304.

131. Greenstein and Immerman 1992, 569. Kennedy's own dictated notes record that after Secretary of State Christian Herter stated his view that the United States should intervene if the Laotian government invoked U.S. commitments under SEATO, Eisenhower "stated also that he felt we should intervene." Notes of Conversation between President-Elect Kennedy and President Eisenhower, January 19, 1961, *FRUS, 1961–1963*, XXIV, Doc. 7.

132. Freedman 2000, 294–295.

133. For overviews of Kennedy's decision making during the Laos crisis, see Kaiser 2000, chap. 2; Freedman 2000, chap. 32.

134. Report Prepared by the Inter-agency Task Force on Laos, *FRUS, 1961–1963*, XXIV, attachment to Doc. 10.

135. Nitze to McNamara (summarizing January 23, 1961, meeting with JFK), January 23, 1961, *FRUS, 1961–1963*, XXIV, Doc. 10.

136. Memorandum of Conference with President Kennedy, February 6, 1961, *FRUS, 1961–1963*, VIII, Doc. 11. Laos would be one of the first three countries (along with Vietnam and Thailand) that the Special Group (CI) was assigned to monitor.

137. McGhee to Rusk (summarizing March 3 meeting with JFK on Laos), March 3, 1961, *FRUS, 1961–1963*, XXIV, Doc. 22.

138. Memorandum of Conference with President Kennedy, March 9, 1961, *FRUS, 1961–1963*, XXIV, Doc. 25.

139. Rostow to JFK, March 7, 1961, *FRUS, 1961–1963*, XXIV, Doc. 24.

140. Galbraith to JFK, May 10, 1961, Galbraith 1998, 70.

141. Kennedy discussed the allies' support for Souvanna in a meeting with Ambassador Brown and again at the March 9 meeting. See Memorandum of Conversation, February 3, 1961, *FRUS, 1961–1963*, XXIV, Doc. 13; Memorandum of Conference with President Kennedy, March 9, 1961. See also Freedman 2000, 299; Kaiser 2000, 40–42.

142. Freedman 2000, 296.

143. For example, Chief of Naval Operations Admiral Arleigh Burke argued on April 29 that "each time you give ground it is harder to stand next time. If we give up Laos we would have to put US forces into Viet-Nam and Thailand. . . . It would be easier to hold now than later." Memorandum of Conversation, April 29, 1961, *FRUS, 1961–1963*, XXIV, Doc. 67.

144. Freedman 2000, 298–299; see also Schlesinger 1965, 310–311; *FRUS, 1961–1963*, XXIV, Doc. 35, note 1.

145. Kennedy did not attend this meeting, but his brother Robert did. Freedman notes that the meeting "revealed the gap that had developed between the military and the civilians." Freedman 2000, 301. For an account of the meeting, see Memorandum of Conversation, April 29, 1961.

146. Schlesinger 1965, 315.
147. Freedman 2000, 303.
148. Memorandum of Conversation, May 31, 1961, *FRUS, 1961–1963*, XXIV, Doc. 103.
149. On these developments, see Freedman 2000, 303–304; Kaiser 2000, 55–56.
150. Quoted in Reeves 1993, 173.
151. Gelb and Betts 1979, 81 (emphasis in original).
152. Rostow to Bundy (summarizing White House meeting of January 28, 1961), January 30, 1961, *FRUS, 1961–1963*, I, Doc. 4.
153. NSAM 12, "Re: Forces in Vietnam," February 6, 1961, *FRUS, 1961–1963*, I, Doc. 9.
154. Gravel 1971, 2:49.
155. NSAM 52, "Vietnam," May 11, 1961, *FRUS, 1961–1963*, I, Doc. 52.
156. Freedman 2000, 310.
157. Taylor and Rostow to JFK, July 27, 1961, *FRUS, 1961–1963*, I, Doc. 107.
158. Memorandum of a Discussion, July 28, 1961, *FRUS, 1961–1963*, I, Doc. 109.
159. Quoted in Kaiser 2000, 102.
160. Taylor's messages are in Gravel 1971, 2:88–92.
161. Ibid., 92. For the official Taylor Report, see Taylor to JFK, November 3, 1961, *FRUS, 1961–1963*, I, Doc. 210.
162. Quoted in Schlesinger 1965, 505. On the bureaucratic debate and recommendations in this period, see Gravel 1971, 2:102–127; Kaiser 2000, 105–121.
163. JFK to Rusk and McNamara, November 14, 1961, *FRUS, 1961–1963*, I, Doc. 252.
164. Khong 1992, 87–95. Khong argues, however, that Kennedy still saw the Malayan, Philippine, and Greek conflicts—and by analogy, the conflict in Vietnam—in terms of aggression, but it was "indirect aggression" rather than the more direct aggression suggested by the Korea analogy. Furthermore, Khong notes that even adherents to the Malayan analogy tended to overestimate the external influence of the Soviet Union in fostering the conflict. See ibid., 87, 229, 233. Nonetheless, it is possible to argue that Kennedy's diagnosis of the conflict still focused to a greater extent on the internal dynamics inside Vietnam than did Johnson's.
165. Notes on the National Security Council Meeting, November 15, 1961, *FRUS, 1961–1963*, I, Doc. 254.
166. NSAM 111, "First Phase of Viet-Nam Program," November 22, 1961, *FRUS, 1961–1963*, I, Doc. 272.
167. Quoted in Macdonald 1992, 215.
168. Hilsman 1967, 53.
169. Roger Hilsman, "A Strategic Concept for South Vietnam," February 2, 1962, *FRUS, 1961–1963*, II, Doc. 42; Robert Thompson, Draft Paper ("Delta Plan"), undated, *FRUS, 1961–1963*, II, Doc. 51. For an overview of the decision making in this period, see Gravel 1971, 2:128–159; see also Blaufarb 1977, chap. 4.

170. On the "agroville" program, see Catton 2002, 63–71; on the origins of the Strategic Hamlet Program, see ibid., chap. 4.

171. Hilsman, "Strategic Concept for South Vietnam" (emphasis omitted).

172. Latham 2000, 185–186.

173. David Halberstam was one important media source; for his description of this period, see Halberstam 1965. See also Freedman 2000, 359–362.

174. See Macdonald 1992, chaps. 8–9. Among others, see also Latham 2000, chap. 5; Carter 2008, chap. 5. On the Diem regime's own goals for the Strategic Hamlet Program, which were arguably somewhat transformative, see Catton 2002, chaps. 4–5; see also Miller 2004 on the origins of Diem's vision for transforming South Vietnam.

175. Carter 2008, 123, 125.

176. See Fitzgerald 1972, 155–158. On the problems with the Strategic Hamlet Program, see also Gelb and Betts 1979, 85–86; Kaiser 2000, chap. 6.

177. Khong 1992, 91–95; see also Blaufarb 1977, 47–49.

178. On the military implementation, see Krepinevich 1986, 67–90; Avant 1994, chap. 3.

179. Galbraith to JFK, November 21, 1961, Galbraith 1998, 91.

180. On the "logic of political survival," see Bueno de Mesquita et al. 2003.

181. See Freedman 2000, chap. 40. Macdonald also sees the coup in the context of the overall reformist effort: see Macdonald 1992, 234–246.

182. Freedman 2000, 397.

183. Gallucci 1975, 25; see also Freedman 2000, chap. 39; Gravel 1971, 2:chap. 4.

184. State to Saigon, August 24, 1963, *FRUS, 1961–1963*, III, Doc. 281. On the bureaucratic maneuvering surrounding the cable, see Kaiser 2000, 227–236.

185. See Memorandum of a Conference with the President, August 27, 1963, *FRUS, 1961–1963*, III, Doc. 303.

186. JFK to McNamara, September 21, 1963, *FRUS, 1961–1963*, IV, Doc. 142.

187. Summary Record of the 519th Meeting of the National Security Council, October 2, 1963, *FRUS, 1961–1963*, IV, Doc. 169.

188. Memorandum of Conference with President Kennedy, October 29, 1963, *FRUS, 1961–1963*, IV, Doc. 234.

189. Freedman 2000, 396.

190. Memorandum of a Conference with President Kennedy, October 29, 1963, *FRUS, 1961–1963*, IV, Doc. 235. Kennedy's concerns about the success of the coup can be found in meetings as early as August 26 and August 27. See Memorandum for the Record of a Meeting at the White House, August 26, 1963, *FRUS, 1961–1963*, III, Doc. 289; and Memorandum of a Conference with the President, August 27, 1963. These concerns are also a prominent feature of the taped conversations of these meetings (the tapes were released by the Kennedy Library in December 2009). For a discussion of how the tapes reveal Kennedy's caution about the success of a coup, but not necessarily about a coup itself, see Prados 2009; see also portions transcribed by the Kennedy Library,

http://www.jfklibrary.org/Historical+Resources/JFK+in+History/
Proposed+Coup+in+Vietnam.htm.

191. Bundy to Lodge, October 29, 1963, *FRUS, 1961–1963*, IV, Doc. 236; Saigon to State, October 30, 1963, *FRUS, 1961–1963*, IV, Doc. 242.

192. Kaiser 2000, 278–279; Freedman 2000, chap. 40.

193. Bundy to Lodge, October 30, 1963, *FRUS, 1961–1963*, IV, Doc. 249.

194. Summary Record of the 519th Meeting of the National Security Council, October 2, 1963.

195. Kaiser makes a similar point, arguing that the August 24, 1963, cable that marked the beginning of serious presidential-level consideration of a coup "reflected a generally held belief . . . that South Vietnam could not survive without fundamental changes." Kaiser 2000, 231.

196. See, for example, Schmitz 1999, 254.

197. Quoted in Kaiser 2000, 277.

198. I have not addressed, for example, the question why Kennedy did not pursue a negotiated settlement or whether he initiated a withdrawal from Vietnam in the fall of 1963. On negotiations, Freedman argues that the advantages of Laos did not exist in Vietnam and that for much of 1962 Kennedy believed counterinsurgency was working. Freedman 2000, 340–341, 356. On the question of withdrawal in late 1963, historians continue to debate Kennedy's intentions. For the argument that Kennedy intended to withdraw, see Newman 1992, chap. 21. Logevall, who argues that Kennedy would not have escalated had he lived, nonetheless rejects this "incipient withdrawal" thesis, arguing that the discussion of withdrawal was a political move aimed at both Diem and U.S. audiences. See Logevall 1999, 69–71 (on "incipient withdrawal") and 395–400 (on why Kennedy would not have escalated).

199. Gaddis 2005, chaps. 7–8.

200. Rostow to JFK, March 29, 1961, quoted in Fordham 2004, 632; see also Shafer 1988, 245. In a study of the use of force since 1945, Fordham (2004) finds that capabilities significantly influence presidential uses of force, and finds only weak empirical evidence that decision makers anticipate future uses of force when constructing military capabilities. Fordham examines aggregate non-nuclear capabilities, however, rather than disaggregating among different types of non-nuclear capabilities such as counterinsurgency and regular war fighting.

201. Freedman 2000, 339.

202. Quoted in Reeves 1993, 484.

203. Bueno de Mesquita and Downs 2006.

204. Transcript of Presidential Recording, August 20, 1962, Naftali 2001, 487.

205. Krepinevich 1986, 27.

206. Herring 1997, 648.

207. Among those who argue that Kennedy would not have escalated are Newman 1992; Logevall 1999; Kaiser 2000; Dallek 2003. Freedman comes to a more complex conclusion: that Kennedy "would have faced a growing mismatch

between his commitment to South Vietnam and the means available to sustain this commitment," and while he would have had to examine the option of taking the war to the North, "unlike Johnson" he would have examined exit options such as negotiations. Freedman 2000, 413.

5. Lyndon B. Johnson

1. See especially Schwartz 2003; see also Gaskin 1989; Dallek 1991; Bator 2008, 310–313. On the evolution of scholarship on Johnson, see Brands 1999a.
2. Although he emphasizes that Democrats tended to take a reformist view of Third World states during the Cold War, Macdonald nonetheless agrees that Johnson is an "anomaly" who did not see reforming other states' institutions as a central U.S. goal. Macdonald 1992, 42.
3. The Pre-presidential Papers at the Lyndon B. Johnson Library in Austin, Texas, include extensive records from Johnson's congressional career, although relatively few private documents written by Johnson himself. The record includes letters to friends and constituents, speech drafts and speech materials, and memos from staffers, particularly George Reedy, who wrote frequently on foreign policy and on issues related to the work of the Preparedness Subcommittee. The Vice Presidential Security File also contains valuable memos and correspondence, and there is a small but useful collection of memoranda of telephone conversations from his years in Congress, a few of which touch on foreign and defense policy. Johnson kept a private diary only during his brief service as an observer of military efforts in the South Pacific during World War II; there are a few comments on preparedness issues. See Lyndon B. Johnson (hereafter LBJ), World War II Diary, PPP-LBJA Subject File, Box 74, LBJL.
4. Notes on a White House meeting, April 30, 1965, quoted in Editorial Note, *FRUS, 1964–1968*, XXXII, Doc. 42.
5. Johnson's support for Eisenhower also stemmed in part from his belief in the primacy of the presidency on matters of national security and foreign policy. On this point, see Caro 2002, 529.
6. See, for example, Goodwin 1991, 256.
7. Dallek's two-volume biography examines the pre-presidential years in depth. See Dallek 1991 and 1998; see also Gaskin 1989; Woods 2006. Caro 2002 is a valuable study of Johnson's Senate years but concentrates primarily on the means through which Johnson accumulated and exercised power, giving less attention to his foreign policy and national security beliefs. Scholarship on the Johnson presidency has also begun to reevaluate Johnson's foreign policy. See, for example, Schwartz 2003; see also Brands 1995, vii; Brands 1999b.
8. Dallek 1991, 9.
9. Gaskin 1989, chap. 2.

10. As Caro notes, Johnson led a series of fights in the Senate that allowed the basic containment strategy, with its internationalist building blocks such as the United Nations and NATO, to continue. On these fights, see Caro 2002, 521–541; Dallek 1991, 433–437.

11. Goodwin 1991, 95–96.

12. LBJ, Address at Pan American Round Table, October 20, 1953, Statements of LBJ, Box 14, LBJL, 2–3.

13. LBJ, Statement on Senate floor, May 14, 1958, Statements of LBJ, Box 24, LBJL, 2–4.

14. LBJ to Joe Pacheck, May 15, 1958, PPP-SP, Box 602, LBJL.

15. Wirtz to LBJ (with enclosure of Wirtz to Aubrey Williams), April 21, 1947, PPP-LBJA Selected Names File, Box 37, LBJL.

16. LBJ to Wirtz, April 29, 1947, PPP-LBJA Selected Names File, Box 37, LBJL.

17. LBJ, "Peace in This Day Is Not Cheap," May 7, 1947, *Congressional Record*, 80th Congress, 1st session, 4695.

18. Harry S. Truman, Special Message to the Congress on Greece and Turkey: The Truman Doctrine, March 12, 1947, *Public Papers of the Presidents of the United States: Harry S. Truman, 1947*, 176–180.

19. JFK, "Aid for Greece and Turkey," April 1, 1947, Kennedy 1964, 967–970.

20. S. Con Res. 91, June 25, 1954, *Congressional Record*, 83rd Congress, 2nd session, 8927.

21. Reedy memo, May 28, 1954, PPP-SP, Box 413, LBJL (emphasis in original).

22. LBJ, Speech on Senate floor, June 22, 1954, *Congressional Record*, 83rd Congress, 2nd session, 8564.

23. Transcript of telcon, LBJ with Dulles, June 28, 1954, Pre-presidential Papers, Notes and Transcripts of LBJ Conversations, 1951–1963, Box 1, LBJL, 2.

24. LBJ to Lynn S. Holmes, May 24, 1954, PPP-SP, Box 297, LBJL. LBJ also called Guatemala a "communist beachhead in our own back yard" in several other letters; see, for example, LBJ to PFC Henry B. Angus, June 3, 1954; and LBJ to Mrs. E. Kelly, June 8, 1954, both in PPP-SP, Box 297, LBJL.

25. LBJ, Speech on Senate floor, June 25, 1954, *Congressional Record*, 83rd Congress, 2nd session, 8922.

26. LBJ to Charles L. Scarborough, June 28, 1954, PPP-SP, Box 297, LBJL.

27. LBJ, Speech to Austin Kiwanis Club, 1947, PPP-HRP, Box 332, LBJL, 2–3.

28. LBJ, Address at University of Houston Commencement Exercises, May 31, 1958, Statements of LBJ, Box 25, LBJL, 4.

29. LBJ, "Aid Arabs? U.S. Must—or Else," *Dallas Times Herald*, August 6, 1958, copy in Statements of LBJ, Box 25, LBJL. On the genesis of the column, see LBJ to Felix R. McKnight, July 30, 1958, and McKnight to LBJ, July 24, 1958, both in PPP-SP, Box 602, LBJL.

30. LBJ, "Challenge of a New Day," May 22, 1948, PPP-HRP, Box 333, LBJL, 4.

31. Ibid., 5.

32. LBJ to Madeline Bynum, January 30, 1951, PPP-SP, Box 223, LBJL.

33. Reedy memo, May 11, 1954, PPP-SP, Box 413, LBJL, 1.

34. See JFK to LBJ, June 28, 1957, White House Famous Names File, Box 5, LBJL.

35. LBJ, Address at University of Houston Commencement Exercises, May 31, 1958, 3.

36. Dallek paints Johnson's vice presidential travels to the Third World as "a kind of New Deal crusade." Dallek 1998, 15; see also Gardner 1995, 52.

37. Kaufman 1987, 80–81.

38. LBJ, "This Vote Will Be Heard around the World," April 2, 1948, PPP-HRP, Box 333, LBJL.

39. LBJ to William G. Goodrich Jr., March 28, 1958, PPP-SP, Box 601, LBJL. See also LBJ to Mrs. Robert Fitch, March 28, 1958; LBJ to B. V. Bartow, March 28, 1958; LBJ to Mark Lemmon, June 11, 1958; and LBJ to Ben W. Jackson, June 19, 1958, all in PPP-SP, Box 601, LBJL.

40. LBJ to Mark Lemmon, June 11, 1958.

41. LBJ, Address at Howard Payne College, April 13, 1957, Statements of LBJ, Box 21, LBJL, 3–4.

42. LBJ to J. E. Brown, May 31, 1951, PPP-SP, Box 223, LBJL.

43. LBJ to Davis B. Carter, November 13, 1953, PPP-SP, Box 249, LBJL. See also LBJ to J. E. Brown, May 31, 1951.

44. The Legislative Reference Service found this pattern in a report, requested by Johnson, summarizing his foreign policy statements. "Foreign Policy Statements of Vice President Johnson, 1949–1962," Legislative Reference Service Report, April 30, 1962, Vice Presidential Aide's Files of George Reedy, LBJL, 18.

45. LBJ to Mrs. Robert Fitch, March 28, 1958; see also LBJ to B. V. Bartow, March 28, 1958; and LBJ to William G. Goodrich Jr., March 28, 1958.

46. Kaufman 1987, 80.

47. LBJ, 1953 guest column, reprinted as "LBJ Deplored Foreign Aid—in 1953," *Human Events*, April 28, 1961, copy in Vice Presidential Papers, Subject Files, Box 79, LBJL.

48. LBJ to Ben W. Jackson, June 19, 1958.

49. LBJ, "Washington News Letter," February 3, 1959, PPP-LBJA Subject File, Box 95, LBJL.

50. Goldman 1969, 76.

51. Geyelin 1966, 27; more generally, see 25–27.

52. On Johnson's interest in ordinary people during his 1961 trip to Asia, see, for example, Bangkok to State, May 20, 1961, *FRUS, 1961–1963*, I, Doc. 57. Johnson's interest in infrastructure was rekindled after a stop in India on the 1961 trip, when he helped Ambassador John Kenneth Galbraith bring small power packs to India. See Russell Baker, "Johnson Turns on a Light for India," *New York Times*, July 30, 1961; Galbraith to LBJ, July 11, 1961; LBJ to Galbraith, July 24, 1961, all in Vice Presidential Papers, Subject Files, Box 79, LBJL.

53. LBJ to Truman, April 5, 1948, copy in PPP-SP, Box 345, LBJL. See also Truman to LBJ, March 22, 1948, copy; LBJ to Truman, March 20, 1948, copy, both in

PPP-SP, Box 345, LBJL. As Dallek notes, this correspondence got significant press attention. Dallek 1991, 294.

54. See the memos to LBJ in PPP-HRP, Box 329, LBJL. On air power, see particularly memos to LBJ dated March 17, April 17, and April 22, 1948.

55. Dallek 1991, 294.

56. Ibid., 382; see also LBJ, "Delay-Defeat-Retreat," July 12, 1950, PPP-SP, Box 346, LBJL.

57. On the politics behind the creation of the subcommittee, see Dallek 1991, 384–387; Caro 2002, 308–311.

58. Dallek 1991, 386.

59. See "Summary of First Thirty-Six Reports of the Senate Preparedness Subcommittee," undated, PPP-SP, Box 346, LBJL. Johnson's biographers differ on the value and sincerity of Johnson's work. Caro sees a politician creating "his own little empire" whereas Dallek acknowledges the political motives driving Johnson's work but also sees "sincere" concern for national security issues. Caro 2002, 314–327; Dallek 1991, 386.

60. On April 3, for example, Johnson and other congressional leaders met with Dulles and JCS chairman Radford about Indochina. See Memorandum for the File of the Secretary of State, April 5, 1954, *FRUS, 1952–1954*, XIII, 1224. Johnson also attended a Dulles-led briefing for members of Congress on May 5, after the Geneva Conference. See Record of the Secretary of State's Briefing for Members of Congress, Held at the Department of State, May 5, 1954, 5:30 p.m., *FRUS, 1952–1954*, XIII, 1471–1477.

61. Prados 1995, 13 (referencing the April 3 meeting noted above).

62. Ibid., 14, 16.

63. Western 2005, 36.

64. LBJ to R. L. Lindley, May 18, 1954, PPP-SP, Box 1194, LBJL. Prados goes so far as to argue that Johnson favored intervention even without allies. See Prados 2007, 234.

65. LBJ to Paul D. Balbin, May 19, 1954, PPP-SP, Box 1194, LBJL.

66. On Johnson's constituent mail, see Prados 1995, 15. For examples of Johnson's letters employing the "caught bluffing" language, see LBJ to Phil Hopkins, May 13, 1954; LBJ to Omar N. Braddock, May 11, 1954; and LBJ to Gus B. Michel, May 5, 1954, all in PPP-SP, Box 1194, LBJL. The "language of strength" is in LBJ to Jack Burrus, May 8, 1954, PPP-SP, Box 1194, LBJL.

67. Only a small portion of Johnson's letters address independence or colonialism. In a letter to a friend, Maston Nixon, Johnson noted that "Asia is gripped by a tremendous revolt against colonialism. . . . I certainly agree with you that we have got to have a policy based upon bringing independence rather than continued dependence to these people." LBJ to Maston Nixon, May 21, 1954, PPP-SP, Box 1194, LBJL. See also LBJ to T. E. Robbins, June 11, 1954, PPP-SP, Box 1195, LBJL.

68. Prados 2007, 234.

69. LBJ, "Washington News Letter," April 24, 1954, PPP-LBJA Subject File, Box 94, LBJL, 1 (emphasis omitted).
70. LBJ to Claude E. Carter, April 23, 1954, PPP-SP, Box 1194, LBJL.
71. LBJ to Omar N. Braddock, May 11, 1954. For similar language, see LBJ to Douglas Page, May 17, 1954, PPP-SP, Box 1194, LBJL.
72. LBJ to W. W. Housewright, May 11, 1954, PPP-SP, Box 1194, LBJL.
73. See, for example, LBJ to W. P. Crouch, May 17, 1954, PPP-SP, Box 1194, LBJL.
74. LBJ, Speech to Jefferson-Jackson Day Dinner, May 6, 1954, Statements of LBJ, Box 15, LBJL, 3.
75. Prados 2007, 15.
76. Johnson explicitly admitted to this "reluctance" in his classified statement to the House Foreign Affairs Committee following the trip, saying he "was unfamiliar with the area" and thought the mission "might accomplish little or nothing." LBJ, Statement before House Foreign Affairs Committee, June 5, 1961, VPSF, Box 11, LBJL, 1.
77. See "Papers for Vice President's Trip," undated, VPSF, Box 1, LBJL; Bowles to LBJ, May 8, 1961, NSF, Box 1, LBJL, 2.
78. LBJ, Speech at Farewell Dinner in Saigon, May 12, 1961 (USIS Release), VPSF, Box 1, LBJL, 1–2. An account of the initial meeting between Johnson and Diem is in Saigon to State, May 13, 1961, *FRUS, 1961–1963*, I, Doc. 54.
79. LBJ to JFK, "Mission to Southeast Asia, India and Pakistan," May 23, 1961, VPSF, Box 1, LBJL, 2.
80. Ibid., 5.
81. Ibid., 6. A similar pattern emerged in his classified statement to the House Foreign Affairs Committee on his return. See LBJ, Statement before House Foreign Affairs Committee, June 5, 1961, 6–7.
82. Paper Prepared by the Vice President, undated, *FRUS, 1961–1963*, I, Doc. 59. An editorial note in the *FRUS* volume indicates that it is "not clear whether this paper was intended to be an annex to the memorandum to the President, a draft of the memorandum itself, or the report from which the Vice President briefed the Cabinet on May 25." Ibid., note 1.
83. LBJ, Statement before House Foreign Affairs Committee, June 5, 1961, 9.
84. Report by the Vice President, undated, *FRUS, 1961–1963*, I, Doc. 60.
85. LBJ, Speech at Farewell Dinner in Saigon, May 12, 1961, 2; LBJ quoted in Halberstam 1972, 135.
86. LBJ, Statement before House Foreign Affairs Committee, June 5, 1961, 14.
87. Among his behind-the-scenes moves during the debate over the Eisenhower Doctrine, Johnson got the Middle East Resolution amended to require the administration to submit economic projects to Congress for advance approval. See undated memo (summarizing Democrats' influence on the Middle East Resolution), PPP-LBJA Subject File, Box 69, LBJL.
88. LBJ, Speech on Senate floor, July 15, 1958, *Congressional Record*, 85th Congress, 2nd session, 13767; Russell Baker, "Critics in Senate Deplore Landing," *New York Times*, July 16, 1958.

89. JFK to V. Veinmayr, July 11, 1958, PPP-SF, Box 693, JFKL; LBJ to Henry Grawunder Sr., July 18, 1958, PPP-SP, Box 602, LBJL.

90. Freedman 2000, 405.

91. Summary Record of a Meeting, the White House, January 28, 1961, *FRUS, 1961–1963*, I, Doc. 3.

92. LBJ, Statement before House Foreign Affairs Committee, June 5, 1961, 7.

93. LBJ to JFK, May 23, 1961, 6. A similar statement is in LBJ, Statement before House Foreign Affairs Committee, June 5, 1961, 7.

94. Memorandum of Conference with President Kennedy, March 9, 1961, *FRUS, 1961–1963*, XXIV, Doc. 25. According to this memorandum, Johnson did not comment in this meeting.

95. Notes, Meeting of National Security Council, May 1, 1961, VPSF, Box 5, LBJL, 2, 4.

96. Memorandum Prepared in the Department of State, undated, *FRUS, 1961–1963*, XXIV, Doc. 451, notes 2–4.

97. On this point, see Goodwin 1991, 170–178.

98. Freedman 2000, 399–400; see also Preston 2006, 47–53.

99. NSAM 283, "U.S. Overseas Internal Defense Training Policy and Objectives," February 13, 1964, NSF, Box 3, LBJL; Forrestal to Bundy, February 11, 1964, NSF, Box 3, LBJL. On Forrestal, see Halberstam 1972, 376–377; Gelb and Betts 1979, 81–82.

100. "Lyndon's Other Bible," *Time*, September 3, 1965; Gardner 1995, 29; on Johnson's interest in meeting with Ward, see Editorial Note, *FRUS, 1964–1968*, IX, Doc. 4.

101. Packenham 1973, 85–87, 92.

102. Ibid., 84, 93.

103. Kaufman 1987, 81.

104. Memorandum for the Record (dictated by McCone), March 18, 1965, *FRUS, 1964–1968*, XXXIII, Doc. 30.

105. NSAM 341, "The Direction, Coordination and Supervision of Interdepartmental Activities Overseas," March 2, 1966, *FRUS, 1964–1968*, XXXIII, Doc. 56. Taylor's report is in Bundy to LBJ, January 19, 1966, with attachment of Taylor's letter to Johnson and full report, *FRUS, 1964–1968*, XXXIII, Doc. 50. The memo and attachments were included with Johnson's "Night Reading," and as the editors of the *FRUS* volume note, there is a marking that indicates that Johnson saw them. Ibid., note 1.

106. Komer to Bundy, January 21, 1966, *FRUS, 1964–1968*, XXXIII, Doc. 51.

107. NSAM 343, "Appointment of Special Assistant to the President for Peaceful Construction in Vietnam," March 28, 1966, *FRUS, 1964–1968*, IV, Doc. 102.

108. On the problems and contradictions of the Alliance, see in particular Levinson and Onís 1970; see also Wiarda 1988.

109. Levinson and Onís 1970, 86–87; Rabe 1999, 122–123, 179.

110. Rabe argues that Kennedy's policies were shifting near the end of his life. Rabe 1999, 175; see also Levinson and Onís 1970, 86; Tulchin 1994, 240–241; Dallek 1998, 96.

111. Among those taking some version of this view are LaFeber 1981; Schoultz 1998, 358; Lawrence 2005, 20. Packenham also calls the Johnson administration's changes "a major shift in U.S. policy toward Latin American political development," though he notes the Kennedy administration's "gradual shift toward more realistic goals." Packenham 1973, 97.

112. Goldman 1969, 75.

113. Rabe 1999, 176.

114. Quoted in Wicker 1968, 196.

115. On this shift in goals, see Levinson and Onís 1970, 87–88; Packenham 1973, 95–97.

116. Tad Szulc, "U.S. May Abandon Effort to Deter Latin Dictators," *New York Times*, March 19, 1964. See also Levinson and Onís 1970, 88; Packenham 1973, 95; Tulchin 1994, 230; Editorial Note, *FRUS, 1964–1968*, XXXI, Doc. 10.

117. Tulchin 1994, 231. It is true that, as Tulchin notes, Johnson was "deeply interested in several specific goals of the Alliance," especially the development of infrastructure, always a favorite Johnson theme in both domestic and foreign affairs. Ibid., 218–219.

118. Latham 2002, 501. On the long-term causes of the riots, see ibid., 501–507.

119. Lawrence 2005, 22.

120. On the crisis and Johnson's response, see, for example, ibid.; Jorden 1984, chaps. 2–4; Dallek 1998, 92–97.

121. This was CIA director John McCone's assessment in the first White House meeting to discuss the crisis, on January 10. Memorandum for the Record, January 10, 1964, *FRUS, 1964–1968*, XXXI, Doc. 368. Johnson repeated this formulation in his call with Russell later that morning. Transcript of telcon, LBJ with Russell, January 10, 1964, *FRUS, 1964–1968*, XXXI, Doc. 369.

122. Transcript of telcon, LBJ with Chiari, January 10, 1964, *FRUS, 1964–1968*, XXXI, Doc. 370.

123. Editorial Note, *FRUS, 1964–1968*, XXXI, Doc. 379.

124. Vance to Taylor, January 22, 1964, *FRUS, 1964–1968*, XXXI, Doc. 381. Johnson discussed his concerns about the security situation in Panama and his request to McNamara to "get ready for the worse if something happened down there" in a telephone conversation with Mann on January 22. See ibid., note 3.

125. Telcon, LBJ with Russell, January 11, 1964, Editorial Note, *FRUS, 1964–1968*, XXXI, Doc. 373.

126. Telcon, LBJ with Bundy, January 11, 1964, Editorial Note, *FRUS, 1964–1968*, XXXI, Doc. 373.

127. Transcript of telcon, LBJ with Mann and Dungan, January 14, 1964, *FRUS, 1964–1968*, XXXI, Doc. 378.

128. Telcon, LBJ with Mann, March 10, 1964, Editorial Note, *FRUS, 1964–1968*, XXXI, Doc. 397.

129. Latham 2002, 514.

130. Memorandum of a Telephone Conversation, November 18, 1964, *FRUS, 1964–1968*, XXXI, Doc. 419.

131. Mansfield to LBJ, January 31, 1964, *FRUS, 1964–1968*, XXXI, Doc. 385.

132. Editorial Note, *FRUS, 1964–1968*, XXXI, Doc. 399. As Eric Goldman notes, the assembled diplomats could not believe Johnson would use an Alliance anniversary to make such a statement. Goldman 1969, 76.

133. Transcript of telcon, LBJ with Russell, February 26, 1964, *FRUS, 1964–1968*, XXXI, Doc. 391.

134. Transcript of telcon, LBJ with Russell, March 9, 1964, *FRUS, 1964–1968*, XXXI, Doc. 396.

135. Telcon, LBJ with Bundy, March 12, 1964, Editorial Note, *FRUS, 1964–1968*, XXXI, Doc. 399. In a meeting later that day, there was a tense moment in which Mann threatened resignation and Johnson threatened to fire him. Jorden 1984, 80.

136. Editorial Note, *FRUS, 1964–1968*, XXXI, Doc. 401.

137. Dallek 1998, 93.

138. Lawrence 2005, 26–28.

139. For early accounts of the Dominican Republic crisis and intervention, see Draper 1968; Slater 1970; Lowenthal 1995. Gleijeses 1978 draws extensively on sources from the Dominican side. More recent accounts based on the documentary record include Brands 1995, 50–61; Felten 1999. See also Dallek 1998, 262–268; Rabe 1999, 191–193; Rabe 2006.

140. Gleijeses 1978, 277–281, chap. 11.

141. Indeed, Lawrence Yates notes that the Lebanon analogy was pertinent to Johnson's decision making during the Dominican Republic crisis. See Yates 1988, 66.

142. See, for example, Brands 1995, 53. Both Tulchin and Dallek argue that the overriding goal of preventing another communist takeover in the hemisphere restricted Johnson's options in Latin America. Tulchin 1994, 227; Dallek 1999, 15.

143. Ball 1982, 329; see also McPherson 2003.

144. Talking Paper—Vice President's Visit to President Bosch, undated, VPSF, Box 3, LBJL, 2.

145. Slater 1970, 16–17.

146. Gleijeses 1978, 75–77, 285–287; see also Draper 1968, 20.

147. Quoted in Schlesinger 1965, 705–706.

148. State to Santo Domingo, October 4, 1963, *FRUS, 1961–1963*, XII, Doc. 359.

149. Santo Domingo to State, May 21, 1964, *FRUS, 1964–1968*, XXXII, Doc. 5.

150. Transcript of telcon, LBJ with Mann, April 26, 1965, *FRUS, 1964–1968*, XXXII, Doc. 22.

151. State to Santo Domingo, April 27, 1965, *FRUS, 1964–1968*, XXXII, Doc. 24.

152. Quoted in Editorial Note, *FRUS, 1964–1968*, XXXII, Doc. 30.

153. Santo Domingo to NSA (message marked "Critic Five"), April 28, 1965, *FRUS, 1964–1968*, XXXII, Doc. 32.

154. Memorandum of telcon, LBJ with Mann, Rusk, and Bundy, April 28, 1965, *FRUS, 1964–1968*, XXXII, Doc. 31.

155. Santo Domingo to NSA, April 28, 1965, *FRUS, 1964–1968*, XXXII, Doc. 36.

156. Transcript of telcon, LBJ with Bundy, April 29, 1965, *FRUS, 1964–1968*, XXXII, Doc. 40.

157. State to Santo Domingo, April 29, 1965, quoted in Brands 1995, 56.

158. Lowenthal 1995, chap. 4; Felten 1999, 103.

159. Valenti's notes are quoted in Editorial Note, *FRUS, 1964–1968*, XXXII, Doc. 42.

160. Felten 1999, 104.

161. Wheeler to Palmer, May 1, 1965, Editorial Note, *FRUS, 1964–1968*, XXXII, Doc. 43.

162. Lowenthal 1995, 123.

163. State to Santo Domingo, April 30, 1965, *FRUS, 1964–1968*, XXXII, Doc. 45.

164. Memorandum for the Record, Meeting on the Dominican Republic, May 2, 1965, *FRUS, 1964–1968*, XXXII, Doc. 51.

165. Transcript of telcon, LBJ with McNamara, May 12, 1965, *FRUS, 1964–1968*, XXXII, Doc. 64.

166. Felten 1999, 109–111.

167. The conversation is mentioned in Memorandum for the Record (drafted on May 13, summarizing meeting at White House, May 12–13, 1965), *FRUS, 1964–1968*, XXXII, Doc. 66.

168. Transcript of telcon, LBJ with Bundy, Mann et al., May 18, 1965, *FRUS, 1964–1968*, XXXII, Doc. 77. On the influence of domestic politics in the crisis, see also McPherson 2003.

169. State to Santo Domingo (listed as being from Johnson), May 22, 1965, *FRUS, 1964–1968*, XXXII, Doc. 89.

170. Felten 1999, 121–122.

171. Quoted in ibid., 121.

172. As acting CIA director Richard Helms wrote to a deputy in December 1965, "the President told the Director and me . . . [that] he expected the Agency to devote the necessary personnel and material resources in the Dominican Republic required to win the presidential election for the candidate favored by the United States Government. . . . He wants to win the election, and he expects the Agency to arrange for this to happen." Helms to Fitzgerald, "Presidential Election in the Dominican Republic," December 29, 1965, *FRUS, 1964–1968*, XXXII, Doc. 151. See also Editorial Note, *FRUS, 1964–1968*, XXXII, Doc. 150; Rabe 2006, 56.

173. On Fulbright's criticism, see Brands 1995, 60–61.

174. Tulchin 1994, 236.
175. On the peacekeeping role of U.S. forces in the Dominican Republic, see Yates 1988, chap. 7.
176. See, for example, Slater 1970, 219–220; Gleijeses 1978, 290–294; Rabe 1999, 191–193; Rabe 2006.
177. LBJ, Radio and Television Report to the American People on the Situation in the Dominican Republic, May 2, 1965, *Public Papers of the Presidents of the United States: Lyndon B. Johnson, 1965*, 469–474.
178. Gleijeses 1978, 299–300; Felten 1999, 126–127.
179. For comprehensive discussions of Johnson's decision to escalate, see, among relatively recent accounts, Logevall 1999; Kaiser 2000. Earlier analyses include Gallucci 1975; Gelb and Betts 1979; Berman 1982; Herring 1996. For a review of scholarship on the U.S. involvement in Vietnam, see Berman and Routh 2003.
180. Those who argue that Johnson was highly constrained in Vietnam include Gelb and Betts 1979, 352–354 (arguing that all the presidents who confronted Vietnam were constrained by their perception of the U.S. commitment); Dallek 1999. Gareth Porter (2005) also sees the war as a product of forces beyond White House control but takes a more structural view, arguing that the United States enjoyed a dominant power position over the Soviet Union at the time of the Vietnam decisions, leading to a more aggressive American posture in Southeast Asia. Logevall (1999) maintains instead that Johnson had real choice in Vietnam and could have withdrawn at many points during what Logevall terms "The Long 1964"; see also Burke et al. 1989, 146–149. On Vietnam as a "war of choice" for the United States, see also Downes 2009, 11–12, 32–34.
181. Logevall 1999, especially 76; see also 78.
182. Dallek 1998, 99.
183. While not making the argument in precisely these terms, Gelb and Betts, for example, argue that "the tightening of the noose on the battlefield after Kennedy's death tightened the range of means that could be used to uphold the objectives." Gelb and Betts 1979, 94–95.
184. Burris to LBJ, "Viet Cong Activity," March 20, 1962, VPSF, Box 5, LBJL.
185. Memorandum of Conversation (drafted by Hilsman), August 31, 1963, *FRUS, 1961–1963*, IV, Doc. 37.
186. Ibid.
187. Ibid., note 7, which quotes from Bromley Smith's summary of this meeting.
188. Memorandum for the Record of Meeting (drafted by McCone on November 25), November 24, 1963, *FRUS, 1961–1963*, IV, Doc. 330.
189. Quoted in Dallek 1998, 99.
190. The NSAM directed that U.S. action should "include not only military but political, economic, social, educational and informational effort. We should seek to turn the tide not only of battle but of belief, and we should seek to

increase not only the control of hamlets but the productivity of this area."
NSAM 273, November 26, 1963, *FRUS, 1961–1963*, IV, Doc. 331.

191. Memorandum for the Record of Discussion at the Daily White House Staff Meeting, November 22, 1963, *FRUS, 1961–1963*, IV, Doc. 322.

192. Mansfield to LBJ, December 7, 1963, *FRUS, 1961–1963*, IV, Doc. 355.

193. Forrestal to LBJ, December 7, 1963, *FRUS, 1961–1963*, IV, Doc. 360.

194. Memorandum by McCone, March 3, 1964, *FRUS, 1964–1968*, I, Doc. 68; see also Gravel 1971, 3:43–44.

195. Among the accounts noting this point are Herring 1996, 121; Kaiser 2000, 289.

196. On Johnson's rejection of military options in this period, see Kaiser 2000, chap. 10.

197. Transcript of telcon, LBJ with Bundy, May 20, 1964, McKee 2007, 781–782.

198. Transcript of telcon, LBJ with RFK, May 28, 1964, McKee 2007, 920; 922–924; on Johnson's relationship with Robert Kennedy, see Dallek 1998, 56–58.

199. LBJ to Taylor, December 30, 1964, *FRUS, 1964–1968*, I, Doc. 477.

200. Cooper to Bundy, March 1, 1965, *FRUS, 1964–1968*, II, Doc. 173.

201. McNamara to Taylor, March 2, 1965, *FRUS, 1964–1968*, II, Doc. 178.

202. Bundy Memorandum, March 16, 1965, *FRUS, 1964–1968*, II, Doc. 200; McCone to Carter, April 1, 1965, *FRUS, 1964–1968*, II, Doc. 230.

203. Khong 1992, 100–101, 110–111.

204. See Editorial Note, *FRUS, 1964–1968*, I, Doc. 403. For accounts of the policy debate surrounding the three options, see Gravel 1971, 3:206–251; Logevall 1999, 255–274; Kaiser 2000, 353–381.

205. Khong 1992, 138–143. In choosing between the two options that might address this problem, Khong notes that limited intervention, or Option C, was preferable to the heavier intervention of Option B because the Korean analogy also counseled for restrained action so as not to provoke counterintervention by the Chinese.

206. Transcript of telcon, LBJ with Russell, May 27, 1964, Beschloss 1997, 364, 369. In this vein, John Zaller argues that it was the anticipated fear of public opinion, which might not favor intervention initially but would punish the president for walking away from the conflict, that drove Johnson to intervene. Notably, he maintains that Kennedy and Johnson analyzed "latent public opinion" along similar lines. See Zaller 2003.

207. Transcript of telcon, LBJ with Bundy, May 27, 1964, Beschloss 1997, 370.

208. Personal Notes of a Meeting with President Johnson, April 1, 1965, *FRUS, 1964–1968*, II, Doc. 229.

209. Herring 1996, 131. A February 12 intelligence assessment "rais[ed] the question whether the situations in South Vietnam and Laos may be on the verge of collapse." See "SNIE 50–64, Short-Term Prospects in Southeast Asia," February 12, 1964, *FRUS, 1964–1968*, I, Doc. 42.

210. Memorandum for the Record of a Meeting, February 20, 1964, *FRUS, 1964–1968*, I, Doc. 54.
211. Transcript of telcon, LBJ with Bundy, May 13, 1964, McKee 2007, 684.
212. Logevall 1999, 122–123.
213. Freedman 2000, 405–406.
214. McNamara to LBJ (report adopted as NSAM 288), March 16, 1964, *FRUS, 1964–1968*, I, Doc. 84; see also NSAM 288, "Implementation of South Vietnam Programs," *FRUS, 1964–1968*, I, Doc. 87; Gravel 1971, 3:50.
215. Gravel 1971, 3:51, 54.
216. Memorandum for the Record of the White House Daily Staff Meeting, March 30, 1964, *FRUS, 1964–1968*, I, Doc. 99.
217. LBJ, Address at Johns Hopkins University, "Peace without Conquest," April 7, 1965, *Public Papers of the Presidents of the United States: Lyndon B. Johnson, 1965*, 394–399. On the speech, see Gardner 1995, chap. 9.
218. Gardner 1995, 190–193, and chap. 6 on the "two wars." On Johnson and the Mekong project, see also Ekbladh 2010, 206–212.
219. Logevall 1999, 371–372; see also Gelb and Betts 1979, 283; Kaiser 2000, 423–427.
220. LBJ, "Peace without Conquest," April 7, 1965.
221. Memorandum of a Meeting, September 9, 1964, *FRUS, 1964–1968*, I, Doc. 343.
222. McNaughton draft memo, "Aims and Options in Southeast Asia," October 13, 1964, Gravel 1971, 3:580–583.
223. Logevall 1999, 272–273.
224. Memorandum of the Meeting of the Executive Committee, November 24, 1964, *FRUS, 1964–1968*, I, Doc. 424. Option A's advocates included Maxwell Taylor and Averell Harriman. See Taylor paper, "The Current Situation in South Viet-Nam—November 1964," undated, *FRUS, 1964–1968*, I, Doc. 426; Logevall 1999, 273. At the staff level, Robert Johnson of the State Department's Policy Planning Staff and CIA Vietnam analyst George Carver also argued for more counterinsurgency efforts. See Robert H. Johnson to William Bundy (with enclosure of Johnson paper "The Case for Option A"), November 18, 1964, Papers of Paul C. Warnke, John McNaughton Files, Box 8, LBJL; Robert H. Johnson to Forrestal (with enclosure of George Carver paper "The Feasibility and Possible Advantages of a Continued Concentration on Counterinsurgency [Option A]"), November 19, 1964, Papers of Paul C. Warnke, John McNaughton Files, Box 8, LBJL. Both these memos are discussed in Kaiser 2000, 362.
225. Notes on a Meeting, December 1, 1964, *FRUS, 1964–1968*, I, Doc. 432.
226. Ibid.
227. Logevall 1999, 270.
228. Bundy handwritten meeting notes, January 27, 1965, Papers of McGeorge Bundy, Box 1, LBJL (the final two sentences are underlined in Bundy's notes). See also Logevall 1999, 318–319. For the "fork in the road" memo, see Bundy to LBJ, January 27, 1965, *FRUS, 1964–1968*, II, Doc. 42.

229. Logevall 1999, 292.
230. Ibid., 314.
231. On the period leading up to this decision, see Gravel 1971, 3:286–332; Gallucci 1975, chap. 3; Kaiser 2000, 393–404.
232. Before approving the request, the president sent the army chief of staff, General Harold K. Johnson, to Saigon to find out what more "can be done within South Vietnam," including "all possible additional actions—political, military, and economic." State to Saigon (McNamara for Taylor), March 2, 1965, *FRUS, 1964–1968*, II, Doc. 178.
233. Logevall 1999, 369; Gelb and Betts 1979, 121; see also Berman 1982, 54.
234. CINCPAC (Commander in Chief, Pacific) to JCS, March 6, 1965, *FRUS, 1964–1968*, II, Doc. 185. For a summary of the three phases of guerrilla warfare, see Krepinevich 1986, 7.
235. For a North Vietnamese account of the development of main-force units in this period, see Military History Institute of Vietnam 2002, chap. 5. Porter, however, argues that the North Vietnamese were very cautious about sending main-force units, for fear of provoking a major U.S. intervention, and went to some lengths to conceal them, thereby limiting their combat effectiveness. Porter 2005, 132–137. He also suggests that the North Vietnamese themselves were influenced by their perceptions of Kennedy and Johnson, viewing Johnson as "more likely to change the character of the war from 'special war' to 'limited war." See ibid., 127.
236. Those arguing for counterinsurgency and pacification include Krepinevich 1986 and Nagl 2005, chaps. 6–7; for the contrasting view emphasizing conventional warfare, see Summers 1982. For the argument that neither strategy would have worked, given the flexibility and resources of the North Vietnamese, see Lebovic 2010, chap. 2.
237. Berman 1982, 82–84, 135–138. As Berman details, those who opposed McNamara's assumption that the Viet Cong had entered the "third phase" included Bundy, Ball, and CIA director William Raborn.
238. Krepinevich 1986, 268; see also 140.
239. Lewy 1978, 86. Avant argues that counterinsurgency was crucial to defeating the main-force units themselves. See Avant 1994, 69–70, 77–78.
240. Quoted in Kaiser 2000, 414; see also Gravel 1971, 3:406.
241. Gelb and Betts 1979, 134.
242. On the expectations for each strategy, see Gravel 1971, 3:479–485; see also Gallucci 1975, 106–110.
243. Gravel 1971, 3:470.
244. McNamara to LBJ, July 1, 1965, *FRUS, 1964–1968*, III, Doc. 38.
245. Berman 1982, 82–91, 135–138. Although Berman notes that little of the correspondence among the president's advisers reached his desk (ibid., 137), some of the dissents citing the lack of evidence for a Viet Cong shift to the "third phase" were addressed directly to Johnson.

246. Ibid., 99, 106, 127–128.
247. Notes of Meeting, July 21, 1965, *FRUS, 1964–1968*, III, Doc. 71. Notes of the same meeting, drafted by Chester Cooper of the NSC, report substantially the same discussion, with Johnson declaring that the "mission should be as limited as we dare make it" before Wheeler, McNamara, and Ball debated the question of large-unit operations (without input from Johnson). See Memorandum for the Record, July 21, 1965, *FRUS, 1964–1968*, III, Doc. 72.
248. Cooper to Bundy, July 21, 1965, *FRUS, 1964–1968*, III, Doc. 73.
249. Bundy to LBJ, Meeting Agenda, undated (but for July 22 meeting), *FRUS, 1964–1968*, III, Doc. 77; Notes of Meeting, July 22, 1965, *FRUS, 1964–1968*, III, Doc. 78.
250. Notes of Meeting, July 22, 1965, *FRUS, 1964–1968*, III, Doc. 76.
251. Fitzgerald 1972, 476; see also chap. 12.
252. Carter 2008, 202.
253. Avant 1994, 84–87; see also Gravel 1971, 2:533–536; Gaddis 2005, 251.
254. Berman 1982, 145–146.
255. For a discussion, see Downes 2009.
256. Krepinevich 1986, 268. For an alternative argument, see Summers 1982.
257. Gravel 1971, 3:475; see also Gelb and Betts 1979, 121; Berman 1982, 145; Logevall 1999.
258. Gelb and Betts 1979, 278.
259. Quoted in Karnow 1983, 415. Others, however, have regarded Johnson as more detached on the question of strategy. See, for example, Herring 1994, 178–179; Bator 2008, 319–321.
260. On this point, see Caverley 2009/2010.
261. State to Saigon, October 4, 1965, quoted in Gravel 1971, 2:543 (emphasis omitted).
262. Herring 1994, 67; see also Hunt 1995, 1. For skeptical views, see Gravel 1971, 2:544; Blaufarb 1977, 232; Gelb and Betts 1979, 283.
263. Telcon, LBJ with Rusk, February 3, 1966, *FRUS, 1964–1968*, IV, Doc. 63. On the Honolulu conference, see also Gravel 1971, 2:548–554.
264. NSAM 343, March 28, 1966; Herring 1994, 71; see also Cooper to LBJ, March 5, 1966, *FRUS, 1964–1968*, IV, attachment to Doc. 90 (sent via Komer). Bundy had recommended a new position that would coordinate nonmilitary operations only. See Bundy to LBJ, February 16, 1966, *FRUS, 1964–1968*, IV, Doc. 77.
265. Herring 1994, 74–82; Gravel 1971, 2:589–621; Blaufarb 1977, 232–239.
266. Blaufarb 1977, 240.
267. Herring 1994, 87.
268. Avant 1994, 101.
269. Herring 1994, 88.
270. Bundy interview with Gordon Goldstein, in Goldstein 2008, 98.
271. Logevall 1999, 398.
272. Porter 2005, 163.

273. Ibid., chap. 7.
274. Roger Hilsman, "A Strategic Concept for South Vietnam," February 2, 1962, *FRUS, 1961–1963*, II, Doc. 42.
275. Gaddis 2005, chaps. 7–8.
276. On Johnson's concern about protecting the Great Society, see Berman 1982, 145–153; Bator 2008.
277. Dallek 2003, 710–711.
278. LBJ, "Washington News Letter," May 21, 1958, PPP-LBJA Subject File, Box 95, LBJL (emphasis omitted).

6. Before and After the Cold War

1. Chollet and Goldgeier 2008, xiv. On the evolution of the purpose of intervention over time, see Finnemore 2003.
2. For a discussion of how America's rise translated into expansionist tendencies (including interventionism), see Zakaria 1998.
3. See, for example, Kissinger 1994, 29–30.
4. Cooper 1983, 271.
5. Beale 1956, 3.
6. Quoted in Collin 1990, 49.
7. Quoted in Beale 1956, 76.
8. Quoted in ibid., 60.
9. Quoted in ibid., 64–65.
10. Ibid., 32–35, 70. On Roosevelt's concept of "civilization," see Ninkovich 1986.
11. Quoted in Ninkovich 1986, 233.
12. Collin 1990, 52.
13. Beale 1956, 29.
14. On the Dominican Republic crisis and intervention, see Collin 1990, chaps. 12–15; Langley 2002, 20–26.
15. Langley 2002, 23.
16. Quoted in ibid.
17. Quoted in ibid., 24.
18. Collin 1990, 399.
19. Quoted in ibid., 400.
20. Ibid., 392.
21. Langley 2002, 115 (emphasis in original).
22. On Wilson's pre-presidential years and the evolution of his beliefs, see Link 1947; Mulder 1978; Ninkovich 1994, chap. 2.
23. Quoted in Link 1947, 27.
24. On the connection between imperialism and reform in Wilson's thinking, see Mulder 1978, chap. 9; Ninkovich 1994, 42.
25. Ninkovich 1994, 40–41.

26. Mulder 1978, 231.

27. Quoted in ibid.

28. Quoted in ibid., 272.

29. Link 1956, 328, 330.

30. Smith 1994, 67–68.

31. On Wilson's intervention in the Dominican Republic, see ibid., 71–73; Langley 2002, chaps. 10–12.

32. Langley 2002, 144.

33. Ibid., 148.

34. See Chollet and Goldgeier 2008, 8.

35. On the stability of elite beliefs even as the international system transitioned to the post–Cold War period, see Murray 1996.

36. Finnemore 2003, 137.

37. Don Oberdorfer, "On Global Matters, Two Candidates' Positions Are Mostly in Sync," *Washington Post*, September 29, 1992.

38. Halberstam 2001, 69–70.

39. Western 2005, chap. 5.

40. See Thomas L. Friedman, "Seeing Foreign Policy in a Rear-View Mirror," *New York Times*, August 23, 1992.

41. Dan Balz and E. J. Dionne Jr., "Democrats Warm Up for a Busy Weekend; Presidential Candidates Clinton, Kerrey, Tsongas Trade Ideas on Eve of Debate Here Sunday," *Washington Post*, December 13, 1991; "Excerpts from Interview with Clinton on Goals for Presidency," *New York Times*, June 28, 1992.

42. Quoted in Thomas L. Friedman, "Turning His Sights Overseas, Clinton Sees a Problem at 1600 Pennsylvania Avenue," *New York Times*, April 2, 1992.

43. "Excerpts from Clinton's Speech on Foreign Policy Leadership," *New York Times*, August 14, 1992.

44. "Excerpts from Speech by Clinton on U.S. Role," *New York Times*, October 2, 1992.

45. Chollet and Goldgeier 2008, 35–37; see also Don Oberdorfer, "On the Stump, Clinton Quietly Got 11 Briefings on Events Overseas," *Washington Post*, November 6, 1992; Thomas L. Friedman, "Clinton's Foreign-Policy Agenda Reaches across Broad Spectrum," *New York Times*, October 4, 1992.

46. For overviews of the crisis in Somalia and the U.S. and UN responses, see Hirsch and Oakley 1995; Lyons and Samatar 1995; Von Hippel 2000, chap. 3; Halberstam 2001, chap. 23; Dobbins et al. 2003, chap. 4; Western 2005, chap. 5.

47. Western 2005, 136–137; Halberstam 2001, 250–252.

48. Dobbins et al. 2003, 58–59.

49. George H. W. Bush, Address to the Nation on the Situation in Somalia, December 4, 1992, *Public Papers of the Presidents of the United States: George Bush, 1992–1993*, 2175–2176.

50. See Lyons and Samatar 1995, 39–43.

51. Clarke and Herbst 1996, 74; see also Lyons and Samatar 1995, 43, 67–68.

52. United Nations Security Council Resolution 814, March 26, 1993, http://daccess
-dds-ny.un.org/doc/UNDOC/GEN/N93/226/18/IMG/N9322618.pdf; see also
Lyons and Samatar 1995, 53; Von Hippel 2000, 63–64; Dobbins et al. 2003,
59–60.

53. United Nations Security Council Resolution 837, June 6, 1993, http://daccess
-dds-ny.un.org/doc/UNDOC/GEN/N93/332/32/IMG/N9333232.pdf.

54. Dobbins et al. 2003, 59–60.

55. Halberstam 2001, 254. On the Clinton administration's early problems in dealing
with foreign policy, including Somalia, see Chollet and Goldgeier 2008, chap. 3.

56. Clarke and Herbst 1996, 73.

57. Hirsch and Oakley 1995, xix.

58. Quoted in Halberstam 2001, 256. In July 1993, Sandy Berger, then the deputy
national security adviser, told reporters, "Let's not lose sight [of UNOSOM's]
objective, which is nation-building." Berger's remarks came in a press briefing by
Treasury Secretary Lloyd Bentsen, July 8, 1993, Woolley and Peters, The
American Presidency Project, http://www.presidency.ucsb.edu/ws/index.php
?pid=60171.

59. Clinton, Remarks at the American University Centennial Celebration, February
26, 1993, *Public Papers of the Presidents of the United States: William J. Clinton, 1993,*
207.

60. Clinton, Radio Address, June 12, 1993, *Public Papers of the Presidents of the United
States: William J. Clinton, 1993,* 840.

61. Clinton, Interview with Foreign Journalists, July 2, 1993, *Public Papers of the
Presidents of the United States: William J. Clinton, 1993,* 987.

62. Madeleine K. Albright, "Yes, There Is a Reason to Be in Somalia," *New York Times,*
August 10, 1993.

63. Clinton, Exchange with Reporters at Yale University in New Haven, October 9,
1993, *Public Papers of the Presidents of the United States: William J. Clinton, 1993,*
1729.

64. Halberstam 2001, 241.

65. Girard 2004, 19, 161.

66. Ibid., 162. On the 1994 Haiti intervention as an effort to bring about internal
political change, primarily directed by the United States despite its officially
multilateral nature, see also Kreps 2007.

67. Quoted in R. W. Apple Jr., "Bush Questions Aid to Moscow in a Policy Talk,"
New York Times, November 20, 1999; see also Dan Balz, "Bush Favors Internationalism; Candidate Calls China a 'Competitor,' Opposes Test Ban Treaty," *Washington Post,* November 20, 1999.

68. Quoted in Terry M. Neal, "In TV Talk, Bush Draws Some Lines," *Washington Post,*
November 22, 1999.

69. First Gore-Bush Presidential Debate, Boston, October 3, 2000, Woolley and
Peters, The American Presidency Project, http://www.presidency.ucsb.edu/ws/
index.php?pid=29418.

70. Second Gore-Bush Presidential Debate, Winston-Salem, N.C., October 11, 2000, Woolley and Peters, The American Presidency Project, http://www.presidency.ucsb.edu/ws/index.php?pid=29419.

71. Quoted in Michael R. Gordon, "Bush Would Stop U.S. Peacekeeping in Balkan Fights," *New York Times*, October 21, 2000; see also Rice 2000.

72. On Clinton's Iraq policy, see Chollet and Goldgeier 2008, chap. 7.

73. See John Lancaster, "In Saddam's Future, a Harder U.S. Line: Bush, Gore Depart from Clinton Policy," *Washington Post*, June 3, 2000; see also Steven Mufson, "A World View of His Own: On Foreign Policy, Bush Parts Ways with Father," *Washington Post*, August 11, 2000.

74. Quoted in Richard L. Berke, "Confident Bush Takes No Risks in First Debate," *New York Times*, December 3, 1999.

75. Second Gore-Bush Presidential Debate, Winston-Salem, N.C., October 11, 2000.

76. On the beliefs of the key Bush foreign policy advisers, see Mann 2004. As Mann describes, though Bush's advisers shared a commitment to American military power, there were important differences among them. Neoconservative advisers such as Deputy Defense Secretary Paul Wolfowitz held internally focused views and supported more intrusive forms of military intervention, including in the Clinton era. But other advisers such as Rice and Powell took a more externally focused view that focused on containment and deterrence, and if necessary, overwhelming conventional force in war.

77. On Rumsfeld's "transformation" agenda for the military, especially in the context of its relationship to the planning for the Iraq War, see Packer 2005, 42; Gordon and Trainor 2006, 3–10.

78. PDD-56 White Paper, "The Clinton Administration's Policy on Managing Complex Contingency Operations," May 1997, http://clinton2.nara.gov/WH/EOP/NSC/html/documents/NSCDoc2.html.

79. Packer 2005, 110.

80. James Fallows, "Bush's Lost Year," *Atlantic Monthly*, October 2004.

81. Serafino and Weiss 2006, 4, 7–8; see also Steven R. Weisman, "Bush Gives State Dept. Priority in Helping Nations to Rebuild," *New York Times*, December 15, 2005.

82. Jervis 2008/2009, 659.

83. Indeed, though many scholars have found that policymakers tend to assimilate new information in light of existing beliefs, Jonathan Renshon finds that aspects of Bush's "operational code" beliefs, as measured through public statements, did change from his early months in the presidency to the period after September 11, 2001. Notably, however, Renshon finds that in the period in which Bush transitioned from governor and candidate to president, his beliefs became more entrenched; furthermore, Renshon finds that Bush's beliefs did not change significantly in the period beginning six months after September 11 to the end of his second term. Renshon interprets this evidence as supporting the idea that

Bush's beliefs changed significantly because of the shock of September 11 but that otherwise his beliefs were relatively consistent. Renshon also finds that only certain dimensions of Bush's worldview changed following September 11. The dimensions studied by Renshon follow the "operational code" criteria and thus differ from the beliefs studied here. See Renshon 2008.

84. Quoted in Woodward 2004, 162.

85. Quoted in ibid., 27.

86. National Security Strategy of the United States of America, September 2002, http://www.globalsecurity.org/military/library/policy/national/nss-020920 .pdf.

87. George W. Bush, Remarks at the American Enterprise Institute Dinner, February 26, 2003, *Public Papers of the Presidents of the United States: George W. Bush, 2003*, 217. For arguments that the Bush Doctrine and the intellectual underpinnings of the Iraq War incorporated what can be termed an internally focused view of other states, see Jervis 2003; Flibbert 2006.

88. George W. Bush, Inaugural Address, January 20, 2005, *Public Papers of the Presidents of the United States: George W. Bush, 2005*, 66.

89. Woodward 2004, 89.

90. Ibid., 284.

91. On Wolfowitz's background and beliefs, see Mann 2004, chap. 2, 73–76; Packer 2005, 24–28.

92. Ricks 2006, 27. Wolfowitz would later sign on to Rumsfeld's efforts to invade Iraq with the smallest force possible, publicly dismissing claims that it would take a huge force to secure postwar Iraq. As he told a House committee before the invasion, "it is hard to conceive that it would take more forces to provide stability in post-Saddam Iraq than it would take to conduct the war itself and to secure the surrender of Saddam's security forces and his army—hard to imagine." Quoted in ibid., 98. Occasionally, Wolfowitz supported efforts to shift the U.S. strategy in a more transformative direction, such as a period early in the insurgency when, as Ricks reports, Wolfowitz expressed interest in a proposal for a "native constabulary force." See ibid., 187. But Wolfowitz fell largely in line with the overall Pentagon approach to the war.

93. George W. Bush, News Conference, March 6, 2003, *Public Papers of the Presidents of the United States: George W. Bush, 2003*, 247.

94. Packer 2005, 60.

95. Ibid., 395; see also Russett 2005, 396; Jervis 2008/2009, 659.

96. See, for example, James Fallows, "Blind into Baghdad," *Atlantic Monthly*, January/ February 2004; Gordon and Trainor 2006; Ricks 2006. Mann notes that a "decapitation of the Iraqi leadership" was not only central to the war plan but also to the "strategy for postwar reconstruction. The aim was not to rebuild Iraq from the ground up but to let Iraqis take over." Mann 2004, 360.

97. Gordon and Trainor 2006, 73.

98. Quoted in ibid., 142.

99. Ricks 2006, 116.
100. Quoted in ibid.
101. Ibid., 117 (Ricks here paraphrases Major Isaiah Wilson).
102. Kreps, for example, argues that "the focus going into Afghanistan was on military targets rather than institution-building after combat." Kreps 2008, 559.
103. Quoted in Packer 2005, 114.
104. On this point, see, for example, ibid.; Gordon and Trainor 2006, 101–105.
105. Wright and Reese 2008, 55–65.
106. Rumsfeld, Remarks at 11th Annual Salute to Freedom, "Beyond Nation Building," February 14, 2003, http://www.defenselink.mil/Speeches/Speech .aspx?SpeechID=337.
107. Woodward 2004, 121–122.
108. Packer 2005, 96.
109. On this point, see Fallows, "Blind into Baghdad."
110. See, for example, Rathmell 2005, 1021–1022; Bensahel 2006, 454–458; Wright and Reese 2008, 70–80.
111. Woodward 2004, 282–283. On ORHA, see Packer 2005, 120–148; see also Woodward 2004, 283–284; Ricks 2006, 80–81, 101–107. On the lack of preparation for the postwar phase, see also O'Hanlon 2004/2005; Battle and Blanton 2007.
112. The planning is summarized in Fallows, "Blind into Baghdad."
113. On Zinni's planning, see Gordon and Trainor 2006, 25–28; Ricks 2006, 33–34.
114. Rathmell 2005, 1027.
115. Bensahel 2006, 458.
116. Gordon and Trainor 2006, 160.
117. Woodward 2004, 329.
118. Gordon and Trainor 2006, 160.
119. Quoted in Woodward 2004, 339–340.
120. Ibid., 340.
121. For a discussion of whether administration officials saw Chalabi as an individual strongman or a potential path to a more democratic solution, see Jervis 2008/2009, 666–667. On Chalabi as a key to Rumsfeld's plan to allow U.S. troops to get out and avoid nation building, see also Evan Thomas and Mark Hosenball, "The Rise and Fall of Chalabi: Bush's Mr. Wrong," Newsweek, May 31, 2004.
122. Quoted in Woodward 2004, 339–340.
123. For discussions of this point, see Byman 2008; Lebovic 2010, 203, 207.
124. Corera 2004, 31.
125. Bensahel 2006, 458.
126. Corera 2004, 31–32.
127. Wright and Reese 2008, 25–26.
128. Rathmell 2005, 1035.

129. Bensahel 2006, 459–461.
130. Ibid., 465–466.
131. Wright and Reese 2008, 92–93.
132. Bensahel 2006, 462.
133. Packer 2005, 186.
134. Bensahel 2006, 462.
135. Wright and Reese 2008, 98.
136. James Fallows, "Why Iraq Has No Army," *Atlantic Monthly*, December 2005.
137. Rathmell 2005, 1035–1036.
138. Packer 2005, 202.
139. On the emergence of the insurgency and the principles of counterinsurgency as applied to Iraq, see ibid., chap. 9; Ricks 2006, chaps. 8–9, 14.
140. Ricks 2006, 152–154; George Packer, "The Lesson of Tal Afar: Is It Too Late for the Administration to Correct Its Course in Iraq?" *New Yorker*, April 10, 2006.
141. On army efforts to develop links with the Iraqi people, see, for example, Bensahel 2006, 465; Wright and Reese 2008, 116–118.
142. Wright and Reese 2008, 70.
143. Bensahel 2006, 471.
144. See *U.S. Army/Marine Corps Counterinsurgency Field Manual* 2007.

7. The Role of Leaders

1. LBJ, Speech on Senate floor, July 15, 1958, *Congressional Record*, 85th Congress, 2nd session, 13767; Russell Baker, "Critics in Senate Deplore Landing," *New York Times*, July 16, 1958; JFK to Herbert J. Spiro, August 8, 1958, PPP-SF, Box 693, JFKL; JFK to Maurice Mordka, March 18, 1958, PPP-SF, Box 691, JFKL.
2. Finnemore 2003.
3. See Bush and Scowcroft 1998, chap. 19; Mann 2004, 189–191.
4. On the U.S. decision not to intervene in Rwanda, see Samantha Power, "Bystanders to Genocide: Why the United States Let the Rwandan Tragedy Happen," *Atlantic Monthly*, September 2001.
5. Madeleine K. Albright, "The End of Intervention," *New York Times*, June 11, 2008.
6. Barack Obama, Speech to Anti-war Rally, October 2, 2002, reprinted in Obama, "Weighing the Costs of Waging War in Iraq," *Hyde Park Herald*, October 30, 2002.
7. Obama 2006, 316–317.
8. See Obama 2004, chaps. 7–14.
9. Barack Obama, remarks to Chicago Council on Global Affairs, April 23, 2007, http://www.thechicagocouncil.org/dynamic_page.php?id=64.
10. Obama, Speech to Anti-war Rally, October 2, 2002.

11. Anne E. Kornblut, Scott Wilson, and Karen DeYoung, "Obama Pressed for Faster Surge," *Washington Post*, December 6, 2009. See also Peter Baker, "How Obama Came to Plan for 'Surge' in Afghanistan," *New York Times*, December 5, 2009. On Secretary of Defense Robert Gates rejecting the idea that the United States was on a nation-building mission, see also Christi Parsons and Julian E. Barnes, "Obama Homed In on an Afghanistan Pullout Date," *Los Angeles Times*, December 4, 2009.

12. Quoted in Bobby Ghosh, "Taking It to the Taliban," *Time*, February 25, 2010. On the transformative aspects of the Marja operation, see also Rajiv Chandrasekaran, "Marines Plan Joint Mission to Eject Insurgents from Last Helmand Stronghold," *Washington Post*, February 10, 2010; Dexter Filkins, "Afghan Offensive Is New War Model," *New York Times*, February 12, 2010, and "Prize on the Battlefields of Marja May Be Momentum," *New York Times*, February 19, 2010.

13. See, for example, Quinlivan 1995/1996.

14. See, for example, the critiques by Stephen Biddle and Stathis Kalyvas of the new Counterinsurgency Field Manual (Biddle 2008; Kalyvas 2008); see also Myerson 2009.

15. On this problem with the analogy between Malaya and Vietnam, see Vertzberger 1990, 332–333; more generally, see Khong 1992, 91–95.

16. Regan 2000b.

17. Quoted in Schlesinger 1965, 704–705.

18. Notes on a White House meeting, April 30, 1965, quoted in Editorial Note, *FRUS, 1964–1968*, XXXII, Doc. 42.

19. Scholars have identified other cleavages in foreign policy beliefs that cut across parties: see, for example, Mead 2001; Nau 2008.

20. J. Owen 2002, 405.

21. See, for example, Friedberg 2000.

22. Litwak 2007, xiv.

23. Rock 1989, chap. 2.

24. Friedberg 2005.

References

Allison, Graham, and Philip Zelikow. 1999. *Essence of Decision: Explaining the Cuban Missile Crisis.* 2nd ed. New York: Longman.

Ambrose, Stephen E. 1967. *Eisenhower and Berlin, 1945: The Decision to Halt at the Elbe.* New York: W. W. Norton.

———. 1970. *The Supreme Commander: The War Years of General Dwight D. Eisenhower.* Jackson: University Press of Mississippi.

———. 1983. *Eisenhower, vol. 1: Soldier, General of the Army, President-Elect, 1890–1952.* New York: Simon and Schuster.

Anderson, David L. 1991. *Trapped by Success: The Eisenhower Administration and Vietnam, 1953–1961.* New York: Columbia University Press.

Arreguín-Toft, Ivan. 2005. *How the Weak Win Wars: A Theory of Asymmetric Conflict.* New York: Cambridge University Press.

Art, Robert J. 1973. "Bureaucratic Politics and American Foreign Policy: A Critique." *Policy Sciences* 4 (4): 467–490.

Atkinson, Rick. 2002. *An Army at Dawn: The War in North Africa, 1942–1943.* New York: Owl Books.

Avant, Deborah D. 1994. *Political Institutions and Military Change: Lessons from Peripheral Wars.* Ithaca, N.Y.: Cornell University Press.

Axelgard, Frederick W. 1991. "US Support for the British Position in Pre-revolutionary Iraq." In *The Iraqi Revolution of 1958: The Old Social Classes Revisited*, edited by Robert A. Fernea and William Roger Louis. New York: I. B. Tauris.

Ball, George W. 1982. *The Past Has Another Pattern: Memoirs.* New York: W. W. Norton.

Batatu, Hanna. 1978. *The Old Social Classes and the Revolutionary Movements of Iraq: A Study of Iraq's Old Landed and Commercial Classes and of Its Communists, Ba'thists, and Free Officers.* Princeton, N.J.: Princeton University Press.

Bator, Francis M. 2008. "No Good Choices: LBJ and the Vietnam/Great Society Connection." *Diplomatic History* 32 (3): 309–340.

Battle, Joyce, and Thomas Blanton, eds. 2007. "Top Secret Polo Step: Iraq War Plan Assumed Only 5,000 U.S. Troops Still There by December 2006." National Security Archive Electronic Briefing Book No. 214. http://www.gwu.edu/~nsarchiv/NSAEBB/NSAEBB214/index.htm.

Baumgartner, Frank R., Bryan D. Jones, and John Wilkerson. Policy Agendas Budget Trends Tool. http://www.policyagendas.org.

Beale, Howard K. 1956. *Theodore Roosevelt and the Rise of America to World Power.* Baltimore: Johns Hopkins University Press.

Bennett, Andrew. 1999. *Condemned to Repetition? The Rise, Fall, and Reprise of Soviet-Russian Military Interventionism, 1973–1996.* Cambridge, Mass.: MIT Press.

Bensahel, Nora. 2006. "Mission Not Accomplished: What Went Wrong with Iraqi Reconstruction." *Journal of Strategic Studies* 29 (3): 453–473.

Berinsky, Adam J. 2009. *In Time of War: Understanding American Public Opinion from World War II to Iraq.* Chicago: University of Chicago Press.

Berman, Larry. 1982. *Planning a Tragedy: The Americanization of the War in Vietnam.* New York: W. W. Norton.

Berman, Larry, and Stephen R. Routh. 2003. "Why the United States Fought in Vietnam." *Annual Review of Political Science* 6:181–204.

Beschloss, Michael R., ed. 1997. *Taking Charge: The Johnson White House Tapes, 1963–1964.* New York: Simon and Schuster.

Betts, Richard K. 1977. *Soldiers, Statesmen, and Cold War Crises.* Cambridge, Mass.: Harvard University Press.

Biddle, Stephen. 2008. "Review of the *U.S. Army/Marine Corps Counterinsurgency Field Manual.*" *Perspectives on Politics* 6 (2): 347–350.

Bill, James A. 1988. *The Eagle and the Lion: The Tragedy of American-Iranian Relations.* New Haven, Conn.: Yale University Press.

Billings-Yun, Melanie. 1988. *Decision against War: Eisenhower and Dien Bien Phu, 1954.* New York: Columbia University Press.

Blaufarb, Douglas S. 1977. *The Counterinsurgency Era: U.S. Doctrine and Performance, 1950 to the Present.* New York: Free Press.

Bose, Meena. 1998. *Shaping and Signaling Presidential Policy: The National Security Decision Making of Eisenhower and Kennedy.* College Station: Texas A&M University Press.

Bowie, Robert R., and Richard H. Immerman. 1998. *Waging Peace: How Eisenhower Shaped an Enduring Cold War Strategy.* New York: Oxford University Press.

Brands, H. W. 1987–1988. "Decisions on American Armed Intervention: Lebanon, Dominican Republic, and Grenada." *Political Science Quarterly* 102 (4): 607–624.

———. 1989. *The Specter of Neutralism: The United States and the Emergence of the Third World, 1947–1960.* New York: Columbia University Press.

———. 1995. *The Wages of Globalism: Lyndon Johnson and the Limits of American Power.* New York: Oxford University Press.

——. 1999a. Introduction to *The Foreign Policies of Lyndon Johnson: Beyond Vietnam*, edited by Brands. College Station: Texas A&M University Press.

——, ed. 1999b. *The Foreign Policies of Lyndon Johnson: Beyond Vietnam*. College Station: Texas A&M University Press.

Brecher, Michael, and Jonathan Wilkenfeld. International Crisis Behavior Project. http://www.cidcm.umd.edu/icb/.

Bueno de Mesquita, Bruce, and George W. Downs. 2006. "Intervention and Democracy." *International Organization* 60 (3): 627–649.

Bueno de Mesquita, Bruce, Alastair Smith, Randolph M. Siverson, and James D. Morrow. 2003. *The Logic of Political Survival*. Cambridge, Mass.: MIT Press.

Bull, Hedley. 1984. Introduction to *Intervention in World Politics*, edited by Bull. Oxford: Clarendon Press.

Bunce, Valerie. 1981. *Do New Leaders Make a Difference? Executive Succession and Public Policy under Capitalism and Socialism*. Princeton, N.J.: Princeton University Press.

Burke, John P., Fred I. Greenstein, Larry Berman, and Richard H. Immerman. 1989. *How Presidents Test Reality: Decisions on Vietnam, 1954 and 1965*. New York: Russell Sage Foundation.

Bush, George, and Brent Scowcroft. 1998. *A World Transformed*. New York: Vintage Books.

Butcher, Harry C. 1946. *My Three Years with Eisenhower*. New York: Simon and Schuster.

Byman, Daniel. 2008. "An Autopsy of the Iraq Debacle: Policy Failure or Bridge Too Far?" *Security Studies* 17 (4): 599–643.

Byman, Daniel L., and Kenneth M. Pollack. 2001. "Let Us Now Praise Great Men: Bringing the Statesman Back In." *International Security* 25 (4): 107–146.

Caro, Robert A. 2002. *Master of the Senate*. New York: Alfred A. Knopf.

Carter, James M. 2008. *Inventing Vietnam: The United States and State Building, 1954–1968*. New York: Cambridge University Press.

Catton, Philip E. 2002. *Diem's Final Failure: Prelude to America's War in Vietnam*. Lawrence: University Press of Kansas.

Caverley, Jonathan D. 2009/2010. "The Myth of Military Myopia: Democracy, Small Wars, and Vietnam." *International Security* 34 (3): 119–157.

Chandler, Alfred D., Jr., Louis Galambos, and Daun van Ee, eds. Various years. *The Papers of Dwight David Eisenhower*. Baltimore: Johns Hopkins University Press.

Chiozza, Giacomo, and Ajin Choi. 2003. "Guess Who Did What: Political Leaders and the Management of Territorial Disputes, 1950–1990." *Journal of Conflict Resolution* 47 (3): 251–278.

Chiozza, Giacomo, and H. E. Goemans. 2004. "International Conflict and the Tenure of Leaders: Is War Still *Ex Post* Inefficient?" *American Journal of Political Science* 48 (3): 604–619.

Chollet, Derek, and James Goldgeier. 2008. *America between the Wars: From 11/9 to 9/11*. New York: Public Affairs.

Clarke, Walter, and Jeffrey Herbst. 1996. "Somalia and the Future of Humanitarian Intervention." *Foreign Affairs* 75 (2): 70–85.

Clutterbuck, Richard L. 1966. *The Long, Long War: Counterinsurgency in Malaya and Vietnam*. New York: Praeger.

Cohen, Raymond. 1979. *Threat Perception in International Crisis*. Madison: University of Wisconsin Press.

Collier, David, and Robert Adcock. 1999. "Democracy and Dichotomies: A Pragmatic Approach to Choices about Concepts." *Annual Review of Political Science* 2:537–565.

Collin, Richard H. 1990. *Theodore Roosevelt's Caribbean: The Panama Canal, the Monroe Doctrine, and the Latin American Context*. Baton Rouge: Louisiana State University Press.

Combs, Jerald A. 1970. *The Jay Treaty: Political Battleground of the Founding Fathers*. Berkeley: University of California Press.

Cooper, John Milton, Jr. 1983. *The Warrior and the Priest: Woodrow Wilson and Theodore Roosevelt*. Cambridge, Mass.: Belknap Press of Harvard University Press.

Corera, Gordon. 2004. "Iraq Provides Lessons in Nation Building." *Jane's Intelligence Review* 16 (1): 30–33.

Cutler, Robert. 1965. *No Time for Rest*. Boston: Little, Brown.

Dallek, Robert. 1991. *Lone Star Rising: Lyndon Johnson and His Times, 1908–1960*. New York: Oxford University Press.

———. 1998. *Flawed Giant: Lyndon Johnson and His Times, 1961–1973*. New York: Oxford University Press.

———. 1999. "Lyndon Johnson as a World Leader." In *The Foreign Policies of Lyndon Johnson: Beyond Vietnam*, edited by H. W. Brands. College Station: Texas A&M University Press.

———. 2003. *An Unfinished Life: John F. Kennedy, 1917–1963*. Boston: Little, Brown.

Darden, Keith A. 2009. *Economic Liberalism and Its Rivals: The Formation of International Institutions among the Post-Soviet States*. New York: Cambridge University Press.

Divine, Robert A. 1981. *Eisenhower and the Cold War*. New York: Oxford University Press.

Dobbins, James, John G. McGinn, Keith Crane, Seth G. Jones, Rollie Lal, Andrew Rathmell, Rachel M. Swanger, and Anga R. Timilsina. 2003. *America's Role in Nation-Building: From Germany to Iraq*. Washington, D.C.: RAND.

Downes, Alexander B. 2009. "How Smart and Tough Are Democracies? Reassessing Theories of Democratic Victory in War." *International Security* 33 (4): 9–51.

Doyle, Michael W. 1986. "Liberalism and World Politics." *American Political Science Review* 80 (4): 1151–1169.

Doyle, Michael W., and Nicholas Sambanis. 2006. *Making War and Building Peace: United Nations Peace Operations*. Princeton, N.J.: Princeton University Press.

Draper, Theodore. 1968. *The Dominican Revolt: A Case Study in American Policy*. New York: Commentary.

Dueck, Colin. 2006. *Reluctant Crusaders: Power, Culture, and Change in American Grand Strategy*. Princeton, N.J.: Princeton University Press.

Duiker, William J. 1994. *U.S. Containment Policy and the Conflict in Indochina*. Stanford, Calif.: Stanford University Press.

Edelstein, David M. 2002. "Managing Uncertainty: Beliefs about Intentions and the Rise of Great Powers." *Security Studies* 12 (1): 1–40.

———. 2008. *Occupational Hazards: Success and Failure in Military Occupation*. Ithaca, N.Y.: Cornell University Press.

Eisenhower, Dwight D. 1965. *Waging Peace, 1956–1961: The White House Years*. Garden City, N.Y.: Doubleday.

Ekbladh, David. 2010. *The Great American Mission: Modernization and the Construction of an American World Order*. Princeton, N.J.: Princeton University Press.

Eveland, Wilbur Crane. 1980. *Ropes of Sand: America's Failure in the Middle East*. New York: W. W. Norton.

Farnham, Barbara. 2003. "The Theory of Democratic Peace and Threat Perception." *International Studies Quarterly* 47 (3): 395–415.

Fearon, James D. 1994. "Domestic Political Audiences and the Escalation of International Disputes." *American Political Science Review* 88 (3): 577–592.

Felten, Peter. 1999. "Yankee, Go Home and Take Me with You: Lyndon Johnson and the Dominican Republic." In *The Foreign Policies of Lyndon Johnson: Beyond Vietnam*, edited by H. W. Brands. College Station: Texas A&M University Press.

Fernea, Robert A., and William Roger Louis, eds. 1991. *The Iraqi Revolution of 1958: The Old Social Classes Revisited*. New York: I. B. Tauris.

Ferrell, Robert H., ed. 1981. *The Eisenhower Diaries*. New York: W. W. Norton.

Finnemore, Martha. 2003. *The Purpose of Intervention: Changing Beliefs about the Use of Force*. Ithaca, N.Y.: Cornell University Press.

Fitzgerald, Frances. 1972. *Fire in the Lake: The Vietnamese and the Americans in Vietnam*. New York: Vintage Books.

Flibbert, Andrew. 2006. "The Road to Baghdad: Ideas and Intellectuals in Explanations of the Iraq War." *Security Studies* 15 (2): 310–352.

Fordham, Benjamin O. 2004. "A Very Sharp Sword: The Influence of Military Capabilities on American Decisions to Use Force." *Journal of Conflict Resolution* 48 (5): 632–656.

———. 2008. "Power or Plenty? Economic Interests, Security Concerns, and American Intervention." *International Studies Quarterly* 52 (4): 737–758.

Fortna, Virginia Page. 2008. *Does Peacekeeping Work? Shaping Belligerents' Choices after Civil War*. Princeton, N.J.: Princeton University Press.

Freedman, Lawrence. 2000. *Kennedy's Wars: Berlin, Cuba, Laos, and Vietnam*. New York: Oxford University Press.

Friedberg, Aaron L. 2000. *In the Shadow of the Garrison State: America's Anti-Statism and Its Cold War Grand Strategy*. Princeton, N.J.: Princeton University Press.

———. 2005. "The Future of U.S.-China Relations: Is Conflict Inevitable?" *International Security* 30 (2): 7–45.

Funk, Arthur L. 1973. "Negotiating the 'Deal with Darlan.'" *Journal of Contemporary History* 8 (2): 81–117.

Gaddis, John Lewis. 2000. *The United States and the Origins of the Cold War, 1941–1947*. Rev. ed. New York: Columbia University Press.

———. 2005. *Strategies of Containment: A Critical Appraisal of American National Security Policy during the Cold War*. Rev. ed. New York: Oxford University Press.

Galbraith, John Kenneth. 1998. *Letters to Kennedy*. Edited by James Goodman. Cambridge, Mass.: Harvard University Press.

Gallucci, Robert L. 1975. *Neither Peace nor Honor: The Politics of American Military Policy in Viet-Nam*. Baltimore: Johns Hopkins University Press.

Galula, David. 2006. *Counterinsurgency Warfare: Theory and Practice*. Westport, Conn.: Praeger Security International.

Gardner, Lloyd C. 1995. *Pay Any Price: Lyndon Johnson and the Wars for Vietnam*. Chicago: Ivan R. Dee.

Gaskin, Thomas Mayhew. 1989. "Senator Lyndon B. Johnson and United States Foreign Policy." PhD diss., University of Washington.

Gelb, Leslie H., and Richard K. Betts. 1979. *The Irony of Vietnam: The System Worked*. Washington, D.C.: Brookings Institution.

Genco, Stephen J. 1974. "The Eisenhower Doctrine: Deterrence in the Middle East, 1957–1958." In *Deterrence in American Foreign Policy: Theory and Practice*, edited by Alexander L. George and Richard Smoke. New York: Columbia University Press.

Gendzier, Irene L. 1997. *Notes from the Minefield: United States Intervention in Lebanon and the Middle East, 1945–1958*. New York: Columbia University Press.

———. 2002. "Oil, Politics, and US Intervention." In *A Revolutionary Year: The Middle East in 1958*, edited by William Roger Louis and Roger Owen. Washington, D.C.: Woodrow Wilson Center Press.

Gent, Stephen E. 2007. "Strange Bedfellows: The Strategic Dynamics of Major Power Military Interventions." *Journal of Politics* 69 (4): 1089–1102.

George, Alexander L. 1969. "The 'Operational Code': A Neglected Approach to the Study of Political Leaders and Decision-Making." *International Studies Quarterly* 13 (2): 190–222.

———. 1972. "Rejoinder to 'Comment' by I. M. Destler" (correspondence related to "The Case for Multiple Advocacy in Making Foreign Policy"). *American Political Science Review* 66 (3): 791–795.

———. 1979. "The Causal Nexus between Cognitive Beliefs and Decision-Making Behavior: The 'Operational Code' Belief System." In *Psychological Models in International Politics*, edited by Lawrence S. Falkowski. Boulder, Colo.: Westview Press.

George, Alexander L., and Andrew Bennett. 2005. *Case Studies and Theory Development in the Social Sciences*. Cambridge, Mass.: MIT Press.

Gerges, Fawaz A. 1994. *The Superpowers and the Middle East: Regional and International Politics, 1955–1967*. Boulder, Colo.: Westview Press.

Geyelin, Philip. 1966. *Lyndon B. Johnson and the World*. New York: Praeger.

Girard, Philippe R. 2004. *Clinton in Haiti: The 1994 U.S. Invasion of Haiti*. New York: Palgrave Macmillan.

Gleijeses, Piero. 1978. *The Dominican Crisis: The 1965 Constitutionalist Revolt and American Intervention*. Translated by Lawrence Lipson. Baltimore: Johns Hopkins University Press.

———. 1991. *Shattered Hope: The Guatemalan Revolution and the United States, 1944–1954*. Princeton, N.J.: Princeton University Press.

Goemans, Henk E., Kristian Skrede Gleditsch, and Giacomo Chiozza. 2009. "Introducing Archigos: A Dataset of Political Leaders." *Journal of Peace Research* 46 (2): 269–283.

Goldgeier, James M. 1994. *Leadership Style and Soviet Foreign Policy: Stalin, Khrushchev, Brezhnev, Gorbachev*. Baltimore: Johns Hopkins University Press.

Goldgeier, James M., and Philip E. Tetlock. 2001. "Psychology and International Relations Theory." *Annual Review of Political Science* 4:67–92.

Goldman, Eric F. 1969. *The Tragedy of Lyndon Johnson*. New York: Alfred A. Knopf.

Goldstein, Gordon M. 2008. *Lessons in Disaster: McGeorge Bundy and the Path to War in Vietnam*. New York: Henry Holt.

Goldstein, Judith, and Robert O. Keohane. 1993. "Ideas and Foreign Policy: An Analytical Framework." In *Ideas and Foreign Policy: Beliefs, Institutions, and Political Change*, edited by Goldstein and Keohane. Ithaca, N.Y.: Cornell University Press.

Goodwin, Doris Kearns. 1991. *Lyndon Johnson and the American Dream*. New York: St. Martin's Griffin.

Gordon, Michael R., and Bernard E. Trainor. 2006. *Cobra II: The Inside Story of the Invasion and Occupation of Iraq*. New York: Pantheon Books.

Gravel, Mike, ed. 1971. *The Pentagon Papers: The Defense Department History of United States Decisionmaking on Vietnam*, vols. 1, 2, and 3. Boston: Beacon Press.

Greenstein, Fred I. 1982. *The Hidden-Hand Presidency: Eisenhower as Leader*. New York: Basic Books.

———. 2004. *The Presidential Difference: Leadership Style from FDR to George W. Bush*. 2nd ed. Princeton, N.J.: Princeton University Press.

Greenstein, Fred I., and Richard H. Immerman. 1992. "What Did Eisenhower Tell Kennedy about Indochina? The Politics of Misperception." *Journal of American History* 79 (2): 568–587.

Guisinger, Alexandra, and Alastair Smith. 2002. "Honest Threats: The Interaction of Reputation and Political Institutions in International Crises." *Journal of Conflict Resolution* 46 (2): 175–200.

Haas, Mark L. 2005. *The Ideological Origins of Great Power Politics, 1789–1989*. Ithaca, N.Y.: Cornell University Press.

Haass, Richard N. 2009. *War of Necessity, War of Choice: A Memoir of Two Iraq Wars*. New York: Simon and Schuster.

Halberstam, David. 1965. *The Making of a Quagmire*. New York: Random House.

———. 1972. *The Best and the Brightest*. New York: Random House.

———. 2001. *War in a Time of Peace: Bush, Clinton, and the Generals*. New York: Scribner.

Hermann, Margaret G., and Charles W. Kegley. 1995. "Rethinking Democracy and International Peace: Perspectives from Political Psychology." *International Studies Quarterly* 39 (4): 511–533.

Herring, George C. 1994. *LBJ and Vietnam: A Different Kind of War*. Austin: University of Texas Press.

———. 1996. *America's Longest War: The United States and Vietnam, 1950–1975*. 3rd ed. New York: McGraw-Hill.

———. 1997. "Lyndon Johnson's War?" *Diplomatic History* 21 (4): 645–650.

Hilsman, Roger. 1967. *To Move a Nation: The Politics of Foreign Policy in the Administration of John F. Kennedy*. New York: Doubleday.

Hirsch, John L., and Robert B. Oakley. 1995. *Somalia and Operation Restore Hope: Reflections on Peacemaking and Peacekeeping*. Washington, D.C.: United States Institute of Peace Press.

Hoffmann, Stanley. 1984. "The Problem of Intervention." In *Intervention in World Politics*, edited by Hedley Bull. Oxford: Clarendon Press.

Holland, Matthew F. 2001. *Eisenhower between the Wars: The Making of a General and Statesman*. Westport, Conn.: Praeger.

Holsti, Ole R. 1962. "The Belief System and National Images: A Case Study." *Journal of Conflict Resolution* 6 (3): 244–252.

Holsti, Ole R., and James N. Rosenau. 1988. "The Domestic and Foreign Policy Beliefs of American Leaders." *Journal of Conflict Resolution* 32 (2): 248–294.

Holt, Daniel D., and James W. Leyerzapf, eds. 1998. *Eisenhower: The Prewar Diaries and Selected Papers, 1905–1941*. Baltimore: Johns Hopkins University Press.

Horowitz, Michael, Rose McDermott, and Allan C. Stam. 2005. "Leader Age, Regime Type, and Violent International Relations." *Journal of Conflict Resolution* 49 (5): 661–685.

Howell, William G. 2003. *Power without Persuasion: The Politics of Direct Presidential Action*. Princeton, N.J.: Princeton University Press.

Howell, William G., and Jon C. Pevehouse. 2007. *While Dangers Gather: Congressional Checks on Presidential War Powers*. Princeton, N.J.: Princeton University Press.

Hunt, Michael H. 2009. *Ideology and U.S. Foreign Policy*. New Haven, Conn.: Yale University Press.

Hunt, Richard A. 1995. *Pacification: The American Struggle for Vietnam's Hearts and Minds*. Boulder, Colo.: Westview.

Huth, Paul K. 1998. "Major Power Intervention in International Crises, 1918–1988." *Journal of Conflict Resolution* 42 (6): 744–770.

Immerman, Richard H. 1979. "Eisenhower and Dulles: Who Made the Decisions?" *Political Psychology* 1 (2): 21–38.

———. 1982. *The CIA in Guatemala: The Foreign Policy of Intervention*. Austin: University of Texas Press.

———. 1990. "Confessions of an Eisenhower Revisionist: An Agonizing Reappraisal." *Diplomatic History* 14 (3): 319–342.

Jentleson, Bruce W. 1992. "The Pretty Prudent Public: Post Post-Vietnam American Opinion on the Use of Military Force." *International Studies Quarterly* 36 (1): 49–73.

Jentleson, Bruce W., and Ariel E. Levite. 1992. "The Analysis of Protracted Foreign Military Intervention." In *Foreign Military Intervention: The Dynamics of Protracted Conflict*, edited by Ariel E. Levite, Bruce W. Jentleson, and Larry Berman. New York: Columbia University Press.

Jervis, Robert. 1976. *Perception and Misperception in International Politics*. Princeton, N.J.: Princeton University Press.

———. 2003. "Understanding the Bush Doctrine." *Political Science Quarterly* 118 (3): 365–388.

———. 2008/2009. "War, Intelligence, and Honesty: A Review Essay." *Political Science Quarterly* 123 (4): 645–675.

Johnston, Alastair Iain. 1995. *Cultural Realism: Strategic Culture and Grand Strategy in Chinese History*. Princeton, N.J.: Princeton University Press.

Jones, Benjamin F., and Benjamin A. Olken. 2005. "Do Leaders Matter? National Leadership and Growth since World War II." *Quarterly Journal of Economics* 120 (3): 835–864.

Jorden, William J. 1984. *Panama Odyssey*. Austin: University of Texas Press.

Kagan, Robert. 2006. *Dangerous Nation: America's Foreign Policy from Its Earliest Days to the Dawn of the Twentieth Century*. New York: Vintage Books.

Kahin, Audrey R., and George McT. Kahin. 1995. *Subversion as Foreign Policy: The Secret Eisenhower and Dulles Debacle in Indonesia*. New York: New Press.

Kaiser, David E. 2000. *American Tragedy: Kennedy, Johnson, and the Origins of the Vietnam War*. Cambridge, Mass.: Belknap Press of Harvard University Press.

Kalyvas, Stathis N. 2008. "Review of the *U.S. Army/Marine Corps Counterinsurgency Field Manual*." *Perspectives on Politics* 6 (2): 351–353.

Karnow, Stanley. 1983. *Vietnam: A History*. New York: Viking Press.

Kaufman, Burton I. 1982. *Trade and Aid: Eisenhower's Foreign Economic Policy, 1953–1961*. Baltimore: Johns Hopkins University Press.

———. 1987. "Foreign Aid and the Balance-of-Payments Problem: Vietnam and Johnson's Foreign Economic Policy." In *The Johnson Years, vol. 2: Vietnam, the Environment, and Science*, edited by Robert A. Divine. Lawrence: University Press of Kansas.

Kegley, Charles W., and Margaret G. Hermann. 1996. "How Democracies Use Intervention: A Neglected Dimension in Studies of the Democratic Peace." *Journal of Peace Research* 33 (3): 309–322.

Kennedy, John F. 1957. "A Democrat Looks at Foreign Policy." *Foreign Affairs* 36 (1): 44–59.

———. 1964. *A Compilation of Statements and Speeches Made during His Service in the United States Senate and House of Representatives*. Washington, D.C.: U.S. Government Printing Office.

Kerr, Malcolm. 1972. "The Lebanese Civil War." In *The International Regulation of Civil Wars*, edited by Evan Luard. New York: New York University Press.

Khong, Yuen Foong. 1992. *Analogies at War: Korea, Munich, Dien Bien Phu, and the Vietnam Decisions of 1965*. Princeton, N.J.: Princeton University Press.

Kier, Elizabeth. 1997. *Imagining War: French and British Military Doctrine between the Wars*. Princeton, N.J.: Princeton University Press.

Kingdon, John W. 1984. *Agendas, Alternatives, and Public Policies*. Boston: Little, Brown.

Kinzer, Stephen. 2006. *Overthrow: America's Century of Regime Change from Hawaii to Iraq*. New York: Times Books.

Kissinger, Henry A. 1964. *A World Restored*. New York: Grosset and Dunlap.

———. 1979. *White House Years*. Boston: Little, Brown.

———. 1994. *Diplomacy*. New York: Simon and Schuster.

Knorr, Klaus. 1976. "Threat Perception." In *Historical Dimensions of National Security Problems*, edited by Knorr. Lawrence: University Press of Kansas.

Krasner, Stephen D. 1972. "Are Bureaucracies Important? (or Allison Wonderland)." *Foreign Policy* 7:159–179.

———. 1978. *Defending the National Interest: Raw Materials Investments and U.S. Foreign Policy*. Princeton, N.J.: Princeton University Press.

———. 1993. "Westphalia and All That." In *Ideas and Foreign Policy: Beliefs, Institutions, and Political Change*, edited by Judith Goldstein and Robert O. Keohane. Ithaca, N.Y.: Cornell University Press.

———. 1999. *Sovereignty: Organized Hypocrisy*. Princeton, N.J.: Princeton University Press.

Krepinevich, Andrew F., Jr. 1986. *The Army and Vietnam*. Baltimore: Johns Hopkins University Press.

Kreps, Sarah E. 2007. "The 1994 Haiti Intervention: A Unilateral Operation in Multilateral Clothes." *Journal of Strategic Studies* 30 (3): 449–474.

———. 2008. "When Does the Mission Determine the Coalition? The Logic of Multilateral Intervention and the Case of Afghanistan." *Security Studies* 17 (3): 531–567.

———. Forthcoming. *Coalitions of Convenience: United States Military Interventions after the Cold War*. Oxford University Press.

Kunz, Diane B. 1991. *The Economic Diplomacy of the Suez Crisis*. Chapel Hill: University of North Carolina Press.

Kyle, Keith. 1991. *Suez*. New York: St. Martin's Press.

LaFeber, Walter. 1981. "Latin American Policy." In *Exploring the Johnson Years*, edited by Robert A. Divine. Austin: University of Texas Press.

Langley, Lester D. 2002. *The Banana Wars: United States Intervention in the Caribbean, 1898–1934*. 2nd ed. Wilmington, Del.: SR Books.

Larson, Deborah Welch. 1985. *Origins of Containment: A Psychological Explanation*. Princeton, N.J.: Princeton University Press.

Latham, Michael E. 2000. *Modernization as Ideology: American Social Science and "Nation Building" in the Kennedy Era*. Chapel Hill: University of North Carolina Press.

———. 2002. "Imperial Legacy and Cold War Credibility: Lyndon Johnson and the Panama Crisis." *Peace and Change* 27 (4): 499–527.

Lawrence, Mark Atwood. 2005. "Exception to the Rule? The Johnson Administration and the Panama Canal." In *Looking Back at LBJ: White House Politics in a New Light*, edited by Mitchell B. Lerner. Lawrence: University Press of Kansas.

Lebovic, James H. 2010. *The Limits of U.S. Military Capability: Lessons from Vietnam and Iraq*. Baltimore: Johns Hopkins University Press.

Legro, Jeffrey W. 1995. *Cooperation under Fire: Anglo-German Restraint during World War II*. Ithaca, N.Y.: Cornell University Press.

Lehman, Kenneth. 1997. "Revolutions and Attributions: Making Sense of Eisenhower Administration Policies in Bolivia and Guatemala." *Diplomatic History* 21 (2): 185–213.

Levinson, Jerome, and Juan de Onís. 1970. *The Alliance That Lost Its Way: A Critical Report on the Alliance for Progress*. Chicago: Quadrangle Books.

Levy, Jack S. 1994. "Learning and Foreign Policy: Sweeping a Conceptual Minefield." *International Organization* 48 (2): 279–312.

Lewy, Guenter. 1978. *America in Vietnam*. New York: Oxford University Press.

Link, Arthur S. 1947. *Wilson: The Road to the White House*. Princeton, N.J.: Princeton University Press.

———. 1956. *Wilson: The New Freedom*. Princeton, N.J.: Princeton University Press.

———, ed. 1983. *The Papers of Woodrow Wilson*, vol. 41. Princeton, N.J.: Princeton University Press.

Little, Douglas. 1996. "His Finest Hour? Eisenhower, Lebanon, and the 1958 Middle East Crisis." *Diplomatic History* 20 (1): 27–54.

———. 2002. *American Orientalism: The United States and the Middle East since 1945*. Chapel Hill: University of North Carolina Press.

———. 2004. "Mission Impossible: The CIA and the Cult of Covert Action in the Middle East." *Diplomatic History* 28 (5): 663–701.

Litwak, Robert S. 2007. *Regime Change: U.S. Strategy through the Prism of 9/11*. Washington, D.C.: Woodrow Wilson Center Press.

Logevall, Fredrik. 1999. *Choosing War: The Lost Chance for Peace and the Escalation of War in Vietnam*. Berkeley: University of California Press.

Lowenthal, Abraham F. 1995. *The Dominican Intervention*. Johns Hopkins Paperbacks ed. Baltimore: Johns Hopkins University Press.

Lyall, Jason, and Isaiah Wilson III. 2009. "Rage against the Machines: Explaining Outcomes in Counterinsurgency Wars." *International Organization* 63 (1): 67–106.

Lyon, Peter. 1974. *Eisenhower: Portrait of the Hero*. Boston: Little, Brown.

Lyons, Terrence, and Ahmed I. Samatar. 1995. *Somalia: State Collapse, Multilateral Intervention, and Strategies for Political Reconstruction*. Washington, D.C.: Brookings Institution.

Macdonald, Douglas J. 1992. *Adventures in Chaos: American Intervention for Reform in the Third World*. Cambridge, Mass.: Harvard University Press.

Mahoney, James, and Gary Goertz. 2004. "The Possibility Principle: Choosing Negative Cases in Comparative Research." *American Political Science Review* 98 (4): 653–669.

Mann, James. 2004. *Rise of the Vulcans: The History of Bush's War Cabinet*. New York: Penguin Books.

Marquis, Jefferson P. 2000. "The Other Warriors: American Social Science and Nation Building in Vietnam." *Diplomatic History* 24 (1): 79–105.

Marten, Kimberly Zisk. 2004. *Enforcing the Peace: Learning from the Imperial Past*. New York: Columbia University Press.

McKee, Guian A., ed. 2007. *The Presidential Recordings: Lyndon B. Johnson*, vol. 6. Series edited by Ernest May and Timothy Naftali. New York: W. W. Norton.

McMahon, Robert J. 1986. "Eisenhower and Third World Nationalism: A Critique of the Revisionists." *Political Science Quarterly* 101 (3): 453–473.

McNamara, Kathleen R. 1998. *The Currency of Ideas: Monetary Politics in the European Union*. Ithaca, N.Y.: Cornell University Press.

McPherson, Alan. 2003. "Misled by Himself: What the Johnson Tapes Reveal about the Dominican Intervention of 1965." *Latin American Research Review* 38 (2): 127–146.

Mead, Walter Russell. 2001. *Special Providence: American Foreign Policy and How It Changed the World*. New York: Alfred A. Knopf.

Meernik, James. 1994. "Presidential Decision Making and the Political Use of Military Force." *International Studies Quarterly* 38 (1): 121–138.

Military History Institute of Vietnam. 2002. *Victory in Vietnam: The Official History of the People's Army of Vietnam, 1954–1975*. Translated by Merle Pribbenow. Lawrence: University Press of Kansas.

Miller, Benjamin. 1998. "The Logic of U.S. Military Interventions in the Post–Cold War Era." *Contemporary Security Policy* 19 (3): 72–109.

Miller, Edward. 2004. "Vision, Power and Agency: The Ascent of Ngo Dinh Diem, 1945–54." *Journal of Southeast Asian Studies* 35 (3): 433–458.

Moe, Terry M. 1995. "The Politics of Structural Choice: Toward a Theory of Public Bureaucracy." In *Organization Theory: From Chester Barnard to the Present and Beyond*, edited by Oliver E. Williamson. Expanded ed. New York: Oxford University Press.

Moravcsik, Andrew. 1997. "Taking Preferences Seriously: A Liberal Theory of International Politics." *International Organization* 51 (4): 513–553.

Morgenthau, Hans J. 1967. "To Intervene or Not to Intervene." *Foreign Affairs* 45 (3): 425–436.

Mueller, John E. 1973. *War, Presidents, and Public Opinion*. New York: John Wiley and Sons.

Mulder, John M. 1978. *Woodrow Wilson: The Years of Preparation*. Princeton, N.J.: Princeton University Press.

Murray, Shoon Kathleen. 1996. *Anchors against Change: American Opinion Leaders' Beliefs after the Cold War*. Ann Arbor: University of Michigan Press.

Myerson, Roger B. 2009. "A Field Manual for the Cradle of Civilization: Theory of Leadership and Lessons of Iraq." *Journal of Conflict Resolution* 53 (3): 470–482.

Naftali, Timothy, ed. 2001. *The Presidential Recordings: John F. Kennedy, the Great Crises*, vol. 1. Series edited by Philip Zelikow, Ernest May, and Timothy Naftali. New York: W. W. Norton.

Nagl, John A. 2005. *Learning to Eat Soup with a Knife: Counterinsurgency Lessons from Malaya and Vietnam*. Chicago: University of Chicago Press.

Nau, Henry R. 2008. "Conservative Internationalism." *Policy Review* 150:3–44.

Newman, John M. 1992. *JFK and Vietnam: Deception, Intrigue, and the Struggle for Power.* New York: Warner Books.

Ninkovich, Frank. 1986. "Theodore Roosevelt: Civilization as Ideology." *Diplomatic History* 10 (3): 221–245.

———. 1994. *Modernity and Power: A History of the Domino Theory in the Twentieth Century.* Chicago: University of Chicago Press.

Obama, Barack. 2004. *Dreams from My Father: A Story of Race and Inheritance.* Rev. ed. New York: Three Rivers Press.

———. 2006. *The Audacity of Hope: Thoughts on Reclaiming the American Dream.* New York: Crown Publishers.

O'Hanlon, Michael E. 2004/2005. "Iraq without a Plan." *Policy Review* 128:33–45.

Osgood, Kenneth A. 2006. *Total Cold War: Eisenhower's Secret Propaganda Battle at Home and Abroad.* Lawrence: University Press of Kansas.

Owen, John M., IV. 1997. *Liberal Peace, Liberal War: American Politics and International Security.* Ithaca, N.Y.: Cornell University Press.

———. 2002. "The Foreign Imposition of Domestic Institutions." *International Organization* 56 (2): 375–409.

Owen, Roger. 2002. "The Dog That Neither Barked nor Bit: The Fear of Oil Shortages." In *A Revolutionary Year: The Middle East in 1958*, edited by William Roger Louis and Roger Owen. Washington, D.C.: Woodrow Wilson Center Press.

Packenham, Robert A. 1973. *Liberal America and the Third World: Political Development Ideas in Foreign Aid and Social Science.* Princeton, N.J.: Princeton University Press.

Packer, George. 2005. *The Assassins' Gate: America in Iraq.* New York: Farrar, Straus and Giroux.

Paris, Roland. 2004. *At War's End: Building Peace after Civil Conflict.* New York: Cambridge University Press.

Pearson, Frederic S., Robert A. Baumann, and Jeffrey J. Pickering. 1994. "Military Intervention and Realpolitik." In *Reconstructing Realpolitik*, edited by Frank W. Wayman and Paul F. Diehl. Ann Arbor: University of Michigan Press.

Peceny, Mark. 1995. "Two Paths to the Promotion of Democracy during U.S. Military Interventions." *International Studies Quarterly* 39 (3): 371–401.

Perret, Geoffrey. 1999. *Eisenhower.* New York: Random House.

Pickering, Jeffrey, and Mark Peceny. 2006. "Forging Democracy at Gunpoint." *International Studies Quarterly* 50 (3): 539–559.

Porter, Gareth. 2005. *Perils of Dominance: Imbalance of Power and the Road to War in Vietnam.* Berkeley: University of California Press.

Posen, Barry R. 1984. *The Sources of Military Doctrine: France, Britain, and Germany between the World Wars.* Ithaca, N.Y.: Cornell University Press.

Post, Jerrold M. 2004. *Leaders and Their Followers in a Dangerous World: The Psychology of Political Behavior.* Ithaca, N.Y.: Cornell University Press.

Prados, John. 1995. *The Hidden History of the Vietnam War.* Chicago: Ivan R. Dee.

———. 2007. "Assessing Dien Bien Phu." In *The First Vietnam War: Colonial Conflict and Cold War Crisis*, edited by Mark Atwood Lawrence and Fredrik Logevall. Cambridge, Mass.: Harvard University Press.

———, ed. 2009. "Kennedy Considered Supporting Coup in South Vietnam, August 1963." National Security Archive Electronic Briefing Book No. 302. http://www.gwu.edu/~nsarchiv/NSAEBB/NSAEBB302/index.htm.

Preston, Andrew. 2006. *The War Council: McGeorge Bundy, the NSC, and Vietnam.* Cambridge, Mass.: Harvard University Press.

Public Papers of the Presidents of the United States. Various years. Washington, D.C.: U.S. Government Printing Office.

Quinlivan, James T. 1995/1996. "Force Requirements in Stability Operations." *Parameters* 25 (4): 59–69.

Rabe, Stephen G. 1988. *Eisenhower and Latin America: The Foreign Policy of Anticommunism.* Chapel Hill: University of North Carolina Press.

———. 1993. "Eisenhower Revisionism: A Decade of Scholarship." *Diplomatic History* 17 (1): 97–115.

———. 1999. *The Most Dangerous Area in the World: John F. Kennedy Confronts Communist Revolution in Latin America.* Chapel Hill: University of North Carolina Press.

———. 2005. *U.S. Intervention in British Guiana: A Cold War Story.* Chapel Hill: University of North Carolina Press.

———. 2006. "The Johnson Doctrine." *Presidential Studies Quarterly* 36 (1): 48–58.

Rathbun, Brian C. 2004. *Partisan Interventions: European Party Politics and Peace Enforcement in the Balkans.* Ithaca, N.Y.: Cornell University Press.

Rathmell, Andrew. 2005. "Planning Post-conflict Reconstruction in Iraq: What Can We Learn?" *International Affairs* 81 (5): 1013–1038.

Reeves, Richard. 1993. *President Kennedy: Profile of Power.* New York: Simon and Schuster.

Regan, Patrick M. 1998. "Choosing to Intervene: Outside Interventions in Internal Conflicts." *Journal of Politics* 60 (3): 754–779.

———. 2000a. *Civil Wars and Foreign Powers: Outside Intervention in Intrastate Conflict.* Ann Arbor: University of Michigan Press.

———. 2000b. "Substituting Policies during U.S. Interventions in Internal Conflicts: A Little of This, a Little of That." *Journal of Conflict Resolution* 44 (1): 90–106.

Reiter, Dan, and Curtis Meek. 1999. "Determinants of Military Strategy, 1903–1994: A Quantitative Empirical Test." *International Studies Quarterly* 43 (2): 363–387.

Renshon, Jonathan. 2008. "Stability and Change in Belief Systems: The Operational Code of George W. Bush." *Journal of Conflict Resolution* 52 (6): 820–849.

Rice, Condoleezza. 2000. "Promoting the National Interest." *Foreign Affairs* 79 (1): 45–62.

Ricks, Thomas E. 2006. *Fiasco: The American Military Adventure in Iraq.* New York: Penguin Press.

Rock, Stephen R. 1989. *Why Peace Breaks Out: Great Power Rapprochement in Historical Perspective.* Chapel Hill: University of North Carolina Press.

Rosen, Stephen Peter. 1991. *Winning the Next War: Innovation and the Modern Military.* Ithaca, N.Y.: Cornell University Press.

———. 2005. *War and Human Nature.* Princeton, N.J.: Princeton University Press.

Rosenau, James N. 1969. "Intervention as a Scientific Concept." *Journal of Conflict Resolution* 13 (2): 149–171.

Rossiter, Clinton, ed. 1961. *The Federalist Papers.* New York: Penguin Books.

Rostow, Walt W. 2003. *Concept and Controversy: Sixty Years of Taking Ideas to Market.* Austin: University of Texas Press.

Rousseau, David L. 2006. *Identifying Threats and Threatening Identities: The Social Construction of Realism and Liberalism.* Stanford, Calif.: Stanford University Press.

Ruggie, John Gerard. 1998. *Constructing the World Polity: Essays on International Institutionalization.* London: Routledge.

Russett, Bruce. 1990. *Controlling the Sword: The Democratic Governance of National Security.* Cambridge, Mass.: Harvard University Press.

———. 2005. "Bushwhacking the Democratic Peace." *International Studies Perspectives* 6 (4): 395–408.

Russett, Bruce, and John R. Oneal. 2001. *Triangulating Peace: Democracy, Interdependence, and International Organizations.* New York: W. W. Norton.

Samuels, Richard J. 2003. *Machiavelli's Children: Leaders and Their Legacies in Italy and Japan.* Ithaca, N.Y.: Cornell University Press.

Scheman, L. Ronald, ed. 1988. *The Alliance for Progress: A Retrospective.* New York: Praeger.

Schlesinger, Arthur M., Jr. 1965. *A Thousand Days: John F. Kennedy in the White House.* New York: Fawcett Premier.

Schlesinger, Stephen, and Stephen Kinzer. 2005. *Bitter Fruit: The Story of the American Coup in Guatemala.* Rev. ed. Cambridge, Mass.: David Rockefeller Center for Latin American Studies, Harvard University.

Schmitz, David F. 1999. *Thank God They're on Our Side: The United States and Right-Wing Dictatorships, 1921–1965.* Chapel Hill: University of North Carolina Press.

Schoultz, Lars. 1998. *Beneath the United States: A History of U.S. Policy toward Latin America.* Cambridge, Mass.: Harvard University Press.

Schwartz, Thomas Alan. 2003. *Lyndon Johnson and Europe: In the Shadow of Vietnam.* Cambridge, Mass.: Harvard University Press.

Scott, James C. 1998. *Seeing Like a State: How Certain Schemes to Improve the Human Condition Have Failed.* New Haven, Conn.: Yale University Press.

Scott, James M. 1996. *Deciding to Intervene: The Reagan Doctrine and American Foreign Policy.* Durham, N.C.: Duke University Press.

Sechser, Todd S. 2004. "Are Soldiers Less War-Prone Than Statesmen?" *Journal of Conflict Resolution* 48 (5): 746–774.

Selverstone, Marc J. 2009. *Constructing the Monolith: The United States, Great Britain, and International Communism, 1945–1950.* Cambridge, Mass.: Harvard University Press.

Serafino, Nina M., and Martin A. Weiss. 2006. *Peacekeeping and Conflict Transitions: Background and Congressional Action on Civilian Capabilities.* Washington, D.C.: Congressional Research Service.

Shafer, D. Michael. 1988. *Deadly Paradigms: The Failure of U.S. Counterinsurgency Policy.* Princeton, N.J.: Princeton University Press.

Slater, Jerome. 1970. *Intervention and Negotiation: The United States and the Dominican Revolution.* New York: Harper and Row.

Smith, Alastair. 1996. "To Intervene or Not to Intervene: A Biased Decision." *Journal of Conflict Resolution* 40 (1): 16–40.

——. 1998. "International Crises and Domestic Politics." *American Political Science Review* 92 (3): 623–638.

Smith, Tony. 1994. *America's Mission: The United States and the Worldwide Struggle for Democracy in the Twentieth Century.* Princeton, N.J.: Princeton University Press.

Snyder, Jack. 1991. *Myths of Empire: Domestic Politics and International Ambition.* Ithaca, N.Y.: Cornell University Press.

Sorensen, Theodore C. 1965. *Kennedy.* New York: Harper and Row.

Spector, Ronald H. 1983. *Advice and Support: The Early Years, 1941–1960.* Washington, D.C.: Center of Military History, United States Army.

Sullivan, Patricia L. 2007. "War Aims and War Outcomes: Why Powerful States Lose Limited Wars." *Journal of Conflict Resolution* 51 (3): 496–524.

Sullivan, Patricia L., and Michael T. Koch. 2009. "Military Intervention by Powerful States, 1945–2003." *Journal of Peace Research* 46 (5): 707–718.

Summers, Harry G., Jr. 1982. *On Strategy: A Critical Analysis of the Vietnam War.* New York: Dell.

Taliaferro, Jeffrey W. 2004. *Balancing Risks: Great Power Intervention in the Periphery.* Ithaca, N.Y.: Cornell University Press.

Tetlock, Philip E. 1998. "Social Psychology and World Politics." In *Handbook of Social Psychology,* 4th ed., edited by Daniel T. Gilbert, Susan T. Fiske, and Gardner Lindzey. New York: McGraw-Hill.

——. 1999. "Theory-Driven Reasoning about Plausible Pasts and Probable Futures in World Politics: Are We Prisoners of Our Preconceptions?" *American Journal of Political Science* 43 (2): 335–366.

Thompson, Robert. 1966. *Defeating Communist Insurgency: The Lessons of Malaya and Vietnam.* New York: Praeger.

Tillema, Herbert K. 1973. *Appeal to Force: American Military Intervention in the Era of Containment.* New York: Crowell.

——. 1989. "Foreign Overt Military Intervention in the Nuclear Age." *Journal of Peace Research* 26 (2): 179–196.

Tulchin, Joseph S. 1994. "The Promise of Progress: U.S. Relations with Latin America during the Administration of Lyndon B. Johnson." In *Lyndon Johnson Confronts the World: American Foreign Policy, 1963–1968,* edited by Warren I. Cohen and Nancy Bernkopf Tucker. New York: Cambridge University Press.

U.S. Army/Marine Corps Counterinsurgency Field Manual. 2007. Chicago: University of Chicago Press.

U.S. Department of State. Various years. *Foreign Relations of the United States.* Washington, D.C.: U.S. Government Printing Office.

Vertzberger, Yaacov Y. I. 1990. *The World in Their Minds: Information Processing, Cognition, and Perception in Foreign Policy Decisionmaking.* Stanford, Calif.: Stanford University Press.

———. 1998. *Risk Taking and Decisionmaking: Foreign Military Intervention Decisions.* Stanford, Calif.: Stanford University Press.

Von Hippel, Karin. 2000. *Democracy by Force: U.S. Military Intervention in the Post–Cold War World.* Cambridge: Cambridge University Press.

Walt, Stephen M. 1987. *The Origins of Alliances.* Ithaca, N.Y.: Cornell University Press.

———. 1996. *Revolution and War.* Ithaca, N.Y.: Cornell University Press.

Walter, Barbara F. 2002. *Committing to Peace: The Successful Settlement of Civil Wars.* Princeton, N.J.: Princeton University Press.

Waltz, Kenneth N. 1959. *Man, the State, and War: A Theoretical Analysis.* New York: Columbia University Press.

———. 1979. *Theory of International Politics.* Reading, Mass.: Addison-Wesley.

Watts, Stephen. 2007. "Constructing Order amid Violence: Comparative Military Interventions in the Era of Peacekeeping and Counter-Terrorism." PhD diss., Cornell University.

Weeks, Jessica L. 2008. "Autocratic Audience Costs: Regime Type and Signaling Resolve." *International Organization* 62 (1): 35–64.

Werner, Suzanne. 1996. "Absolute and Limited War: The Possibility of Foreign-Imposed Regime Change." *International Interactions* 22 (1): 67–88.

Westad, Odd Arne. 2005. *The Global Cold War: Third World Interventions and the Making of Our Times.* New York: Cambridge University Press.

Western, Jon. 2005. *Selling Intervention and War: The Presidency, the Media, and the American Public.* Baltimore: Johns Hopkins University Press.

Wiarda, Howard J. 1988. "Did the Alliance 'Lose Its Way,' or Were Its Assumptions All Wrong from the Beginning and Are Those Assumptions Still with Us?" In *The Alliance for Progress: A Retrospective*, edited by L. Ronald Scheman. New York: Praeger.

Wicker, Tom. 1968. *JFK and LBJ: The Influence of Personality upon Politics.* Baltimore: Pelican Books.

Woods, Randall B. 2006. *LBJ: Architect of American Ambition.* New York: Free Press.

Woodward, Bob. 2004. *Plan of Attack.* New York: Simon and Schuster.

Woolley, John T., and Gerhard Peters. The American Presidency Project. http://www.presidency.ucsb.edu.

Wright, Donald P., and Timothy R. Reese. 2008. *On Point II: Transition to the New Campaign; The United States Army in Operation Iraqi Freedom, May 2003–January 2005.* Fort Leavenworth, Kan.: Combat Studies Institute Press.

Yaqub, Salim. 2004. *Containing Arab Nationalism: The Eisenhower Doctrine and the Middle East.* Chapel Hill: University of North Carolina Press.

Yarhi-Milo, Keren. 2009. "Knowing Thy Adversary: Assessments of Intentions in International Relations." PhD diss., University of Pennsylvania.

Yates, Lawrence A. 1988. *Power Pack: U.S. Intervention in the Dominican Republic, 1965–1966*. Fort Leavenworth, Kan.: Combat Studies Institute, U.S. Army Command and General Staff College.

Zakaria, Fareed. 1998. *From Wealth to Power: The Unusual Origins of America's World Role*. Princeton, N.J.: Princeton University Press.

Zaller, John R. 1992. *The Nature and Origins of Mass Opinion*. New York: Cambridge University Press.

———. 2003. "Coming to Grips with V. O. Key's Concept of Latent Opinion." In *Electoral Democracy*, edited by Michael B. MacKuen and George Rabinowitz. Ann Arbor: University of Michigan Press.

Index

Note: Page numbers in *italics* indicate figures; those with a *t* indicate tables.